positions asia critique

intimate industries:

restructuring (im)material labor in asia

volume 24   number 1   february 2016

Contents

Guest Editors' Introduction

Intimate Industries: Restructuring (Im)Material Labor in Asia

Rhacel Salazar Parreñas, Hung Cam Thai, and Rachel Silvey

Introduction

Markets of affect, care, reproduction, and sex have long inhabited a transnational terrain,[1] yet the institutionalization of their production has escaped theorization. Inviting their study is the rise and expansion of transnational market processes of commercial intimacy, which now reach a wide range of sectors that are increasingly formalized. Some of the new intimate industries that have sprung up in Asia in recent years are international marriage brokerages, Internet pornography businesses, overseas call centers, adoption centers, migrant care work training centers, wildlife tourism companies, and private surrogacy clinics. As we see in this volume, these industries have been organized, institutionalized, and incorporated with relative rapidity into the global political economy, with important implications for the meaning, form, and valuation of labor.

positions 24:1 DOI 10.1215/10679847-3320017

The performance of intimate labor within the context of intimate relations underlies the formation of intimate industries. This includes exchanges of labor considered "priceless" or "not for sale," or only to be given "freely" or "for love." *Intimate labor* is defined by Eileen Boris and Rhacel Parreñas as the work of forging, sustaining, nurturing, maintaining, and managing interpersonal ties, as well as the work of tending to the sexual, bodily, health, hygiene, and care needs of individuals.[2] *Intimate relations*, as broadly defined by Nicole Constable, are the "relationships that are—or give the impression of being—physically and/or emotionally close, personal, sexually intimate, private, caring or loving."[3] Viviana Zelizer adds that intimate relations involve some level of dependency and trust; relations become intimate when "the interactions within them depend on particularized knowledge received, and attention provided by, at least one person—knowledge and attention that are not widely available to third parties. The knowledge involved includes such elements as shared secrets, interpersonal rituals, bodily information, awareness of personal vulnerability, and shared memory of embarrassing situations. The attention involved includes such elements as terms of endearment, bodily services, private languages, emotional support, and correction of embarrassing defects."[4] We would add that intimate relations tend almost always to operate in an unequal terrain in which one party performs the maintenance of intimacy more than does the other.

Intimate industries produce, enable, promote, and market some relational connections while disrupting or rearranging other, previously existing social relations. For instance, the industries that help maintain or create an idealized family formation or domestic lifestyle for the consumers of intimate labor often rely upon the separation of the migrant who performs such intimate labor from her family and community of origin.[5] The articles collected here examine such trade-offs and their complex meanings and implications for the workers themselves. The authors explore these social processes through the industries that organize, enable, or delimit the trade in domestic labor (Nicole Constable, Pei-Chia Lan), marriage migration (Danièle Bélanger), companionship and romance (Hae Yeon Choo), sex work (Constable), pornographic performance (Celine Parreñas Shimizu), surrogate mothering and ova donation (Sharmila Rudrappa, Daisy Deomampo), and live, interpersonal cosmetics sales (Eileen Otis). Other authors trace the reorganization of these industries through various sites where intimate labor is exchanged, including call centers in India (Akhil Gupta and Purnima Mankekar), wildlife rehabilitation tourism centers in Indonesia (Juno Salazar Parreñas), adoption centers in China (Leslie Wang), and the dance bars and public streets of Mumbai (Chaitanya Lakkimsetti).

Affective Labor, Immaterial Labor, and the Commodification of Intimate Industries

Intimate industries rely on *affective labor*, or work that "produces or manipulates affects such as feelings of ease, well-being, satisfaction, excitement or passion."[6] The term *affect*, as used here, refers to work aimed at producing or modifying emotional experiences in other people (i.e., employers, consumers, clients). Affective labor figures prominently in service and care work because the purpose of these industries is not only to produce specific results (e.g., a rapid response, a clean house, a safe child) but also and at least as importantly to invoke a feeling in others (e.g., entitlement, superiority, relief, affirmation, pleasure). Affective labor is animated through relationships between humans, other species, and objects.[7] Attention to specific affective relationships permits insight into the ways that race, gender, ethnicity, and nationality are refracted in hierarchical regimes of intimate labor and reproduced through everyday interactions. Pei-Chia Lan (this volume) contrasts the varying expectations of the performance of affective labor by foreign caregivers in Japan and Taiwan. She argues that in Taiwan, elderly employers expect the demonstration of servility and deference, while their counterparts in Japan value the qualities of being expressive and emotional—traits that employers characterize as foreign or un-Japanese.

Our examination of intimate industries expands upon Michael Hardt and Antonio Negri's concept of *immaterial labor*, which they define as the production of service, cultural products, knowledge, and communication.[8] Although their concept of immaterial labor is compelling, it fails to capture the inequalities of shifting technologies and markets of social reproduction. In particular, while their concept underplays the gendered and racialized divisions of intimate labor, our focus on the politics of intimate industries emphasizes the dynamics of such inequalities. Hardt and Negri's concept of immaterial labor also underemphasizes the physical labor required in the production of intimacy in that the concept refers primarily to symbolic, informational, and cognitive activities (see Gupta and Mankekar, this volume).

Our discussion of intimate industries also builds on the seminal work of Ara Wilson and her examination of intimate economies. Wilson shows how social and cultural meanings of intimacy—specifically our identities and relationships—define markets, and the ways in which markets likewise shape intimacy. As she notes, "economic systems are not separate from intimate life."[9] Diverging slightly from Wilson, this volume does not map the emergence of various economic systems in Asia nor show how such systems are shaped by intimate norms (e.g., kin economy, folk economy, and moral economy). Instead, our volume looks at configurations of labor in global capitalism; the experiences engendered in such labors, including the bodily, sensory, and emotional states of being they elicit; the cultural and social transformations encouraged in the rise of intimate industries; and the formation of identities in the transnational commercialization of intimacy in Asia. We extend Wilson's conceptualization by highlighting the social processes through which intimacy is commodified and by zeroing in on the industry-scale dimensions of what Zelizer calls the "purchase of intimacy."[10]

Examining intimate industries allows us to see how the contested cultural logics of race, gender, and nation shape political economic relations within Asia and between Asia and the global political economy. Intimate industries have grown in conjunction with the commodification of intimacy, wherein "intimacy or intimate relations can be treated, understood, or thought of as if they have entered the market."[11] We emphasize that these are industries of intimacy in order to focus on the organized, regulated, and marketized characteristics of the expanding commercialization of domestic, sexual, emotional, and affective labor. The cases collected in this volume illustrate both the contested, political nature of the making of these markets, as well as the long history of stratification by race, gender, and nation that are reinforced through intimate labor.

Commodifying the Family and the Domestic Sphere

This volume shows how the analysis of intimate industries reveals the mutual constitution of intimate relations and market processes. Significantly, intimate industries transect informal economies of gift exchanges and love-based transactions. As the markets for intimacy grow, trade in the intimate is intertwined with new constitutions of femininity (Otis) and emergent constitutions of racialized families (Deomampo), as well as with the maintenance of traditional gendered caring regimes (Lan). The availability of intimate labor for pay is, of course, not a new phenomenon either in Asia or elsewhere, but the scope and scale of the global commodification of intimacy are historically unprecedented. As intimate labor markets in Asia have taken on new spatial forms, so too have the nature, texture, and boundaries of the domestic sphere been reworked socially and spatially. Moreover, particular configurations of race, ones specific to the historic Orientalization and colonian encounters in Asia, reverberate in intimate market relations.

A number of studies in this volume explicate the association between intimacy and the domestic sphere by showing how the "hostile worlds" of private and public economies are merged through expenditures.[12] These studies illuminate the exchange and distribution of valued resources, from the mundane sensorial satisfaction of touch (Parreñas), to the morally charged act of purchasing sexual pleasure (Constable, Lakkimsetti), and to the broader issue of paying for a life through adoption (Wang) or for a child through surrogacy (Deomampo, Rudrappa).[13] The articles in this volume show not only the practices of intimate industries but also how value is created across different domains of social relations. Daisy Deomampo's article on race selection in gestational surrogacy illustrates the ways exotic views of race lead to varying racial systems in pricing, whereby the eggs of darker-skinned women are given greater value by Western purchasers than by Indian sellers. However, Sharmila Rudrappa warns against celebrating the preference for dark skin by purchasers of gestational surrogacy because this preference is embedded in essentialist views of an Indian "other" whose foreignness is what makes her desirable in this relational context. Danièle Bélanger's article shows the ways in which marriages are commercialized through brokerage systems in Vietnam. She finds that the commercialization of marriage brokerage means that paid brokers are now doing the work that was historically designated as unpaid family labor. The commodification of marriages challenges the conventional view that intimate unions are based solely on interfamilial private gift exchanges such as dowries or bride price.

We emphasize the spatiality of Asian intimate industries as the frontier of such commodity exchanges under globalization. The various articles in this volume show that market transactions of intimacy are mediated not only by money but also by what Wolfgang Haug refers to as consumer aesthetics of fantasy and longing for "commodified goods."[14] These aesthetics move social practices and relations outside the moral boundaries of kin and community. In such commodified relations, private unpaid transactions are imagined into new paradigms of expenditures and pleasures. The proliferation of markets for the kinds of intimate labor that were once associated with the unpaid domestic sphere in Asia (e.g., arranged marriages via kinship ties) represents the growth of a major monetized sector not only within Asia's regional economies but also in the context of global and transnational economic exchange. The global scope of the industries is exemplified by the sex and caring industries (see Constable, Lan), and also by those industries linked to technology and reproduction such as call centers (Gupta and Mankekar) and adoption centers (Wang). Whereas research on intimate labor associated with the so-called family and the domestic sphere has focused on migration and on migrants from poorer countries to wealthier ones,[15] this volume addresses how intimate industries are produced and anchored in Asia, as well as how they travel through global markets. Indeed, mobility for both workers and consumers in the intimate industries of Asia is not confined to travel of the elite business classes nor the migration of low-wage workers but is increasingly also linked to middle-income consumers who travel within Asia for services, goods, relationships, and experiences tied to this industry.[16]

These thriving new forms of labor, trade, and consumption raise crucial questions about what Arlie Hochschild calls the "commodity frontier."[17] Hochschild points out that in globalization, the commodity frontier is the place where elements of intimate and domestic life become objects of sale, and where market forces and the private self combine to shape the subjective meanings of objects and possessions. Furthermore, she argues that these elements of intimacies that are being bought and sold are the "new gold" of globalization.[18] An example of this new gold is offered by Rudrappa (this volume) in the context of the commercialization of surrogate mothering, which in late capitalism is characterized by commodity exchanges that reach all the way into women's wombs. Likewise, Constable (this volume) examines the importance of surplus reproductive labor (i.e., the new gold) of women migrant workers in relation to three intersecting intimate industries in Asia: domestic work, sex tourism, and adoption. Drawing on her work on these three industries, she illustrates the intersectionalities and hierarchies of class, gender, race, and nationality within the region. Her article highlights the significance of surplus labor—as it spills out of one intimate industry to fuel the expansion of another—extracting labor value from intimate laborers' bodies and work.

Moral Economies of Commercial Intimacy

The commodification of intimacy in Asia operates within multiple and oftentimes conflicting moral economies. These conflicts show up in moral anxieties and debates about the regulation of bodies, sexuality, and the boundaries of publicity and privacy, all of which influence market policies instituted by government regimes. We use the term *moral economies* to refer to the ways that social norms intersect with the making of exchange value.[19] The articles in this volume show that markets and intimacies tend not to inhabit different domains in practice. To reiterate, the intersections of intimacy and money do not elicit a "hostile worlds" view.[20] The articles here show that people subscribe simultaneously to both moral injunctions and financial incentives, and that there are no simple divisions between moral and money-based prerogatives. As such, the concept of intimate industries challenges classical theories of exchange from Marcel Mauss to Georg Simmel that emphasize reciprocity and obligations. In particular, attention to intimate industries provides a counterpoint to Simmel's argument that commodity exchange offers consumers and workers freedom from the constraints of obligations and community.[21]

In contrast to Simmel's expectations, the commercialization of intimacy may help to uphold the fulfillment of cultural traditions. We see this in the case of Taiwan, where the outsourcing of elder care to foreign domestic workers allows adult children to fulfill their filial duty (Lan), and in Vietnam, where participating in matchmaking industries allows individuals to fulfill kinship obligations (Bélanger). This is also the case in Hong Kong (Constable), where the moral anxieties generated by commercial intimacies vary across markets: money for adoption and sex are constructed as immoral and hence barred by state regimes, but compensation for care is clearly morally acceptable. The commercialization of intimacy does not necessarily wreak moral havoc, but it may uphold the broad moral order that reinforces entrenched political economic inequalities of globalization. We see this with the feelings of moral superiority that motivate Western Christians to adopt special needs children in China (Wang), and that drive Westerners to find pleasure and meaning in helping the downtrodden, including animals (Parreñas).

What moral boundaries are invoked, and by whom, in the regulation of different intimate industries? Interestingly, within neoliberal discourse, market forces in and of themselves tend to be understood as natural and inevitable, and by extension, beyond moral reproach. But when capitalist markets intrude into what has been considered private, moral hackles are raised across the political spectrum. The boundaries between what counts as a public as opposed to a private good are cultural struggles in which women's bodies and sexual morality are central features. Sometimes the moral terrain appears relatively straightforward, such as in the context of cosmetics sales and the production of a feminine "beauty proletariat" in China (Otis) or in the making of a modern consumer or entrepreneurial subject in the global economy. When commercial intimacies uphold traditions, such as filial piety (Lan) and the reproduction of a particular family ideal (Bélanger), they seem to give both employers and consumers of the labor the moral flexibility to redefine the fulfillment of traditional roles. Often the moral stature of the employer or the consumer is maintained or enhanced by the labor of the intimate employee. In other cases, however, intimate laborers mobilize and rework moral regimes to their own benefit, such as when hostess club workers and domestic workers frame their labor as morally upstanding in part because of the income it provides to their families.[22] We see an example of this shakier terrain in the case of hostess clubs in South Korea that produce a distinct moral economy of romance and love, one that both challenges romantic views of true love and promotes shifting cultural mores of love. The palatability of these changes is made morally acceptable by the presumed motivation in hostess club–based partnerships, which is to form a family or aspire to monogamy (Choo).

Commercialized sex generates its own intense moral anxieties. When it comes to sexual commerce, a stringent moral regime is sometimes forcefully expressed top down in state discourse, ignoring other regimes of morality that may be more pronouncedly bottom up.[23] The top-down state governance of intimacy, such as the surveillance of international marriages to uncover instances of human trafficking in Vietnam (Bélanger), does not reflect the economic and cultural desires of the people involved in the industry. Attempts to morally bar commercial sex and their restrictive governance (e.g., in relation to marriage migration [Bélanger]) and bar dancing (Lakkimsetti) thus lead to a "contradictory discourse of the state" (Lakkimsetti), which simultaneously promotes capitalist enterprise and at the same time suppresses the emerging markets of intimate industries.

The moral conflicts engendered by the commercialization of intimacy emerge not only from the threat of the "hostile worlds" view but also by a seemingly state-induced angst over the recent relative slowdown in manufacturing production in Asia. Declining rates of growth prompt political contestation of what constitutes productive labor and what constitutes unproductive labor in these shifting economies. In India, a class divide was created by the 2005 ban on dance bars, which allowed bar dancing to continue in three-star and fancier hotels. Examining this class divide, Lakkimsetti (this volume) notes how the blatant and excessive flow of cash in low-end dance bars (in contrast with discrete exchanges in high-end places) aggravates the moral anxieties of state officials. In low-end dance bars, economic exchanges center on the purchase of visceral sexual pleasures, while economic exchanges in high-end dance bars also include financial exchanges among men. For example, in Vietnam, as in many parts of Asia and elsewhere, business deals among male elites are often decided in settings that allow them to purchase sexual pleasures. Indeed, scholars have argued convincingly that recent economic development in Asia depends upon the sexual labor in these industries.[24] Because low-end bar dancing produces neither material nor immaterial labor, however, it is easily dismissed as unproductive labor. This suggests that the constitution of affect is given lesser value because of its dismissal as immoral in the context of low-end dance bars.

Lakkimsetti's research explains the ways that the regulation of intimate industries reflects the moral anxiety over commercial sex, as well as the moral view of affective labor as unproductive. Similarly, the anxiety over commercial adoption that Rudrappa (this volume) observed is caused not only by its disruption of the view of the family as sacred but also by the "unproductive" nature of the commodified labor in this economic exchange. The moral denigration and heightened regulation of affective labor when it is exchanged by women in lower-class settings reinforce the devaluation of gendered, racialized, and classed labor.

The commercialization of intimacy is converging with multiple moral anxieties in Asia, some of which concern the growing importance of the region in the shifting global economy, and many of which revolve around women's bodies, sexuality, labor, and domesticity. These anxieties concern not only the cultural transformations engendered by commercial intimacy but also the economic insecurities generated by the rapidly changing economic landscapes of Asia.

Bodies and Biopolitics

As Ann Laura Stoler shows for colonial Indonesian society, the norms regarding appropriate domesticity, gendered sexual morality, and acceptable affective attachments provide windows onto the racial politics of imperial rule.[25] We are interested in understanding the contemporary, global, and comparative echoes of her argument for analyzing the ways that intimate industries figure in Asia's changing political and economic landscape.[26] Through attention to the socially and economically productive effects of gender and other forms of difference within intimate industries, the articles collected here expand the spaces, subjects, and processes often considered central to shaping the economic sphere. We argue that a focus on the geographies of intimate industries helps to explain how racialized and gendered subjects are slotted into production systems. More broadly, placing intimate industries at the center of analysis destabilizes the meanings of core concepts (e.g., value, labor, alienation) in critical political economy research and thereby opens space for fresh conceptual interventions and frameworks.

Intimate industries rely on embodied labor. But the bodies in question are not classical Marxian laboring bodies. According to David Harvey, the laboring body is positioned in relation to capital circulation and accumulation, and labor is understood as a form of metabolic exchange between the human body and its environment.[27] In this view, labor (and by extension, human life itself) is objectified in capitalism because labor is appropriated as a power independent of the producer. However, as Gupta and Mankekar (in this volume) demonstrate, the terrain of alienation characteristic of a capitalistic system is accentuated in intimate industries. Their study of call center workers in contemporary Bangalore illustrates how participation in the performance and exchange of affect leads to specific characteristics of labor alienation, and these take particular tolls on these workers' psyches and bodies.

Indeed, many of the articles in this volume push broadly Marxian conceptions of labor into deeper ongoing engagement with feminist theories of social reproduction and Foucauldian conceptions of biopolitics. In contrast with essentialist and universalist approaches to the body, contemporary analyses of social reproduction and biopolitics examine the often invisible and taken-for-granted, everyday practices that regulate and govern the social differentiation of bodies.[28] As Wendy Harcourt puts it, "population statistics, medical records, thumbprints on our passports, identity cards that state our height and eye colour, magazines that advertise ideal bodies, are all part of biopolitical strategies that categorize . . . bodies."[29] Examining such strategies is central to understanding the gendered economy of labor, and in particular the ongoing reinforcements of social norms with respect to which bodies belong in which work spaces, which workers are expected to provide what kinds of care or intimacy, and who is considered a legitimate consumer of intimate labor.

Although laboring bodies in intimate industries in Asia are often constructed as low-value, disposable, or easily replaceable commodities, the body can be mobilized as a site for contestation. As Shimizu (this volume) shows in her research on Asian male porn stars, strategic invocations of bodily images and stories can perform and produce cultural value. Making such connections has the potential to open up new political and economic futures.[30] This work stresses the power of economic subjects to resignify the systems of valuation they inhabit, whether as desirable sexual subjects in pornography (Shimizu) or as ethical subjects voluntarily laboring to shovel the "shit" of elephants (Parreñas). This in turn allows people in intimate industries, even if minimally, locally, or temporarily, to rescript aspects of their positions and subjectivities in relation to capitalist development.[31]

In a very basic sense, the central concern of this special issue is to put people as embodied subjects back into narratives of economic change. The collection aims to provide a corrective to the disembodied research approaches that remain commonplace in the social sciences. It acknowledges and explores the corporeal and relational nature of labor and economic change. It thus attends in particular to the ways in which intimate laborers themselves interpret, define, and live in their economic contexts. As a whole, understanding intimate industries "strengthens the vision of globalization from below; alters the participants, practices, and potentials of economic development; and reconfigures the imaginary of economic transformation."[32] Indeed, these articles show that intimate industries, and the people who labor within them, are integral to shaping the specific nature of Asia's contemporary role in the global economy.

Notes

This volume is the result of a workshop titled Rethinking Global Capitalism through Intimate industries in Asia, held at Pomona College on March 7–8, 2013, with funding from the Pacific Basin Institute of Pomona College and the Social Science and Humanities Research Council of Canada (File No: 646-2011-1164), as well as the SSHRC Partnership Project titled Gender, Migration and the Work of Care: Comparative Perspectives (File NO: 895-2012-1021). This support is greatly appreciated.

1. Thanh-Dam Truong, *Sex, Money and Morality: Prostitution and Tourism in Southeast Asia*

(London: Zed Books, 1990); Rhacel Salazar Parreñas, "Migrant Filipina Domestic Workers and the International Division of Reproductive Labor," *Gender and Society* 14, no. 4 (2000): 560–81.

2. Eileen Boris and Rhacel Parreñas, eds., *Intimate Labors: Cultures, Technologies, and the Politics of Care* (Stanford, CA: Stanford University Press, 2010).

3. Nicole Constable, "The Commodification of Intimacy: Marriage, Sex and Reproductive Labor," *Annual Review of Anthropology* 38 (2009): 49–64. See p. 50.

4. Viviana Zelizer, *The Purchase of Intimacy* (Princeton, NJ: Princeton University Press, 2005), 14.

5. Rhacel Salazar Parreñas, *Children of Global Migration: Transnational Families and Gendered Woes* (Stanford, CA: Stanford University Press, 2005); Geraldine Pratt, *Families Apart: Migrant Mothers and the Conflicts of Labor and Love* (Minneapolis: University of Minnesota Press, 2012).

6. Michael Hardt, "Affective Labor," *boundary 2* 26, no. 2 (1999): 89–100. See p. 96.

7. Ariel Ducey, "Technologies of Caring Labor: From Objects to Affect," in *Intimate Labors*, ed. Eileen Boris and Rhacel Salazar Parreñas (Stanford, CA: Stanford University Press, 2010), 18–32.

8. Michael Hardt and Antonio Negri, *Empire* (Cambridge, MA: Harvard University Press, 2001).

9. Ara Wilson, *The Intimate Economies of Bangkok* (Berkeley: University of California Press, 2004), 11.

10. Zelizer, *Purchase of Intimacy*.

11. Constable, "Commodification of Intimacy," 50.

12. Ibid.

13. Zelizer, *Purchase of Intimacy*.

14. Wolfgang Haug, *Commodity Aesthetics, Ideology, and Culture* (New York: International General Press, 1987).

15. Barbara Ehrenreich and Arlie Russell Hochschild, *Global Woman: Nannies, Maids, and Sex Workers in the New Economy* (New York: Metropolitan Books, 2002).

16. Hung Cam Thai, *Insufficient Funds: The Culture of Money in Low-Wage Transnational Families* (Stanford, CA: Stanford University Press, 2014).

17. Arlie Russell Hochschild, "The Commodity Frontier," in *Self, Social Structure, and Beliefs*, ed. Jeffrey C. Alexander, Gary T. Marx, and Christine L. Williams (Berkeley: University of California Press, 2000), 38–56.

18. Arlie Russell Hochschild, "Love and Gold," in Ehrenreich and Hochschild, *Global Woman*, 15–30.

19. James C. Scott's *Moral Economy of the Peasant: Subsistence and Rebellion in Southeast Asia* (New Haven, CT: Yale University Press, 1976) is a classic analysis of another kind of moral economy. Scott's main argument is that peasants participate in a moral economy of patron-

client relations that provides some social protection to weaker classes in times of shortage or crisis. He shows that peasants accustomed to such moral economies were likely to rebel or incite revolution when market incursions began to disrupt their traditional social economies. Samuel Popkin's subsequent *The Rational Peasant* (Berkeley: University of California Press, 1979) seeks to refute Scott's argument, emphasizing instead that peasants are rational economic actors who prefer free markets to feudal systems. Our understanding of moral economies differs from both these classic streams of thought in political anthropology in that we emphasize the mutual imbrication of rationalities/moralities and economies/cultures.

20. Zelizer, *Purchase of Intimacy.*

21. Marcel Mauss, *The Gift: The Form and Reason for Exchange in Archaic Societies* (New York: W.W. Norton, 2000); Georg Simmel, "Faithfulness and Gratitude," in *The Gift: An Interdisplinary Perspective*, ed. Aafke E. Komter (Amsterdam: Amsterdam University Press, 1996), 39–48.

22. For a discussion of hostess club workers, see Rhacel Salazar Parreñas, *Illicit Flirtations: Labor, Migration, and Sex Trafficking in Tokyo* (Stanford, CA: Stanford University Press, 2011). For domestic workers, see Pierrette Hondagneu-Sotelo and Ernestine Avila, "'I'm Here, but I'm There': The Meanings of Transnational Latina Motherhood," *Gender and Society* 11, no. 5 (1997): 548–71.

23. Parreñas, *Illicit Flirtations.*

24. See, for example, Kimberly Kay Hoang, *Chasing the Tiger: Sex Work and Finance Capital in Vietnam's New Global Economy* (Berkeley: University of California Press, forthcoming); Thu Huong Vo-Nguyen, *The Ironies of Freedom: Sex, Culture, and Neoliberal Governance in Vietnam* (Seattle: University of Washington Press, 2008); Anne Allison, *Nightwork: Sexuality, Pleasure, and Corporate Masculinity in a Tokyo Hostess Club* (Chicago: University of Chicago Press, 1994).

25. Ann L. Stoler, *Carnal Knowledge and Imperial Power: Race and the Intimate in Colonial Rule* (Berkeley: University of California Press, 2002). Over the last ten years, the literature examining the relationships between intimacy and empire has grown rapidly.

26. Stoler has also written about these issues as they apply to the history of North America: Ann L. Stoler, ed., *Haunted by Empire: Geographies of Intimacy in North American History* (Durham, NC: Duke University Press, 2006).

27. David Harvey, "The Body as an Accumulation Strategy," *Environment and Planning D: Society and Space* 16, no. 4 (1998): 401–21.

28. Isabella Bakker and Rachel Silvey, eds., *Beyond States and Markets: The Challenges of Social Reproduction* (New York: Routledge, 2007).

29. Wendy Harcourt, *Body Politics in Development: Critical Debates in Gender and Development* (London: Zed Books, 2009), 20.

30. For a review of recent work in this vein, see Rachel Silvey and Katharine Rankin, "Development Studies: Critical Development Studies and Political Geographic Imaginaries," *Progress in Human Geography* 35, no. 5 (2010): 696–704.

31. J. K. Gibson-Graham, *A Postcapitalist Politics* (Minneapolis: University of Minnesota Press, 2006).

32. Maliha Safri and Julie Graham, "The Global Household: Toward a Feminist Postcapitalist International Political Economy," *Signs* 36, no. 1 (2010): 99–125. See p. 100.

Intimate Encounters: Affective Labor in Call Centers

Purnima Mankekar and Akhil Gupta

Introduction

In this article, we examine the affective regimes generated by the labor practices of call center workers in Bangalore. We argue that these affective regimes generate forms of alienation and intimacy that are coimplicated rather than in opposition to each other. We seek to extend Karl Marx's theorization of alienation and, in so doing, rethink conceptions of intimacy predicated on assumptions of authentic self-hood.[1] In contesting the presumption that the intimate is in contradistinction to the public, we join scholarly conversations that trace how relations of intimacy are constructed through processes of labor.[2] Furthermore, we examine how intimacy and capital are mutually imbricated: just as intimate relations have been recast by capital[3] so too is the production of capital refracted by relations of intimacy.[4]

positions 24:1 DOI 10.1215/10679847-3320029
Copyright 2016 by Duke University Press

In our analysis of intimate encounters and affective labor, we draw upon several years of intensive ethnographic field research in call centers in the southern Indian city of Bangalore. In the course of our research, we conducted interviews and participation observation in call centers of three different sizes. Our informants ranged from chief executive officers (CEOs), chief operating officers (COOs), the venture capitalists who have helped set up call centers, to managers, supervisors, team leaders, and call center agents situated at the lowest rungs of the professional ladder. We sat in on recruitment interviews, "induction sessions," training, and "barged" calls by listening in on conversations between agents and clients. In addition to doing ethnographic research in call centers, we also conducted interviews, engaged in participant observation, and compiled oral histories with call center employees off-site, that is, in their homes and in spaces of leisure: one of our objectives was to trace how the relationship between work and leisure is reconstituted through affective labor.

In what follows, we focus on intimate encounters between call center agents and their overseas customers, drawing upon, and extending, theorizations of intimate labor by Eileen Boris and Rhacel Salazar Parreñas.[5] Boris and Parreñas posit that intimate labor refers to work that "exposes personal information that would leave one vulnerable if others had access to such knowledge."[6] It includes a spectrum of work including bill collection, elder care, domestic work, sex work, and various forms of therapy.[7] In conjunction with their framework, we examine call center agents' intimate encounters with customers, and hence interrogate conceptions of intimacy predicated on face-to-face interactions. Boris and Parreñas argue that attentiveness is a hallmark of intimate labor and point out that not all service labor is intimate labor; for example, fast-food workers do not perform intimate labor.[8] Our research contributes to these ongoing discussions by foregrounding how theories of affective labor enable us to rethink the relationship between intimate labor and capitalism in the contemporary moment.

We begin our analysis of affective labor in call centers by situating the business process outsourcing (BPO) industry in a global context in which the liberalization of the Indian economy occurred and by outlining some of its distinctive structural characteristics. This background is important because it helps us to understand the larger context for the production of intimacy in call centers. Next, we examine the consequences of untimely work—questions of time and temporality—for establishing relations of intimacy. We conclude by reflecting on how affective labor in call centers provokes us to rethink our assumptions about intimacy based on spatial and temporal contiguity and, equally, about the relationship between intimacy and capitalism.

The Structure of the BPO Industry in India

Business process outsourcing (BPO hereafter) refers to a range of long-distance services provided by Indian companies to corporations (mostly) in the West. The first companies in this business were involved with data entry and data transcription. However, it was only when the business quickly grew in voice processes or call centers that the industry attracted international attention. Subsequently, BPO work has quickly diversified to a range of back-office processes such as finance, accounting, data processing, secretarial work, human relations (HR) services, and procurement and logistics. One of the high-growth areas in India has been in what is sometimes called knowledge process outsourcing (KPO), represented by such activities as lawyers writing briefs and doing legal research for companies in the United Kingdom and the United States, or radiologists reading scans for hospitals in the United States. The term *call center* has now been largely replaced in reportage and popular parlance by *BPO* because call centers have become relatively less important in recent years, accounting for only 42 percent of the total BPO industry in 2011–12.[9]

It is essential that we situate BPOs within a longer history of outsourcing and offshoring from the United States. This process began with the offshoring of manufacturing in the 1980s, and it was part of the larger project of increasing profits for capitalists at the same time as putting downward pressure on the wages of domestic workers by expanding the spatial reach of capitalism.[10] Aided and abetted by the US state, as exemplified by then President Ronald Reagan, US corporations started manufacturing products in sites such as Japan, Korea, and Southeast Asia where labor costs were lower. Although this initially elicited resistance from traditional, manufacturing-based unions and the working class, Reagan's war against unions was, by and large, supported by middle-class workers in the service sector, whose jobs were *not* threatened by the offshoring of manufacturing industries. The service sector was already then the dominant sector of the US economy and, since it was growing, the accelerated erosion of manufacturing did not result in a major recession in the United States.

At first, service-sector jobs were seen as being immune to offshoring because they either depended upon higher-end cognitive and symbolic labor ("immaterial labor") that was concentrated in the global North or location-specific tasks that required geographical proximity. However, unexpected shifts in both sectors have led to the movement of such jobs to the global South, but the development of an information technology (IT)-enabled tele-communications infrastructure and increased Taylorization was central to both. We will take up each of these developments in turn.

The growth of India as an IT powerhouse had its origins in the seg-mentation of "intellectual" labor into creative and routine tasks. India's IT boom has been led by the breaking down of software product development into higher-end functions, which continue, for the most part, to be done in places like Silicon Valley, and lower-end maintenance and coding func-tions, which were offshored to places like India, where a large population of scientists and engineers were available for a fraction of what it would cost to hire them in the global North.[11] What made such offshoring of routine tasks feasible was the development of low-cost, reliable satellite links that enabled the exchange of code in real time.

The same technologies of Taylorization, and inexpensive communication systems, have also contributed to the offshoring of other types of services. Taylorization enabled the geographical separation of different parts of any given service industry. Even services that depend on the proximity of the client to the customer, like hair cutting, massage, and examination by a doc-tor, can be separated into communication, accounting, and service delivery components. Thus, call centers were established, first in the United States and the United Kingdom, to handle the communications component of cus-tomers' interactions with banks, airlines, taxi fleets, and the like. Account-ing functions were increasingly moved out of the doctor's office and the airline counter and relocated in locations where cheaper, low-cost labor was available. Once this geographical separation was successfully accomplished, it made sense to move the call center or accounting office to the lowest-cost location, for example, from Omaha to Bangalore. Once again, the development of inexpensive and high-quality telecommunications infrastructure was critical in enabling such a move. Although the primary reason these jobs are being moved has to do with cost savings, there is a big difference between the cultural resources needed to do a job as a call center agent and those needed for back-office work such as accounting. The cost-enabled global geographical dispersion of communicative and affective domains of labor in the service industries has had unintended cultural and political consequences for the development of global capitalism. In this article, we track some dimensions of this process.

Given the history of the offshoring of manufacturing, it is ironic that the outsourcing of services to offshore call centers has now become the focus of such intense public debate and xenophobic nationalism. Call centers in the West historically tend to be relatively small (around 250 people) and hire employees with low levels of skill. Call center jobs are perceived by most employees to be dead-end positions, with few prospects for learning or advancement. Thus, when call-center jobs first started moving to India to take advantage of discrepancies in labor cost (an Indian worker starts at approximately one-tenth the minimum wage paid to a worker in the United States), one would not have anticipated the outcry that followed. The jobs that were being "lost" were low-skill, low-paying jobs without career prospects.

In the United States, controversies surrounding the outsourcing of jobs to India partake of a longer genealogy of racialized (and racist) discourses about the relationship between labor, high technology, and Asia and Asians. In the United States, as Lee and Wong point out, Asians are represented as occupying a fraught relationship with technology, either as "nimble-fingered" female laborers working in computer factories or as "geeks" writing code.[12] These discourses racialize Asians in specific ways.[13] The outrage against call-center agents located in India draws on white supremacist discourses of the irrevocable alterity of Asians: that so-called American jobs are being "given to" (or "stolen by") Asians only adds fuel to the xenophobic fire.[14] Located within a global political economy that is striated by race as much as it is by gender and national location, call center agents in India are always-already racialized by virtue of working in this industry. Part of the explanation for the outrage in the West to call centers in India—the barely concealed racism, the linguistic chauvinism—is that these call centers represent something larger than themselves. They are seen as the beachhead to the outsourcing of other, higher-paying service-sector jobs held by (white, male) middle-class people in the West.[15]

That such fears are not well founded is evident from the fact that the overall impact of outsourcing remains relatively small: of the approximately $2 trillion spent on information technology (IT) and business process industries in 2013 worldwide, Indian companies accounted for less than 5 percent of the total. In India, the BPO industry is classified as part of the IT sector and is called information technology enabled services (ITES). IT/ITES are represented by one trade association, the National Association of Software and Services Companies (NASSCOM), and account for $100 billion in annual revenue. Of this, BPOs earned $16 billion, or about 16 percent.[16] In 2011–12, the BPO industry employed approximately 880,000 people in India,[17] of which slightly less than half were employed in call centers.

Since the first call center in India opened in 1999, BPOs have constituted a "sunrise" sector of the Indian economy. In a little over a decade, the industry has grown from zero to just under a million employees. Rapid growth has been accompanied by very fast technological change, so that the industry shifts in focus and strategy with dizzying speed. Because fixed costs are relatively small, new companies can be set up quickly. This has created a highly competitive field, in which no single company has more than 2 percent of the global BPO market. Such intense competition, combined with rapid growth rates, and a limited pool of potential employees with English-language skills, has resulted in turnover rates that approach 40 percent annually.

When we started our fieldwork in 2009, BPO employees were paid a very good wage compared to other workers in the service sector in India. By 2012, most agents were being hired out of high school and were at least eighteen years of age. If they worked in a call center representing companies in the United States or the United Kingdom, they started out with a base salary of Rs. 10,000 to Rs. 12,000 a month (roughly US$200 to $250 a month). They were picked up and dropped off at home in shared company cabs and were provided subsidized food in the cafeteria. In addition, they were given medical insurance (sometimes covering their parents and siblings as well). However, the most attractive part of the job usually consisted of the additional money they made in the form of bonuses. BPO jobs offered strong incentives to get higher scores in performance metrics. An agent who consistently performed very well could double her salary within a year through bonuses, incentives, and overtime. Many companies withheld bonuses in the first year, and used the lure of bonuses in the second year to keep their best agents from switching jobs and companies. The best-performing agents were frequently promoted to team leader (TL) within the first two years. Subsequent promotions depended upon the company, but since the industry was expanding so rapidly, people often received promotions within three years. One of the main reasons people quit their jobs was that they were not promoted as quickly as they expected. Rapid promotions also meant that the higher echelons of any company were staffed by exceedingly young executives; apart from the CEOs, most second-tier managers were in their late twenties or early thirties. Having worked in BPOs since graduating college at the age of twenty or twenty-one, they were all "veterans" of the industry: eight to ten years later, they sometimes found themselves near the apex of the organizational pyramid.

At the time that we started our intensive research in Bangalore in 2009, the rapid rate of growth in BPOs was slowing down owing to a complex mix of factors. The industry was more mature; it had less of the atmosphere of a study hall in a college dorm, and more of a professional, fast-paced, no-nonsense, bureaucratic workplace. More people had started approaching BPOs as a career rather than a temporary job. With a global recession, and a downward squeeze on margins, companies were expanding less rapidly. Therefore, opportunities for new jobs contracted, and there was a reduction in turnover as agents started staying in their jobs longer. The result was that promotions were slower, and starting salaries stagnated. Many new recruits were disappointed that the atmosphere at work was less "fun" than they had expected. Agents who had been at the job for two or three years were also frustrated that they were not being promoted quickly enough.

Affects and Affective Labor in Call Centers

In this section, we outline some of the ways that theories of affect and affective labor enable us to understand the intimate encounters between call center agents and their overseas customers. Our conception of affective labor is in dialogue with Michael Hardt's work and with feminist theorizations of work and labor.[18] Hardt describes affective labor as a category of labor that builds on feminist critiques of gendered labor such as emotional labor, kin work, and care in both waged and unwaged economies and, hence, extends the work of French and Italian Marxists on cognitive labor to include the affective.[19] He posits, "The term affective labor is meant to bring together elements from these two different streams and grasp simultaneously the corporeal and intellectual aspects of the new forms of production, recognizing that such labor engages at once with rational intelligence and with passions or feeling."[20] Hardt situates affective labor alongside forms of immaterial labor entailed in the production, for instance, of code, information, ideas, and images.[21]

Our conception of affective labor also draws on theories of affect that underscore the distinction between affects and emotions. As Brian Massumi, Lawrence Grossberg, Patricia Clough, and several other scholars have argued, affects and emotions operate on different registers: emotions are affects recognized retroactively through language and are contingent on subjective experience.[22] Conceptually, then, emotions remain tied to tropes of the interiority of the subject. In contrast, in our characterization of the labor of call center agents as affective labor, we theorize affect as a field of intensities that circulates between bodies and objects and between and across bodies; as existing alongside, barely beneath, and in excess of cognition; and as transgressing binaries of mind versus body, and private feeling versus collective sentiment.[23] Affects cannot be located solely in an individual subject, nor can they be relegated to the psyche or to subjective feelings.

Thus, diverging from the pathbreaking scholarship of Arlie Hochschild, who highlights the manipulation and control of emotions in how workers produce particular feelings for clients (as in the case of flight attendants),[24] we wish to problematize the purported dichotomy between "false" identities and the purportedly authentic selves of call center agents:[25] in our larger project, we are concerned with how the affective labor of agents is, in fact, generative of subjectivity. Put another way, rather than assume that individual workers are the locus or "source" of affects, we are interested in how affective labor *produces* them as particular kinds of laboring subjects. Moreover, our conceptualization of affective labor enables us to conceive of the work of call center agents not solely in terms of their interpellation by ideological or disciplinary apparatuses of labor but also in terms of their capacity to act and be acted upon, to navigate space and time, and to experience and inhabit their bodies in specific ways.

Throughout our research, the call centers we worked in were saturated with the intensity of affect. Elsewhere, each of us has described the raw energy that crackled and swirled around us when we first entered "the floor"—the area where call center agents made their calls.[26] Within a few moments of walking in, we were swept up into its high-energy atmosphere: the floor represented all the speed-up and electricity of a newsroom just before a deadline.[27] Agents sat in cubicles in a large room that was humming with the sound of their voices as they spoke in low tones to their customers. Scanning the faces and bodies of the agents, we saw a plethora of expressions: the intense concentration woven into the tightness of a young woman's body as she leaned forward in her chair to persuade a customer to clinch a deal, the determined smile of another young woman as she attempted to coax her customer to divulge information demanded by the client company, the sagging shoulders of a young man as he realized that his customer was being "noncompliant." Every now and then, we would hear cries of "oh shit—I lost him (or her)!" when a customer hung up. Their team leader paced the aisles, periodically glancing at the screens of agents, sometimes stopping to answer a question they might have and, from time to time, clapping someone on their back to congratulate them for a job well done. We have never been able to get accustomed to the affective intensities, the electric charge, of the floor in any of the call centers where we conduct our research: to this day, every time we "barge" calls with our informants, we are physically exhausted and emotionally spent by the time we leave.

Hardt argues that the concept of affective labor is a way to bridge two streams of research: feminist critiques of labor that centrally involve affects (see above), and the interventions of French and Italian economists and labor sociologists who, employing terms such as *cognitive labor* and the *new cogni-tariat*, point to the increasingly intellectual character of productive practices and the labor market.[28] Clough goes beyond merging these two streams by drawing attention to the manner in which the techno-scientific mediates bodily practices. Affective labor, then, foregrounds how emotional, intel-lectual, and corporeal forms of work, together with technologies, matter, and materials, are implicated in the labor of call center agents. Call center agents are not involved in producing "just talk." They generate happiness or frustration in clients; they create profits for their company and for the corporation that has hired their company; they (re)produce the intangibles of "brand image" for the product that they service as an important source of value to the corporate client; they produce stress, corporeal and emotional, for themselves, as well as forms of sociality with clients and other workers; and they also produce a wage that allows for the reproduction of labor in the family.

Affects (and affective labor) are often experienced in the body yet cannot be "biologized." To a large degree, call center work consists of the gen-eration and modulation of affect, in that it problematizes the boundaries between cognition, corporeality, and emotion. Fundamentally, as argued by Hardt, "affective labor is ontological."[29] In the call centers where we con-ducted our ethnographic research, affective labor had to be learned. Affec-tive training *reconstituted* the work habits, daily routines, and speech pat-terns of call center agents—habits of the mind as well as the body. All the trainers, team leaders, and call center agents we worked with emphasized the importance of cultivating attention, solicitude, empathy, and intimacy—affective regimes that blur the distinction between thought, feeling, and corporeality. In training sessions, agents were taught not only how to make calls and conduct business but, equally importantly, how to groom them-selves, use deodorants, how to enter and leave elevators, how to stand in the hallways and, last but not least, how to use Western-style toilets.

The agents' ability to meet quotas set by their supervisors was predicated on their ability to assume culturally appropriate affects in interactions with their clients. The call center agents with whom we worked were trained to adopt particular kinds of affective repertoires—of courtesy, familiarity, friendliness, helpfulness, and, above all, caring—thus underscoring the centrality of certain modes of affect to their self-constitution and self-regulation as laboring subjects. Since modes of courtesy and friendliness in the United States or the United Kingdom (the main markets for Indian call centers) are very different from those in India, our informants learned culturally specific modes of effecting the right affect in their voice. Thus, for example, several agents working on US "processes" (projects) had to unlearn ostensibly "Indian" modes of respect for authority and deference in favor of adopting "American" speech patterns of informality and assertiveness. In contrast, agents working on UK processes had to deploy speech patterns that were much more formal to index "British" forms of courtesy and hierarchy.

Much of the training focused on such nuances and on the retraining of the body and the voice to produce the right affect in agents' unscripted encounters with customers. In training, agents were often told to smile when speaking to customers. The idea was that, even though customers could not see them smiling, they would be able to "hear" the agents' smiles in their voices. As one agent, Veronica, repeatedly told us, "It is all in the voice. You have to distill your emotions into your voice." The modulation of voice involves emotion, cognition, and the body at the same time that it is shaped by culturally specific discourses such as those of nationality, gender, class, deference, and/or authority.

Critics emphasize the alienation of the call center worker by noting the high volume of calls that agents handle and the intense surveillance to which they are subjected. Certainly, that labor in call centers is affective in no way takes away from the fact that many facets of the work are repetitive and highly Taylorized: these aspects of call center work do resemble an assembly line. Additionally, the industry's struggles to come up with appropriate metrics for "worker productivity" showed up in the changing goals that workers were expected to realize. In the early years of the call center industry, the emphasis was on the time agents spent on each call. However, after we started intensive fieldwork in 2009, presumably because of consumer complaints, companies shifted their strategy to emphasize "customer satisfaction" as measured by a "customer satisfaction index." Companies noted that consumers who called back were often angry because their problems had not been resolved in the first call and these customers were more likely to express displeasure at customer service. Thus, agents were told to ensure that customers were satisfied during the first call so that they did not have to call again. The criteria therefore shifted to handling the largest number of calls while, simultaneously, ensuring that customers were happy with the service they received. More than any "objective" measure, the effectivity of affective labor was measured by the "happiness" of the person at the other end. Workers now had to labor to please their customers without knowing which actions would result in a "good" rating versus a "bad" one, and without any control over the consumers' contexts. Since affective labor depends on interaction, the "output" is always uncertain, even less than the worker's control over a product being made on an assembly line. It is for this reason that we contend that call center work cannot be categorized as just another example of Taylorized, assembly-line production, no different than producing cars, washing machines, or electronics: in this important sense, then, the affective labor of our informants was distinct from the labor of factory workers.

The affectivity of the labor of call center agents raises some interesting conundrums about alienation. Among the ways that Marx describes alienation in the *Economic and Philosophical Manuscripts of 1844* is the alienation of the worker in the act of production itself.[30] The routinization of work in call centers, along with the intense surveillance of agents, represents one facet of the alienated labor of call center agents. In Marxian terms, the self-estrangement of call center agents is symptomatized by the fact that their labor does not comprise spontaneous activity.[31] At the same time, in contrast to Marx's description of estranged labor as leading to the alienation of the worker from species-being, call center agents produce a distinct form of sociality that problematizes assumptions about pre-alienated subjects who, through their affective labor, engage in intimate encounters with their clients. The work of call center agents foregrounds how affective labor itself produces intimate encounters and, in the process, is generative of particular kinds of laboring subjects, thus blurring the boundaries between "pre-alienated" and alienated self-hood.[32]

Nevertheless, this is a form of sociality produced under conditions that, as Marx points out, engenders the reproduction of relations of capital and begets the dominion of the one (the capitalist) who does not produce.[33] It is a form of sociality that is formed by a four-cornered relationship between the international capitalist firm, the domestic capitalist, the domestic agent, and the (usually) international client. Thus, it is a field constituted by intersecting forms of inequality. Further, the affective labor of the call center agents with whom we worked did result in the production of surplus: hotel bookings were made, tickets on flights sold, computers repaired, and so on. However, the fact that their labor depended on empathetic engagement and intimacy made for forms of alienation that were different from conventional production. The alienation registered by loss of control over time and the pace of one's work,[34] by shift work, and by constant surveillance is familiar from product assembly lines, but the affective labor that produces and, indeed, aims for "customer satisfaction" has no equivalent in those forms of production: customer satisfaction, in other words, is the primary "product" of these forms of labor.

Certainly, surveillance was an important component of the environment in which these agents worked and set the parameters for their affective labor.[35] We observed that, even as agents' success in their job depended on their ability to produce appropriate affects, they were also bound to the parameters set in the script they had to follow. This script was usually provided by the client company, and protocols for beginning a call and the signing-off had to be followed to the letter. All calls were recorded in their entirety and subjected to random checks by the quality assurance team; a complaint from a customer to the client company could potentially cause not only the agent in question to lose his or her job but, if the complaint was serious, for the BPO to lose its contract.

The Untimely and the Intimate

The untimely nature of the work of our informants, and the scrambled temporalities it generated, shaped a range of intimate relations implicating their bodies, each other, and their customers. Their affective labor was thoroughly enmeshed in temporalizing processes on multiple levels. They worked in shifts that depended on the place for which they were providing services. For example, processes catering to US clients often took place in three shifts: 6:30 p.m.–3:30 a.m. (the most desirable of the US shifts); 9:30 p.m.–6:30 a.m.; and, the graveyard shift, 12:30 a.m. to 9:30 a.m. If they could find such work, most of our informants preferred to work for UK processes, which began at 1:30 p.m. or 2:30 p.m. and lasted for nine hours, because at such a job, they felt that they could get home at a "decent" time.

The scrambled temporalities of their affective labor had corporeal consequences for our informants. Because their experience of time was shaped by the time of a far-away place, agents experienced a radical disruption of their body clocks. Working at night and sleeping in the day disrupted their sleep cycles, resulting in chronic insomnia, depression, a suppressed immune system, and, in the case of young women, the disruption of menstrual and ovulation cycles. In addition to the intrinsically intimate experience of having their circadian rhythms disturbed, call center agents also experienced a disruption of their social life. Their interactions with family members, neighbors, and friends—indeed with all those who did not work the same hours—were severely curtailed, resulting in what A. Aneesh has termed "social death."[36]

The stringent monitoring of agents' time at work produced another form of alienation. The times at which they logged in and out of their workstations were automatically recorded and carefully monitored.[37] This information was archived as part of a large data file on each employee and was consulted by supervisors and managers when they made decisions on raises and perks and about whom to fire. Agents were graded by a letter grade every quarter. If an agent consistently received a D grade, he or she was fired. Regimes of temporality shaped the imperative to be productive: the time-discipline of working in a call center meant that agents had to meet strict hourly or daily targets; at the same time, because customer satisfaction was paramount, agents hesitated to rush through a call: in these circumstances, adopting the right affect was critical.[38]

In most of the call centers where we did our ethnographic work, agents were permitted two coffee breaks and one dinner break. Indeed, the rhythms of the body had to be brought into synchrony with the time-discipline of the call center, thus foregrounding the entanglement of labor, temporality, and intimacy. For instance, the time-discipline of the call center meant that, while agents were permitted bathroom breaks, every time they had to leave their cubicle to go to the bathroom they would have to log off and then log back on when they returned. This information, too, was recorded in their process logs. This became a serious problem if an agent felt under the weather or became ill while at work. They would have to get the team leader's permission in order to take a break, something that many agents, particularly women suffering from menstrual cramps, experienced as a humiliating invasion of their privacy.

Theorists of affect insist that it animates the social.[39] The affective labor of our informants was both predicated on sociality and was, simultaneously, productive of sociality. Thus, while we broadly agree with Aneesh's claim that call center agents experienced social death, affective labor was also generative of specific forms of sociality. Like many kinds of service work, their work was intensely social, even as their labor was predicated on interactions that were highly structured by the demands of capital. The relations of sociality surrounding a call center extended beyond the company itself. Many new recruits confided to us that they applied for a job in a particular company either with a friend, or because a friend was already working there. It was often the case that when agents left for another company, their friends would accompany them. Even though agents were required to compete aggressively with each other, companies went out of their way to cultivate social relationships among agents and would organize parties, trips to pubs and restaurants, and retreats at fancy spas and resorts—all of which were termed "team-building exercises" designed to get agents to "bond."[40]

The managers we spoke with emphasized that, for workers to function effectively as a team, it was necessary that they formed social relationships with each other: this was their primary motivation for organizing frequent team-building events such as parties and outings and taking agents on all-expenses-paid retreats. Agents frequently entered into intimate social and, at times, sexual relationships with each other, in part because their hours of work cut them off from other friends and community members. Intimate friendships were cultivated over dinner and coffee breaks in the office and in the cabs and vans that transported them between their homes and work. A great deal of intense socializing occurred after work, and sexual liaisons occasionally sprung up at out-of-town retreats.[41]

The affective labor of call center agents was thus productive of a range of intimacies, all of which underscore the coimbrication of intimacy and productive processes. Several of our informants entered into marriages and sexual liaisons with colleagues, including premarital and extramarital relationships. In a social context in which arranged marriages continued to be the norm and gender segregation was still relatively stringent, these relationships were, predictably, deemed highly transgressive. The fact that many of these relationships developed between agents of different castes, regional affiliations, and religions made them all the more transgressive; it is perhaps no surprise, then, that call centers were stereotypically represented in popular media as spaces that encouraged licentious behavior on the part of young people beyond the disciplining gaze of parents and community members.

Grossly exaggerated as these stereotypes were, it was clear to us that, for most agents, working in call centers afforded the opportunity to get to know people of the opposite sex, sometimes intimately. It is also true that, given that most of our informants were in their early twenties, the temptation to enter into sexual relationships with coworkers proved irresistible to some of them. On their part, managers were deeply ambivalent about sexual liaisons among agents. Closed-circuit TVs were everywhere in the companies where we did our ethnographic work—in work areas, meeting rooms, photocopy rooms, hallways, entryways and lobbies, stairwells, and company cafeterias—ostensibly to discourage the abuse of drugs. However, as many agents reported, the real motivation was to discourage sexual liaisons in the workplace.

Thus, although managers and supervisors claimed to adopt a "don't ask, don't tell" policy toward sexual liaisons at work, they were nervous about workplace romances. As one COO said, "I don't *want* to care what my agents do outside this building but I have to—because it affects how they work. For instance, if there is a break up [or] a pregnancy we have to face the music—or if they start a relationship they want to work in the same process." Managers also felt that they had to keep an eye on what happened after agents left the premises. They would keep tabs on the logs kept by the cab drivers assigned to transport workers, and drivers were instructed to let supervisors know whether agents asked to be dropped off (or picked up from) addresses different from those in their personnel files. In large part, this surveillance was a response to the bad press and controversies sparked by the specter of young people of different genders doing night work and spending money in restaurants and pubs, but COOs and managers were also worried that romance would unsettle relationships in the workplace.

One team leader complained to us about how much he hated it when agents formed sexual relationships. He insisted that it disrupted the dynamics of the entire team and, therefore, hampered its productivity. He proceeded to describe to us the many managerial challenges that ensued when a romantic triangle had developed between three of his agents. Another manager told us about how, when agents became romantically involved, they would beg to be placed in the same process, but, after their break-up, one of them would then entreat him to be transferred to another team. Yet another supervisor informed us that she was being harassed by the parents of a young woman who had formed a romantic attachment with a man of a different religion. She felt caught between a rock and a hard place: on the one hand, she did not want to antagonize the couple because they were highly productive workers; at the same time, she was getting exhausted from having to field calls from the angry parents and was becoming increasingly worried that they would stir trouble for the company by either showing up at the office and making a scene or reporting what was happening to the local media. Yet, as evident from the numerous sexual liaisons we came across during our fieldwork, the surveillance exercised by the company had its limits: the erotic energies of these young people undermined the efforts of managers and team leaders to regulate the relationships that developed among them and underscored the "lines of flight"—the eruptive potential—of erotics.[42]

Thus, because of these intimate encounters, call centers became erotically charged social spaces. As noted above, in many cases, young men and women were working alongside each other for the first time in their lives; this, combined with how the rhythms of their work led to their being cut off from other social interactions, made it almost inevitable that some of them entered into intimate relationships with one another. Further, the very fact that these relationships were socially taboo sometimes made them all the more irresistible. The stigma attached to working in a call center and doing night work, persistent media hype about the so-called scandals that brewed in these spaces, and the surveillance to which agents were subjected within and beyond the workplace all had the paradoxical effect of recursively constituting call centers as erotically charged spaces.

As noted above, we do not conceptualize intimacy, erotic or otherwise, in opposition to alienated labor, or as a locus of authenticity. Instead, we are concerned with how realms of intimacy are themselves shaped by technology and suffused with the work of capital. First, the affective labor of agents and their interactions with customers were, quite literally, mediated by information technology. For instance, for outbound calls, a dialer software program identified which customer to call, and for inbound calls, some basic data elicited over the phone gave the agent detailed information about the consumer's spending habits, household, and so forth. Thus, despite the fact that agents could not see the people they were talking to, they learned intimate details of their customers' lives. One agent eloquently described the situation in this manner: "We learn as much about a customer as their own family—in some cases, we know things about them that even their own family members don't know." Customers often shared intimate details of their lives with agents: why they had credit card charges from a foreign country, why their phone bill was so high that month, who came to get them when their car broke down, and so on. Intimacy, thus, became a constitutive part of the affective labor performed by many call center agents.

It is important to note that some of the agents we worked with were deeply ambivalent about the intimacy that they had to establish with customers. One young man, Andy, felt torn about the intimate conversations that had developed between him and an elderly customer in the United Kingdom. Andy claimed that this customer kept calling for customer service and would ask for him by name. Despite the team leader's efforts to shield Andy from his repeated calls, he would refuse to speak with anybody else. Once on the phone, this customer would talk for hours about his deceased wife, sometimes weeping with grief, on other occasions bitterly angry that she had "left" him. At first, Andy was deeply sympathetic and did nothing to discourage him, but, as time went on, he began to dread these calls because they lasted so long and, equally importantly, because he felt emotionally drained by them.

Intimate encounters with clients could also become coercive. Another agent, Annie, spoke of how she had to put up with the sexual innuendoes of a customer. She was working on an inbound process, with customers calling in with questions about a particular software program. One customer had surmised that she was Indian and kept asking her if she was a virgin. This customer's discourse highlights the mutual imbrication of Orientalist and racialized discourses about Indian women's sexuality. Annie avoided "escalating" the call to her supervisor because she was afraid that the supervisor would blame her for encouraging the customer. Therefore, the customer kept calling back, ostensibly with questions about the software, and asked for Annie by name. When she eventually asked her supervisor to forward the call to another agent, the customer claimed that she had given him bad advice and that was why he continued to have problems with his software. The supervisor then insisted that she handle all his calls, and the customer continued to harass her. In this instance, and in others like it, intimate encounters across transnational space acquired the form of racialized sexual harassment.

We assert that the affective labor of call center agents entails the production and modulation of affects and is, therefore, unlike the labor of factory workers, agricultural laborers, and artisans and craftspeople for whom the production of affects per se is neither at the core of the productive process nor its end-product. However much affect may be involved in the production of goods and commodities in the act of laboring, the labor itself is not about the management and modulation of affect, nor is the "product" one that produces the equivalent of "customer satisfaction." The difference between the work of call center agents and, for example, factory workers or farmers is not that one is affective and the other is not, but that affect has a very different position in each of these productive processes. In short, we wish to argue that we need to pay attention to *how* labor is affective in different cases.

Theorists of affect foreground how bodies of workers become nodes in the circulation of intensities between subjects and between subjects and objects.[43] We believe that these forms of affective intensities are particularly salient in labor contexts shaped by information technology. Framing the work of our informants, and the intimacies thus produced, in terms of affective labor enables us to glean the porosity of their bodies to technology, to the scrambled temporalities generated by the labor process, and to the work discipline to which they were subject. As we note above, some of these changes were intimately corporeal—as with the widespread disruption of circadian rhythms or of the menstrual and ovulation cycles of some of our women informants.

The affective labor of call center workers hence implicated emotions, cognition, and bodies all at once. Conceptualizing the work of call center agents as affective labor enables us to foreground the intimacies engendered not as epiphenomenal but as intrinsic to the productive process and, therefore, as an intimate industry. In short, foregrounding the affective labor of our informants allows us to underscore the institutionalization of the production of these intimacies; in so doing, we join with the editors of this volume who emphasize the "organized, regulated, and marketized characteristics of the expanding commercialization of domestic, sexual, emotional, and affective labor" (this volume, 4).

Conclusion: Intimate Encounters across Time and Space

As Lauren Berlant points out, "intimacy builds worlds; it creates spaces and usurps places meant for other kinds of relations."[44] The affective labor of call center agents is service work and is, hence, not about the production of a tangible commodity. It is also intimate labor provided at a distance. Intimacy implies a proximity that may be physical, corporeal, emotional, and/or geographical. The affective labor of our informants underscored the ways in which it reconstituted their very experience of time and space, proximity and distance. On the one hand, their success at work was contingent on their construction of a relationship of proximity with their clients, eliciting and producing affects that generated intimate encounters. However, although these workers did not engage in physical travel, their virtual and imaginative travel was generative of new modalities of proximity that compel us to review our definitions of proximity and distance. There is a voluminous literature on the global care chain comprising workers who migrate from the global South to wealthier nations to provide care and services;[45] the virtual and imaginative travel of call center workers, however, provokes us to rethink the place of movement, in conjunction with our assumptions about proximity and distance, in formations of intimacy.[46]

At the same time, call centers in India are predicated on labor arbitrage (the difference between the cost of labor in metropolitan and peripheral regions); hence, they also index the global expansion of capitalism for the extraction of surplus value. Call center agents work with scripts under conditions of time management and surveillance that resemble those of an assembly line, and yet they are engaged in a form of labor that requires cross-cultural resources of empathy and understanding. Agents have to marshal these resources for instrumental ends, such as making a sale, and yet their engagement with customers goes well beyond the instrumental. As in the story of the old man who missed his wife, many agents repeatedly told us that what they liked most about their jobs was that they got to know people in the West—how they lived, what they thought, and so on. In short, these jobs condensed an extraordinarily rich and contradictory set of determinations and meanings that need careful unpacking.

Nicole Constable provides us with an insightful and capacious definition of intimate relationships as "social relationships that are—or give the impression of being—physically and/or emotionally close, personal, sexually intimate, private, caring, or loving."[47] She argues that new technologies have transformed landscapes of intimacy. Many of our informants spoke of how their work in call centers reconfigured their relations with their family members, close friends, and partners in profound ways. Beyond the obvious effects that their work had on their social lives, it also shaped their relationships with their very bodies, their experiences of time and temporality, and how they navigated the multiple chronotopes that they were expected to simultaneously inhabit.

More broadly, then, as a central component of the information technology–enabled services (ITES) industry in India, call centers present a unique opportunity to rethink not just intimacy but the relationship between technology and intimacy and the workings of capital itself. So far, we have examined how landscapes of intimacy were reconstituted through the affective labor of call center workers. We are also concerned not just with how capitalism transforms intimacy but also with how certain relations of intimacy are generative of capitalism. Sylvia Yanagisako posits that capitalist production is produced not solely by instrumental action but, equally, by affective action and sentiment.[48] Similarly, Ara Wilson has pointed to the myriad ways in which capitalism is shaped by economies that are moral and affective, what she terms "the intimacies of global capitalism."[49] We join with these scholars in underscoring that the intimate encounters produced by the affective labors of call center agents were not secondary to capitalist production but were central to it. These encounters, therefore, constitute a vital component of the intimate industries proliferating in the current historical conjuncture.

As we have argued above, our informants' participation in the generation of profit—after all, labor arbitrage is the main reason for outsourcing— was predicated on the modulation of affect and on new ways of inhabiting their bodies. Our participant observation at training sessions in call centers brought home to us the ways in which the call center agent's body had to be reshaped in accordance with the demands of the job; yet, this reshaping of the body, and its resulting permeability to practices of affective labor, extended beyond the training session and, indeed, the workplace.[50] In *The Woman in the Body*, Emily Martin insightfully points to how the temporality of capital, its time-discipline, reconfigures the bodies of women. In analogical fashion, the bodies of call center workers are rendered malleable to the demands of their work with consequences that include the disruption of circadian rhythms from having to simultaneously inhabit multiple time zones, and ailments ranging from carpal tunnel syndrome and orthopedic problems to depression and, in the case of women agents, to irregular menstrual cycles and infertility—all of which foreground how these forms of affective labor, and the time-discipline they entail, are deeply corporeal.[51] The editors of this volume posit, "In a very basic sense, the central concern of this [work] is to put people as embodied subjects back into narratives of economic exchange. . . . It acknowledges and explores the corporeal and relational nature of labor and economic change" (12). Theories of affective labor enable us to examine the relationship between capitalism and embodiment by foregrounding the corporeal body whose bodily processes are being reshaped by the logics of capital and technology, in short, not just the laboring body but the feeling body.

In sum, the affective regimes of call centers enable us to rethink the relationship between technology, sociality, and intimacy, between the technological and the corporeal, and between humans and the tools (machines) we use to do our labor. Call center agents were taught to make the customer feel comfortable. They were trained to follow the cadences of the customer's speech, to make small talk to fill up dead time over the phone, and to open up the possibility of confidences being conveyed by soliciting information from customers. Whether it was a credit card charge or a hotel booking, customers provided details of their lives to which strangers would not necessarily be privy. Agents had to respond to such information in a manner that was sympathetic and engaged but "professional" in ways that perhaps parallel the engaged reactions of a healthcare professional or a counselor. Yet such interactions were mediated by technology, both the technology that enabled high-quality, "live" conversation with someone halfway across the world as well as the complex dialing technology that connected callers and agents.

We concur here with the work of scholars like Ariel Ducey and Boris and Parreñas, who resist the search for authenticity in their work on intimate labor.[52] For, while the affective regimes generated by call center work produce forms of alienation and social death for agents, the forms of intimacy enabled by these labor practices are much more complex than the easy dichotomies about commodified versus authentic relationships. Theories of affect—and, hence, of affective labor—imply a divergence from conceptions of consciousness predicated on assumptions of interiority. Theories of affect and affective labor enable us to problematize binaries that seem to be persistent in social theory: that of body versus mind and reason versus passion.

Conceptions of affective labor have epistemological and political implications in terms of how we may conceptualize the subjectivities of workers in intimate industries like call centers. Kathi Weeks asks, "What are the ways by which one can advance a theory of agency without deploying a model of the subject as it supposedly once was or is now beyond the reach of capital?"[53] Drawing on Baruch Spinoza's insistence on the ethical dimensions of affect, the affective labor of our informants allows us to think of their agency in terms of potentiality—as opposed to the unproductive binary of compliance versus resistance.[54] Encapsulating but also transecting emotional, cognitive, and corporeal labor, the affective labor of the call center agents with whom we worked reminds us of the centrality of affect to what Kathleen Stewart has termed processes of "worlding": the *generative* capacity to navigate the world, to be acted upon, and to act in the world.[55]

Notes

1. Karl Marx, *Economic and Philosophical Manuscripts of 1844, The Marx-Engels Reader*, 2nd ed., ed. Robert C. Tucker (New York: W.W. Norton, 1978); Lauren Berlant, ed., *Intimacy* (Chicago: University of Chicago Press, 2000).

2. Eileen Boris and Rhacel Salazar Parreñas, eds., introduction to *Intimate Labors: Cultures, Technologies and the Politics of Care* (Stanford: Stanford University Press, 2010), 1–11; Kalindi Vora, "The Transmission of Care: Affective Economies and Indian Call Centers," in Boris and Parreñas, *Intimate Labors*, 33–48.

3. Anthony Giddens, *The Transformation of Intimacy: Sexuality, Love, and Eroticism in Modern Societies* (Stanford: Stanford University Press, 1992).

4. Ara Wilson, *The Intimate Economies of Bangkok: Tomboys, Tycoons, and Avon Ladies in the Global City* (Berkeley: University of California Press, 2004); compare Yanagisako on the centrality of sentiment to capital: Sylvia Yanagisako, *Producing Culture and Capital: Family Firms in Italy* (Princeton, NJ: Princeton University Press, 2002).

5. Boris and Parreñas, introduction.

6. Ibid., 5.

7. Ibid.

8. Ibid., 4.

9. In 2004–5, this figure was over 60 percent. See Dilip Maitra, "India to Remain the BPO Capital of the World," *Deccan Herald*, October 18, 2012, www.deccanherald.com/content/233910/india-remain-bpo-capital-world.html.

10. Inderpal Grewal, *Transnational America: Feminisms, Diasporas, Neoliberalisms* (Durham, NC: Duke University Press, 2005); Aihwa Ong, *Neoliberalism as Exception: Mutations in Citizenship and Sovereignty* (Durham, NC: Duke University Press, 2006); Vora, "Transmission of Care."

11. This picture has been considerably altered by the reverse migration of Indian scientists and engineers, who have established India as a leading center of research and development. The software industry in India is now moving into product development and basic research in a big way, and many midlevel corporate executives are being lured back to India for jobs with multinational companies. As a result, the wage differentials between the United States and India have also shrunk.

12. Rachel Lee and Sau-Ling Cynthia Wong, eds., *Asian America.Net: Ethnicity, Nationalism, and Cyberspace* (New York: Routledge, 2003).

13. Ibid.; see also Ong, *Neoliberalism as Exception*.

14. Purnima Mankekar, "Becoming Entrepreneurial Subjects: Neoliberalism and Media," in *The State in India after Liberalization*, ed. Akhil Gupta and K. Sivaramakrishnan, 213–31 (New York: Routledge, 2011).

15. See Ong, *Neoliberalism as Exception*.

16. The comparable figure in the Philippines, now the world's largest hub for call centers, is $11 billion.

17. Maitra, "India to Remain."

18. For instance, see Kathi Weeks, "Life within and against Work: Affective Labor, Feminist Critique, and Post-Fordist Politics," *Ephemera* 7, no. 1 (2007): 233–49; see also Dyer-Witherford, Nick, "Empire, Immaterial Labor, the New Combinations, and the Global Worker" *Rethinking Marxism* 13, no. 3-4: 70–80 (2001); Hardt, Michael, and Antonio Negri. *Multitude: War and Democracy in the Age of Empire* (London: Penguin, 2005).

19. Michael Hardt, "What Affects Are Good For," in *The Affective Turn: Theorizing the Social*, ed. Patricia Clough (Durham, NC: Duke University Press, 2007), ix–xiii, xi.

20. Ibid.

21. Ibid., xii. The term *immaterial labor* is drawn from the work of Italian Marxists, who use it to refer to functions that generate and communicate symbolic activity but do not result in the production of a tangible commodity. Neither Michael Hardt ("Affective Labor," *Boundary 2* 26, no. 2 [1999]: 89–100) nor we conflate affective and immaterial labor, but parsing the relationship between these two terms is beyond the scope of this article. We prefer affective labor as an analytic because, first, it does not assume a teleological narrative in which immaterial labor forms the apex of the development of capitalism. Second, the move to services has resulted in the rapid growth of affective labor that involves a lot of hard bodily labor, as in elder care, nursing, and so forth. Third, unlike the term *immaterial labor*, *affective labor* does not resurrect the dichotomy of body versus mind and the crafting of real objects versus the manipulation of symbols. Instead, we follow Patricia Clough's suggestion that we look to the configurations of bodies, technologies, and matter that are involved in different forms of production. See Patricia Clough, introduction to *The Affective Turn: Theorizing the Social*, ed. Patricia Clough and Jean Halley (Durham, NC: Duke University Press, 2007), 1–33, 2.

22. Brian Massumi, *Parables for the Virtual: Movement, Affect, Sensation* (Durham, NC: Duke University Press, 2002); Lawrence Grossberg, "Affect's Future: Rediscovering the Virtual in the Actual" (interview by Melissa Gregg and Gregory J. Seigworth), in *Affect Theory Reader*, ed. Gregory J. Seigworth and Melissa Gregg (Durham, NC: Duke University Press, 2010), 309–38; Clough, introduction.

23. Massumi, *Parables for the Virtual*; Clough, "Introduction."

24. Arlie Hochschild, *The Managed Heart: Commercialization of Human Feeling* (Berkeley: University of California Press, 2012).

25. Mankekar, "Becoming Entrepreneurial Subjects."

26. Ibid., 215–16."

27. Gupta and Sharma, "Introduction," *The Anthropology of the State*, 1.

28. Hardt, "What Affects Are Good For," xi.

29. Hardt, "Affective Labor," 99.

30. Marx, *Economic and Philosophical Manuscripts*.

31. Ibid., 74.

32. See Weeks, "Life Within," 243.

33. Marx, *Economic and Philosophical Manuscripts*, 78.

34. Although working according to the clock no longer has a high affective charge today, it did when it was first introduced into industrial capitalism. See E. P. Thompson, "Time, Work-Discipline, and Industrial Capitalism," *Past and Present* 38, no. 1 (1967): 56–97.

35. See Carla Freeman's excellent descriptions of gendered surveillance in informatics, in *High Tech and High Heels in the Global Economy: Women, Work, and Pink-Collar Identities in the Caribbean* (Durham, NC: Duke University Press, 2000), 28.

36. A. Aneesh, *Virtual Migration: The Programming of Globalization* (Durham, NC: Duke University Press, 2006); see also Reena Patel, *Working the Night Shift: Women in India's Call Center Industry* (Stanford, CA: Stanford University Press, 2010).

37. See also Vora, "Transmission of Care."

38. See Emily Martin, *The Woman in the Body* (New York: Beacon Press, 1987); and Thompson's "Time" on the time-discipline of capitalism.

39. See, for instance, Kathleen Stewart, *Ordinary Affects* (Durham, NC: Duke University Press, 2007).

40. On affects, affective labor, and sociality in the workplace, see Melissa Gregg, "On Friday Night Drinks: Workplace Affects in the Age of the Cubicle," in *The Affect Theory Reader*, ed. Melissa Gregg and Gregory J. Seigworth (Durham, NC: Duke University Press, 2010), 250–68.

41. In the case of agents who did not live with their families, these parties were held in homes because the city of Bangalore imposed an 11:00 p.m. curfew on bars and restaurants in response to increasing moral panics over the "lewd behavior" of young people, including call center agents. In this manner the city, as it were, was involved in practicing surveillance and regulating the social lives of agents.

42. Gilles Deleuze, "Desire and Pleasure," in *Foucault and His Interlocutors*, ed. Arnold I. Davidson (Chicago: University of Chicago Press, 1998), 185–94.

43. Massumi, *Parables for the Virtual*; Clough, "Introduction"; Mankekar, "Becoming Entrepreneurial Subjects."

44. Berlant, *Intimacy*, 2.

45. See, especially, Rhacel Salazar Parreñas, *Servants of Globalization: Women, Migration, and Domestic Work* (Stanford, CA: Stanford University Press, 2001).

46. Compare Aneesh, *Virtual Migration*.

47. Nicole Constable, "The Commodification of Intimacy: Marriage, Sex, and Reproductive Labor," *Annual Review of Anthropology* 38 (2009): 49–64, 50.

48. Yanagisako, *Producing Culture and Capital*.

49. Wilson, *Intimate Economies of Bangkok*. See also Lisa Rofel, *Desiring China: Experiments in Neoliberalism, Sexuality, and Public Culture* (Durham, NC: Duke University Press, 2007), for

an important discussion of the mutual imbrication of desire and capitalism, and Purnima Mankekar, "Becoming Entrepreneurial Subjects: Neoliberalism and Media," in *The State in India after Liberalization*, ed. Akhil Gupta and K. Sivaramakrishnan (New York: Routledge, 2011), 213–31, on the romance of capitalism in neoliberal discourses in India.

50. Ariel Ducey, "More than a Job: Meaning, Affect, and Training Health Care Workers," in *The Affective Turn: Theorizing the Social*, ed. Patricia Clough with Jean Halley (Durham, NC: Duke University Press, 2007), 187–208.

51. Martin, *Woman in the Body*.

52. Ducey, "More than a Job"; and Boris and Parreñas, "Introduction."

53. Weeks, "Life Within," 245.

54. See also Saba Mahmood's critique of the liberal "resistant" subject in *Politics of Piety: The Islamic Revival and the Feminist Subject* (Princeton, NJ: Princeton University Press, 2011).

55. Stewart, *Ordinary Affects*.

Reproductive Labor at the Intersection of Three Intimate Industries: Domestic Work, Sex Tourism, and Adoption

Nicole Constable

Introduction

Estranged from her husband in Indonesia, Mia[1] came from central Java to work in Hong Kong as a domestic worker when she was in her twenties. In Hong Kong she worked for three different Chinese employers, paid back her recruitment debts, and regularly sent remittances to her mother, who took care of her two children in Java. While working for her third employer, she met an American at a bar. He was in Hong Kong working temporarily for a small business, and she began to see him and sleep with him regularly. After a few months, shortly after she learned that she was pregnant, he returned to his home country, and she never heard from him again. Meanwhile, when they learned that she was pregnant, her employers terminated her contract. Unwilling to return home in her condition, she overstayed her visa, worked

positions 24:1   DOI 10.1215/10679847-3320041

illegally, and stayed with friends in a cheap, crowded boarding house. Mia struggled with her decision about what to do with the baby, especially since it would be born "out of wedlock" and she already had two children to support. Like many other women I knew, she did not want to become a mother again. She first took behind-the-counter drugs to "throw the baby away" (i.e., cause a miscarriage), to no effect. Despite strong and persistent pressure and criticism from friends and acquaintances who urged her to take the baby to Indonesia, she decided, with the support of a nongovernmental organization (NGO), to "adopt the baby" (i.e., give the baby for adoption). The child was adopted almost a year later by a well-off expatriate couple in Hong Kong. Mia imagined the child would live in a fancy home, have a good education, and experience advantages that her children in Indonesia could not dream of. One day, when the child grew up, she hoped they would meet again. She had left a note to that effect in the baby's adoption file.

This article explores, ethnographically and critically, the contributions of migrant women like Mia to three intersecting sectors of "intimate industries" in Asia: domestic work, sex tourism, and adoption. While domestic work, sex work, and adoption have individually received much scholarly attention, the intersections between them have not. Here I consider how migrant women's "contributions" to these three sectors can be better understood if we consider both their paid and unpaid activities as "work." Most women I knew received formal pay only for domestic work and did *not* consider going to bars or giving a child for adoption "work." Yet, drawing from both feminist and Marxist thought, I ask what we can learn by looking at migrant women's intimate re/productive contributions to these three "intimate industries"? Their reproductive labor in each sector, I argue below, is obtained at low cost or no cost because of the type of activity and the way in which their laboring bodies are differently valued from those of locals and citizens. The intersections and overlaps between these otherwise distinct sectors illustrate the critical significance of global and regional class hierarchies and the intersections of gender, migration, race, and nationality within the context of late global capitalism. These intersections are especially pertinent for understanding the situations of those who perform less-valued (and less formally remunerated) activities or forms of immaterial labor that have been largely overlooked by Michael Hardt and Antonio Negri in their influential work on late global capitalism and empire.[2] Moreover, these three intimate industries allow us to consider the ongoing value of the nineteenth-century Marxist notion of "surplus labor" in a new context. The cases discussed below describe what I call the unpaid or low-paid "intimate surplus labor" or the unrecognized reproductive and intimate contributions of "immaterial labor" provided by migrant women within the contemporary political economy.

These three service sectors (as opposed to manufacturing industries) are among the many contemporary industries that provide services for clients or customers who seek assistance in finding marriage partners, children to adopt, sexual services, elderly and child caregivers, household workers, and other intimate, affective, or reproductive services. Brokers who work to recruit, promote, and facilitate access to intimate services of various sorts, and who are among the main financial beneficiaries of these industries, have begun to receive critical scholarly attention. Largely overlooked in scholarly literature, however, are the connections between different sectors such as domestic work and sex work. Especially little attention has been paid to how unpaid labor contributes to the success of many such industries. For example, one economic sector can inadvertently fuel another, providing additional labor or indirectly boosting profits, as in the case of migrant domestic workers who casually participate in the entertainment or sex industry.

Here I focus on how the formal and ongoing recruitment of Filipino and Indonesian domestic workers to do low-paid household and care work in Hong Kong is linked to two other industries for which domestic workers often unknowingly but voluntarily contribute what might be seen as free or very low-paid intimate labor of other sorts: the informal sex industry and, more recently and occasionally, what is popularly and informally referred to as the "adoption industry."[3] The free, informal, or unpaid voluntary labor of migrant women, as discussed below, can be seen as a contemporary permutation of David Ricardo's labor theory of value in which "surplus labor" creates the "surplus value" upon which capitalist profits are based. Ricardo and Karl Marx's notions of how labor created value in nineteenth-century Europe are still provocative: Workers were paid less than the value that their labor added to the goods they produced or services they provided. The difference between what workers were paid and the value of the products of their labor (what they sold for) represented "surplus value" based on "surplus labor" and contributed to capitalists' profits. In late modern intimate industries, who works, what is understood as "work," and who profits is perhaps less clear cut than in the classic cases of Ricardo and Marx's time, but the notion of surplus labor is nonetheless useful.

These intersecting industries also point to complex patterns of what Shellee Colen calls "reproductive stratification," by which she means that *both* "physical and social reproductive tasks are accomplished differentially according to inequalities that are based on hierarchies of class, race, ethnicity, gender, place in a global economy, and migration status and that are structured by social, economic, and political forces."[4] While Colen refers mainly to reproductive stratification between domestic workers and their employers, this article builds on Colen's work by expanding the scope of reproductive labor performed by migrant domestic workers to include a wider range of labor—particularly intimate labor that includes caretaking and sexual service work—and biopower. My use of *biopower* builds on Hardt's view of biopower's having "the potential of affective labor" and the "power of the creation of life."[5] Yet Hardt excludes biological procreation: "Biopolitical production here consists primarily in the labor involved in the creation of life—not the activities of procreation but the creation of life precisely in the production and reproduction of affects."[6] I argue that although affective reproductive labor and biological reproductive labor differ from each other in significant ways, as discussed below and in several other contributions to this issue, they are related to market processes in different ways. As Sharmila Rudrappa argues in this volume, parents who hire surrogates, like those who hire domestic workers, often prefer to view the relationship and transaction as financially based, whereas most adoptive parents strongly resist such a view of adoption. Yet brokers and facilitators in each of these sectors earn their living by facilitating access to procreative and nonprocreative intimate and reproductive labor of others.

Building on earlier research among domestic workers, here I utilize ethnographic and online materials gathered from 2010 through 2012.[7] Ethnographic research focused on migrant workers' romantic and sexual relationships, pregnancies, and motherhood in Hong Kong, while online research included analysis of two websites dedicated to sex tourism. Below I first outline some patterns of the "domestic worker industry," particularly the recruitment of Indonesian and Filipino domestic workers to Hong Kong and elsewhere, highlighting patterns of economic flows and the role of brokers. Concepts of reproductive labor and intimate surplus labor are used to discuss who (in the absence of capitalist "owners" of productive industries) profits or benefits from the migrant domestic worker industry and how. Second, I turn to the topic of sex tourism and to the role of informal Internet forums that promote particular images, advice, and information for men who pursue their "hobby" and want to meet "DHs" (domestic helpers) in Hong Kong. I consider some of the industry's parameters, including local laws and policies about soliciting and prostitution, formal and informal affective labor of Internet forums, and the ways in which this wider industry and its customers (who themselves contribute unpaid immaterial labor online) profit from the intimate and informal surplus labor of domestic workers. Third, I turn to adoption and to the difficult issues—especially moral and ethical ones—that adoption raises in relation to other forms of affective and intimate labor provided by migrant domestic workers. Regardless of the intentions of employers of domestic workers, men who pursue their sexual "hobby," and couples who adopt children, and despite the active and thoughtful choices made by migrant women that can yield certain benefits (including money, pleasure, hope, and freedom), these examples nonetheless reveal a fundamental inequity of who benefits and in what ways from these three industries and about the alignment of global privileges of class, race, gender, and nationality in stratified intimate and reproductive labor.[8]

Reproductive Labor and the Migrant Domestic Worker Industry

Exploitative recruitment practices faced by migrant domestic workers have long been criticized, and the mainstream international media has recently taken note.[9] In Hong Kong, foreign domestic workers have filed legal complaints against illegal charges and unscrupulous loans associated with the recruitment process. Hong Kong does not permit employment agencies to charge workers more than 10 percent of one month's wages (less than HK$400 or US$50 in 2012), but this has not prevented recruitment agencies in Indonesia and the Philippines from charging far more. In Indonesia, for example, women are advanced "pocket money" by recruiters and then, in order to get a job, must promise to repay it with steep interest, plus alleged costs of training centers, applications, paperwork, and medical examinations. For Indonesian recruits, this often amounts to almost seven months' wages. Should they lose their jobs before then, they are pressured by Hong Kong loan collectors to pay their debts. Those who profit from this industry include agency owners and their employees; formal and informal subcontractors that include the recruits' neighbors, community leaders, and relatives; owners and workers at associated loan agencies; affiliated agencies in Hong Kong; and actual employers, who as of 2013 are largely spared recruitment costs other than travel and wages.[10]

In Hong Kong, many parties benefit from the inexpensive labor of migrant domestic workers. Foreign women fill a critical niche that local women are loath to fill. Foreign workers cost far less than locals, and given their unrestricted work hours, and the requirement that they "live in," they receive much less than the local hourly minimum wage, which was, at the time of my research, HK$28 (US$3.60 in 2011 and 2012) and was increased to HK$32.50 in 2015. Employers, especially women who are otherwise responsible for the household duties performed by domestic workers (cooking, cleaning, caregiving), benefit from having more leisure time or from working in more lucrative occupations. Employers span a wide salary range and occupational spectrum. Some perform low-level sales and clerical work, barely meeting the annual household income required to hire a domestic worker; others are securely middle or upper-middle class. Hong Kong depends on and benefits from this inexpensive neoliberal solution to providing child and elderly care.

Domestic workers and their own families, of course, can benefit too. Employers are required to provide domestic workers with room and board, and they can earn US$500 per month. The wage, low by Hong Kong standards, is more than many well-educated workers and professionals earn at home. If all goes well and loans and agency fees are repaid, workers can save or remit funds to their families. Officially recorded remittances from abroad accounted for 11.7 percent of the gross domestic product (GDP) in the Philippines and 1.3 percent of that in Indonesia in 2009; in 2010 $21.3

billion were remitted to the Philippines and $7.1 billion to Indonesia,[11] but the gross regional domestic product figures for some migrant-sending regions of Indonesia, for example East Java, are estimated to be as much as 42 percent.[12] Domestic workers can also benefit in nonmaterial ways. They enjoy the modernity of Hong Kong, the opportunity to escape familial and other conflicts at home, and the chance to experience greater freedom and adventure. For Indonesian domestic workers in particular, mainly in their twenties and on average several years younger than Filipinas, Hong Kong offers escape from family supervision and the pressure to marry young.

Several points warrant emphasis. First, in order to become a domestic worker in Hong Kong, women must adhere to a pattern of stratified reproduction. Roughly half are married and have children at home, but they forego their own reproductive tasks, usually delegating the care of their own children to a female family member, often the maternal grandmother, while providing cheap and affordable reproductive labor for their employers, in what Rhacel Parreñas describes as a chain of care.[13] While their employers are free to have children, domestic workers are prohibited from bringing children or family members to Hong Kong. Although they are legally entitled to maternity benefits, there are significant barriers to their giving birth in Hong Kong, including the common practice of getting fired when they are discovered to be pregnant.[14] Domestic workers' reproductive labor as "maids" is in this sense what Evelyn Nakano Glen describes as the "array of activities and relationships involved in maintaining people both on a daily basis and intergenerationally."[15] This includes the time-consuming, affective, and service work of cooking, feeding, cleaning, and child care and elderly care—labor once provided by unpaid female household members.

Surplus labor, as noted, is commonly understood as the labor expended beyond what is necessary for subsistence.[16] Capitalist systems, according to Marx, depend on those who labor and others who benefit and profit from the surplus labor of others. Surplus labor refers to profits earned from paying low wages or getting work done for free. In other words, a person's labor may provide her with a living wage, but it also benefits others who are more advantageously situated within a capitalist system. Although scholars debate whether Marx's labor theory of value considered domestic work unproductive labor that does not create surplus value or as "reproductive and even productive labor that, since it creates surplus value either directly or indirectly, must be conceived as an integral part of capitalist production,"[17] for my purposes, it is clear that the longer her hours and the lower her wages, the more Hong Kong employers benefit from domestic workers. In Hong Kong, maximum work hours are not regulated, but many domestic workers work more than eighty hours a week. By law they are entitled a day off each week. On that day, relieving the workweek tedium and loneliness, women take part in a variety of activities in which they are not just "workers." They take part in religious gatherings at churches or mosques; political activism; social service and empowerment activities; volunteer work at elderly homes; fund-raising for local and overseas charity causes such as tsunami, typhoon, and earthquake disaster relief back home; music and dance performances; and beauty contests and talent shows. Women meet boyfriends and girlfriends and rendezvous in guesthouses and public spaces. Some work part time. Some spend time socializing at bars and clubs before returning to their employers' homes before their nighttime curfews. It is this latter activity, motivated largely by a desire for fun, friends, relaxation, and an escape from the narrow identity of "domestic helper," that potentially connects migrant women to the wider sex industry, which I turn to next.

Immaterial Labor and the Sex Industry

Research for this section is based partly on two English-language nonprofit Internet websites that provide information about the sex industry: The World Sex Guide and The International Sex Guide. Both provide forums for heterosexual men to discuss what some refer to as their "hobby" of having sex with women in different regions of the world. Both websites have forums devoted to particular countries and geographic regions. My research involved perusing several hundred postings about Hong Kong, particularly those that focused on domestic workers.[18] In relation to Hardt and Negri's idea of immaterial labor, these websites are interesting because they are apparently nonprofit and their content depends entirely on voluntary participation and contributions of members, some of whom have spent many hours posting experiences and offering advice. Despite the free labor from its members, these forums serve as informal advertising and promotion of particular sex-industry businesses and establishments, with posters frequently listing the names of their favorite bars and clubs (e.g., New Makati, Neptune III, which closed in December 2012, and many others) and providing evaluations of and tips about locating saunas, karaoke nightclubs (or hostess clubs), massage parlors, and brothels.[19]

Some "senior members" of the forums, self-ascribed experienced "punters" (slang for johns, consumers, or customers), have over a thousand posts. Some are Hong Kong residents or frequent business visitors. The vast majority are men. Less experienced punters or "newbies" to Hong Kong often pose questions and are referred to general guides and additional websites or receive advice for procuring sex in Hong Kong. Several discussion threads have to do with what one labels "horny DHs" (domestic helpers). Some posters provide advice on how to get sex for free or for as little as the cost of a meal and a taxi home; others occasionally criticize this as exploitation of poor women who are deeply in debt, have been recently fired, and who dabble in this business only out of temporary desperation. Whereas men acknowledge that there are Filipino and Indonesian professionals, DHs are depicted as not quite professionals and sometimes as innocent targets as opposed to Chinese and other "WGs" (working girls), who are rarely—if ever—talked about in terms of exploitation.[20]

A popular subtheme of Hong Kong discussions about DHs involves how to spot them, when and where to meet them, whether and how much to pay them, how to treat them, how many drinks to buy them before shifting to another prospect (when it is clear they are not interested in having sex), and the shades of grey between "professional" WGs who have a fixed price for particular services and other types of women one might meet in bars. These range from the professionals who work full time at the bar, those who are paid a commission on drinks (some of whom will be willing to have sex for money), and those who simply go to a bar during their free time to have fun, sometimes to meet a man, and perhaps make a little extra money from sex. Some women—especially domestic workers who go to bars on Sunday afternoons—are out for fun, sometimes hoping to meet someone for flirtation or a fling, a meaningful relationship and possibly an advantageous marriage, or to be treated to a meal and make a bit of extra money.[21] Some of the postings reflect an understanding that domestic workers who are between contracts, on recognizance papers, or are overstayers are more likely to have financial or other pragmatic motives for being there, including the hope of finding a man who is a resident and could sign her employment contract.[22] Few postings seem to directly or indirectly raise the possibility that women might strategically perform and utilize various common stereotypes about DHs so as to gain men's sympathy and their financial assistance (see also Hae Yeon Choo in this volume).[23] This might include telling stories of crushing debts from recruitment fees, being fired and having no place to stay, or having family crises that require money at home, all of which might well be the truth.

In 2011, Jim, from the United States, bragged online about his exploits with a Hong Kong DH. He claimed he successfully convinced a beautiful, sexy, unsuspecting Filipina virgin that he was her "boyfriend." By buying her dinner and drinks, giving her small gifts and taxi fare, sweet-talking her and treating her like his "girlfriend" (holding hands, touching her gently in public, and spending time with her), she agreed to spend the night with him and to have oral sex but not to have intercourse because she was a virgin. On their second night together, she agreed to have intercourse. By treating her well, he told forum readers, he got sex for free. Pointing to the distinction between "mongers" (or punters) who pay for sex, and "players" who use charm and finesse to get it, he and others advised readers on where to go to meet DHs and on how to treat them so as to spend much less money than with a WG. Jim enthusiastically recounted his good fortune in having free sex with a virgin. Interestingly, some domestic workers I spoke to about Jim's post echoed the reaction of two academics I talked to, raising the question of who had fooled whom. Perhaps the woman had strung him along, convincing him that she was a virgin to maintain his interest and prolong his attention over a period of time? In other words, men and women can both manipulate such situations to their advantage. Women's apparently unpaid intimate surplus labor may serve as an investment into a murky moral economy in which rewards can take different forms and fit into unpredictable time frames and gambles.[24]

A book about the lives of expatriates in Hong Kong describes the experiences of Hamish, a British expatriate who does regular rounds of pubs in Wanchai:

Hamish knows that "working girls" fall into two categories. There are professionals, prostitutes who are "very, very expensive" and Filipino or Indonesian maids freelancing on the side. The latter will "fuck your brains out for the price of a gin and tonic." Alternatively they may want to form intimate alliances of various kinds with (Chinese and Western) men of financial substance who can buy them presents or give them small amounts of money. Hamish astutely connects the labor force around what he calls the "girlie bars" and the maids he sees in Statue Square on Sundays in what he dismissively calls the "birdcage" because of its concentration of women chattering. Some of them freelance in a variety of ways in Wanchai. He identifies a spectrum of Southeast Asian female migration circumstances in which "gweilo" [foreign] men are a resource for accumulating money and opportunities. Intimate relationships with wealthier men supplement low wages. Marriage offers a route out to another kind of life altogether. . . . The emotional and the financial are interconnected. It is easy, Hamish says wistfully, for men of his age to fall in love with younger women: especially when they are beautiful. Love, sex, and money form a powerful matrix in the Wanchai night.[25]

Wanchai bars, which are well known in the sex industry and largely oriented toward Western expatriates and military men on leave, must work to attract women customers by having ladies' nights and offering them cheap or free drinks. They offer women free drinks or a cut on the cost of drinks that men buy them. One former domestic worker I knew regularly frequented several Wanchai bars with two former domestic worker friends. They wore makeup and tight sexy clothing and struck provocative homoerotic poses. Men responded by buying them more drinks in an effort to further lower their inhibitions and to get them to behave more flirtatiously and seductively. Domestic workers on their day off and freelancers who function much like hostesses in other settings flatter men and offer them attention and are thus essential to the popularity of bars and their ability to attract male customers.[26] As the forum posts suggest, some women are there only to drink and socialize or to make money from drinks and have fun, but others are open to—or hoping for—something more, as the following examples illustrate.

Wahyu, an Indonesian in her early thirties, left two children behind in Indonesia when she went to work in Taiwan and then in Hong Kong with a domestic worker visa. Although the details of her early experiences as a domestic worker in Hong Kong were never clear to me, she spent at least her day off in bars, and when she was terminated, a bar owner or manager agreed to sign her domestic worker contract, and she spent more time at the bar. Eventually, she overstayed her visa and continued to work in Wanchai. She recounted making money in Taiwan and Hong Kong bars and spending several months in prison for selling drugs, but she was released early because she was pregnant. When I met her, she had recently given birth. The father was a European man she'd met at a Wanchai bar who traveled to Hong Kong on monthly business. She said that she knew he was married and would never leave his wife, but she considered him her "boyfriend" because she saw him regularly over several months. He did not use protection, and she had expected, based on his cavalier dismissal of her concerns about pregnancy (saying they would "deal with it"), that he would help her in some way, perhaps by providing financial support or paying for an abortion. Whenever he was in town, she stayed in his hotel room. When she told him she was pregnant, they had uncharacteristically rough sex; she speculated that he had tried to cause a miscarriage. Then she never saw or heard from him again. Originally, she planned to put the baby up for adoption, but later, inspired by a friend who filed a paternity claim against the Hong Kong resident father of her child, Wahyu decided to pursue him legally to prove paternity and secure child support. She had the man's business card and contact information in Europe, and other pertinent information, so she approached a migrant worker organization in the hope of finding a lawyer.

Anti, an Indonesian domestic worker in her twenties, went with her friends to a Wanchai bar on their Sunday off for fun. She recounted that she and her friends were invited by a group of men—mostly white men and a few Pakistanis—to a man's birthday party in an upscale hotel. Anti agreed to join her friends, and she remembered a lot of drinking and dancing. The next morning, she awoke naked and alone in the hotel room with only vague memories of coming in and out of consciousness while she was being raped by several men. When she learned that she was pregnant, she took illegally obtained abortive drugs, bled a little, and hoped that the pregnancy had ended. When it turned out she had not miscarried as planned, she decided on adoption. After she gave birth, she only glanced at the infant, who was soon placed in a group home for babies awaiting adoption. She saw the baby once more at the home when she officially gave up her parental rights (she thought the baby looked like her, offering no hint as to the ethnicity or race of the biological father). In a scenario recounted to her by the social worker who had assisted her with the process, and echoing Mia's expectations, she assumed her child would be adopted by a wealthy expatriate family in Hong Kong and would have a better future than she could provide. Taking an "out of wedlock" baby home was out of the question. She was unmarried, assumed to be a virgin, and she hoped her family would never learn about her pregnancy. She processed a new work contract, spent a few weeks in Jakarta (without returning home to her family), and soon went back to work for a new Hong Kong employer less than two months after the birth.

Wanchai bars, linked to earlier times of US military R & R in Hong Kong, are notoriously aimed at attracting Western men, even though the military presence has dropped substantially. Some also welcome other nationalities of clientele, including Africans and Pakistanis, some of whom are Hong Kong residents or visitors, others of whom are undocumented workers. Certain bars and neighborhoods cater to different ethnic groups and nationalities. Areas of Tsim Sha Tsui cater exclusively to Chinese men and areas of Yaumatei and Jordan cater to South Asian and Nepalese men. Domestic workers know where to go to meet men of different nationalities. One Filipina described meeting her friends and praying at the mosque on Sundays, then shedding their modest clothing and head covers and going to a Wanchai bar in the afternoon where they would meet their Pakistani and Sri Lankan husbands and boyfriends before returning home to their employers' flats on Sunday evening. Besides bars and clubs, there are many public spaces, including several parks and shopping areas, where male migrants from different parts of Asia and Africa, as well as asylum seekers and torture claimants from Africa and South Asia, meet foreign domestic workers.[27]

The first intersection between industries involves domestic workers who visit bars on their days off, made up and dressed up to counteract the harsh monotony of their work, to flirt, drink, sing, dance, and socialize. In contrast to their lives as migrant workers, where "good workers" are constructed as "just workers" (not mothers, wives, or lovers), bars offer opportunities to be sexy and feminine, to meet men for attention, sex, money, or love. The women's presence—a form of intimate surplus labor—contributes to the attraction of the bar to male customers. Men are drawn by the chance to meet attractive women distinguished by class, race, gender, and migrant identities, who raise the possibility of cheap or free sex, compared with that procured from professional WGs. In the second intersection, such sexual relationships can lead to unwanted pregnancy and sometimes to adoption.

Adoption of Domestic Workers' Babies

One nongovernmental organization estimates that there are around six thousand migrant mothers and their babies in Hong Kong, not including those who have returned home pregnant or with their children.[28] Given the lack of quantitative data, it is difficult to say how many domestic workers become pregnant in Hong Kong, how many have legal or illegal abortions, and how many give birth in Hong Kong or go home to do so.

Many migrant mothers take their babies home to the Philippines or Indonesia and leave them temporarily with a family member to look after or to raise as their own, while they return to migrant work and send remittances to support the child. In most such cases, birth mothers try to earn money to support the child. I knew one Indonesian mother who was said to have "sold" her baby to a childless woman in Jakarta (a returned migrant worker she had met in Hong Kong). The birth mother said that the woman was trying to extort money from her, while the woman in Jakarta claimed that the birth mother had demanded that *she* pay for the child. While I was never sure whose story was true, after less than a month, the birth mother retrieved the baby and was overjoyed that her brother and his wife agreed to raise the child as theirs.

In several cases, including some that transpired over a decade ago, Filipino domestic workers arranged to adopt the unwanted children of other domestic workers. Legal adoptions (as opposed to informal fostering) took place either in Hong Kong (through the Philippine consulate) or in the Philippines. Two Filipina adoptive mothers said that they had their own names put on the child's birth certificate. Only a small number of domestic workers give their children for adoption in Hong Kong, and those who do often go back to work as quickly as they can after the baby is delivered. Some adoptions of domestic workers' children are arranged privately, with legal assistance and possibly with economic compensation for the birth mother. Such private arrangements are difficult to learn about.[29] Nonprivate adoptions of domestic workers' children are fairly recent and must go through the Social Welfare Department (SWD). The SWD was unwilling or unable to tell me how many adoptions were of children born to domestic workers, but it is clear that the number is fairly small, probably well under fifty a year.

I visited one of three possible institutional residences for locally born babies awaiting local adoption in Hong Kong. Of the twenty-five available cribs at this residence, the vast majority were used by Chinese babies born of young unwed Hong Kong Chinese women. Over the past few years, I was told, the number of babies born of Indonesian domestic worker mothers increased from one or two babies (out of twenty-five housed at any one time) to five or even seven at a time. These numbers might inadvertently overstate the number of babies of migrant mothers because the time frame for adopting babies of Hong Kong Chinese mothers is much shorter than for migrant mothers. Chinese babies are often adopted within two or three months, but the adoption of babies of migrant women, especially women who are married abroad, requires a time-consuming process of "tracing" or attempting to trace her legal husband overseas to get his permission for the adoption, even if he is not the father.[30] For the mothers, the process of releasing their children for adoption is complex and time-consuming and includes registering the birth, obtaining a birth certificate at the birth registry, and participating in counseling sessions with SWD social workers who often try to convince them to take the baby home; mothers who delay the child-release process or disappear or return home without completing it significantly prolong the process. Some babies have remained in the institutional residence for a year or more, not because of a shortage of prospective adoptive parents but because of the legal requirements to release the baby for adoption.

Most of the babies of migrant mothers in the residence over the past few years were "mixed race" and had Indonesian birth mothers. Many of the biological fathers of babies with darker skin or eyes were presumed to be South Asian or African. Others looked more like their mothers (Indonesian), and when I asked the staff member about their fathers, I was told that they could have been of any number of other nationalities, including Asians (perhaps Chinese or Nepalese) or whites. The staff member at the institutional residence could not recall any babies with Filipina birth mothers and she confirmed that "mixed" babies were adopted mostly—or entirely—by white or mixed-race expatriate couples. Another part of the building housed babies and young children with more severe special needs; most had been left behind by mainland Chinese mothers. If they were adopted at all, they would likely be adopted in the West; some had gone to the United States.

John and Mary Smith, a British expatriate couple who had lived in Hong Kong several years, could not have a child of their own for medical reasons, so they decided to adopt locally. John was a professional with a good income, and Mary was happy to put aside her career to be a mother (with the help of a domestic worker who would help with child care and household work). The Smiths' circumstances were financially very good, and they lived in a prestigious area of Hong Kong. Mary described the process, including the application form, classes she and John had to attend, home visits by social workers occurring before they were deemed eligible to adopt and again before the adoption was finalized, and the wait and eventual final legal approval of the adoption. The Smiths' baby's birth mother was an Indonesian domestic worker and the biological father was reputedly a foreign "trader" who had come to Hong Kong briefly on business. As Mary explained, she knew several well-off white expatriate families with "mixed-race" adopted children, several belonging to the same play group. According to Mary, several other adoptive parents, and staff in the adoption industry, Chinese locals prefer to adopt children who "look like them" (i.e., are Chinese), so "mixed-race" children are often adopted by white expatriates who are said to "care less about race" or occasionally by mixed-race couples.

The term *broker*—as a person who coordinates, arranges, or facilitates commercial transactions between buyers and sellers—applies fairly comfortably to the domestic worker sector and refers to the recruiters and agencies of various levels that make money from recruiting domestic workers and their affective and reproductive labor for overseas markets, including Hong Kong. The term also applies fairly easily to the sex work sector with regard to workers who are recruited to work as "entertainers," many of whom come to Hong Kong to work for short stints on tourist visas or for longer periods on work visas. It also applies loosely to touts and informal online sex industry websites that help punters to access the sexual services they desire. Applied to adoption (like marriage), the terms *broker* and *industry* sit less comfortably, primarily because of a common popular and current aversion—in the West and increasingly in Asia—to equating intimate and affective familial relationships with the commodification or the "purchase of intimacy."[31] Associating children (or wives) with commodities undoubtedly touches a sensitive nerve, one that often triggers concerns about trafficking or the "sale" of women and children.

Adoptive expatriate parents in Hong Kong often react defensively to the idea that adoptions are economic transactions or a form of "buying babies." Those who might be considered "brokers" or facilitators in this industry are equally wary of such terms. In the case of the adoption of babies of domestic workers who go through institutional channels (i.e., that are not arranged privately), the process can involve a variety of "middlemen," including migrant worker social workers and advocates or advisors at nongovernmental organizations who provide pregnant women or mothers with information about adoption and help them to navigate the bureaucratic procedures. Such organizations conceive of their work as "helping" the birth mother, the child, and the adoptive family. The process also includes SWD social workers and Immigration Department officers who often see their primary role as gatekeepers whose duty is to persuade errant migrant women to take responsibility for their babies and take them home, not "abandon" them in Hong Kong. Ultimately, if the birth mother remains firm about adoption, then social workers must give approval. Others involved in the process of releasing such children for adoption include an NGO called International Social Services, which is responsible for tracing the birth mother's husband (if she is married) for permission to adopt, even when he is not the father. The institutional home for the child awaiting adoption and a series of other volunteers, paid service providers, and medical practitioners look after the child before the institutional adoption process is finalized. The legal system is also involved, and a judge approves the final legal adoption. Many such "facilitators" are paid for their work facilitating the adoption of children by the adoptive parents, but the birth mother is not.

Domestic work, sex work, and biological reproduction might all be said to produce services or "value" for different sectors of intimate industries. In each case, the labor is understood differently, but all three are devalued because of the way that gender, race, and migration status align. Each form of intimate activity (domestic work, unpaid sex or entertainment work, and procreative work) involves different sorts of bodily effort, different kinds of emotions, affect, and pleasures. Housework involves long hours, isolation, and lonely, tedious, and repetitive work, often with little or no pleasure and low pay. The tedium of their work and their official designation as "domestic helpers" (not permitted to have families or lovers) propel some women to seek companionship, entertainment, or sexual pleasures on their day off. Because women frequent bars for fun and pleasure, to be something other than "domestic helpers," bars attract male patrons who seek the presence or the intimate attention of DHs. For these men, it is ostensibly possible to have sex with DHs for far less than with professional sex workers. Yet sexual encounters risk unwanted pregnancies, which, in some cases, support an adoption industry. In each case, lines are crossed but also blurred. Women's reproductive procreative labor—much like low-paid reproductive household labor—is devalued in this context, partly because pregnancy is considered instinctual, not skilled or creative work deserving of compensation.

A striking difference between the social construction of domestic work, sex work, and the procreative labor of adoptive birth mothers has to do with monetary remuneration. Most would agree that migrant domestic workers should be paid for their work. WGs are paid by definition, although domestic workers who casually or informally participate in the sex industry and have drinks or sex with men they meet in bars are often paid far less than professional prostitutes and often depend on men's kindness, sympathy, and generosity. In other words, their immaterial service work or voluntary affective labor is often not considered work at all, by them or others. They and their customers may prefer that the financial arrangement be hidden or disguised as more of a voluntary exchange in the guise of gifts that are exchanged for intimacy. Some women may agree to have sex with men for fun or the price of a few drinks and taxi fare. In some cases, it is likely that the inflated amount requested for taxi fare is in fact a subtle way of preserving the impression of the GFE (girlfriend experience) and serves as real pay for services.[32] In some cases, women seek companionship and a "boyfriend experience." In the case of the procreative reproductive work of birth mothers, there is a widespread view that they should not be paid. The case of adoption stands in striking contrast to surrogacy and egg donation (see Sharmila Rudrappa and Daisy Deomampo in this volume); payment to an adoptive birth mother for her reproductive labor raises fears of child trafficking and questions about the birth mother's ethics and morals, whereas surrogacy can be justified as renting a womb and as a financial arrangement. Although Hong Kong birth mothers can receive medical care (with costs covered by welfare or charities), I have never heard of anyone (in Hong Kong or elsewhere) advocating to pay birth mothers for their time and labor (as one might a surrogate or an egg donor). Similar to the notion that payment for organ donation might promote unethical exploitation of the poor who might willingly sell kidneys and other organs out of necessity or desperation, paying birth mothers for their biological labor is seen as a slippery ethical slope that could fuel a market for babies. Hong Kong officials go to great lengths to assure that a woman and her husband (if she has one) or the biological father (if she knows how to reach him) are willing to release the child for adoption, and they often pressure birth mothers to keep their children. Most Hong Kong government officials (including the Indonesian consul) consider such babies the birth mother's rightful responsibility. Organizations that support adoption often see it as a way to give the child a better future, to "help" the birth mother, relieving her of an unwanted burden.

Commenting on the idea of birth mothers getting paid for their children, Jumati, an Indonesian domestic worker and the birth mother of a child who had been adopted a few years earlier, spoke to me several times over a year and a half about the pressure she had experienced from many sides *not* to give her child for adoption. While she credited a helpful and sympathetic NGO for helping her to make up her mind on what to do and to follow the procedures to give her child for adoption, she experienced pressure from staff at the Indonesian consulate, her immigration officer, SWD social workers, and from Indonesian friends and acquaintances not to do so. They said, "It is your child, how can you give it away?" "You are the mother, you should keep it." "It is wrong not to keep your baby." She told me that what finally shut her friends up and stopped them from pressuring her was when she finally told them, in a burst of impatience, that the NGO had paid her for the child. "I told them they [the NGO] gave me a few thousand [HK] dollars. That they gave me money!" This explanation seemed to provide a satisfactory and conversation-stopping explanation; it also points to an economic logic that other Indonesian women well understood. To Jumati and her friends, the idea of receiving compensation for providing a child to childless and wealthy expatriate family, made sense.[33] Unfortunately, for the NGO involved, however, her story fueled the stubborn and persistent rumor that they "buy and sell babies," a charge they continuously defended themselves against.[34]

Conclusion: Intimate Labor within a System of Global Inequality

What can be said about these three forms of intimate labor and their ties to global inequality? How does one sector provide labor and "products" for another? The case of migrant domestic workers is a well-studied example. Women who can afford to, often outsource household duties to women of different race, class, and national origins. New recruits of migrant women from poorer regions of the world move to wealthier regions to fill these roles, and a variety of brokers and subbrokers at home and abroad profit. The sending states benefit from the employment opportunities and remittances they generate, while the receiving states benefit from the neoliberal market solution to what might otherwise be considered government responsibility.

Similarly, the sex industry is regulated and controlled by the Hong Kong government. Although prostitution is legal, brothels and solicitation are not. "Crackdowns" on brothels regularly appear in the local news. While police raids are commonly heard of and migrant women are often arrested for sex-work-related offenses (I have witnessed on several occasions mainland Chinese women who are presumably caught soliciting being arrested by the police in the Jordan and Yaumatei area), migrant women with valid domestic worker visas who go to bars and work casually or informally and who can pass as customers are relatively safe. Clearly, many bars and clubs—including their owners, managers, and employees—benefit from attracting male customers and depend on the continuing attraction of having many young and sexy available Southeast Asian women around for potential hookups and paid services. Some bars hire men or women of different nationalities. For example, Filipino men have long been musicians and performers in Hong Kong, and Nepalese men are bartenders or bouncers, while Nepalese women are waitresses because many have local residence and can therefore work legally for low wages. Many nationalities of women are represented in the Hong Kong sex industry, but Filipino and Indonesian domestic workers and former domestic workers form a unique and significant part of it, partly because they are considered friendlier and more accessible to Western and other foreign men than local and mainland Chinese women or South Asian women, and partly because they are less expensive, a possible bargain, and sometimes "free" compared with WGs. This reputation extends beyond Western and white expatriates and is shared by many of Hong Kong's ethnic minority men and migrants from South Asia and Africa.[35]

Many of the sixty-five or more domestic workers I knew who were pregnant or had babies became pregnant with a long-term partner or someone they considered "like a husband." Some became pregnant accidentally or as a result of alcohol use. In several cases, women I knew said they became pregnant as a result of rape.[36] Given the many social pressures against doing so, relatively few women chose to give their children up for adoption, especially those who had an ongoing relationship with the father. But some did, and their reproductive labor was never considered "work." On the contrary, domestic workers who got pregnant were seen by employers as the opposite of "good workers," and those who gave up their children were also "bad mothers." Some NGO counselors and social workers understood adoption as a way to "help" the birth mother and the child. Expatriate adoptive parents described the child as a "gift"—but one they could never reciprocate, since they did not know the birth mother.

Ultimately, the examples described above illustrate how the various intimate labors of migrant domestic workers spill out in unplanned and unintended ways, propelled by global capitalist logics of intimate affective and reproductive surplus labor. The work migrant women do—well beyond their paid household work—benefits privileged employers, consumers, adoptive parents, as well as many others who own, manage, or work in the wider commercial sectors of intimate industries. Domestic workers create profits and contribute to the incomes of those who work in sex-related industries. They support the adoption-related "industry" not only by justifying the compensated work of those whose work is recognized as useful labor—lawyers, caregivers, NGO staff, social workers, and others—but by contributing the stratified reproductive labor that helps to fill the material demand for babies among childless and privileged expatriates who would otherwise compete with local Chinese parents who receive priority in adopting higher-demand Chinese babies. Of course, domestic workers can also benefit or derive pleasure from their activities in relation to all three sectors, but their activities and choices are always circumscribed by the constraints of class, gender, race, and migratory status.

Notes

Rhacel Salazar Parreñas, Hung Cam Thai, and Rachel Silvey organized the conference in which this paper was first presented. I woud like to thank them, the conference participants, and Joseph Alter, Sealing Cheng, Hae Yeon Choo, Marianne Novy, and Sharmila Rudrappa for their helpful comments.

1. This and other names are pseudonyms.
2. Michael Hardt and Antonio Negri, *Empire* (Cambridge, MA: Harvard University Press, 2000); and Michael Hardt and Antonio Negri, *Multitude: War and Democracy in the Age of Empire* (New York: Penguin, 2004). Mary Hawkesworth, "The Gendered Ontology of *Multitude*," *Political Theory* 34, no. 3 (2006): 357–64, has a trenchant critique of Hardt and Negri's work. She writes:

   > In conceptualizing immaterial labor, rather than 'service work' as the hegemonic form of labor under globalization, Hardt and Negri privilege the elite sectors of service work (knowledge production, information technology, finance) dominated by men, eliding the heavily embodied service sectors populated by women ("care work," domestic labor, sex work). In most of its iterations, immaterial labor is conflated with intellectual labor, cognitive labor, problem solving, symbolic and analytic tasks, and linguistic expression, spheres long associated in the history of Western political thought with male capacities. (358)

   Hawkesworth also notes that they discuss reproduction, but that their examples suggest that "it is an all-male affair" (358).

3. Marriage could also be considered a reproductive intimate industry, but due to space limitations and the fact that most domestic workers who marry in Hong Kong do not meet partners through marriage brokers or the marriage industry per se, I am not including mar-

riage in the present discussion. But see Pei-Chia Lan, "New Global Politics of Reproductive Labor: Gendered Labor and Marriage Migration," *Sociology Compass*, no. 6 (2008): 1801–15.

4. Shellee Colen, "'Like a Mother to Them': Stratified Reproduction and West Indian Child-care Workers and Employers in New York," in *Conceiving the New World Order: The Global Politics of Reproduction*, ed. Faye D. Ginsburg and Rayna Rapp (Berkeley: University of California Press, 1995), 78–102, 78.

5. Michael Hardt, "Affective Labor," *boundary 2* 26, no. 2 (1999): 89–100, 98.

6. Ibid., 99.

7. See Nicole Constable, *Maid to Order in Hong Kong: Stories of Migrant Workers* (Ithaca, NY: Cornell University Press, 2007); and *Born out of Place: Migrant Mothers, Babies, and the Politics of Labor in Hong Kong* (Berkeley: University of California Press, 2014).

8. Brooke M. Beloso "Sex, Work, and the Feminist Erasure of Class," *Signs* 38, no. 1 (2012): 47–70.

9. Sheridan Prass and Cathy Chan, "Indentured Service, Hong Kong Style," *Bloomsburg Business-week*, November 15, 2012, www.businessweek.com/articles/2012-11-15/indentured-servitude -hong-kong-style.

10. Johan Lindquist, "*Petugas Lapangan*, Field Agent," *Indonesia* 87 (2009): 55–57. Wayne Palmer, "Costly Inducements: Pocket Money Given to Intending Migrant Domestic Workers Comes at a Price," *Inside Indonesia*, April–June 2010, www.insideindonesia.org/feature-editions/costly -inducements.

11. *Migration and Remittances Factbook*, 2nd ed. (Washington DC: The World Bank, 2011), 24, siteresources.worldbank.org/INTLAC/Resources/Factbook2011-Ebook.pdf.

12. Frances Barnes, *Indonesia Country Report*, n.d., www.ausaid.gov.au/Publications/Documents /indonesia_study.pdf (accessed January 15, 2014).

13. Rhacel Salazar Parreñas, *Servants of Globalization: Women, Migration, and Domestic Work* (Stanford, CA: Stanford University Press, 2001).

14. Constable, *Born out of Place*.

15. Evelyn Nakano Glenn, "From Servitude to Service Work: Historical Continuities in the Racial Division of Paid Reproductive Labor," *Signs: Journal of Women in Culture and Society* 18, no. 1 (1992): 1–43, 1.

16. Karl Marx, *Capital*, vol. 1 (London: Electric Book, 1967), 312–13.

17. Kathi Weeks, *The Problem of Work: Feminism, Marxism, Antiwork Politics, and Postwork Images* (Durham, NC: Duke University Press, 2011), 119.

18. I did not obtain permission to quote materials from these websites, so the materials I describe here are broadly summarized. Jim is a pseudonym.

19. Prostitution is legal in Hong Kong, but running a brothel, making money from someone else's prostitution, and soliciting or advertising for prostitution is not.

20. No such sympathy or concern was expressed for Mainland Chinese migrant sex workers or Hong Kong locals. Many men are reluctant to visit establishments or meet sex workers

with whom they cannot communicate. Language barriers may prevent them from gaining sympathy for other migrant sex workers. Discussions of Chinese establishments and services tend to focus on how to access services and negotiate transactions. Filipinos often speak some English, as do many Indonesians who worked in Singapore or have English-speaking boyfriends.

21. In the course of my research, I met and was told of several married couples who originally met in bars. I learned of a few cases of men who signed women's domestic worker contracts. In some cases the woman worked and was paid for domestic work, and in other cases, this was a way for the person to remain in Hong Kong and work "illegally."

22. Recognizance papers are given to people who file claims with the Hong Kong government in accordance with the United Nations (UN) Convention against Torture or with the UN High Commissioner for Refugees (UNHCR) in accordance with the UN Convention on Refugees (see Constable, *Born out of Place*). Former domestic workers who file such claims, like other claimants, receive minimal social support and are not legally permitted to work. These claims generally allow them to remain in Hong Kong for up to several years while their cases are processed.

23. Except for the sexual aspect, my relationship with them was somewhat similar to their relationships or "friendships" with men they met in bars. They rarely asked me for money directly but suggested we eat together and (correctly) assumed I would pay. They told me about their financial difficulties, especially emergencies that arose after leaving Hong Kong, in the hope that I could help. One advantage of having friends with jobs and money is that they might be good resources in times of need. Given women's lack of money, they were remarkably generous with their peers. They hoped that the men they met in bars and with whom they had developed friendships or sexual relationships, like other friends, would help them financially.

24. In contrast to later posts about how to spot desperate DHs who would be satisfied for simply cab fare, Jim's post did not seem to be criticized as exploitation.

25. Caroline Knowles and Douglas Harper, *Hong Kong: Migrant Lives, Landscapes, and Journeys* (Chicago: University of Chicago Press, 2009), 188–89.

26. On hostesses, see Rhacel Salazar Parreñas, *Illicit Flirtations: Labor, Migration, and Sex Trafficking in Tokyo* (Stanford, CA: Stanford University Press, 2011); and Anne Allison, *Nightwork: Sexuality, Pleasure, and Corporate Masculinity in a Tokyo Hostess Club* (Chicago: University of Chicago Press, 1994).

27. Constable, *Born out of Place*.

28. See PathFinders *Annual Report 2011, available at* www.pathfinders.org.hk. Another estimate is that there are 3,000 pregnant domestic workers per year, 1 percent of the total population of 300,000 foreign domestic workers.

29. In her historical study of US adoptions in the 1950s and 1960s, Rickie Solinger's *Wake Up Little Susie* (New York: Routledge, 2000) found that 39 percent of the middle-class white

women she knew of chose "black-market" independent adoptions with the likely help of lawyers or obstetricians. In those black-market deals, which were opposed by policy makers and social service providers, the birth mother "was paid money to cover her prenatal care and living costs, her delivery expenses, and an additional sum in exchange for the baby" (32).

30. If the woman is unmarried or can prove the husband is not the father, the process can be shorter.

31. See Viviana Zelizer, *The Purchase of Intimacy* (Princeton, NJ: Princeton University Press, 2005); and Nicole Constable, "The Commodification of Intimacy: Marriage, Sex, and Reproductive Labor," *Annual Review of Anthropology* 38 (2009): 49–64.

32. My guess would be that many women do not spend the taxi fare on taxis but take far less expensive modes of transportation and keep the money. Men tell of giving women several hundred Hong Kong dollars, which seems highly inflated. On the GFE, see Elizabeth Bernstein, *Temporarily Yours: Intimacy, Authenticity, and the Commerce of Sex* (Chicago: University of Chicago Press, 2007).

33. Jumati was not rejecting motherhood altogether. She already had children back home who depended on her remittances. Adopting out her baby made it possible to go back to work again and send home remittances.

34. Solinger, in *Wake Up Little Susie*, shows that adoption in the United States in the 1950s and 1960s (pre–*Roe v. Wade*) was an opportunity for redemption of white single mothers who could be "cured" if they expressed remorse at their sexual promiscuity (and did not succumb to the black market) but that it offered no such opportunities for black women. Solinger points to market factors in which white women produced valuable "commodities," whereas black babies lacked market value (29). "White babies . . . entered a healthy sellers' market, with up to ten couples competing for every one adoptable infant" (30).

35. A story I heard several times, once by an African migrant worker, was about a well-known Indian prostitute who returned to Chungking Mansions in Kowloon after a long time away. She reputedly turned to the nearest man and said, "Where have all the prostitutes gone?" He replied, "They have been replaced by domestic helper girlfriends."

36. One social worker bluntly said that she *never* believes stories of rape. Some cases I knew of undoubtedly constituted rape. My role was not been to judge the "truth" but to contemplate the meaning of such stories and the cross-cultural misunderstandings that occur between men and women over sex. One African man told me that any woman who enters a man's room is "fair game." Another man, a recent arrival to Hong Kong, was surprised to learn that a man was arrested for molesting a woman in an elevator (it was captured by a security camera). He was also surprised that drunkenness is not a valid defense for sexual assault.

Beyond the Brokers:

Local Marriage Migration Industries of Rural Vietnam

Danièle Bélanger

Introduction

On January 1, 2013, the Vietnamese press reported on several successful police raids in hotels in Can Tho City where Chinese men were meeting Vietnamese women with the objective of finding a wife.[1] According to these reports, the men were fined and ordered out of the country for activities not allowed under the terms of their visas. A few days earlier, VNExpress published a story on a ring of nine Vietnamese and seven Chinese involved in trafficking Vietnamese girls to China.[2] In another report, a high-ranking official expressed fears for the future of Vietnamese men due to the shortage of women caused by marriage out-migration. Concerns over men's ability to marry are exacerbated by the recent increase in sex ratios at birth due to the practice of sex-selective abortion, which has created a shortage

positions 24:1   DOI 10.1215/10679847-3320053
Copyright 2016 by Duke University Press

of young girls. In 2010, the head of the Department of Population and Family Planning shocked citizens by stating in the mass media that, in the future, Vietnamese men might have to go to Africa to find wives, a very catastrophic scenario for a nation striving for "population quality."[3] Reports also threaten that men's inability to marry could increase the number of sex-related crimes.[4]

Three arguments have been generated by the mass media and government officials through these narratives. First, women, particularly poor and uneducated women, are vulnerable to human trafficking for the purpose of marriage or prostitution and are, therefore, in need of rescue. Second, this alarming situation is fueled by traffickers and brokers with ill intentions who deprive Vietnam of its young women. Third, this situation is skewing the marriage market and creating an alarming situation for men, since women who marry foreigners become immigrants in their husband's country of residence. The demographic imbalance caused by international marriage migration could be further aggravated by the recent spread of sex selection in favor of boys in Vietnam. While the original reporting on international marriage and the industry around it focused on tragic cases of women being deceived, trafficked, abused, and even murdered, recent reports also emphasize the plight of men suffering the consequences of this migration flow.[5] Vietnamese men are the new victims of marriage migration and sex selection.

Against the backdrop of anxieties around gender, marriage, sexuality, nationalism, mobility, and human trafficking, sparked by the out-migration of women for the purpose of marriage, this article examines how the marriage industry is structured and organized at the local level in Vietnamese marriage migrants' communities of origin. The study focuses on marriages between Vietnamese women and Asian men, particularly men from Taiwan, South Korea, and China. First, it documents how the local-level Vietnamese intimate industry of international marriage has evolved since the beginning of the trend in the early to mid-1990s. Second, it examines the parallel development of a local industry catering to single men. I show how these two separate intimate industries are highly gendered, contested, and constantly changing. I argue that the industry is embedded in both formal and informal institutions because local-level industry actors must succeed in the delicate juggling act of combating international marriage, often framed by the central state apparatus as human trafficking, while participating in the industry that offers international marriage-related services. As in many other sectors of transition economies, such as China and Vietnam, private- and public-sector activities are often embedded, with individuals in powerful positions within the state being well situated to carry on private sideline businesses.

The fine-grain ethnographic approach provides evidence that relationships embedded in the local industry outrun the commodification lens. Village relationships around the marriage industry are imbued with desires, empathy, proximity, and hope, as well as with materialistic rationalities of profit making. The wedding organizer who marries his or her cousin to a South Korean man is both a businessperson and a cousin; the commune cadre with a daughter who marries a Taiwanese man is both a leader attempting to prevent marriage migration and a parent trying to help his or her daughter succeed abroad. Intimacies and the marriage industry overlap in many ways.

This analysis is based on fieldwork conducted in two provinces of Vietnam between March and December of 2012. In total, ninety-nine interviews were conducted with local leaders, members of the local marriage industries, and various community members with the broader objective of shedding light on how the international marriage migration of women impacts their communities of origin.

The International Marriage Industry in the Asian Context

Previous research provides rich narratives of men and women in brokered marriages in different settings. Nicole Constable's pioneering study provides a seminal account of the complexity of motives and power relations in relationships formed through Internet dating agencies.[6] Her work contributes significantly in unsettling the simplistic depictions of men's and women's relationships in these marriages. Hung Cam Thai's inquiry into marriages between Vietnamese-American men and Vietnamese women in Vietnam challenges essentialist views of female hypergamy—the idea that poor women of the developing world marry men from developed countries mostly for economic reasons—as the central process in these marriages.[7] His examination of couples formed by working-class Vietnamese-American men and well-educated Vietnamese women provides further evidence into the complexity of transnational marriages. Scholars of cross-border unions, such as Constable and Thai, and others like Tomoko Nakamatsu and Melody Lu, categorically reject the association frequently made between "mail-order brides," brokered marriages, and trafficking of third world vulnerable women.[8] All these studies consistently identify agency as being central to these migrations and marriages. Moreover, narratives collected by these scholars all powerfully convey the place of longing, desire, and love in marriages organized through private networks, matchmaking agencies, private brokers, or Internet dating sites. These ethnographies also unsettle stereotypes associated with men in these marriages.

The smaller body of studies inquiring into the role of agencies and brokers in transnational "arranged" marriages within Asia document the process and structure of recruitment, matchmaking, and transit of partners across borders. The research is located within the "migration industry" paradigm and examines how the movement of brides across borders is facilitated and organized by intermediary agencies and private brokers. Hong-zen Wang and Shu-minh Chang provide one of the first accounts of the transnational brokerage process between Taiwan and Vietnam in which they argue that, without the strong role of the migration industry, fewer marriage migrants would have moved within Asia.[9] They emphasize the commodification of the marriage itself and how competition in the marriage industry leads to lower prices and increased commodification of women. On the Taiwanese side, they describe the work of organized Taiwanese agencies that run offices in Vietnam. These representatives in Vietnam deal with Vietnamese agencies called "big matchmakers" who send "small matchmakers" to communities where potential brides live. In Taiwan and Vietnam, some individual agents also act as matchmakers. They are usually already married Taiwanese-Vietnamese couples who can use their networks to match couples. On the Vietnamese side, they observe that big and small matchmakers are often Vietnamese ethnic Chinese who can navigate relations in both Vietnamese and Chinese languages and cultural worlds. Recent accounts of transnational activities among Vietnamese-Taiwanese couples document how these couples may use their ethnic and language capital to enter the matchmaking business and benefit by making income from their transnational marriage and family.[10] This research lends further support to the criticism of the female hypergamy framework, since these studies indicate how both men and women may benefit from a cross-border marriage.

Lu focuses on the marriage industry between Taiwanese men and women from mainland China.[11] She documents the strong role of Taiwanese matchmakers in defining preference and orienting choices with respect to foreign brides. She also examines how the commercial activities around China-Taiwan marriages go beyond an industry and how the personal networks and relationships in these transactions are embedded. She also argues against the idea that international marriages are a form of human trafficking and underscores women's agency in entering these unions. Dong Hoon Seol studies a one-week marriage tour undertaken by a group of South Korean men and provides a detailed description of the matchmaking process.[12] He documents how the marriage industry operates transnationally between Vietnam and South Korea and how South Korean men and their parents engage with members of the industry.

The research on international marriages and the matchmaking industry situates international marriages between Vietnamese women and East Asian men within the development of networks through investment, manufacturing, and the "export" of Vietnamese labor. Some Taiwanese who owned factories used their pool of young Vietnamese female workers for international matchmaking. Research also indicates that brokers involved in the recruitment of brides had previous experience in the recruitment of migrant workers destined to Taiwan or South Korea.[13] International marriages must be situated, therefore, within Vietnam's insertion into global capitalism and the development of business and diplomatic relations with East Asian countries. Regional inequalities, high unemployment, and poverty rates in Vietnam are also factors in the marriage and labor migration flows from Vietnam to East Asian countries. World system theories, thus, provide a useful lens to understand the flows of brokered marriage migrants within Asia.

Other scholars underscore that there is a blurred line between the recruitment of foreign labor and foreign wives and the categorization of migrant women as either wives or workers.[14] Along the same line, Sara Friedman conceptualizes marriage migrants as intimate laborers, alongside other migrant women, such as domestic workers and sex workers.[15] When considering reproductive work a form of intimate labor, the industry that facilitates the mobility of this labor fits well with the concept of the intimate industry.[16]

My analysis builds on these previous works, while broadening the discussion in two ways. First, my approach to the intimate industry shifts the gaze from the large transnational processes of matchmaking as the central object of study to the local dynamics in emigrant women's communities of origin. My interest lies in how, at the local level, community-level cadres and community members perceive the marriage industry and participate in it. I expand the notion of the marriage industry to various types of local businesses, such as wedding shop services, private guesthouses for future brides, guesthouses for international couples, language trainers, marriage counselors, and small local brokers. I also include the matchmaking activities that have recently developed to assist single men in finding brides. Second, this approach leads me to examine the contradictory discourses of the state with respect to the marriage industry. Here, I contrast the discourse of the central state apparatus conveyed to the public through the mass media (discussed in a previous analysis[17]) with the local cadres' perception of international marriage and its local industry. I also document the emergence of local services for single men who bring in women from other provinces. To sum up, I examine the local services around the exit, transit, and entry of women. I contrast the dominant state discourse around international marriage and its industry, generally equated with human trafficking, with local actors' discourse and roles in simultaneously reproducing and distancing themselves from this discourse, while being part of the industry.

Marriage Migration from Vietnam

Vietnamese women entered the international marriage markets in the early 1990s. In Taiwan and South Korea, they form the second largest number of immigrant spouses after women from mainland China.[18] The emigration of women who married foreign Asian men began in the south of the country and after 2000 spread to the north. The two provinces we study in this article, Can Tho and Hai Phong, are believed to be among the most important places of origin of emigrant spouses migrating to Taiwan and South Korea.

While most women married Taiwanese men in the 1990s, unions with South Korean men increased significantly after 2000. For local women, South Korea is primarily seen through the lens of hugely popular soap operas in which South Korean men are glamorized as being gentle, handsome, and responsible, and South Korean society is represented as being advanced, modern, and wealthy. Dramatic reports about women who returned after being brutally abused in Taiwan could have altered the local perception of the desirability of Taiwanese men in the early and mid-2000s. Recently, numerous media accounts and local officials have been reporting on the increase in marriages to Chinese men.

As argued by Lu, matchmaking agencies in Taiwan and South Korea also play a key role in the way foreign brides are marketed. Vietnamese women are portrayed as being young, virginal, docile, and pretty.[19] Importantly, they look East Asian, and their children will not be easily distinguishable from "pure" Taiwanese or South Korean children.[20] For some Vietnamese women, international marriage is an alternative to labor migration, which is too costly for many families. Chain migration plays a key role in sustaining the migration. Once a group of women has migrated, they assist in marrying their sisters, cousins, and friends to foreign men; consequently, chain migration can lead to the development of a local "marriage migration culture." In some localities, the phenomenon becomes so widespread that it is seen as a very desirable option for many young women and their families.[21]

The Vietnamese government expresses its opinions on international marriage migration with Asian men in Vietnamese media. All mass media are state owned, tightly controlled, and censored by the state; they are referred to as "the mouth of the Communist party." A thorough media content analysis based on 643 items published between 2000 and 2010 on international marriages between Vietnamese women and foreign Asian men revealed very negative social constructions of the Vietnamese brides, the men who marry them, and the marriages in general. This analysis revealed four dominant narratives that speak to changes in Vietnamese society: (1) shifts in notions of gender, sexuality, and marriage; (2) emerging discourses around class making; (3) emerging discourse on human trafficking; and (4) shifting roles of the media. With respect to the parallel between the marriage migration industry and human trafficking, we noted that

> the current "moral crusade" against human trafficking for the purpose of obtaining sex workers has taken under its wing the sub-phenomenon of marriage migration. For the media, marriage migration provides a powerful example of how well-organized, widespread, and terrible human trafficking has become. At the same time, stories of raids, arrests, and convictions convince readers that the government is being pro-active in protecting its weak female citizens who fall victim to traffickers.[22]

In contrast to these very negative and dramatic portrayals, previous research indicates some positive aspects of international marriage migration in the migrant women's communities of origin. In a previous study, we showed how most daughters send significant remittances to their natal families. We also documented how this migration alters the gender system by increasing the status of girls in families.[23] Because they have the option of marrying locally or internationally, girls and their parents can demand more in marriage transactions, for example, a higher bride price, which is a form of reverse dowry. But the ability of women migrants to support their parents stands as the most significant reason that alters the gender preference for sons. While media reports and state discourse tend to equate marriage migration with human trafficking, leaders, families, and other villagers do not make this association. They simply mention that most women do well, and a few are not lucky (*khong may*). Daughters married abroad are not constructed locally in negative terms but rather as responsible daughters who emigrated to help their parents and seek a better life. As transnational daughters, they are expected to send remittances for their own natal family while caring for their new foreign husband and, often, his parents.[24] In this context, villagers regard the marriage industry as being a facilitator for both marriages and international migration and necessary for navigating the complicated legal aspects of marrying a foreigner and then emigrating internationally from Vietnam.

Despite the significant positive dimensions of this migration for young women and their families, most reports continue to be negative. Women are referred to as "women who marry foreigners," but never migrants. The gendering of migration flows explains, in part, the government's glamorization of labor migration (typically associated with men even though many women become migrant workers) and its demonization of marriage migration (as a threat to the nation, Vietnamese women, and the future of men).[25]

Fieldwork

The fieldwork was conducted in the provinces of Hai Phong (120 kilometers north of Hanoi) and Can Tho (185 kilometers south of Saigon) between March and December of 2012. In each province, two communities (located in the same district) in which large numbers of women were marrying foreign men and emigrating abroad afterward were selected. This analysis is part of a larger project on the impact of female out-migration on marriage, men, family relations, labor market opportunities, and internal migration. In the southern communities, marriage migration was very prevalent in the 1990s. We could obtain complete village marriage registration data only for the 2005–2012 period. Over the past eight years, approximately 10 percent of all marriages registered were between a local woman and foreign man (9 percent in one village and 11 percent in the other one). In the northern locations, where the phenomenon is more recent, the proportions were much higher: 32 percent and 41 percent of all marriages registered between 2005 and 2012 were between a local woman and a foreign man.

A total of ninety-nine interviews were conducted in the four communities studied. Most participants agreed to have their interviews recorded. My assistant and I took detailed notes on our daily conversations with key informants. The study participants included village officials, business owners, families with daughters married abroad, families with single sons, and families with a daughter-in-law from another province. The present analysis draws extensively from key informants who were directly or indirectly involved in the marriage industry and other study participants. Lengthy and frequent discussions were held with one woman who ran a wedding-service business and another who provided language training and counseling to women candidates for international marriage to Taiwanese and Chinese men. Two other informants, a man and a woman, owned guesthouses that catered to international couples (a local woman and a foreign husband), their children, and the husband's relatives, who may come to Vietnam to visit the wife's family. Families with daughters married to foreign men shared their experience about the marriage industry. The information on the matchmaking services that cater to single village men comes from families who resorted to an interprovincial matchmaking service for their sons and the married sons themselves. The analysis also uses observations and insight from many participants with whom we conversed informally during fieldwork.

Some actors refused to meet with us, especially matchmakers who felt particularly vulnerable, given the tendency to associate their work with human trafficking. To obtain interviews with the two hotel owners, we had to use personal contacts and be persistent. Both refused to be recorded. We had no difficulty collecting data from the parents of men, or men themselves, who used matchmaking services to find a wife from another province.

"It Takes a Village"

While we have no longitudinal data to quantitatively document the rapid expansion of local businesses that have emerged around international marriages and the emigration of female spouses from the village, leaders and villagers alike elaborated at length during interviews on the recent growth of this local line of business.

Some businesses that already existed prior to the international marriage boom began to design services to respond to the needs of international couples and their families; others were created specifically around its growth. Beauty parlors, hair salons, marriage outfit rental, language training, translation services, and tour guide services for prospecting grooms form one part of the local intimate industry and show how the intimate industry goes much beyond matchmaking, the typical focus of existing research. Moreover, this industry does not die after the wedding; it continues through the maintenance of transnational family ties through, for instance, services provided around return visits, remittances received, the sending of children to visit (or live with) maternal grandparents, and the need for travel abroad of maternal relatives. Services that enable and facilitate transnational intimacies are part of the intimate industry.

The different types of marriage that have developed in the villages we studied involve multiple actors. Those who support and organize the marriages of local women and men to spouses from other countries or other provinces match and introduce future spouses, but they also prepare, transport, train, dress, and beautify them. In these processes, new relationships, alliances, and networks develop; it takes a village for the industry to run smoothly and safely.

Being a successful actor in the local industry effectively required distancing oneself from anything related to human trafficking. Study participants involved in the local industry systematically asserted that they knew nothing about brokers. This tension was particularly obvious with the two hotel owners who catered exclusively to foreign men and their Vietnamese wives. Because police generally target hotels when they organize raids looking for matchmaker-traffickers and men "buying" Vietnamese wives, the owners feared their businesses would appear to be suspicious. Participating in our research provided a way for people to publicly assert that they had "nothing to hide." Participants reiterated that international marriages are perfectly legal when women are in agreement and all bureaucratic procedures followed; but the suspicion around the practice, sparked by negative stereotyping on the part of the state, required a constant negotiation and reassertion of one's legitimacy and legality as a business owner. The common imbrication of legal and less legal practices under one roof is a reality that study participants did not comment on. In this section, I summarize the narratives of four individuals who were active in the local marriage industry.

Em Kim: The Wedding Shop Owner

Em Kim is a young woman who runs a wedding shop where customers can rent wedding attire for the groom, bride, and all other family members. Em Kim also offers a full range of services, including wedding photography (including beautifying Photoshop work) and videotaping, as well as makeup, laser body hair removal, and hairstyling for the brides. The groom and other wedding attendees (mother of groom, mother of the bride, sisters, close friends, etc.) also come to Em Kim for some of these services. Em Kim's husband is the vice-resident of the commune and is proud of his wife's successful business.

In the early 1990s, Em Kim started taking wedding photos, a skill she learned from her husband who studied photography in his youth. Meeting with numerous international couples, she decided to expand her services and went to the city of Hai Phong to learn additional skills (doing makeup, hair-styles, etc.). In the first half of 2000, her business grew with the large inflow of Taiwanese men marrying into the village. At that time, the matchmaker only introduced the woman to a man, and, once the couple agreed to marry, the family took care of the wedding and called upon Em Kim to organize everything. She coordinated numerous weddings and was busy seven days a week, so she hired an assistant who worked with her full time. Eventually, the assistant also married a foreign man. Gradually, however, the industry changed, and more brokers offered "full packages" to the bride's family. A package included the selection of the groom, the wedding in the city of Hai Phong (often a collective wedding in which many couples were married at once), paperwork, and language training. The package also included all the services Em Kim offered to her customers. As the industry's activities relocated to the city of Hai Phong, she gradually lost her business. A broker offered her work doing makeup, but, since she would be paid by the broker and not the client, she calculated that she would make too little money. Another change that impacted her business was the gradual shift to South Korean grooms instead of Taiwanese grooms. The brokers that facilitated these marriages dealt with another business offering similar services. At some point, Em Kim was invited to become a broker herself, since she knew so many people. After hesitating, she decided that, since her husband was a high-ranking cadre of the People's Committee of the village, it was too risky for her to work in the business. At the same time, it was precisely her husband's powerful position in the local People's Committee that contributed to her good reputation as a wedding shop owner. About her decision not to be involved in matchmaking, Em Kim says:

To say the truth, I do not find that being a matchmaker is good; I am a sincere person. I know that matchmakers play an important role in helping people, but there are also negative aspects to this job. I am very afraid that people will talk (negative rumors). If the matchmaking succeeds, people will express gratitude. But if there are complications, I would be very worried, especially that my husband is a commune cadre. Recently, a matchmaker was caught and then they talked about her in the newspaper and on TV.[26]

Chi Lan: The Commune Cadre and Chinese-Language Teacher

We first met Chi Lan in her capacity as the president of the local Women's Union in a village in Can Tho Province. She introduced us to study participants because she knew everyone well and could easily identify potential participants. Her house was our main base, and we informally interacted with her every day between interviews. Over the course of the fieldwork, Chi Lan told us that she was responsible for a club called the "Club that aims at reducing the negative consequences of international marriages." We met her and her copresident to discuss the objectives and activities of this club. The group meets every two or three months, and mothers with daughters of marrying age are recruited and encouraged to attend the meeting. The group gathers, and the two organizers provide tea and cake to participants while discussing cases in which women who married foreigners had experienced abuse, failed marriages, and even death. The group leaders gathered their "evidence" of the risks of international marriages from newspaper articles and gossip. According to the two women, their activities were successful and contributed to the reduction in the number of women who married abroad over the previous few years. They also counsel young women who want to marry abroad. This government-funded counseling basically consists of instilling fear and discouraging women from making the choice to marry abroad. Chi Lan also runs a private business that includes several services. First, she offers private Chinese-language lessons to women who marry Taiwanese men and are preparing for their preemigration interview. Chi Lan says:

I know Chinese because my father was Chinese. I am a Viet Hoa [ethnic Chinese Vietnamese]. I teach the girls two hours a day, five days a week, at a cost of 800,000 VN dong per month per student [approximately US$40]. They come to study in my home. I have three to six per class. I only teach how to speak. I teach them to understand and properly answer a list of two hundred questions that they might be asked during the interview. If they fail the interview the first time, they come back, study more, and try again. I had the list of two hundred interview questions from a friend who works in the Ministry of Justice in the city. In the last twenty years, I have taught so many girls I cannot count how many. I also provide mediating and counseling services over the cell phone. Sometimes the girls call me from Taiwan and ask me to speak to their husband or parents-in-law if they have a problem. Sometimes the girls' parents in the village want to call their daughters and ask me to speak with the husband or in-laws.[27]

The increase in women marrying South Korean men reduced the number of clients in Lan's language-teaching business. This reduction in students led her to develop other services, such as counseling and guiding Taiwanese men who were coming to her village looking for a spouse. During our stay, Chi Lan spent several days helping a Taiwanese man withdraw money in a nearby town and served as a tourist guide for him in the city of Can Tho. At the local level, she was the best-positioned expert in international marriages. In her official capacity, she tries to discourage international marriages by alerting families and girls to the risks involved. Women who still decide to go, however, could obtain her help, assistance, and services.

When we met with Chi Lan's superior, the president of the People's Committee, he told us that the activities of the local club she was running were very important to him and that he followed the matter very closely. He did not designate the club as strictly a Women's Union matter; rather, he, as president, valued it highly and paid a great deal of attention to it. He was very careful in stating that the commune does not want to prevent international marriages because most families who have daughters abroad benefit from the positive economic impact. When asked, he did recognize how the entire local economy was benefiting from the inflow of remittances sent by emigrant spouses. This money stimulates construction, investment in health and education, and international connections. This positive discourse contrasts sharply with the official stance that continues to equate international marriage with human trafficking. Despite his recognition of the positive aspects, it is his job to prevent the negative consequences of this migration flow. The club is a very effective initiative because it reaches out to mothers who can prevent their daughters from marrying abroad. The president further explained how the idea of the club came from the provincial and national levels of the Women's Union. His commune, along with several others, was chosen as a pilot project. The project was terminated, but his commune decided to continue the activity, since, according to him, the results had been positive.

Chi Van: The Town Guesthouse Owner

Chi Van owns and runs a guesthouse in a town close to villages where many women married abroad. Chi Van describes having entered the business of hosting international couples as "accidental." First, she built a large house in 2000, and some people asked her if she could rent rooms. She then officially started her business. Most of her clients are married couples, along with the husband's relatives (parents, siblings, etc.), who visit the wife's family during holidays. We met a few families with children in the hallway. Chi Van speaks very cautiously about how she manages her guesthouse, obviously worried that we might think she engages in illicit activities. She states several times that foreign men do not come to her hotel to "choose" or "try" a spouse; she hosts only officially registered and married couples. In the course of the interview, she tells us how her two sons are policemen and how her husband is the director of a notary public office. Throughout the interview, she overtly uses these strong connections with the state apparatus to claim the legitimacy of her business. Over the decade she has been running this business, the number of guests has declined. She attributes this trend to the greater tendency for visiting couples to stay with the wife's parents because remittances sent by the couple to the wife's natal family are generally used to improve housing conditions. Once parents-in-law have a better home, they can host their daughter and her foreign husband and the couple no longer needs to stay in a guesthouse or hotel. She also explains how the transfer of matchmaking activities and weddings from the villages to Saigon has also harmed her local business, since she used to have large groups of guests for local weddings with a foreign groom. Toward the end of the conversation, she reveals that she is Vietnamese of Chinese ethnicity and speaks Chinese. Thus, she specializes in Chinese-speaking guests from Malaysia, Taiwan, and China but also has families with spouses from South Korea.

Anh Thanh: The Village Guesthouse Owner

In one of the villages where we conducted fieldwork, we noted a very affluent guesthouse. The size and style of the building drastically contrasted with most of the other dwellings, which were made of steel sheets and had dirt floors. We asked a local cadre who was helping us identify study participants to take us to this place. The cadre proudly told us how the owner of this beautiful mansion was his relative and close friend. We soon found out that the owner is a good friend of other local cadres as well. After a very long negotiation and waiting time, the owner accepted our request to be interviewed, but he refused to be recorded. He described to us the types of guests he hosts. First, men who have already chosen a spouse and are waiting for the wedding registration stay there, but brides are not allowed, since the wedding is not yet registered (the family wedding is not sufficient). Second, much of his business consists of already married couples who come to visit and prefer not to stay with their families. Third, some foreign men come to the village through the local broker and stay there while "choosing" a local spouse. Lastly, some women from other provinces might be brought there by a broker and introduced to foreign men. Anh Thanh had excellent relationships with the local authorities, while his wife was running the guesthouse and dealing with brokers, interpreters, and other intermediaries.

Anh Thanh talks about his business as a safe place for international matchmaking; he sees himself as providing an important service to the community. During our visit, negotiations were underway between two brokers and Anh Thanh's wife. The guesthouse seemed to be a hub of activities around the local marriage industry. We were told that the guesthouse has had an influx of Chinese men coming to find wives.

These four narratives provide insightful information regarding the local marriage industry in rural Vietnam in Hai Phong and Can Tho provinces. First, the development and greater organization of the industry entailed the transfer of the wedding process from the realm of the bride's family and village to a commercial and collective process located in a large city and managed by a matchmaker.[28] In this process, local actors involved in the industry may see their benefits vanish. In the case of Em Kim, the relocation of international marriage to the city of Hai Phong meant that she no longer had her customers in the village. The increasing number of marriages to South Korean husbands at the expense of Taiwanese ones is another change in the industry that harmed her. In addition, Chi Lan lost Chinese-language students with the increased migration to South Korea. She, however, managed to expand her services swiftly and used her Chinese ethnic social capital in several new ways. As a language teacher, counselor, interpreter, and guide, she maintained her position in the local industry.

Second, narratives underscore how those involved in the industry must negotiate the state position on international marriage as often being linked to human trafficking. Our study participants were concerned about the perceptions others might have of their businesses. The two owners of guesthouses enthusiastically elaborated on their connections to state actors as a narrative strategy to prove their legitimacy and noninvolvement in illegal matchmaking activities. This concern was not as acute ten years ago, but, as the antitrafficking rhetoric and interventions were gaining momentum, they had to develop new strategies to prove their legitimacy. During our fieldwork, the story of one broker who had recently been arrested and convicted on human trafficking charges circulated and was repeatedly reported to us as an example of the dangers faced by those in the industry. Unlike other individuals, the arrested woman was guilty of not having been careful enough and not having maintained good "relations" (*khong can than, khong co quan he*).

Third, our interviews with village cadres indicate how cadres close to communities where international marriages take place do not buy into the government's negative rhetoric. To the contrary, they discuss the positive economic benefits that come from these unions through the large amounts of remittances. They see how the local economy gains through a boom in the construction of new houses, house renovations, and an investment in education. In addition, siblings get assistance in getting married, parents' livelihoods are improved, and health-care costs are covered. At the same time, however, cadres must pay attention to the state's negative stance on international marriages by undertaking activities that express a concern for the risks and vulnerability inherent in these marriages. Interestingly, in one village, leaders told us that, when women return to Vietnam after the end of their marriage abroad, they are labeled victims of human trafficking and receive free training. The leaders and administrators, thus, strategically use the category to provide resources to return migrants.

Fourth, the imbrications of public and private, formal and informal institutions suggest that the success of actors in the marriage industry requires a three-party relationship to be sustainable. The case of Chi Lan is particularly telling: despite all the changes in the marriage industry, Chi Lan managed to redefine her niche and protect her business. Her powerful position as president of the Women's Union legitimized her services as "a form of help" rather than "suspicious and trafficking-like activities." As president of the Women's Union, she meets families who are considering international marriage. While officially alerting them to the risks involved, she also forms relationships instrumental in the development of her own business. Her official position gives her legitimacy and social capital, which, when combined with her ethnic social capital, puts her in a unique position to maintain herself in both the public and the private realms. She weaves her activities together in a particularly effective way. Her close connection to the Ministry of Justice is instrumental in providing desirable and marketable language training designed for the very specific needs of the learners.

In Em Kim's case, the connection to the local state first contributes to the success of her business but later contributes to the gradual withdrawal from the international marriage industry. She was offered a part in the new industry relocated in the city of Hai Phong, but she declined. Em Kim's logic for refusing reveals interesting tensions. On the one hand, she feels safe working in the commune under the gaze of her fellow villagers, and, as the wife of a government official, she has legitimacy and a certain degree of "protection" from suspicion. On the other hand, the offer to become a matchmaker is tempting, but the risk is too high. The "matchmaking equals trafficking" discourse looms large over her decision, and she cannot compromise her husband's reputation and position. She accepts the decline in her business and, when we last talked to her, had decided to start selling private health-care insurance to newlywed couples from the village.

Finally, the stories of Em Kim and Chi Van highlight how previously negative (and often hidden) constructions of Chinese origins have become a source of social capital. Speaking the Chinese language is a key asset in today's southern Vietnam, where Taiwanese businesses are established and, also, where Vietnamese-Taiwanese couples come to visit and, in some cases, invest. Wang and Chang note the key role that ethnic Chinese Vietnamese played at the beginning of the marriage industry in the South.[29] In our study, we see how ethnicity and language can, in combination with ties to formal institutions, provide a particularly strong combination for surviving in a contested, unstable, and fragile industry.

New Developments in the Local Industry

Evidence of changes in the local industry surfaced in Hai Phong, where some participants discussed the recent development of activities around the "transit" of women from other provinces. Some local matchmakers have become intermediaries in other locations and moved away from working with local female candidates to international marriage migration. Because they are conveniently situated geographically and South Korean matchmakers are used to going to Hai Phong, they now use the village as a base to bring women from other locations, provide them with training, and have them wait for a few months until the next marriage tour. One informant, Em Hung, provided a rich account of the transit activities that were taking place in a very large residence that served as a transit house and was considered inaccessible by leaders and villagers.

Em Hung was married to a woman who divorced him and went abroad to marry a South Korean man. Her case is often mentioned by men and parents of single sons to show how unreliable women can be: "Even if you marry a local girl, you are not sure things will work out. She could leave the husband and marry a foreign man!" Em Hung is a retired cadre of the commune People's Committee. He is knowledgeable about the marriage industry in his village. His back den, where we sit during the interview, looks onto the very large house, which he observes daily. This house was built by a woman who married in South Korea and returned to her village to work as a local broker. In the last few years, she developed a new line of business: bringing in women from other provinces for international marriages. Women migrate internally and live in this house while waiting to be chosen to go abroad. According to Em Hung and other villagers, women living there never leave the house and never interact with villagers. He observes them on the balconies and through the windows. He knows exactly how many there are, when they arrive, how long they stay, and when men come to choose a spouse. He knows when they either leave the house to spend time in their home villages before migrating or go abroad directly from there. Em Hung explains that his village has become a transit area for women who marry foreigners because of the expertise the local industry has developed. This locally based business is in response to the monopolization of the industry by big brokers located in the city of Hai Phong. Since local girls marry in Hai Phong and pay their brokers there, local brokers are bringing in women from elsewhere. When asked about this house, community leaders say that they know it exists and that it is a private guesthouse. They all know the two people who run the place and do not interfere, saying it is none of their business. In sum, by developing the village into a transit area for women en route to marriage migration, local actors have found another use for their social capital by creating new types of services and activities. These observations provide further support to the idea that the marriage industry is contested and fluid.

Besides the development of one of the villages of Hai Phong into a transit location for brides to be, an increased array of services for local single men trying to find a spouse is another striking development of the local industry. Our desire to study the situation of single men created a particular embarrassment and discomfort among local male leaders in the villages. In the north, in particular, our request to meet families with single men considered "old to marry" (*kho lay vo*) or "too old to marry" (*e roi*) sparked jokes among cadres. Cadres recognized the difficulty for local men who were looking for women to marry in the current context, but they quickly assured us that men do eventually find wives.

The fieldwork shows that internal migration flows are central to providing other opportunities for young men to meet young women. Young men and women from different provinces met in factories or as internal migrants in Ho Chi Minh City or Hai Phong. Once a marriage takes place, personal networks could lead to other introductions and marriages. Young people could also meet while wandering around the city on fancy motorbikes and through cell phone texting.[30] After young men reach the age of twenty-four or twenty-five years, they become more ashamed of seeking a girlfriend on their own and often give up this strategy. By twenty-eight to thirty years of age, they perceive themselves as the pathetic competitors of younger and more attractive men. The shame of being single often prevents them from actively seeking a spouse.

But opportunities created through internal migration and personal networks are insufficient. A local industry has also developed whereby arranged marriages are organized between local men and women from other provinces or, in some cases, women belonging to ethnic minorities. In the Hai Phong villages, an itinerant woman selling traditional medicines, referred to as an ethnic minority woman, regularly traveled between Hai Phong and mountainous provinces and began making introductions. She brought photos of young women, which she showed to families with single sons. If one family was interested in a woman, they arranged a visit to her home village (usually the man with his parents or another relative). As the demand grew, she became more organized and charged a fee, but all participants stressed how this fee is simply a modest expression of their gratitude for her introduction.[31] This resembles the process of international marriages in the beginning. The groom and his family travel once to the woman's province and meet the bride and her parents. The trip involves significant expenses, since the family will typically rent a car and a driver to undertake the trip. On the first visit, if the families agree, the wedding is planned. During the months that follow, the man might visit his future bride a few times on his own, but this may not be possible if the family is poor and the province is far from the man's village. On the wedding date, the family travels again to the wife's village and a wedding is organized there. The wife is brought back to the husband's village, and most families do not organize another wedding party.[32]

According to men and their parents who chose this option, the bride price was less than that for a local woman, but the travel and transportation costs were higher. Wives from other provinces we interviewed generally perceived their marriage migration as improving their lives despite being a great distance from their parents and sometimes feeling homesick. This form of marriage existed in the South prior to the surge in international marriages, but it developed as the local women began to emigrate. In the northern location, where endogamy was a more rigid prescription and preferred form of marriage, this pattern is very recent and signifies an important change in the social construction of an acceptable marriage and a desirable spouse. For "older" men who did not bring a spouse from elsewhere, options included marrying divorced women, young widows, or women who had returned from being married abroad.

Conclusion: Beyond the Brokers

This article calls for a broadening of the conceptualization of the marriage industry in the Asian context. A local approach shifts the gaze from transnational brokers and allows us to capture a more hidden part of the infrastructure. This novel approach, illustrated with the case of Vietnam, makes four important points.

First, the evidence provided in this article shows the local marriage industry as constantly evolving. As marriage migration itself reconfigures local demography, local networks, and local businesses, new developments occur and local actors adapt, transform, and redefine the industry in which they are located. Competition between local- and provincial-level actors who want to reap the benefits of this lucrative industry pushed local-level actors to reinvent themselves. In the northern locations, one important shift has been the development of the "import" of women from other provinces, both for the purpose of foreign marriage (women transiting in the village) and marriage to local single men. The industry around the "export" of local women, thus, gave way to a new one that brings in women.

Second, the role of the state emerges from this analysis as ambivalent. Local-level state representatives are sitting between two chairs. On the one hand, it is their own daughters, sisters, and neighbors who deal with the local industry when marrying a foreign man and migrating abroad; it is also their own sons and nephews who have difficulty finding a wife and must resort to a local broker who will find them an ethnic minority woman from a remote province. It may also be their wives, sisters, brothers, and friends who are reaping the benefits of the numerous transactions involved in such marriages. They might be involved themselves, in fact, by not being able to find a wife or by running a side business within the marriage industry. As local leaders, they also witness firsthand the direct impact—generally positive, but sometimes negative—of the end of village endogamy. They see the enormous economic benefits of remittances. On the other hand, they must endorse the narrative coming from the central state apparatus, which views marriage migration as human trafficking and, therefore, as a phenomenon to be monitored, controlled, and eventually eradicated.

This state-produced ambiguity around marriage migration is highly gendered. The moralistic take on the international marriage migration of village women disseminated in the national media is set in a patriarchal order threatened by women's emancipation from Vietnamese men. In contrast, the emerging local industry that assists men in finding wives is never constructed as threatening and commodified; rather, it is seen as being particularly beneficial for men, their parents, and the entire community. The village patrilineal family lines will be maintained via these "imported" wives belonging to minority ethnic groups. Interestingly, the same patriarchal social constructions exist in the receiving countries of Vietnamese brides that tolerate ethnic others in the name of perpetuating a patrilineal, patrilocal, and patriarchal kinship system in a changing society. In the study locations, ethnic minority women were perceived favorably by men's parents; they are seen as being hardworking, less demanding, and completely available, since they are far from their own families and friends. Among Taiwanese and South Korean families, the same logic justifies marriage to a foreign bride from Vietnam or elsewhere.[33] In more practical terms, the role of local state actors is revealed through the private and public practices of monitoring and criticizing the industry but also through maintaining and developing the local industry in a tense political climate around a phenomenon linked to human trafficking and illicit activities. The fact that our informants working in the industry were all close to local state authorities suggests the importance of co-opting local power to start, strive at, and survive in the business.

Finally, the fine-grain analysis provided here unsettles the notion of this intimate industry as being driven by materialist rationalities. In our field sites, actors in the industry are often also involved in international marriages in various other ways and, in some cases, as direct protagonists. The overlap in roles and experiences draws attention to the multiple layers of intimacies that emerge in village life around marriage and migration.

Notes

1. "Người Trung Quốc 'tuyển' vợ tại khách sạn bị phạt" (Arrest of Chinese Men Selecting Wives at a Hotel), VNExpress, January 1, 2013, www.vnexpress.net/gl/xahoi/2013/01/nguoi -trung-quoc-tuyen-vo-tai-khach-san-bi-phat/.

2. "7 người Trung Quốc 'tuyển' vợ tại khách sạn" (Seven Chinese Select Wives at a Hotel), VNExpress, December 29, 2012, www.vnexpress.net/gl/xa-hoi/2012/12/7-nguoi-trung-quoc-tuyen -vo-tai-khach-san/.

3. "'Đàn ông Việt có thể phải sang châu Phi tìm vợ'" (Vietnamese Men Might Have to Go to Africa to Find Wives), VNExpress, November 27, 2010, www.giadinh.vnexpress.net/tin -tuc/to-am/dan-ong-viet-co-the-phai-sang-chau-phi-tim-vo-2274145.html.

4. "The Boy Boom," *Thanh Nien*, September 6 2010. The article states that "the trend will make it difficult for millions of Vietnamese men to find wives . . . experts also warn of increasing sex-related crimes if the highly unnatural gender imbalance is not addressed," www.thanhniennews.com/index/pages/20100808154954.aspx.

5. For a thorough analysis of Vietnamese mass media, see Danièle Bélanger, Khuat Thu Hong, and Tran Giang Linh, "Transnational Marriages between Vietnamese Women and Asian Men in Vietnamese Online Media," *Journal of Vietnamese Studies* 8, no. 2 (2013): 81–114.

6. Nicole Constable, *Romance on a Global State: Pen Pals, Virtual Ethnography, and "Mail Order" Marriages* (Berkeley: University of California Press 2003).

7. Hung Cam Thai, *For Better or For Worse: Vietnamese International Marriages in the New Global Economy* (New Brunswick, NJ: Rutgers University Press, 2008).

8. Tomoko Nakamatsu, "No Love, No Happy Ending?: The Place of Romantic Love in the Marriage Business and Brokered Cross-Cultural Marriages," in *International Marriages in the Time of Globalization*, ed. Elli K. Heikkila and Brenda S. A. Yeoh, 19–34 (New York: Nova Science, 2010); Melody Chia-We Lu, *Gender, Marriage, and Migration: Contemporary Marriages between Mainland China and Taiwan*. Ph.D. thesis, University of Leiden, 2008.

9. Hong-zen Wang and Shu-minh Chang, "The Commodification of International Marriages: Cross-Border Marriage Business in Taiwan and Viet Nam," *International Migration* 40, no. 6 (2002): 93–116.

10. Hong-zen Wang, "Gendered Transnationalism from Below: Capital, Women and Family in Cross-Border Marriages between Taiwan and Vietnam," in Heikkila and Yeoh, *International Marriages*; and Danièle Bélanger and Hong-zen Wang, "Transnationalism from Below: Evidence from Vietnam-Taiwan Cross-Border Marriages," *Asia Pacific Migration Journal* 21, no. 3 (2012): 291–316.

11. Lu, *Gender, Marriage, and Migration*.

12. Dong Hoon Seol, "International Matchmaking Agencies in Korea and Their Regulating Practices." Paper presented at the Meeting on Cross Border Marriages in East and Southeast Asia. Academia Sinica, October 2006.

13. Lu, *Gender, Marriage, and Migration*. Wang and Chang, "Commodification of International Marriages."

14. See Nicolas Piper and Mina Roces, eds., *Wife or Worker? Asian Women and Migration* (Lanham, MD: Rowman and Littlefield, 2003), for a discussion of the irrelevance of categorizing immigrants as either wives or workers, since most migrant women play both roles. See Danièle Bélanger and Hong-zen Wang, "Becoming a Migrant: Vietnamese Emigration to East Asia, *Pacific Affairs* 86, no. 1 (2013): 31–50, for a discussion of how candidates to migration are not sorted a priori as either migrant worker or foreign bride; rather, they navigate a complex and costly migration industry to make choices while dealing with numerous constraints.

15. Sara L. Friedman, "Rethinking Intimate Labor through Inter-Asian Migrations: Insights from the 2011 Bellagio Conference," *Asia and Pacific Migration Journal* 20, no. 2 (2011): 253–61.

16. For a discussion of the concept of "intimate labors," see Ellen Boris and Rhacel Salazar Parreñas, eds., *Intimate Labors: Cultures, Technologies, and the Politics of Care* (Palo Alto: Stanford University Press 2010). Check city: Berkeley or Palo Alto?

17. Danièle Bélanger et al., "Transnational Marriages between Vietnamese Women and Asian Men in Vietnamese Online Media," *Journal of Vietnamese Studies*, 2013.

18. Danièle Bélanger, "Marriages with Foreign Women in East Asia: Bride Trafficking or Voluntary Migration?," *Population and Societies*, no. 469 (July–August 2010): 4 pp., www.ined .fr/fichier/s_rubrique/19137/population.societies.2010.469.mariages.foreign.women.en.pdf.

19. Chinese women who speak Chinese (or Korean for Chinese of Korean ethnicity) are older and more experienced. Filipino women are "branded" as educated and good English speakers, despite their darker skin and Southeast Asian physical appearance.

20. Danièle Bélanger, "The House and the Classroom: Vietnamese Immigrant Spouses in South Korea and Taiwan," *Population and Societies* 3, no. 1 (2007): 39–59.

21. Danièle Bélanger, Tran Giang Linh, and Le Bach Duong, "Marriage Migrants as Emigrants: Remittances of Marriage Migrant Women from Vietnam to their Natal Families" *Asian Population Studies* 7, no. 2 (2011): 89–105. Our previous research indicates that some parents strongly encourage their daughters to marry abroad, while others are extremely opposed to it.

22. Bélanger et al., "Transnational Marriages between Vietnamese Women and Asian Men in Vietnamese Online Media."

23. Danièle Bélanger and Tran Giang Linh, "The Impact of Transnational Migration on Gender and Marriage in Sending Communities of Vietnam," *Current Sociology* 59, no. 1 (2011): 59–77.

24. Hung Cam Thai, "The Dual Role of Transnational Daughters and Transnational Wives: Monetary Intentions, Expectations and Dilemmas," *Global Networks* 12, no. 2 (2012): 216–32.

25. In fact, one could argue that the economic impact of marriage migration could be more significant, since migrant women have more rights abroad than migrant workers and they do not have to incur a large debt to marry a foreigner and migrate.

26. Em Kim, Hay Tay Province, June 2012.

27. Chi Lan, Can Tho Province, December 2012.

28. Wang and Chang, in "Commodification of International Marriages," documented this trend in the late 1990s, and, for them, this transfer reflected a greater commodification of international marriage.

29. Ibid.

30. In the four communities, we had only one case of Internet dating. The two individuals were more educated than most of our study participants. This marriage was an uxorilocal marriage, and the man justified this choice as a way to maximize his business activities by having networks in two provinces and communes. He and his wife ran a store selling construction material, mostly for building and renovating houses.

31. The fee was between US$150 and $300.

32. This type of marriage also harms local wedding shops, since no wedding is organized in the groom's home village.

33. Another industry that caters to single men is the sex industry. When asked about their sex lives, most men speak openly about the existence of specialized services that are easily available whenever needed. For others, it was a tense topic, and some men revealed painfully and shamefully that they never had sex. Our study did not investigate whether any sex services existed specifically for single men. When we asked local informants, they did not feel it was the case. To be sure, Can Tho City and Hai Phong City, both located relatively close to the villages we studied, offered plenty of commercial sex services to men coming from surrounding villages.

The Materiality of Intimacy in Wildlife Rehabilitation: Rethinking Ethical Capitalism through Embodied Encounters with Animals in Southeast Asia

Juno Salazar Parreñas

Introduction

The dry season heat baked the heaps of elephant dung. Working as a volunteer with nineteen others at Elephant Sanctuary in northern Thailand in April 2010, I was expected to shovel muck from the elephants' pen into the back of a small dump truck. In the dusty piles of elephant excrement, I could see the debris of corn stalks that we had harvested by hand with machetes the day before. After dumping the manure, the truck drove away and we walked to another part of the park to meet it. There at the vegetable patch, we stood in Fordist assembly lines of four, taking turns to walk five meters and pass each other thirty-pound buckets of droppings from the truck to the crops. We paid to perform all this labor ourselves and came from far away places to do so: Britain, Germany, Australia, Canada, the United States,

positions 24:1 DOI 10.1215/10679847-3320065
Copyright 2016 by Duke University Press

and even Chile.[1] We paid to cut corn stalks by hand in sweltering dry heat. We paid to shovel dusty elephant dung. We paid to haul buckets of manure to organically fertilize a vegetable plot. These actions raise a simple question: Why? Why did we, people who had been strangers merely days earlier, pay to perform bodily labor in Thailand that had us handling animal feces and smelling each other's human sweat, all in the sweltering dry season heat?

The reason, I argue here, is that commercial volunteerism involving wildlife offers the possibility of gaining meaningful bodily intimacy with exotic animals through material forms. Handling specific animals' dung is one of the means through which people intimately connect with animals.[2] The other is touch. This article focuses on intimate relationships between two kinds of actors: workers both paid and unpaid on one hand and animals such as elephants, orangutans, and sun bears on the other. The "shit work" of wildlife husbandry offers a way to see how intimacy in intimate industries is obtained through encounters with material effects.

Intimacy as a concept helps reference both physical proximity with other bodies and direct contact with bodily matter. Like the intimacy involved in sex work and nursing, intimacy in the context of wildlife rehabilitation is manifested through physical proximity that affords direct contact with material, bodily forms and with it sensory confrontations of smell and touch. This contact produces knowledge of the other that is specific to a moment shared between individuals that would otherwise be unknown. Such an understanding of intimacy expands Viviana Zelizer's definition of intimacy and its association with "the personal" to include nonhuman actors.[3] It builds on fleshy ideas of intimacy and mutual vulnerability described by Elizabeth Povinelli in fleshy, carnal encounters between ethnographer and ethnographic subject.[4]

Wildlife rehabilitation is an intimate industry distinct from the meat industry precisely because of the former's investment in individuals. While workers in the meat industry handle the bodies of billions of individual animals every year, meatpackers process individuals into mass quantities of uniform and disaggregated packaged parts of flesh.[5] The work of meat processing is carnal; the close proximity between workers and the animals they handle exposes them to zoonotic illnesses like bird flu.[6] This conveys an intimacy in which transfers of illness are possible. Yet, this intimacy differs from the intimacy of intimate industries because of the lack of "the personal" in their processing of flesh. Processing meat is about erasing individuality, of depersonalizing the experience of consuming flesh. Wildlife rehabilitation is about the promotion of individuality, of personalizing the animal face of conservation and species loss through the individuated charisma of charismatic fauna.[7]

In the world of wildlife rehabilitation, animals are privileged for their individuality. Forms of copresence with these individuated animals are forms of intimacy that cross a distance between species. Copresence resulting from the act of individuals caring for individual animals produces forms of knowledge and feeling that are impossible to mediate through sight and sound alone. New video technologies including "critter cams" can mediate connections and intimate knowledge, yet they cannot mediate the driving force for commercial volunteerism involving wildlife: the possibilities for direct bodily engagement and intimate encounters afforded by copresence with an animal endemic to a specific area.[8]

The ubiquity of technologically mediated forms of intimacy likely adds to the value of real, in-the-flesh copresence, such that volunteers treat hard labor necessary in wildlife rehabilitation efforts as a commodity to be consumed. Hard labor for actual animals and copresence with these specific individuals is a vacation for which commercial volunteers pay hundreds and even thousands of dollars for a week or two. Although these animals may no longer be circulating in the pet or logging trades as what Rosemary-Claire Collard calls "lively commodities," they have become crucial actors in a new form of commodification: the phenomenon of paying to perform intimate labor with animals.[9] Thus, wildlife rehabilitation and commercial volunteerism together have to be understood as an intimate industry.

The commercialization of wildlife rehabilitation produces a contact zone across social strata, producing a new space for encounters otherwise impossible, yet one that reiterates a history of local social inequalities.[10] As this article shows, commodification enables contact with animals that commercial volunteers from abroad as well as many locals would otherwise not encounter. These forms of contact disrupt ideas of labor insofar as menial tasks are not the work of low-wage laborers but a commodified form consumed by paying volunteers. Yet, this work depends on the low-wage labor of highland locals who have lived at the periphery of lowland state and society. Commercial volunteerism involving wildlife in Southeast Asia disrupts ideas of menial labor while at the same time reiterates Southeast Asian social inequalities. These different issues converge in a material substance: animal excrement.

This article engages the materiality of intimacy through excrement and touch involving three kinds of animals: elephants in northern Thailand that formerly worked in timber camps or in cities as wandering tourist attractions; Bornean orangutans displaced from their habitats and kept in wildlife centers in Sarawak, Malaysia, for the purpose of rehabilitation; and sun bears that are also displaced from their habitats and are housed in the same Sarawakian wildlife centers with the hope for an eventual release to the wild. All these bodily encounters are trans-specifically experienced in wildlife rehabilitation.[11] Tracing connections with bodies and bodily functions, whether human or nonhuman, serves as an example of how intimacy and intimate industries can and should be understood through materiality.

Commercial volunteerism involving animals is an intimate industry, one that relies on a connection between people and animals to a specific place. The nonhuman animals in the story with which I begin are Asian elephants endemic to Thailand. The commercialization of experiences with these creatures offers a point of comparison to commodified encounters with wildlife endemic to Malaysian Borneo. These engagements are expensive, priced beyond the means of locals, and conducted by transnational volunteers who can see manual labor as a novelty. The initiatives I compare in this article engage hard labor, volunteers paying to physically assist low-wage local workers, and possibilities of intimacy with nonhuman animals that are endemic and thereby emblematic of the areas in which these volunteering efforts take place.

Today, the activities of approximately 1.6 million commercial volunteers per year generate a value between $1.7 and $2.6 billion US dollars. It is estimated that 90 percent of these commercial volunteers travel to Asia, Latin America, and Africa.[12] A typical week-long visit to the elephant sanctuary cost around $325 USD in 2010.[13] It included food, accommodations, and local transportation from Chiang Mai to the sanctuary and to different corn fields near the sanctuary throughout that week. A commercial volunteer experience at Lundu Wildlife Center in Malaysia through ENdangered Great Ape Experiences (ENGAGE) with semiwild orangutans in 2010 cost about $2,000 USD for one month and $1,000 USD for a fortnight.[14] Volunteers to Lundu come for the semiwild orangutans but find themselves caring about other animals such as sun bears.

Paying to perform menial labor is a behavior of a kind of animal different from *homo economicus* or, in other words, the rational, maximizing individual in liberal political economy.[15] Manual labor in the context of commercial volunteerism is not held in contempt and disdain, as it has been historically and cross-culturally.[16] Instead, hard labor is a postindustrial virtue that can be understood in relation to what Slavoj Žižek calls "cultural capitalism" or "ethical capitalism."[17] Žižek identifies this phenomenon in the discourse of environmentalism and social good in the advertisement and consumption of commodities. His examples include voting for which charities receive corporate social-responsibility funds and purchasing a pair of shoes for one's own consumption that will also provide a pair of shoes for a child in need in the global South. Yet all of Žižek's examples iterate the cleanliness and distance experienced by elites from far away. Consumption alone cannot make sense of commercial volunteerism; it cannot make sense of the the literal and conceptual work performed through bodily labor in Southeast Asia for the sake of animals.

Malayan sun bears, Bornean orangutans, and Asian elephants are all very different. Yet a comparison of the work involving them offers ways to address three questions in which bodies matter in intimate industries: First, what forms of intimacy take place in the ecotourism industry of wildlife rehabilitation? Second, how does the literal "shit" in "shit labor" mediate different kinds of relations? Third, how does deep history spanning millennia establish the context and effects in which physical intimacy across species occurs?

Taking into account encounters between humans and three different species makes this ethnographic account literally "multispecies."[18] I spent seventeen months over a span of two years between 2008 and 2010 in Sarawak, Malaysia. There, I spent nine months at Lundu Wildlife Center, where my focus prioritized semiwild orangutans and the people caring for them. Yet, relations with other species, such as bears, gibbons, and birds, were significant to the work that takes place at the site. Encounters, fascinations, and efforts with sun bears could not be ignored. This site offered a point of contrast and comparison to other sites specializing in both wildlife rehabilitation and commercial volunteerism, including the elephant sanctuary in Thailand, where I spent a week as a commercial volunteer.

The stories I share are not just circulations of symbols and representations, but encounters with real, fleshy, and material bodies.[19] Examining such bodily encounters highlights the subjective and social qualities of the ambiguous boundaries between intimacy and disgust. Elizabeth Povinelli, for instance, has written about sharing lice and manually bursting pustular sores with her Aboriginal kin in Australia as forms of embodied sociality, which outsiders may find disgusting.

The line between disgust and intimacy is different for Julie Livingston in her study of an oncology ward in Botswana. There, nurses cleaning necrotic flesh—a source of disgust for the patients themselves—is a rehumanizing process. The work nurses do in Livingston's study pulls such acts away from sensations of disgust and returns feelings and actions to the realm of intimacy. These nurses perform a profession in which intimacy is about reestablishing human life in the face of death in the way that human sociality for Povinelli is about sharing affliction.

At the wildlife center, handling animal bodies is not about a reification of humanity or human sociality. Rather, it is about affirming life and livelihoods through commodified forms of intimacy. Commercial volunteers do not find their handling of excreta disgusting like, for instance, slaughterhouse workers who must use high-power hoses to wash out intestines and who find that flecks of excreta and ingesta have breached the barriers of their protective goggles and helmets.[20] For commercial volunteers in a Thai elephant sanctuary, handling excreta can be fetishized as a direct insertion of oneself into a vegetarian cycle of life: herbivore dung becomes organic fertilizer for a vegetable garden that sustains life. It also becomes stationery paper and greeting cards for sale at the sanctuary's gift shop. Orangutan and bear dung in Malaysia has no direct utilitarian value as paper or as fertilizer. Yet, as we will see, it is nonetheless fetishized as the material effects of a sustained life for endangered animals.

The wildlife center and animal sanctuary, insofar as they are sites for commercial volunteerism, are sites of biopolitics in which paying volunteers and animal handlers can engage in the "power to foster life" with the sweat from their own bodies.[21] Following Michel Foucault, *biopower* references the governance of bodies as both members of populations and as individuals.[22] Scholars of colonial and postcolonial studies locate biopower in the concern about forms of intimacy underwriting colonial endeavors and postcolonial conditions, which in turn shape European bourgeois understandings of order.[23] For instance, Ann Stoler has explained how in the late colonial order the biopolitical question of how to live was fraught with anxieties about class-specific, racially coded, gendered forms, such as the legal ambiguity of mixed-race children produced through relations between Dutch men and Sumatran women and the care of Dutch children by Javanese servants.[24] Like the factory, the school, the army, and the prison, the wildlife center is one such example of Foucauldian biopower insofar that commercial volunteerism with wildlife becomes a life-affirming capitalist form through its commercialized opportunity to individually support the life of a population with one's own body.

As is evident in the stories I present, postcolonial conditions shape the transnational care economy of commercial animal volunteer tourism. The experience of living with and caring for nonhuman animals adds to these discussions in postcolonial studies by showing that the weight of colonial legacies is burdened by nonhuman actors as well. While Thailand was never formally colonized as Malaysia was by Britain, its "crypto-colonial" legacy formed by competing European colonial powers at its borders makes a colonial and postcolonial framework relevant to understanding the transnational dynamics at work.[25] Transnational volunteers from the global North visiting Thailand and Malaysia perceive that commercial volunteerism offers support to local efforts. The custodial labor they perform supports the centers. Such labors are not acts of stewardship: these are not attempts at technical and managerial control.[26] Rather, this labor is hands-on, connected to animals' bodily functions, and dirty. This labor is about being a custodian in postcolonial contexts.[27]

In what follows, I first explain how custodial labor involving encounters between endemic animals, transnational volunteers, and socially stratified locals relies on intimacy. I then ask readers to consider the work feces forces upon custodians. I then examine how possibilities and impossibilities of touching nonhuman, living beings shape the commodification of intimacy and the dangers and pleasures of trans-specific encounters in commercial volunteerism. These examples illustrate two points: First, commercial volunteerism allows contact with creatures that would otherwise be impossible to have. Second, the materiality with which animals confront custodians serves as a reminder that all intimate labor, and by extension intimate industries, entails confrontations with fleshy bodiliness.

Custodial Labor

I use the term *custodial labor* to name the efforts in which different actors experience unequal distributions of risk through post-industrial commercial volunteers' desire to gain meaningfulness through hard labor.[28] Meaningfulness is particularly achieved in the affective interface between bodies in close proximity to each other. What is ultimately a fleeting moment for foreign volunteers is the everyday for animals and workers who stay at the site. Custodial labor identifies the literal custodial labor on-site: shoveling dung, washing cages, and feeding animals. At the same time, it indicates the differences that are inherent when people who are paid little and people who pay a lot of money to be there together perform the same work.

The cost of volunteering is expensive, and yet the wages paid to animal handlers are low. Resources amassed at these sites are dispensed in such a way that the provision of food and care given for the animals entails the utilization of cheap labor performed by locally displaced persons. In the case of elephant rehabilitation, many of the mahouts are from hill tribes at the Burmese border. In the case of orangutan rehabilitation, animal keepers are often indigenous Iban and Bidayuh workers generationally new to wage labor.

Both commercial volunteerism and animal care require supportive labor. At the elephant sanctuary at Thailand, each elephant has a mahout. None of the mahouts I met spoke English. A staff guide, one who graduated from the local university and is proficient in English, leads a group of commercial volunteers. A typical course of study for these leaders was often tourism and hotel studies. As guides, they instruct volunteers on how to conduct farm labor that supports the elephants' livelihood: cutting corn with machetes, shoveling dung, and washing literally tons of vegetables for the elephants' consumption. They also point out particular elephants and tell stories about their individual life histories. The guides mediate the volunteers' entry and participation at Elephant Sanctuary—from farm labor to cuddling baby elephants. Here, the stratification of work is clear: hill-based mahouts who do not speak English and are without formal education occupy the lower rung, followed by English-speaking Thai college graduates and the foreign volunteers who work at the site—a number of whom raise funds for the site in their home countries. All these participants follow Dok, the Thai animal advocate and visionary who opened the site in 1996 and has operated it since. Her fame has been extended through international media outlets such as National Geographic, BBC, and CNN.

Volunteers' days at Dok's elephant sanctuary were filled with manual farm labor that supported the efforts of the park, either directly in the form of harvesting elephant fodder or indirectly in the form of fertilizing the garden plot for human consumption. Each night involved a rotation of cultural activities, all of which conveyed a firm sense of national ethnicity. One such night was a Buddhist ceremony led by visiting monks, and another was a Thai language lesson that consisted of key polite phrases. For weary volunteers unused to hard labor, there was even a Thai massage service offered by local village women for a fee at the park. The elephant sanctuary also had a videographer on-site, a recent college graduate whose job was to document the volunteer group and produce a DVD for each volunteer. The video depicted volunteers at all their tasks for the week: cutting corn, bathing elephants in the river, and feeding them. Interactions between mahouts and volunteers were very limited. Language was a serious barrier between them. The mahouts and volunteers ate the same meals that were prepared by Dok and a host of staff and volunteers, but in separate areas of the very large sheltered veranda. Workers' houses were at a distance from volunteers' accommodations.[29]

Similarly, the work of orangutan rehabilitation also entails an array of workers. Lundu Wildlife Center, which specializes in orangutan rehabilitation, is run by a private-public partnership between the privatized branch of the Sarawak's Forestry Department and ENGAGE, a small transnational volunteering company with headquarters in Great Britain. Labor stratification was not as clearly defined here, but it was nevertheless apparent. Commercial volunteers assisted low-wage animal handlers, who were employed as subcontractors by the Forestry Corporation. Two of the animal handlers were ethnically Bidayuh, six were Iban, and one was Malay. About half of the animal handlers spoke English, and they were paid an extra stipend for mediating between the volunteers and the work to be done at the site. Not surprisingly, this was a source of jealousy between workers.[30] Compensation of this kind officially ceased at the request of the Forestry Corporation, but nevertheless carried on in the form of unofficially distributed cash "incentives." Volunteers did not partake in a cultural program of ethnic tourism or cultural consumption as elaborately stylized as in the Thai elephant sanctuary. However, they attended a dinner at the Iban longhouse just outside the park's gates in which a number of the park's staff members reside. The event took place at the longhouse's *ruai* (veranda) and featured a traditional dance. Volunteers lived in staff housing where their neighbors were two of the keepers and their families, as well as Forestry Corporation staff members.

The relations that make up these sites reinforce the social stratification specific to their regions. Elephant Sanctuary is a microcosm of Chiang Mai society and its inequalities between educated Thais and peripheral hill people, much in the way that orangutan rehabilitation sites in Sarawak reflect multiculturalism and distinctions between urban and rural people that are specific to Sarawak.[31] At the same time, these sites disrupt hierarchies in an unexpected way: menial labor that does not require expertise or specialization becomes a commodity itself. Through the act of completing tasks as work parties, volunteers become a group, in which individual acts and contributions become efforts greater than themselves. Thus, a volunteer at an orangutan rehabilitation center can share a sentiment that is also relevant at an elephant sanctuary: "I can know that I have made a small contribution to a big problem about conservation." Through individual participation in volunteering groups, individuals with the resources to participate in commercial volunteerism can personally feel part of a greater mission. The mission in which they engage is purposely secular. The discourse of commercial volunteerism is marked by the absence of any religious ideology in goals or motivations. They come not for salvation but for a professed interest in animals and conservation.[32]

Volunteers literally pay a price for these initiatives. However, both wage laborers and the animals with which they work pay a price as well: regular contact with a transient set of volunteers, whether weekly (elephant sanctuary) or monthly (orangutan rehabilitation center). Because workers and animals stay, while volunteers come and go, workers and animals face the possibility of transferring illness from animals to humans (zoonosis) or from humans to animals (anthroponosis). For wage workers in orangutan rehabilitation centers, the possibilities of injury are serious. They may lose the functioning of their limbs or digits if an orangutan bites into their tendon, which has happened at the site. Likewise, animals trained for rehabilitation are subjected to punishment. Using sticks during "jungle training skills" is the way keepers compel orangutans to stay in the trees and avoid the company of humans on the ground.[33] The possibility of injury due to the close proximity with which handlers work with animals serves as an example of how risk produced through intimacy is borne by workers and not by commercial volunteers.

The help offered through commercial volunteerism has provisions. With the interest in supporting local efforts comes skepticism about local or traditional animal-handling efforts, especially those that foreigners might consider cruel. One evening of the elephant volunteering week is devoted to watching a documentary about *phaajan*, the ceremonial training process in which mahouts "break" elephants and force them to succumb to human domination through the experience of significant pain over time. The process, usually spanning three to six days and reccurring throughout a set of weeks, includes repeatedly puncturing elephants' flesh with nails attached to rods and tying them in such ways that they receive rope burns whenever they move. *Phaajan*, traditionally used for conscripting elephants for the work of logging, continues as the primary way to train elephants to carry people.

Dok's advocacy through the elephant sanctuary against *phaajan* helped to define how her organization promotes and fosters different kinds of encounters between humans and elephants. Her own personal background of having grown up in a highland village as the granddaughter of a shaman diverted the accusation that commercial volunteers perform a colonial discourse of animal rescue.[34] Because she was a Thai national, her supporters were not merely foreign, white animal advocates demonstrating an animal studies example of Gayatri Spivak's famous assertion about "white men saving brown women from brown men," in which "brown women" are substituted with similarly racialized "endemic animals."[35] Rather, their work can be understood as a self-consciously enacted postcolonial effort to support local initiatives to save local wildlife. Nevertheless, such efforts were always fraught and never without ambivalence.

Animal advocacy, when pitted against local efforts, was commonly understood as an attempted exercise of white colonial hegemony, especially in Sarawak, Malaysia. Early in my research visit, a junior officer confided to me that she does not like how visitors come to Malaysia and "tell us what to do" in regard to animal care.[36] Nearly two years later toward the end of my research visit, the British project manager on-site seemed to respond to that critique in a private conversation with me. He explained, "We're not here to be, 'oh we're white people, we know everything,' because we don't. We're just here to help. . . . "[37] Yet the project manager felt that his organization's efforts were due credit.[38] He went on, "So we come to Lin [the junior officer] with some suggestions and then she comes back to us, two days later, tells us she's decided we're going to do this plan and then she has *our* idea on fancy Forestry Corporation paper."[39] ENGAGE's endeavors are fashioned as specifically postcolonial efforts in which locals must take the lead. Yet solutions and conduct are defined by the foreign agency. In this case, there was ambivalence between wanting the suggestion to be adopted and wanting recognition for having conceived it.

The ongoing argument between the local junior officer Lin and the British project coordinator Tom not only demonstrates the obvious point that commercial volunteerism is fraught with postcolonial legacies. In addition, their discord, along with struggles between Dok's elephant sanctuary and *phajaan* practitioners, shows that animal care in Asia is utterly shaped by commercial interests. Lin and Tom argue about the credit due to their respective organizations, Forestry Corporation, based in the former postcolony of Sarawak, and ENGAGE, based in the former metropole of London. Meanwhile, the elephant sanctuary attempts to promote another kind of commodified human-animal experience to counter the traditional tourist experience of riding an elephant that relies on punitive training through *phajaan*.

Wildlife rehabilitation in Asia poses a serious challenge for applied ethicists and other philosophers in animal studies. Sue Donaldson argues that "commercialization pressures are too dangerous" to the interests of animals, while Lori Gruen sees commercial animal enterprises as antithetical to the enterprise of semiwild sanctuaries.[40] These philosophers aspire to noncommercial, noncapitalist animal sanctuaries, yet the commodification of intimacy with animals in Asia enables unique, potentially life-affirming and life-changing encounters to be shared by a greater number of people than would otherwise be possible if such animal rehabilitation efforts were only about the animals and not also about volunteers paying to perform manual labor for the sake of wildlife. Feminist sociologists and anthropologists such as Viviana Zelizer and Ara Wilson show that there is no space free of economic contexts.[41] Although analytic philosophers set forth normative ideas in which animals should be free from the constraints of commerce, Southeast Asian elephant sanctuaries and wildlife centers are made possible only through commercialism.

My intention is not to laud commercialism for opening opportunities for encounters that would otherwise be impossible. Nor is my goal to vilify commercialism as inherently bad for animals. Instead, my aim is to investigate how commercialism works to reinforce human social hierarchies while producing forms of animal captivity and human-animal intimacy.

Shit Work

Layang was seventeen years old when he began working at an orangutan rehabilitation center. On his first day of work, without any training, he was given a broom and dustpan and told to shovel scat in a cage in which eight fully grown adult orangutans were kept. Here he was, seventeen years later, now thirty-four, telling professionals from Britain how to use a shovel for the same purpose. But this time was very different: there weren't any apes in the cage. Volunteers were allowed to enter the cages only once the orangutans were in their outside enclosures. It was far too dangerous for them because orangutans are about eight times stronger than humans. The immersion through which Layang learned how to become an animal keeper was difficult to demand of anyone. He was one of only two at the site who had the experience that could facilitate the courage needed to enter a cage with an adult orangutan in it. Indeed, he exercised his courage with other animals on-site.

Lundu Wildlife Center held other animals in states of captivity. For two months, a sun bear was kept in a cage within the orangutan night den. The bear simply had nowhere else to go. He was confiscated from an illegal menagerie, and the other two bear enclosures each had four bears in them. Sun bears of Borneo may be the smallest bears in the world, but they are reputed to be the most aggressive. Sun bears and orangutans would rarely interact with each other in the wild, since orangutans stay high in the trees and sun bears are on the ground and active at night. While the orangutans at the rehabilitation site were able to go outside to an open-air walled enclosure, the sun bear in the orangutan night den was kept in his cell for twenty-four hours, seven days a week. The sun bear could look through a two-square-foot barred cage and see the enclosure of Lisbet the orangutan. Whenever Lisbet saw the bear, she would take a rock and throw it at the enclosure from a distance; the bear would scurry away and retreat deeper in the cage.

On my first day observing animal husbandry, Layang entered the bear's cage when the bear was still in it. This was very shocking to me at the time because I had just barely ended my zookeeper internship at the Oakland Zoo in the United States, where I cared for a sun bear. Sweeping up scat with a broom and dustpan, selecting one clump by hand with a plastic bag to be frozen (thereby transforming it from "shit" to "stool sample"), and then mopping and squeegeeing the floor were all parts of my daily existence as a zookeeper intern in the United States. In this sense, handling feces was the primary form of intimacy in accredited US zoos. At the Oakland Zoo, as it is in every accredited zoo in the United States, every encounter with a sun bear must be mediated through sliding doors and mesh fencing. Entering a cage with a bear in it was akin to risking one's own life.

Why did Layang risk his life by entering the bear's cell? The answer might have been his interest in demonstrating his own expertise, to prove his fearlessness at having physical proximity with an infamously aggressive creature. Perhaps this demonstration of fearlessness was provokingly gendered and classed in opposition to my tech-wear-clad, bespectacled, US-educated but local-looking self. Undeniably, there was a simple answer: it was to clean shit.

The cage was as small as a prison cell, no more than ten feet cubed. In one hand Layang carried a small fire hose, in the other, half a small watermelon. He opened the cage and presented the watermelon to the charging bear. With one hand, Layang pushed the watermelon toward the bear's face, projecting the watermelon away from his body. He then used the hose to wash the floor and the two metal platforms attached to the wall inside the cell. Whenever the bear stepped near him, he doused him with water. Once the bear finished the watermelon, rind included, he went for Layang, who would spray him directly with the hose. The situation looked precarious enough for me to offer Layang sugar cane from the bucket of food I carried. He declined while using the hose as his sole defense against the approaching bear. A moment later, Layang asked for the sugar cane. I gave it to him, and he placed it on the top platform. The bear went for it, but his paws couldn't get a proper grip on the wet and slippery platform, so he fell and hit his head on a beam. Layang laughed while taking the sugar cane from the top level to the level on which the bear writhed. The bear tore into it. Layang then closed the gate, which had been open the entire time of the cleaning, and secured the lock.

Such risk taking was difficult for me to understand, especially having been so thoroughly schooled in the practices at accredited US zoos. When Tom asked how accompanying Layang went, I shared my surprise at Layang's entering the bear's cell with the bear still in it. He said, "The other option is to have the bear live in his own shit." Contrary to Tom's opinion, washing away bear feces could be done *without* risk of injury by taking the hose and carefully aiming and shooting the droppings away. Layang, however, preferred the thrilling option.

The larger bear facility was located at the more isolated area of the park and also required attention. Cleaning it entailed three options: risking one's bodily integrity to wash away dung, exercising patience in mosquito-ridden mud and shooting away droppings with a garden hose, or letting the bears

live in their own shit. Keepers who were paid incentives chose the second—
including Layang, likely because four bears at once are harder to fend off
than one. Keepers who did not gain incentives from the volunteering company chose the third option. Such refusals can be perceived as subversive
acts of resistance.[42] However, such subversions are at the expense of others, namely, the captive sun bears at the site. Volunteer labor was meant to
supplement the park's local labor. It supplemented it by offering the most
tedious of all animal husbandry tasks: washing away shit.

Cleaning an orangutan enclosure was tedious work. Two volunteers
would accompany a keeper, whose job was to bring the orangutans out to
their cages one by one through the sliding cage doors. Volunteers were not
allowed to touch the orangutans. Their only contact was indirectly through
cleaning muck and through handing them enrichment devices such as coco-
nuts that the volunteers wrapped in paper and tied up with twine.[43] Volunteers would enter an empty cell wearing rubber boots and carrying either a
bucket of soapy water and a scrubbing broom or a broom and dustpan (figure 1). The tropical humidity and frequent downpours meant that the stains
caused by rusted wrought iron never left the walls. The unequal level of
the concrete floor, slowly shifting because of erosion beneath it, meant that
puddles on the ground always lingered. One cage required pushing and lift-
ing a heavy bin of water. The bin, not surprisingly, would also contain fecal
material, along with other waste: rambutan and banana fruit peelings or
empty water bottles that had been filled with reconstituted milk or stuffed
with sand for their enrichment. The tedium was a source of sarcasm; as one
volunteer said on a night spent drinking beer before her final day of work,
"I'm looking forward to sweeping up shit!'

Through the tedious task of cleaning feces, volunteers discovered the
orangutans' individuality. Efran, for instance, had the easiest cage to clean
up because he would neatly defecate in one of the two rooms of his cell. Gas
and Lisbet were far from tidy—the moisture of their cells from puddles
caused by rainwater seepage and their own urine meant that their feces,
in various states of disintegration, would cling to the dustpan. Since the
bears were housed in fours, their individuality could not be deciphered. The
volunteers couldn't distinguish one bear's shit from another's. Intimacy here

Figure 1 A volunteer scrubs a cage while an orangutan stares, Malaysia 2009.
Photo by Juno Salazar Parreñas

for volunteers was gained through the individuation of orangutan scat, but it was unobtainable in the piles of bear scat.

Likewise, elephant feces did not mediate individuality for volunteers at Elephant Sanctuary. Elephant fecal matter became manure, intimately tied to our bodily labor of harvesting corn stalks. While orangutan feces acts as a conduit of intimate knowledge about specific individuals, elephant feces serves as a conduit of a biological cycle that intimately connected our bodies to the bodies of the elephants for which we cared. This kind of intimate knowledge and participation in this kind of intimate bodily cycle with exotic animals was obtainable only to foreign volunteers from the global North through commercialized volunteerism.

Touch and Go

Elephants, orangutans, and sun bears all have two kinds of histories: individual life histories and species-specific evolutionary histories. The confla-
tion of these two kinds of histories is especially apparent when thinking
about orangutans. Any interspecies encounter between individuals entails a
confrontation with both kinds of history. As fellow hominids, orangutans
are imagined as our relatives in the Family of Man.[44] Sharing 97 percent
of DNA conveys a sense of kinship. That perceived intimacy of kinship
between humans and orangutans is built on an evolutionary family tree
that began 14 million years ago, when the last common ancestor for hominids lived.[45] The evolutionary history of orangutans and humans is more of
a history of departures from each other than it is a history of kinship and
intimacy. Orangutan rehabilitation, then, brings individuals closely together
in the context of 14 million years of separation.

Elephants have played key roles in the history of civilization in Asia,
especially in war and in timber harvesting, dating from five thousand years
ago.[46] Yet biologists do not consider these animals domesticated. Rather,
they are considered working animals taken into captivity.[47] Elephants in
Southeast Asia that work for people in the timber industry were wild and
made tame through forms of punitive training such as *phaajan*.

Sun bears have even fewer shared histories with humans than orangutans
or elephants. Relatively little is known of these mammals. Only in 2007
did the International Union for the Conservation of Nature reclassify them
from "data deficient" to "vulnerable." Unlike elephants and orangutans, sun
bears are unknown to volunteers until the moment they encounter them in
close enough proximity to hear them bark or see them climb, all from a safe
distance.

These evolutionary histories matter when thinking about individual histories of intimacy across species. In this sense, having an individual history
of intimacy entails a history of sociality, a history of individuals in close
proximity to each other in which being with each other shapes how these
individuals experience their worlds. The sun bears' human-bear world is
shaped by bars and captivity and expressed through stereotypical behavioral disorders such as pacing in circles.[48] The elephants' human-elephant

world is shaped through conscripted labor vis-à-vis hauling timber, carrying humans, and painting pictures at zoos. The orangutans' human-orangutan world is shaped through social relations imposed upon the most solitary of the hominids. Bodily contact through touch is in one respect the culmination of intimacy across species. Whether the pain of a bite or the touch of a kiss, these different forms of trans-specific bodily intimacy show the dangers and pleasures of custodial labor involving animals.

When I arrived at Lundu Wildlife Center for fieldwork about orangutan rehabilitation in October 2008, the junior officer Lin shared a story with me, paraphrased as follows, which also perhaps served as a warning to me to not get too close:

> A nature conservation volunteer was here for three weeks. A "stupid girl," according to Lin. She would just try to get closer to the orangutan Ching [who was famous for attacking women, especially those racialized as "local"]. And Ching felt threatened, so she bit her foot. She needed fourteen stitches. So when she came to the keeper, she was smiling and said the orangutan bit me. The keeper was so worried because there was blood. And she just said, "Oh I'll be okay, it's nothing." So when they told the parents, the parents were not surprised because they said the girl was really stubborn. Lin then said, "The girl was smaller than me! I suppose she needed to prove something, to prove that she was brave."[49]

The intimacy the girl achieved in the moment when the orangutan Ching sank her large teeth into the girl's foot was met with a smile and was, without a doubt, full of pain. Indeed, feet and hands as extremities of limbs have the greatest sensitivity for humans.[50] Perhaps the girl's smile was joy at intimate contact, at whatever cost. Perhaps it was chagrin at having been seriously injured. Regardless of whatever reasons could be imagined, the conclusion was the same: physical proximity with orangutans was dangerous. Bites from orangutans were serious (figure 2). It would be folly to confuse large eyes, furry bodies, and calm presence with cuddliness.

Volunteers were strictly forbidden from cuddling or any other form of touching the orangutans. As Tom, the British volunteer manager on-site, said to me in an interview when I asked him about physical contact with orangutans:

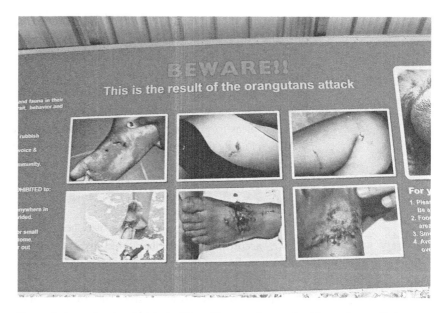

Figure 1 A warning sign depicts six different images of organutan bites on human flesh, Malaysia 2010. Photo by Juno Salazar Parreñas

People [in general] want direct access; people want to touch. With orangutan, as I'm sure you'll know, there's issues for herpes-simplex transmission that kills a lot of orangutans. The common cold kills just as many. Diarrhea, flu . . . so there's zero contact on all of our programs, with all animals. That makes us slightly less palatable than some other programs. A lot of people will want to pay a lot of money if they want to hug an orangutan, or a baby orangutan, to hold a turtle in their hands, or to touch a gorilla. We don't allow any contact. We think it's just the wrong style. The whole point of ecotourism is that you're meant to be doing things altruistically for the benefit of the animal that you're interested in, or the community that you're interested in. It's a bit selfish to try to go up and touch what should be a wild animal. It's not what needs to be done. Unfortunately, in the Western community . . . the orangutan has played quite a role as this cute, cuddly baby that's just like a human, and we selectively filter away volunteers that come with that mindset. There's no contact, they're not cute—they are obviously cute, but that's not why you come here. You come here at the moment to make something, to build things in the middle of the jungle, and work really, really hard and if you're lucky, we'll let you see an orangutan. When they're here, there is a lot more involvement with the orangutan than they're expecting.[51]

Anthroponotic illness was a serious problem that Tom's volunteering company sought to address. Indeed, ENGAGE's approach served to distinguish them from their competitors, including another volunteering company operating in Malaysia, whose literally hands-on involvement at another rehabilitation site in Malaysia has contributed to high mortality rates among infant orangutans.[52] Transient visitors meant transient illness, which was proven the next year when H1N1 became a global pandemic. If the volunteers were carriers, then they could make the zoonotic illness anthroponotic if transferred to an orangutan.[53] ENGAGE responded to the possibility by requiring volunteers to wear surgical masks when in the orangutan areas.

Tom's statement also conveyed postcolonial sentiments in his critique of Western desires to touch exotic animals. A fleeting moment of pleasure for volunteers could have a long-lasting impact on orangutans' behavior. I myself saw the transformation of the orangutan Katrin from one who never made eye contact with humans and had limited encounters to her copying her cell mate Lisbet, who would make direct eye contact and stretch out her arm in order to communicate a demand upon the human beholder of her gaze—whether for food or attention. The problem was that they are too close to humans, evolutionarily speaking, for they adapted to the humans in their company.[54] Evolutionary intimacy descended from a common ancestor shared 14 million years ago forbade physical intimacy with an orangutan. Captive orangutans have an estimated life span of about fifty years. Living at the Lundu Wildlife Center, such an orangutan would potentially encounter a new group of people every two or four weeks. That would mean their lives would be shaped by constant interaction with new humans, whom they are apt to mimic. If they too closely mimicked humans, they would not have the skills to survive on their own if they were to be released and allowed to live autonomously in the forest. Ultimately, eventual release was the intention of orangutan rehabilitation efforts.

Figure 3 The author receives a "kiss" from an elephant while standing near dung, Thailand 2010. Photo taken by unknown

Histories of elephant evolution and millennia of working together with humans allowed for an intimacy with animals that was simply impossible at the orangutan rehabilitation center. Volunteers took pleasure in bathing with elephants in the river, where they could douse them with buckets of water and stroke the water into their gray, wrinkled, and freckled skin that changed from leathery to slick. Volunteers would wear shorts with bikini tops or t-shirts when frolicking with elephants. This close contact happened on the first day of the volunteering experience. After bathing, an elephant would be led to an area where volunteers were clustered so that the elephant could "kiss" each one (figure 3). The mahout used positive reinforcement: for every "kiss" the elephant gave a human, the elephant received a small food treat. Some of the volunteers delighted in the kiss. Others seemed a bit thrown off by the mucous. Every kiss elicited a round of laughter.

Throughout the week, volunteers could freely have contact with elephants, especially in the late afternoon when all the farm labor was done. They could wander upon Dok herself singing a lullaby to a baby elephant nesting on the dusty ground of a roofed shelter. If there were not too many volunteers, they could each snuggle with a baby elephant and take a photo of having done so. This kind of contact contributes to the immense popularity of this site. Bookings are taken online throughout the year, and volunteers often come back to repeat the experience.

Volunteers' engagements of intimacy were focused on connections between individual humans and individual elephants; intimacy between volunteers was often awkward, and connections between people were often limited to pleasantries. Despite participation in common group activities, cohesion in the group did not easily arise. In the time I volunteered, a distinction arose between a clique of three volunteers who had volunteered together previously and other volunteers, including another repeat volunteer whose previous experience occurred at a different time from the other returnees. Their demonstration of the routines familiar to them but not to newcomers, their knowledge of specific elephants, and their disinterest in other volunteers and in events not directly involving elephants conveyed a superiority of a greater commitment to the cause, which caused subtle tension in the group. Those outside this clique would take communal meals together and engage in small talk about travel, their lives back home, and cultural distinctions between their home country and Thailand. Conversations would become uneven and stilted upon certain personal discoveries, such as when a volunteer revealed that her job in Great Britian was to handle deportees, including children. In short, volunteers experienced greater intimacy with elephants than with each other, save for encounters with each other's sweat and smell when laboring.

Intimacy gained by touching a sun bear was never something openly desired by volunteers. Instead, a common concern was their conditions of captivity. Volunteers took turns monitoring their climbing activities, in anticipation of their eventual but unknown release elsewhere. Indeed, Layang entered the bear cage only once in my presence. After two months of having been housed in the orangutan night den, the bear was transferred to the quarantine two days later. At the quarantine, the bear's dwelling was even smaller than the one he had in the orangutan area. It was eight feet wide, eight feet long, and ten feet tall, and it was to house the bear around the clock until an eventual release could be realized.

Species-specific evolutionary histories give us clues as to how individual intimacy with a nonhuman "other" thoroughly transforms the life of that animal. The desire to touch an elephant can be met without forcing domination. Indeed, the sociality of elephants can welcome such trans-specific affections. Touching a bear promises the loss of a finger, given their predatory disposition and the speed with which they move. Contact with a bear has to be done through other material objects, whether water coming out of a hose or a piece of watermelon. Touching an orangutan offers both pleasure and danger. The pleasure of connecting across species is inextricably entwined with the tactile sensation of danger upon this encounter with difference. In other words, the sensation of feeling coarse fur and a clammy, muscular hand poses the danger of potentially sharing infections with the orangutan, transforming the orangutan's behaviors, and experiencing the potential pain and inevitable infection from an orangutan biting into one's flesh.[55] These encounters transform the humans, too. The danger of being too close to an orangutan instills a respect for keeping a distance. Such a response is appropriate for a primate whose life is famous for being solitary. To be intimate with an orangutan is to gain intimate knowledge about the orangutan, not to come into intimate contact. In other words, it is about directly coming into contact with bodily effects and not necessarily actual bodies. This helps to remind us that the effects of bodies can stand in for actual bodies. All are nonetheless forms of embodiment. Thus, intimacy as embodied copresence helps to make sense of how bodies are crucial in intimate industries.

Conclusion

Custodial labor, exemplified by volunteers from the global North paying to perform some of the "shit work" of custodians in the global South, reveals the ways in which intimacy is inevitably about fleshy bodies and animal bodiliness, whether human or nonhuman. When volunteers shovel elephant dung, they can see for themselves the fruit of their labors in the form of corn stalk roughage that they harvested before it went through the elephants' digestive tract. From this image, we can see how they are directly connecting themselves and their backbreaking labor to the elephants' intimate bodily cycles. If the hard labor activities of cutting corn and shoveling is about embodiment, then shoveled fecal matter is about volunteers' bodily contact with the material effects of elephants' bodies. This is intimacy. Intimacy is also the moment when volunteers feel the slippery mucus of an elephant kiss on their faces.

Close encounters with orangutans through custodial labor shows us other forms of intimacy. Intimate knowledge is one such form. It is conveyed in the ability to differentiate orangutans through their stools and in the perceptiveness to signs of individual orangutans' habits, such as where in their cages they tend to have their bowel movements. Intimacy with orangutans is not about touch, especially since direct tactile contact is forbidden for volunteers. For species that otherwise would never come into contact with humans, such as arboreal apes or nocturnal sun bears, being in close proximity and having copresence is already an intimate act. This is apparent when being physically close to an animal might lead to a bite if a respectful distance is not kept.

Mucus and saliva carrying bacteria that can be shared across the divides of human and nonhuman, the texture and smell of scat on wet or dry days, and the possibility of teeth digging into flesh and blood and sending ripples of sensations throughout one's nerves are all material effects of intimacy. Nonhuman animals force us to think of intimacy through material and bodily evidence. Thinking through flesh, feces, and saliva suggests that what appears to be specifically human intimacy is indeed a sign of animal embodiment. Intimacy, in this respect, is experienced through the materiality of bodies.

The idea of keeping a respectful distance with a nonhuman animal while in intimate copresence highlights the complex ways postcoloniality frames the industry of commercial volunteerism. Commercial volunteerism is the flip side to call center outsourcing: people from the global North pay to perform work that is specific to the global South.[56] They pay a lot of money to perform hard labor and are rewarded with the satisfaction of embodiment. This contrasts with call center work in Bangalore, as highlighted by Akhil Gupta and Purnima Mankekar in this issue, in which demands for intimacy through sexual harassment and the desperation of loneliness are disembodied and technologically mediated.

Embodiment drives commercial volunteerism with wildlife, whether that embodiment is through flesh, droppings, or saliva. This serves as a reminder that the materiality of intimacy in intimate industries, and specifically commercial volunteerism, offers something more than what Slavoj Žižek calls "ethical capitalism." While Žižek uses the term to discuss the connection between "egotistic consumerism and altruistic charity," the term is limited to clean acts of consumption.[57] At the elephant sanctuary and wildlife center, animals are not consumed as commodities of ethical capitalism, as is the case for Starbucks and its fair-trade coffee or TOMS, which donates a pair of shoes to a child in need for every pair of shoes purchased. Rather, the participation in commercial volunteerism with wildlife is about dirty and embodied forms of participation in the industry of commercial volunteerism. The dirtiness of various kinds of animal dung, the viscosity of elephant mucus, and the risk of illness exchange are all defining aspects of commercial volunteerism involving wildlife in Southeast Asia. All are about intimacy with bodies. The custodial stories of cleaning up after and caring for elephants, sun bears, and orangutans can help guide other inquiries into intimate industries by serving as a reminder that intimacy is both fleshy and shitty.

Notes

This research was supported by Fulbright-IIE and a travel grant from the Association of South East Asian Nations (ASEAN). Writing was supported during 2012–13 at the Agrarian Studies Program at Yale University and 2013–14 at the Rutgers Center for Historical Analysis. Readings done in Summer 2012 at the Animal Studies Institute–Human Animal Studies at Wesleyan University informed this paper. All proper names have been given pseudonyms to protect the privacy of research subjects. The author thanks Jame Mukherjee, Gabriel Rosenberg, Matthew Bender, Jim Scott, K. "Shivi" Sivaramakrishnan, Lori Gruen, Noah Tamarkin, Akhil Gupta, Rhaçel Parreñas, Rachel Silvey, Hung Thai, Ju Hui Judy Han, Nicole Constable, Purnima Mankekar, and fellow Intimate Industry workshop participants for their helpful engagement. With the exception of geographic names, all proper names in the article are pseudonyms.

1. Nearly everyone in the group of twenty hailed from the global North, and the one Chilean in our group was of German descent. The commercial volunteers I met in Thailand fell under four basic categories: Thirteen out of twenty were professionals taking brief vaca-

tions; three, including the Chilean, were recent university graduates; two were on gap years taking breaks from their education that they planned to resume; and two were pensioners from the United Kingdom. Another group of commercial volunteers were present at the camp at the same time. They were a school group from a boarding school in the US West that catered to wealthy students with disciplinary problems. Their group consisted of twelve boys and six male teachers. Our interactions with them were limited.

2. I use the term *commercial volunteerism* as a synonym of volunteer tourism. Yet unlike the term *volunteer tourism*, the term *commercial volunteerism* emphasizes the paradox inherent in the commodification of volunteer labor. The commodification of volunteerism, in which people pay to perform work themselves, is ubiquitous in Great Britain as well as Australia, New Zealand, and Canada. It has yet to gain popularity among US consumers. See, for instance, Wanda Vrasti, *Volunteer Tourism in the Global South: Giving Back in Neoliberal Times* (London: Routledge, 2013); as well as Peter Smith and Jim Butcher, *Volunteer Tourism and Development* (London: Routledge, 2013).

3. Viviana Zelizer offers a definition for intimate relations in *The Purchase of Intimacy* (Princeton, NJ: Princeton University Press, 2005). She writes, "Let us think of relations as intimate to the extent that interactions within them depend on particularized knowledge received, and attention provided by, at least one person—knowledge and attention that are not widely available to third parties. The knowledge involved includes such elements as shared secrets, interpersonal rituals, bodily information, awareness of personal vulnerability, and shared memory of embarrassing situations" (14). This expansive definition can include relations involving sexual contact, actual bodies, and secret knowledge. By including animals in this framework for understanding the nexus of intimacy, economy, and social relations, I seek to further stress the materiality of bodies at stake.

4. Elizabeth A. Povinelli, *The Empire of Love: Toward a Theory of Intimacy, Genealogy, and Carnality* (Durham, NC: Duke University Press, 2006).

5. Tim Pachirat's *Every Twelve Seconds* vividly describes how individual cows, each distinct with different hides, colors, and spots, all lose their individuality in the process of being shot, skinned, and eviscerated to become beef and beef parts (New Haven, CT: Yale University Press, 2012). In a way, Pachirat adds substance to the conceptual distinction between cow and beef. See Edmund Leach, "Anthropological Aspects of Language: Animal Categories and Verbal Abuse," in *New Directions in the Study of Language*, ed. Eric H. Lenneberg (Cambridge: Cambridge University Press, 1964), 123–56.

6. Natalie Porter, "Bird Flu Biopower: Strategies for Multispecies Coexistence in Việt Nam," *AMET American Ethnologist* 40, no. 1 (2013).

7. Jaime Lorimer, "Nonhuman Charisma," *Environment and Planning D: Society and Space* 25, no. 5 (2007): 911–32; Maan Barua, Meredith Root-Bernstein, Richard J. Ladle, and Paul Jepson, "Defining Flagship Uses Is Critical for Flagship Selection: A Critique of the IUCN Climate Change Flagship Fleet," *Ambio* 40, no. 4 (2011): 431–35.

8. Donna Haraway, *When Species Meet* (Minneapolis: University of Minnesota Press, 2008), 249–64; for more on the concept of copresence, see Donna Haraway, *The Companion Species Manifesto* (Chicago: Prickly Paradigm Press, 2003).

9. Rosemary-Claire Collard, "Putting Animals Back Together, Taking Commodities Apart," *Annals of the Association of American Geographers* 104, no. 1 (2014): 151–65.

10. Mary Louise Pratt, *Imperial Eyes: Travel Writing and Transculturation.* (New York: Routledge, 1992); Donna Haraway, *When Species Meet.* (Minneapolis: University of Minnesota Press, 2008).

11. For more on trans-specific relations, see Eduardo Kohn, "How Dogs Dream: Amazonian Natures and the Politics of Species Engagement," *American Ethnologist* 34, no. 1 (2008); and Rheana (Juno) Salazar Parreñas, "Producing Affect: Transnational Volunteerism in a Malaysian Orangutan Rehabilitation Center," *American Ethnologist* 39, no. 4 (2012): 673–87. Wildlife rehabilitation in Southeast Asia is for endemic animals that are displaced by destruction of their former habitats. They are not necessarily ill or injured, although they sometimes are when they come into the care of Forestry Corporation.

12. ATLAS, *Volunteer Tourism: A Global Analysis* (Arnhem, Netherlands: Tourism Research and Marketing, 2008).

13. In northern Thailand, the average monthly income in 2007 was 13,568 baht or about $452 USD. See Thailand's National Statistics Office, Household Socio-economic Survey 2007 (Bangkok, Thailand: National Statistics Office, 2007).

14. In Sarawak, the mean monthly gross household income in 2009 was 3,581 MYR or about $1,193 USD. See Malaysia's Household Income Survey, 1970–2014, Table 2 (Putra Jaya, Malaysia: Department of Statistics, 2015). The figures are available online at www.epu.gov.my/en/household-income-poverty.

15. John Stewart Mill, *Essays on Some Unsettled Questions of Political Economy* (London: Longmans Green, 1877). Adam Smith, *An Inquiry into the Nature and Causes of the Wealth of Nations* (Oxford: Clarendon Press, 1976).

16. Judith Rollins, *Between Women: Domestics and their Employers* (Philadelphia, PA: Temple University Press, 1985), 23–24. Aban Mehta, *The Domestic Servant Class* (Bombay, Popular Book Depot, 1960).

17. Slavoj Žižek, *Living in the End Times* (London: Verso, 2010), 356.

18. S. Eben Kirksey and Stefan Helmreich, "The Emergence of Multispecies Ethnography," *Cultural Anthropology* 25, no. 4 (2010): 545–76.

19. Mel Y. Chen, *Animacies: Biopolitics, Racial Mattering, and Queer Affect* (Durham, NC: Duke University Press, 2012).

20. Tim Pachirat, *Every 12 Seconds* (New Haven, CT: Yale University Press, 2011). Pachirat's coworker, whom he calls Ramon, had to work in the "gut room." An afternoon's work left bits of intestine in his hair and was bad enough to compel him to find work elsewhere.

21. Michel Foucault in *History of Sexuality, Part 1*, writes, "The ancient right to *take* life or *let* live was replaced by a power to *foster* life or disallow it to the point of death" (138).

22. Michel Foucault, *History of Sexuality: Volume 1* (New York: Vintage Books, 1978). See also *Society Must Be Defended* (New York, Picador, 1997).

23. Povinelli, *Empire of Love*; J. A. Mbembe, *Notes provisoires sur la postcolonie (On the Post-colony)*, Studies on the History of Society and Culture 41 (Berkeley: University of California Press, 2001); Warwick Anderson, *Colonial Pathologies: American Tropical Medicine, Race, and Hygiene in the Philippines* (Durham, NC: Duke University Press); Mary Douglas, *Purity and Danger: An Analysis of Concepts of Pollution and Taboo* (London: Routledge and K. Paul, 1966).

24. Ann Laura Stoler, *Race and the Education of Desire* (Durham, NC: Duke University Press, 1995).

25. Michael Herzfeld, "The Absent Presence: Discourses of Crypto-Colonialism," *South Atlantic Quarterly* 101, no. 4 (2002): 899–926; Thongchai Winichakul, *Siam Mapped: A History of the Geo-Body of a Nation* (Honolulu: University of Hawai'i Press, 1994).

26. Timothy Mitchell, *Rule of Experts: Egypt, Techno-Politics, Modernity* (Berkeley: University of California Press, 2002); James C. Scott, *Seeing Like a State* (New Haven, CT: Yale University Press, 1998).

27. For more on the cultural aspects of what counts as clean or dirty, please see the classic work by Mary Douglas, *Purity and Danger* (London: Routledge, 1966).

28. Rheana "Juno" Salazar Parreñas, "Producing Affect: Transnational Volunteerism in a Malaysian Orangutan Rehabilitation Center," *American Ethnologist* 39, no. 4 (2012): 673–87.

29. The work of commercial volunteerism here differs from "muddy labor" performed by Japanese volunteers in Burma, who define volunteerism through the intimacy of communal living and collective labor alongside their Burmese hosts. See Chika Watanabe, "Muddy Labor: A Japanese Aid Ethic of Collective Intimacy in Myanmar," *Cultural Anthropology* 29, no. 4 (2014): 648–71.

30. For more on social jealousy, see Marina Welker, *Enacting the Corporation* (Berkeley: University of California Press, 2014).

31. For more on the history and politics of multicultural distinctions, social stratification, and the urban/rural divide in Sarawak, see Michael Leigh, *The Rising Moon: Political Change in Sarawak* (Sydney: Sydney University Press, 1974).

32. Ju Hui Judy Han at the Intimate Industries Workshop brilliantly illustrated the motivations of Korean Christian missionary women, which offers a point of contrast to the orientations of commercial volunteers.

33. Punishment is a typical strategy used in wildlife rehabilitation. The idea is to train animals to be averse to people. See, for instance, Rosemary-Claire Collard, "Putting Animals Back Together, Taking Commodities Apart," *Annals of the Association of American Geographers* 104, no. 1 (2014): 151–65.

34. Crystal Rogers, *Mad Dogs and an Englishwoman : The Memoirs of Crystal Rogers* (New Delhi: Penguin Books, 2000).

35. Gayatri Chakravorty Spivak, "Can the Subaltern Speak?," in *Marxism and the Interpretation*

of Culture, ed. Cary Nelson and Lawrence Grossberg (Urbana: University of Illinois Press, 1988), 271–313, 297. Timothy Mitchell in his *Rule of Experts* poses a question in homage to Spivak and her contention with subaltern studies: can the mosquito speak? His answer in the affirmative shows the agency of mosquitos and parasites in Egypt during World War II. The connection between postcolonial theory and animal studies is not to say that animals are the ultimate subaltern in a competition for the dubious honor of being most oppressed. I do not think that animals can be compared as being more or less subaltern than historical subjects implicated in nineteenth-century writing about *sati* or the ritualistic burning of widows. Instead, my point is that the efforts of commercial volunteers from England and other places of the global North see their work as supporting local efforts against local threats upon local wildlife, and that the plight of local wildlife is a global problem of biodiversity loss for which they feel compelled to personally help alleviate. This is a postcolonial iteration of a classic colonial theme of improvement. See, for instance, Mitchell's *Rule of Experts*, Tania Li's *The Will to Improve* (Durham, NC: Duke University Press, 2007).

36. "Lin," interview by the author, Sarawak, Malaysia, November 24, 2008.

37. "Tom," interview by the author, Sarawak, Malaysia, February 8, 2010.

38. For more on the concept of authorial credit, see Bruno Latour and Steve Woolgar, *Laboratory Life: The Social Construction of Scientific Facts*, vol. 80, Sage Library of Social Research (Beverly Hills, CA: Sage, 1979).

39. "Tom," interview by the author.

40. Sue Donaldson, *Zoopolis: A Political Theory of Animal Rights* (Oxford: Oxford University Press, 2011), 138; Lori Gruen, *Ethics and Animals: An Introduction*, Cambridge Applied Ethics (Cambridge: Cambridge University Press, 2011).

41. Ara Wilson, *The Intimate Economies of Bangkok: Tomboys, Tycoons, and Avon Ladies in the Global City* (Berkeley: University of California Press, 2004). Viviana A. Rotman Zelizer, *The Purchase of Intimacy* (Princeton, NJ: Princeton University Press, 2005).

42. Timothy Pachirat, *Every Twelve Seconds* (New Haven, CT: Yale University Press, 2011); James C. Scott, *The Art of Not Being Governed: An Anarchist History of Upland Southeast Asia* (New Haven, CT: Yale University Press, 2009).

43. The idea of enrichment is to provide mental stimulation for animals in captivity. Thus, orangutans enjoy untying knots and taking apart puzzles for food treats.

44. Donna Jeanne Haraway, *Primate Visions: Gender, Race, and Nature in the World of Modern Science* (New York: Routledge, 1989).

45. Andrew Hill and Steven Ward, "Origin of the Hominidae: The Record of African Large Hominoid Evolution between 14 My and 4 My," *American Journal of Physical Anthropology* 31, issue suppl. no. 9 (1988): 49–83.

46. Rangarajan Mahesh, *India's Wildlife History: An Introduction* (Delhi: Permanent Black in association with Ranthambhore Foundation, 2001); R. Sukumar, *The Asian Elephant: Ecology and Management* (Cambridge: Cambridge University Press, 1989).

47. Charles Santiapillai, *The Asian Elephant: An Action Plan for Its Conservation* (Gland, Switzerland: IUCN, 1990).

48. Laurel Braitman, *Animal Madness: How Anxious Dogs, Compulsive Parrots, and Elephants in Recovery Help Us Understand Ourselves* (New York: Simon and Schuster, 2014).

49. Field notes, November 17, 2008.

50. Flavia Mancini, Armando Bauleo, Jonathan Cole, Fausta Lui, Carlo A. Porro, Patrick Haggard, and Gian Domenico Iannetti, "Whole-Body Mapping of Spatial Acuity for Pain and Touch," *Annals of Neurology* 75, no. 6 (2014): 917–24.

51. "Tom," interview with author, November 18, 2008.

52. Noko Kuze et al., "Reproductive Parameters over a 37–Year Period of Free-Ranging Female Borneo Orangutans at Sepilok Orangutan Rehabilitation Centre," *Primates* 49, no. 2 (2008): 126–34.

53. Michael P. Muehlenbein, Leigh Ann Martinez, Andrea Lemke, Laurentius Ambu, Senthilvel Nathan, Sylvia Alsisto, and Rosman Sakong, "Unhealthy Travelers Present Challenges to Sustainable Primate Ecotourism," *Travel Medicine and Infectious Disease* 8, no. 3 (2010): 169–75.

54. Anne Russon, *Orangutans: Wizards of the Rain Forest* (Toronto: Key Porter Books, 1999).

55. The assertion that orangutan bites inevitably led to infection was frequently stated to me by a number of different people when I conducted field research in Sarawak.

56. Khalindi Vora, "The Transmission of Care: Affective Economies and Indian Call Centers," in *Intimate Labors: Cultures, Technologies, and the Politics of Care*, ed. Eileen Boris and Rhacel Salazar Parreñas, 33–48 (Stanford, CA: Stanford University Press, 2010).

57. Žižek, *Living*, 356.

Producing Global Adoptability of Special Needs Children in China

Leslie Wang

Introduction

On a cold December evening in 2007, I stood nervously waiting on a dark, crowded train platform in a small central Chinese city. The distinctive scent of burning coal permeated the frigid air as several old men rolled past with carts, loudly hawking a mind-boggling variety of instant noodles, red cellophane–wrapped sausages, and cheap cigarettes. Like several of the other passengers waiting to catch the overnight train to Beijing, I was carrying a lively one-year-old child. Yet unlike the others, the rambunctious toddler that was presently writhing around in my arms, screeching in protest as she attempted to slip out of my grasp, was not my own.

The girl's English-speaking nurses called her Emma,[1] although her documents bore the Chinese name that she had been given by her orphanage. Emma suffered from a rare condition called retinoblastoma, a child-

positions 24:1 DOI 10.1215/10679847-3320077
Copyright 2016 by Duke University Press

hood cancer that had claimed the sight in her left eye and was threatening vision in her right, and possibly even her life. Though it was impossible to know for certain, this illness was most likely the reason that she had been abandoned to state care. As part of my volunteering duties for Tomorrow's Children, a Western evangelical Christian organization dedicated to caring for unwanted special needs youth, I had been given the task of escorting the child back to Beijing. Preparations had been made for her to fly to Hong Kong and immediately undergo surgery and chemotherapy.

Emma's health situation was urgent, though it was not readily apparent, given that her intense level of energy seemed somehow to increase as the night wore on. We boarded the train and settled into the bottom bunk of a dimly lit soft-sleeper car filled with businessmen. The girl bounced up and down on the bed, babbling happily, and pounded the wall repeatedly with her tiny hand as the businessmen snored overhead. I lay awake the entire evening, terrified to let her out of my sight. When we reached Beijing the following morning, I passed her over to a waiting volunteer and heaved an enormous sigh of relief.

Emma spent the next two years in Hong Kong undergoing multiple costly procedures to save her young life. After completing my fieldwork, I kept up with her progress through the organization's monthly newsletters, where I learned that Emma's cloudy left eye had been removed and she was undergoing chemotherapy, laser treatment, and radiation in order to maintain vision on the right side. The newsletter from March 2009 asked funders to donate $20,000 to cover her latest course of radiation treatment. Against tremendous odds, the toddler's cancer subsequently went into total remission, and she returned to Beijing in July 2009. I did not hear about her again for a year and a half, when it was jubilantly announced that the now four-year-old child had been matched with a foreign family and was awaiting the arrival of her new adoptive parents. The newsletter rejoiced, "[Emma] is indeed one of our many miracles. Without the help of [her doctors], their team, friends and supporters, she would not be alive today. We are hopeful for a very bright future for her with her new family."[2]

In 2007, *Time Magazine* announced that we had entered "the Chinese century" and predicted that the People's Republic of China (PRC) would soon surpass the United States as the world's most powerful national economy.[3] Indeed, since first "opening up" (*gaige kaifang*) to global capitalism in 1978, the PRC has experienced meteoric rates of growth credited with alleviating poverty for more than 600 million people.[4] As the United States's second largest trading partner and an increasingly influential force in the global economy, China is simultaneously viewed as a land of free-wheeling economic opportunity and as a dangerous threat to the industrialized world. A recent poll from the Pew Research Center's Global Attitudes Project found that three quarters of US citizens surveyed consider the nation to be untrustworthy, and 26 percent named China "as the country that represents the greatest danger to the U.S.," higher than both Iran and North Korea.[5]

China is in tremendous flux, undergoing unprecedented economic growth and prosperity while remaining a developing country whose per capita income was ranked 114th in the world in 2011.[6] Akin to other postsocialist contexts, economic privatization in the PRC has also been accompanied by political decentralization. In particular, the central government has largely retreated from its responsibilities in the public sector and eliminated millions of government jobs and a range of social welfare benefits. Expectations of cradle-to-grave employment security once guaranteed through the socialist "iron rice bowl" (*tie fanwan*) have completely disappeared and been replaced by individual family responsibility. Consequently, the reform era has been characterized by an anxious sense of competition over resources and widening disparities between social classes.

Research on China and globalization has tended to focus myopically on the large-scale implications of rapid development, manufacturing, and industrialization.[7] Few studies have considered the fundamental ways in which global capitalism has transformed the "private" realm of families and intimate relationships or how these macro-level changes have reshaped individual lives, especially those of children. Over the past several decades, the life chances of China's youngest members have been profoundly altered by an unwieldy combination of economic pressures, stringent fertility regulations that limit most couples to one or two offspring,[8] and a long-standing cultural preference for sons. These constraints have led to the relinquishment of countless—possibly millions—of healthy girls and special needs youth of both sexes to government care since the beginning of market reforms.

Because of the sweeping family planning campaigns in the late 1980s and early 1990s, state orphanages began to fill with abandoned children.[9] At that time, the Chinese government turned to transnational adoption as a possible solution to this predicament while still being able to enforce strict fertility regulations locally. In the years since its implementation, sending children overseas has been extremely lucrative for the PRC. Hundreds of millions of dollars of foreign resources have poured into the Chinese economy, both through adoptions and the subsequent donations sent by parents to children's welfare institutes. Parents routinely spend US$20,000–$30,000 per adoption, including foreign agency fees, expenses for a ten-to-fourteen-day mandatory trip to China that at least one parent is required to make to retrieve their child, plus an obligatory cash donation to the orphanage that has increased to US$5,000 in recent years. Additionally, the migration of Chinese children to Western families has opened an avenue for the global humanitarian aid industry to reach state-run orphanages. Consequently, local authorities have welcomed numerous foreign nongovernmental organizations (NGOs) to use their own resources to provide care for relinquished youth.[10]

China's embrace of global capitalism has contributed to both a skyrocketing demand for its manufactured goods and an intense (some might even say insatiable) desire for its children, culminating in "one of the most privileged forms of diaspora and immigration" in the contemporary era.[11] Between 1992 and 2010, the PRC government facilitated the adoption of more than 130,000 children—most of them healthy females—to affluent foreigners residing in sixteen first-world nations. The United States has received the majority of these youth.[12] Although numbers have fallen precipitously in recent years for reasons that will be explored later in this article, from 2000 until the present day, China has been ranked the top "sending country" of adoptable children in the world.

Over the past two decades, healthy female adoptees have been the subject of intense concern and scrutiny. Nearly every aspect of their experiences has been assessed through studies that measure their physiological development, psychological well-being, and racial/ethnic cultural identity formation, to name just a few. Surprisingly little, however, has been written about special needs children such as Emma who have been adopted with increasing frequency through an alternative plan known as the "Waiting Child

Program."[13] As I will examine further, she and the thousands of other ill, disabled, and older youth who comprise the official Chinese state-defined category of "special needs" disrupt commonplace understandings about children's ready adoptability and their intrinsic value to foreign families. While most research highlights the demand for children by families within rich "receiving countries," this article redirects attention to the changing *supply* of adoptable youth in the "sending country."

Intercountry adoption has been critiqued for treating children as commodities. Yet, this argument is based on an a priori assumption that parents consider all adoptees to be inherently appealing (i.e., young and/or healthy). Children who may face long-term physical and possibly mental limitations that can require costly medical and professional services challenge the notion that young adoptees are a "tabula rasa" that parents can mold according to their own wishes. Undoubtedly, adoption agencies are playing an integral role in marketing older and disabled children to Western parents, a topic that researchers have begun to investigate.[14] However, the aim of this article is to explore the intimate labor (which Eileen Boris and Rhacel Parreñas define as "work that involves embodied and affective interactions in the service of social reproduction") that occurs in China *prior to adoption* and transforms locally marginalized special needs youth into internationally desirable daughters and sons.[15]

Feminist scholars have theorized how the logic of the market has infiltrated the most intimate processes of family life and personal relationships. In *The Outsourced Self,* Arlie Hochschild contends that busy first-world citizens have come to rely on commodified services and expertise to help them navigate once-private domains of life such as love, friendship, and childcare.[16] The outsourcing of intimate labor has become increasingly global in scope, as millions of poor migrants have moved from developing to industrialized nations to perform care and service work for middle-class professionals. Researchers have demonstrated how the stratified provision of caring labor has reinforced inequalities between nations and individuals in the global economy.[17]

In this article, I suggest that first-world citizens are not the only ones who benefit from outsourced intimacy. Chinese government authorities have also profited from being able to outsource intimate labor to affluent, foreign child-saving groups that are part of the global humanitarian aid industry. This essay is based on more than a year of ethnographic fieldwork that I conducted with the Tomorrow's Children Foundation, a Western faith-based NGO that used first-world medical practices to care for sick and dying abandoned youth. Although many children passed away in their facilities, a considerable number were also nursed back to health and ultimately adopted by foreign families. I will demonstrate how this organization produced globally desirable special needs children through costly intensive emotional and material investment in their well-being.

I begin by situating this case within the domestic Chinese context that has led to the large-scale abandonment of special needs youth and a description of the methodological approach of this project. Next I provide an overview of shifting marketplace of Chinese adoption and the changing population of available children. Lastly, drawing from ethnographic insights garnered from fieldwork conducted in four Tomorrow's Children medical foster homes in China between 2006 and 2007, I analyze practices of outsourced intimate labor used to transform marginalized outcasts into global citizens—a process that highlights the commodity thinking and market forces underlying practices of international adoption.

Background, Data, and Methods

Before examining the details of this case, it is important to situate it within the contemporary Chinese context and the combination of factors that have resulted in special needs children being adopted abroad. Because of stringent family planning regulations such as the now defunct one-child policy, the total fertility rate has plummeted. Simultaneously, the number of those born with congenital issues has skyrocketed. According to official statistics that were released in 2007, every thirty seconds, a child is born with a disability or illness in the PRC.[18] Because Chinese society is still dominated by norms of filial piety and the expectation that offspring will care for parents in old age, there is widespread agreement that individuals born with any kind of abnormality (but particularly those with mental disabilities) lack value because they are less able to become productive laborers in the future.[19] The idea that handicapped children disrupt the natural order of family and lineage is compounded by a strong cultural stigma against any type of congenital disease or deformity; a child's disability tends to be interpreted as symbolic punishment for the wrongdoings of parents, particularly mothers.[20] Yet rather than trying to change the larger cultural mindset toward disability, state authorities have tended to blame the situation on the "backwardness" of rural people.[21]

A government survey reported that in 2005 there were 573,000 orphaned children spread across the country. Those with special needs constituted 37.3 percent of institutionalized youth in cities and composed 66.6 percent of the total in rural areas.[22] A follow-up study released by UNICEF China in 2010 found that the numbers of orphaned children had risen to 712,000, a 24 percent increase from only five years earlier.[23] It did not, however, provide new figures on the number of special needs children in state care. Researchers have argued that the Chinese government is largely responsible for the large-scale abandonment of these children, pointing to the near-total lack of social welfare provisions for families with sick or disabled offspring.[24] Chinese state authorities have also contributed to the stigmatization of special needs youth by publicly labeling them societal burdens and a hindrance to China's global economic progress.[25] As the central state has retreated from the public sector in recent years, responsibility for parentless children has been pushed onto local-level governments. The dearth of child welfare resources has led local authorities to engage in a growing number of collaborations with foreign humanitarian organizations as a way to make ends meet.

I first learned about Tomorrow's Children in the summer of 2005 when a colleague mentioned a beautiful foreign foster home on the rural outskirts of Beijing that provided first-world medical care to abandoned children. I visited the home for the first time that summer and met the Dunlops, a white evangelical Christian couple from Australia who had originally gone to Beijing in 1997 to pursue work opportunities. Within several years of being in China, they felt a calling to devote themselves to providing care for extremely sick, institutionalized children and opened the first Tomorrow's Children foster home in 2003. Barbara Dunlop was a Western-trained physician and handled all the children's medical care, while her husband Peter dealt with the administrative and financial aspects of their rapidly expanding organization.

The group's original mission was to provide nonhospice palliative care to children with operable issues and treatable diseases who would have almost no chance of survival had they stayed in an institution. The first medical foster home accommodated up to fifty-six children at a time; they were sent from child welfare institutes across the country and suffered from an extensive range of illnesses and disabilities. The group used its global religious and business contacts to obtain pro bono or reduced-fee surgeries for children in regions with more advanced medical technology, such as the United States, Singapore, and Hong Kong. Children were often sent abroad for months at a time for surgery and recuperation. After being deemed completely healthy, usually by the age of two or three, they were generally placed on the foreign adoption list (some children were adopted with long-term illnesses or prior to undergoing major surgeries, although this was far less common). Though the organization could not directly arrange adoptions, which are controlled by the Chinese state, most children were eventually placed with Western Christian families.

Tomorrow's Children worked hard to develop a close working relationship with the Chinese Ministry of Civil Affairs, the government branch responsible for orphans, the elderly, and the impoverished. As a result, the organization was asked to build similar facilities in central China to provide hospice care for infants and young children with a low likelihood of survival or future adoption. In the decade since the organization was founded, it has experienced incredible growth. According to figures available on its website, the group now operates five separate units that care for around three hundred babies and employ over five hundred local staff. In 2012, the units took in 293 new admissions and organized hospital surgery or treatment for 193 babies. Two-hundred and sixty-one of its children were internationally adopted between 2006 and 2012.[26] The units were also supported by a steady stream of Western volunteers who provided labor, donations, and specialized skills during both short- and long-term stays.

The foster homes provided medical and emotional care that was based on Christian principles of self-sacrifice and aiding those in need. The Dunlops describe having been "inspired by God's will" to devote their lives to caring for "the least of these" (a reference to Bible verse Matthew 25:40, "The King will reply, 'I tell you the truth, whatever you did for one of the least of these brothers of mine, you did for me.'"). Because Chinese law prohibits proselytizing, the group funneled its energy into work with neglected youth in order to set an example that it hoped locals would eventually follow. Erica Bornstein has called this approach "lifestyle evangelism" or "the process of living a life in the manner of Christ, providing an example, and showing non-believers Christianity through the life that was led."[27] By using their own funds to administer to sick and disabled babies who were seen as having little value to local society, the organization was able to serve a dual purpose: it filled a major gap in the Chinese child welfare system while also accomplishing its own goals of alleviating suffering and helping to facilitate the international adoption of children.

Nearly all the volunteers in the units (other than myself) were evangelical Christians, and it seemed to surprise them to hear that secular people also performed charity work. During a tour of the Beijing home, Barbara pointed to a picture of the head surgeon of a prestigious US medical school who could be counted on in emergencies to catch a plane to Beijing to operate on a dying child. Reflecting on his generosity, she added with some incredulity, "and he's not even a Christian!" My own lack of religious conviction appeared to be overridden by the fact that I could speak Mandarin and was able to volunteer full time during the extremely critical first few months after the opening of one of the organization's palliative care units in central China.

This article is based on ethnographic fieldwork that I conducted over five separate research trips to four Tomorrow's Children medical foster homes between November 2006 and September 2007. In total, I carried out three months of participant observation and informal interviews with Western volunteers and Chinese *ayis* (caregivers/nannies). I also performed translation, helped with child care, dealt with Chinese medical practitioners, oriented new volunteers to the area, as well as completed simple office administration. All parties were aware of my researcher status. Because of the political sensitivity of issues, I did not tape-record any interviews but instead transcribed them from memory soon afterward. Later, I coded all my written materials, including interviews, observational data, and general field notes. During data analysis, I employed a grounded theory approach, inductively focusing themes that emerged from the data.[28]

Commodification and the Changing Market of Chinese Children

In this section, I turn to a discussion of Chinese adoptions in light of practices of commodification and the shifting international availability of children. Special needs adoption from China first officially began in September 2000, when laws allowing older and disabled youth to be adopted through an alternative known as the Waiting Child Program were implemented.[29] According to one US adoption agency's description, the children available through this plan "are generally older [aged eight to thirteen] and/or with minor to significant medical or physical conditions. Examples include, but are not limited to, children with repaired or unrepaired cleft lips or palates, repaired or unrepaired heart defects, missing or webbed fingers or toes, hepatitis B, and vision or hearing impairments."[30]

Adoption has long been the subject of intense ethical debates concerning whether children themselves are bought and sold, or whether commodification exists only in the services and transactions that allow them to be legally exchanged between families, institutions, and nations. Earlier waves of adoption to the United States were primarily motivated by Christian altruism that emerged from US wartime occupation in Asia.[31] However, over time, the spread of global capitalism has created a "free market" in children whereby altruistic motivations have become overshadowed by consumer/parental preferences.[32] According to David Eng, "the logics of global capitalism are ones that commodify and colonize not just an ever-expanding field of objects . . . but also and increasingly subjects themselves, including young children."[33]

Nonetheless, shifts in China's transnational adoption program also suggest that parental preferences are in fact malleable and contingent upon children's availability. Even though special needs youth have been adoptable since 2000, they were not seen as particularly desirable until relatively recently. Instead, most Western parents have been interested in obtaining a "typical" Chinese adoptee—that is, a healthy female infant or toddler no older than eighteen months of age. Since the early 1990s, images of smiling young Asian girls, often attired in red silk dresses and flanked by adoring white parents, have been reinforced through news accounts, advertisements, and a major story line in *Sex and the City*.

Scholars have identified multiple factors that have led Chinese girls to become intensely sought after by US citizens, reasons that are both gendered and racialized. In general, most adoptive parents express a desire for a daughter rather than a son, a preference that intersects with prevalent cultural stereotypes of "submissive" Asian females who are considered easily assimilable into white families.[34] These biases are especially obvious in comparison to the largely negative depictions of African American children available through the domestic foster care system.[35] Moreover, Chinese girls have also been credited with validating Western parental subjectivities; Ann Anagnost has suggested that adoption has helped to placate the desires of white middle-class actors whose value and self-worth hinge on becoming a parent.[36]

When China's international adoption program first commenced, thousands of first-world citizens rushed to submit applications. The PRC quickly developed a stellar international reputation for running a smooth, reliable, and honest program that all but guaranteed the arrival of a healthy girl within a relatively brief one-year time frame. Orphanage officials and adoption agencies assured eager parents that Chinese birth mothers didn't drink or smoke—evidence that they actually "wanted" their pregnancy—but had abandoned their daughters as a result of the one-child policy and patriarchal pressure to produce a son. It was commonly assumed that all adoptable babies were anonymously left under bridges, in crowded marketplaces, at hospitals, and outside orphanage gates where they were sure to be found. Adoptions from the PRC surged, peaking in 2005 with 14,493 children sent abroad, more than half of them to the United States.[37]

Although in the 1990s it was very likely that most healthy girls were legitimately abandoned, over time, the immense profit margin and lax enforcement on either side of the Pacific contributed to practices of child trafficking in China.[38] According to researcher Brian Stuy, the regions of the country with the highest rates of transnational adoption were also the most likely to have participated in baby-buying programs that specifically targeted healthy infant girls.[39] In 2006, the Chinese government discovered that state orphanages in Hunan Province that supplied large numbers of babies had purchased as many as one thousand children who were suspected of being abducted.[40]

As a result, the nation severely scaled back its international adoption program and began encouraging placements of older and disabled children through the Waiting Child Program. The government has incentivized the adoption of these youth by expediting the process, with most adoptions occurring within a year-and-a-half time frame, as opposed to the five years' or longer wait that prospective parents currently face for a healthy infant.[41] It has also relaxed its stipulations regarding who can adopt. The shift in the population of available children led the China Center of Adoption Affairs to revise a 2006 policy outlawing adoptions by foreign single parents; since 2010 the government has permitted heterosexual unmarried females to obtain a "special focus" child—a category that includes older youth, those with significant and/or multiple medical conditions, and children whom no one else has claimed for adoption after their files have been available to agencies for thirty days.[42]

The prevailing understanding of such youth is that they are truly unwanted, although at least one large state orphanage in Henan Province was found to have knowingly adopted out children older than fourteen (the official cut-off age for adoption in China) who actually had birth families that may have sought to keep them.[43] While this major transition ended a fifteen-year trend in which an estimated 95 percent of adoptees were healthy girls, the fact that so many foreigners are now interested in adopting special needs children speaks to the ways in which the Chinese government has been able to repackage international adoption to fit its own objectives. In 2009, the last year for which figures were published, special needs youth constituted nearly *half* of all foreign adoptees; this was a huge jump from 2005, when they did not add up to even one-tenth of adoptive placements (see table 1 below).[44]

Table 1: Special Needs Adoptions from China, 2005–9

World Totals	*2005*	*2006*	*2007*	*2008*	*2009*
Total # Adoptions	14,221	10,646	7858	5531	5294
Special needs adoptions	1285	2131	2365	2604	2583
Total proportion special needs	9 percent	20 percent	30 percent	47 percent	48.8 percent

More recently, an article that was published in the *China Daily*, the official newspaper of the PRC government, reported that only about three thousand children were adopted by foreigners in 2012, of which 74 percent were disabled or older.[45]

Chinese special needs youth elicit particular forms of sympathy from the international community that motivate the work of faith-based groups.[46] The timing of these changes has been significant in that the radically reduced availability of healthy infants from the PRC occurred simultaneously with the growth of the US evangelical Christian adoption movement. Since the mid-2000s, leaders of US mega-churches have persuaded followers of a looming global orphan crisis, encouraging families to adopt needy children as a way to demonstrate faith.[47] Within just a few years, hundreds of churches have established "orphan-care" ministries that have guided thousands of families through the process of adopting both domestically and abroad, a significant portion of which have involved older and disabled children.[48]

As policies have shifted and the overall numbers of international adoptions have fallen, Western adoption agencies have also launched their own campaigns to encourage special needs placements. In the words of one US adoption administrator, "Adoption puts a price on children that makes them more valuable . . . valuable to rescue and valuable to take care of."[49] Despite the possibilities for corruption, international adoption has raised the social value of certain children and brought about an immense upgrading of facilities and care practices within many Chinese institutions. Because of domestic factors that have made healthy girls largely unattainable, the international social value of special needs youth has been heightened instead—a trend that has been facilitated by the entry of the global humanitarian aid industry into local Chinese society. In the next section, I discuss the intimate labor performed within Western medical units that enhanced children's desirability within the global marketplace of adoption.

**Outsourced Intimacy and the Creation
of "Priceless" Special Needs Children**

The special needs youth that were cared for by Tomorrow's Children were recipients of tremendous first-world care, knowledge, and resources largely unavailable to local people. As such, those who were eventually adopted internationally could be considered literal embodiments of reproductive labor that is performed in China for consumption by the global North. The Western organization's care practices were motivated by religious principles as well as rigorous middle-class child-rearing standards. Sharon Hays has argued that first-world parenting has become increasingly "child-centered, expert-guided, emotionally absorbing, labor-intensive, and financially expensive."[50] In the foster homes, this approach took material form in terms of care practices that sought to develop children's potential and ease their transition into a non-Chinese household.

The child-centeredness of the organization was evident in the intensive tracking of babies' physical health and emotional well-being that included detail-oriented and individualizing practices of care that resource-poor local state institutions typically would or could not perform. The foster homes enforced a fairly clear division of labor in the units whereby Chinese ayis performed most physical child-caring tasks—including feeding and medication, bathing, clothing, changing diapers, and putting them to sleep—while Western volunteers attended to children's medical and emotional needs.

In general, ayis were drawn from the local working-class population. All were women and most were mothers, many being hired after they were laid off from jobs in state-run work units (*danwei*). Each nanny was assigned to care for the same two to three babies every day in order to promote bonding and, according to Barbara Dunlop, to prevent everyone "from just gravitating towards the little cuties." Caregivers were each trained to follow a uniform set of Western care standards that sought to keep babies on consistent routines. For their efforts they were paid between US$60 and $75 dollars per month for shifts that lasted eight hours in the Beijing home (an independently operated unit that could set its own hours) and twelve hours in all the other units, which were built within state-run institutions and obligated to adhere to local procedures. Their wages were exceedingly low, not only on a global level but also in comparison to the average salaries of the local areas around the foster homes. In addition to their other labor-intensive duties, ayis were also required to track each minute detail of children's physical progress during their work shifts; using clipboards that passed between daytime and evening caregivers, they recorded the frequency of urination and bowel movements, temperature, feedings, medications, and any changes in condition.

While ayis focused primarily on children's physical circumstances, Western volunteers sought to encourage children's emotional and mental development. Both short- and long-term visitors went to great lengths to encourage sick and disabled youth to live up to their fullest potential—regardless of whether that potential might be quite limited. A wide array of play and educational activities was presented to children, whose interests were noted and encouraged over time. Volunteers' methods aligned with what Annette Lareau has termed "concerted cultivation," a US middle-class practice in which parents expose offspring to educational and extracurricular activities to foster skills that allow them to reproduce their own class status in the future.[51] Within the foster homes, this approach enhanced sick and disabled children's sociability, cognitive capacities, and, ultimately, their international adoptability within a context in which healthy infants are no longer accessible.

The most obvious example of concerted cultivation was the daily English classes that mentally capable toddlers in the Beijing foster home began at the age of two, which I sat in on as an observer. The space itself bore an uncanny resemblance to a first-world preschool classroom, complete with tiny wooden tables and chairs, bilingual posters on the wall featuring animals and the English alphabet, and a soft-tiled multicolored foam mat in the corner surrounded by shelves full of new toys. The classes were taught by a pleasant, bespectacled, white British woman named Nicky who had moved to China with her husband a year earlier to serve as a full-time volunteer with the organization. The highly devout young couple had committed to staying for three years. Nicky was not trained as a teacher, nor did she speak much Mandarin, but she managed to keep the group of six youth (aged two to four) organized and entertained for the full forty-five-minute class session.

After greeting one another with "good morning," three children quickly plopped down at a table and began forming colorful shapes out of Play-Doh. The other group sat at a different table, concentrating hard while composing pictures on red magnetic Etch A Sketch toys that were shaken fiercely every few minutes. Squeezed somewhat comically into tiny seats among the six children were five adult women—the teacher, another British short-term volunteer, two Chinese ayis, and myself. During these activities, some of the children displayed quite remarkable English skills. One three-year-old boy who would soon be adopted counted to ten and was able to name all the parts of the face. Gazing at him fondly, the ayi who had cared for him since he was a baby remarked upon his intelligence and proudly added that she had also taught him to count to fifty in Chinese.

The children engaged in supervised play for about twenty-five minutes, followed by snack time. Nicky then instructed the group to sit down in a line on the foam mat, where they sang classic Western children's songs, including "Row, Row, Row Your Boat," "Head, Shoulders, Knees, and Toes," and "Twinkle, Twinkle Little Star." All the children enthusiastically bobbed their heads and hummed along happily with the familiar melodies, though it wasn't clear whether they understood the lyrics.

While the children were occupied, I had a short conversation with the two ayis, who asked me why foreigners want to adopt Chinese children (this was a question I was repeatedly asked by local people during my fieldwork). I gave a vastly oversimplified response regarding foreign parents sometimes not being able to have their own offspring or wanting to give a child a home. The women looked at one another, nonplussed. One of the ayis stated, "Chinese people prefer to take care of their own [biological] children," the other nodding her head in agreement. I asked what they thought about the Western approach to child rearing that predominated in the foster home. Clucking her tongue in disagreement, one caregiver critiqued volunteers for always following the child's lead. "They do whatever the child wants to do" (*Haizi xiang zuo shenme, jiu zuo shenme*), she asserted.

Intensive Financial Investment and Children's Adoptability

Providing for children's medical and daily life needs in a Western middle-class manner was not only labor intensive, it was also incredibly costly in financial terms. Sara Dorow has noted that in her visits to orphanages that participated in international adoption, ayis were deeply aware of the irony that the abandoned children in their care often experienced better living conditions than they themselves did.[52] This gap in material conditions was even more apparent in facilities run by affluent foreigners. Indeed, Tomorrow's Children's gleaming supply rooms were filled from floor to ceiling with new donated clothing packed and labeled according to size, item, and season. Large metal shelves were lined with seemingly endless supplies of disposable diapers, toiletries, formula, and snacks. The cabinets in the medical examination rooms were also filled with various over-the-counter and prescription medications as well as specialized tools, such as otoscopes, catheters, and pediatric-sized colostomy bags. Many of these items were either unavailable in China or prohibitively expensive; to get around this obstacle, Tomorrow's Children relied on travelers from the United States, the United Kingdom, and Australia to transport supplies to Beijing in their luggage.

The organization was also able to keep up with an estimated US$160,000 per month in running costs through private donations from individuals, churches, schools, and even multinational corporations such as Shell, UPS, Virgin Atlantic, and General Electric—demonstrating the ways in which the interests of the humanitarian sector and foreign private industry often overlap in China. According to a financial report on its website, in 2012 alone Tomorrow's Children received nearly US$3.6 *million* in contributions, of which it spent roughly US$500,000 on baby supplies for the three hundred children in its care and US$2.15 million on payroll expenses for its five hundred local employees.[53] Even though many surgeries and treatments were provided pro bono, the organization also spent large amounts of its own funds on major medical expenditures each year. For example, in 2011 it covered forty-two heart cases, eighty cleft lip and palate cases, thirteen anorectal/bowel defects, thirteen genital defects, and four biliary atresia needing liver transplants, which altogether cost the organization more than half a million US dollars.

Thus, the investment that the group made in its children was a complex combination of care and commodified practices that required extensive financial resources, time, and professional expertise. Every instance in which a child was sent out for international surgery—a process that could take months for preparation and recovery—he or she was accompanied by both a Chinese caregiver and a Western volunteer who stayed the entire time. A recent newsletter recounted the story of a little boy named Brian who was admitted to one of the foster homes in 2008 at three months of age with complex medical needs. In addition to being hospitalized locally, he traveled to Hong Kong multiple times to receive treatments for several ailments, totaling ten separate hospital stays in just four years. Just after his fourth birthday, Brian was well enough to leave China to "join his Forever Family." The newsletter emphasized his readiness to go abroad, noting, "His English is almost as good as his Chinese and he has an uncanny ability to grab onto your heart the moment you see him."[54] Thus, it's possible to see how Brian's renewed physical health and Western-oriented disposition was the product of costly outsourced intimacy in China.

International Adoption as the Ultimate Goal for Children

Although for myriad reasons only a portion of the children cared for by the foster homes were sent abroad, all the material and emotional investment in them indicated that international (rather than domestic) adoption was the ultimate objective. In their work, the Dunlops utilized a discourse of family and kinship, describing the medical units as "normal, home-like settings" where they treated each child as one of their own. The organization also promoted the formation of emotional bonds between ayis and children, describing on its website, "Nannies have the complete responsibility of feeding, bathing and playing with their babies. They are also trained to give prescribed medicines, just like any mother."[55] Unsurprisingly, ayis who cared for the same children around the clock for years at a time often became extremely attached. Despite women's long-term efforts and deep attachments, in reality they were generally treated as paid, temporary maternal substitutes until children could be retrieved by their foreign "forever families."

Although most Western foster homes in China that administer to special needs children are careful to not be overly involved with adoption processes, they sometimes play a direct role in facilitating placements. Anna High found that on rare occasions certain organizations draw on "personal contacts within the China Center of Adoption Affairs or a particularly foreigner-friendly state orphanage to match a difficult special needs case" with a willing family.[56] Tomorrow's Children founder Barbara Dunlop had very clear opinions on adoption and spoke candidly about her preference that children be sent abroad rather than placed locally. She presumed that Chinese people adopt for self-interested purposes, while foreign Christian families love children unconditionally:

> Actually, I'm a bit fearful of domestic adoption. We have families willing to pay the fees for local people to adopt because they think it's a good idea, but sometimes I think Chinese people adopt for the wrong reasons. Like adopting a twelve-year-old to be a maid in your house, that kind of thing, and the fact that they might not treat these children the same as they would blood relatives. In China there's really no child protection laws; people don't know anything about this. Here we have Western Christian families who will love the child no matter what, and that is what I would prefer for these children.

Nonetheless, the large numbers of babies and caregivers spread across five different special care units meant that there were occasions in which nannies did successfully adopt children. Yet some local women learned that this situation was not only frowned-upon by their employers, it also ran counter to the market logic that was employed by Chinese state authorities when considering the "best interests" of adoptable youth. Barbara described a situation where an orphanage refused to allow one of her working-class ayis to adopt a baby: "The officials didn't see any reason to let her adopt a child when they could give it to a Western couple who would pay $4,000 US to the orphanage and be able to provide a good life and education for it. They didn't want to let a woman from the countryside adopt because they didn't think she could provide as good of a life." That children would be better off overseas was a notion that was also commonly shared by local people as well, even those who might be interested in adoption. One afternoon, I went for a walk with two ayis and the children in their care. The nannies and I sat on a bench and chatted while the toddlers ran around in a nearby playground. Xiao Wang, a woman in her forties who had a fifteen-year-old son, engaged me in a discussion about adoption. After asking the requisite questions as to why foreigners are so interested in Chinese children, she inquired as to whether PRC citizens were also able to adopt. I informed her that not only could local people adopt, but they could also often choose the child themselves and that a number of international sponsors were willing to pay the fee. Xiao Wang's face lit up momentarily but soon clouded over, as she quickly talked herself out of the possibility: "I really like this little girl and would be interested in adopting her. I've been with her since she was little . . . but what kind of conditions (*tiaojian*) could I provide for her? What kind of life could she have here compared with being raised in a foreign country?"

Conclusion

Since first opening its international adoption program, China has had a paradoxical relationship with the global North, where it is considered both an untrustworthy economic competitor as well as a major source of highly desirable daughters and sons. While studies of globalization tend to separate economics from the private sphere, this article has sought to illuminate the relationship between the PRC's central role in the global economy and its position as the top producer of adoptable youth in the world. Because of the commodified practices that define it, international adoption cannot be considered solely through the lens of unwanted babies needing families. Instead, this legal market in children involves a constellation of constantly shifting local and global social, political, and economic factors.

Barbara Yngvesson has argued that more attention must be paid to the role that nation-states play in producing children for the global market, facilitating the conditions in which local parents feel compelled to abandon their offspring.[57] Rapid Chinese economic development has fundamentally altered family structure and heightened expectations of offspring, contributing to the devaluation of special needs children. Heavy competition over scarce resources and the market logic that characterizes the Chinese reform era has created a social hierarchy whereby "some bodies are recognized as having more value than others and therefore more deserving of the rights of citizenship."[58] In the face of immense financial pressures, fertility regulations, cultural bias, and the total lack of social welfare provisions for families with disabled and ill children, certain youth have been far more likely to be relinquished by their parents.

Although it has been waning in recent years, the intimate industry of international adoption has created a financial incentive for China to maintain a consistent population of adoptable youth, and parentless children have served as a national resource that has generated substantial income for the nation's social welfare system. As the availability of healthy girls has declined, the social value of special needs children has substantially increased, in part owing to the intense growth of the US Christian adoption movement. In outsourcing the care of locally stigmatized sick and disabled youth to foreign faith-based humanitarian organizations such as Tomorrow's Children, Chinese state authorities have been able to effectively relieve themselves of responsibility for children's welfare while reaping financial benefits should babies be rehabilitated enough to be sent overseas.

This article has sought to challenge the notion that all children who are available for international adoption are inherently desirable. It is often assumed that it is the physical process of migration from poor to rich nations that transforms children from neglected social outcasts into first-world subjects deserving of rights, privileges, and social recognition. For the tens of thousands of healthy Chinese girls who have been adopted by foreign families, this may certainly be the case. However, I've suggested that the global appeal of special needs youth is not entirely commonsensical and points to commodification as a process. For the babies who were cared for by Tomorrow's Children, their attractiveness to parents was the outcome of a lengthy period of intensive material expenditure, emotional investment, and practices of concerted cultivation that transformed them into "priceless" daughters and sons who were readily incorporable into white Western families.[59]

Somewhat ironically, the Chinese government's outsourcing of intimate labor to Christian child savers within the global aid industry has exposed some of the country's least valued members to a first-world quality of life, one that was intended to prepare them for a future middle-class existence abroad. Though state authorities and Western humanitarian groups might disagree on the personal potential of special needs individuals, their interests were in fact aligned by having the same end goal to place children in foreign families. Western parents who pursue a special needs adoption often commit themselves to expending extensive additional labor and vast financial resources on their child. Nonetheless, a good portion of these parents are evangelical Christians whose desire to take a disabled or ill child into their homes extends from a larger first-world commitment to help the less fortunate, an undertaking that allows them to perform moral superiority and altruism through their care of marginalized Others.[60]

China's international adoption program has not only placed children in loving families, but it has also served governmental interests by creating a bridge to the global North and bolstering its relationship with the United States in particular.[61] The shifts in China's adoption industry are deeply symbolic of the nation's rapid global rise. It is highly significant that as the PRC ascends higher in the world economy, the number of children it sends abroad has dramatically declined. Although it is often framed as an issue of child trafficking versus orphan rescue, the transnational circulation of children involves a blend of care and commodified practices that fit somewhere between these two extremes. Ultimately, it remains to be seen whether international adoption from the PRC continues and what form it might take, or whether we will eventually look back at this trend as a remarkable, short-lived phase of China's path to modernization.

Notes

1. All proper names, including that of the organization for which I worked, have been given pseudonyms to protect anonymity.

2. Monthly online newsletter, *Tomorrow's Children Foundation*, January 2011.

3. Michael Elliott, "China Takes on the World," *TIME Magazine*, January 22, 2007, www .time.com/time/ magazine/article/0,9171,1576831,00.html.

4. World Bank, "China Overview," www.worldbank.org/en/country/china/overview.

5. Pew Research Center Global Attitudes Project, "U.S. Public, Experts Differ on China Policies," September 18, 2012.

6. World Bank, "China Overview."

7. For example, see Doug Guthrie, *China and Globalization: The Social, Economic and Political Transformation of Chinese Society* (Hoboken, NJ: Routledge, 2006).

8. The Chinese Communist Party officially announced that it will allow all families to have two children, thus ending the one-child policy after thirty-five years, on October 29, 2015. It should be noted, however, that the effects of decades of stringent fertility regulations, including labor shortages, a rapidly aging population, and skewed sex ratios might not be resolved with the dissolution of this policy. Martin King Whyte, Wang Feng, and Yong Cai, "Challenging Myths about China's One-Child Policy," *China Journal* (2015), 74, 144–59.

9. For an explanation of why Chinese orphanages received a large number of children in the 1980s and early 1990s, see Kay Ann Johnson, *Wanting a Daughter, Needing a Son: Abandonment, Adoption, and Orphanage Care in China* (St. Paul, MN: Yeong and Yeong, 2004).

10. Leslie Wang, "Importing Western Childhoods into a Chinese State-Run Orphanage," *Qualitative Sociology* 33, no. 2 (2010): 137–59.

11. David Eng, "Transnational Adoption and Queer Diasporas," *Social Text* 21, no. 3 (2003): 1–37, 1.

12. Peter Selman, "The Global Decline of Intercountry Adoption: What Lies Ahead?," *Social Policy and Society* 11, no. 3 (2012): 381–97.

13. According to the Great Wall China Adoption Agency website, children are classified as special needs if they have "any level of diagnosed physical, medical, or developmental needs" or are a healthy child between the ages of eight and fourteen. Chinese state regulations stipulate that children above the age of fourteen are no longer eligible for adoption. See Children's House International Adoptions, childrenshouseinternational.com/china/ (accessed October 1, 2015).

14. Sarah MacDonald, "Facing the Decline: Changes and Challenges in Transnational Adoption Since 2004" (paper presented at the Association for the Study of Adoption and Culture Conference, Scripps College, March 20, 2012).

15. Rhacel Parreñas and Eileen Boris, eds., *Intimate Labors: Cultures, Technologies, and the Politics of Care* (Palo Alto, CA: Stanford University Press, 2010), 7.

16. Arlie Hochschild, *The Outsourced Self: Intimate Life in Market Times* (New York: MacMillan, 2012).

17. Leslie Wang, "Unequal Logics of Care: Gender, Globalization and Volunteer Work of Expatriate Wives in China," *Gender and Society* 27, no. 2 (2013): 538–60.

18. Yu Hinan, "Baby Born with Birth Defects Every 30 Seconds," *China Daily*, October 30, 2007, www.chinadaily.com.cn/cndy/2007-10/30/content_6214736.htm.

19. Zhou Xun, "The Discourse of Disability in Modern China," *Patterns of Prejudice* 36, no.1 (2002): 104–12.

20. Eleanor Holroyd, "Chinese Cultural Influences on Parental Caregiving: Obligations toward Children with Disabilities," *Qualitative Health Research* 13, no.1 (2003): 4–19.

21. Frank Dikotter, *Imperfect Conceptions: Medical Knowledge, Birth Defects and Eugenics in China* (New York: Columbia University Press, 1998).

22. Xiaoyuan Shang and Jianpeng Cheng, "Zhongguo gu'er zhuangkuang fenxi" ("Analysis of the Situation of China's Orphans") *Youth Studies* 10 (2006): 8–12.

23 UNICEF China, *Zhongguo ertong fuli zhengce baogao* 中国儿童福利政策报告 2011 (*Child Welfare in China: Stocktaking Report 2011*), www.unicefchina.org/cn/uploadfile/2012/0207/20120207020819518.pdf (accessed October 1, 2015).

24. Xiaoyuan Shang, Karen Fisher, and Jiawen Xie, "Discrimination against children with Disability in China," *International Journal of Social Welfare* 20, no. 3 (2011): 298–308.

25. "Rising Birth Defects," *China Daily*, September 15, 2009, www.chinadaily.com.cn/opinion/2009-09/15/content_8691526.htm.

26. Tomorrow's Children website.

27. Erica Bornstein, "Developing Faith: Theologies of Economic Development in Zimbabwe," *Journal of Religion in Africa* 32, no. 1 (2002): 4–31, 11.

28. Barney Glaser and Anselm Strauss, *The Discovery of Grounded Theory: Strategies for Qualitative Research* (London: Wiedenfeld and Nicholson, 1967).

29. Tony Tan, Kofi Marfo, and Robert Dedrick, "Special Needs Adoption from China: Exploring Child-Level Indicators, Adoptive Family Characteristics, and Correlates of Behavioral Adjustment," *Children and Youth Services Review* 29, no. 10 (2007): 1269–85.

30. www.asiadopt.org/waiting-children/why-a-waiting-child (accessed January 15, 2013).

31. Altruistic motivations were most apparent in the adoption of Korean children, of which more than 150,000 were adopted overseas between 1955 and 1998. For a detailed discussion of Korean adoption, see Eleana Kim, *Adopted Territory: Transnational Korean Adoptees and the Politics of Belonging* (Durham, NC: Duke University Press Books, 2010).

32. Michelle Bratcher Goodwin, "Baby Markets," in *Baby Markets: Money and the New Politics of Creating Families* (Oxford: Cambridge University Press, 2010), 1–22.

33. David Eng, "Political Economics of Passion: Transnational Adoption and Global Woman: Roundtable on Global Woman," *Studies in Gender and Sexuality* 7, no. 1 (2006): 49–59, 52.

34. Mariagiovanna Baccara et al., "Gender and Racial Biases: Evidence from Child Adoption," CESifo Working Paper no. 2921 (2012), papers.ssrn.com/sol3/papers.cfm?abstract_id=1545711 (accessed September 25, 2015).

35. Sara Dorow, "Racialized Choices: Chinese Adoption and the 'White Noise' of Blackness," *Critical Sociology* 32, nos. 2–3 (2006): 357–79.

36. Ann Anagnost, "Scenes of Misrecognition: Maternal Citizenship in the Age of Transnational Adoption," *positions* 8, no. 2 (2000): 389–421.

37. Peter Selman, "International Adoptions from the People's Republic of China." Newcastle University. Unpublished manuscript. Available on request from the author at pfselman@yahoo.co.uk.

38. David Smolin, "Child Laundering: How the Intercountry Adoption System Legitimizes and Incentivizes the Practices of Buying, Trafficking, Kidnapping, and Stealing Children," Working Paper 749, bepress Legal Series (August 29, 2005).

39. Personal communication, June, 12, 2012.

40. Patricia Meier and Zhang Xiaole. "Sold into Adoption: The Hunan Baby Trafficking Scandal Exposes Vulnerabilities in Chinese Adoptions to the United States," *Cumberland Law Review* 39, no.1 (2008): 87.

41. Holt International Adoption, www.holtinternational.org/china/ccop.shtml (accessed September 20, 2015).

42. Joint Council on International Children's Services, www.jointcouncil.org/china-opens -adoption-to-single-women/ (accessed April 12, 2013).

43. Brian H. Stuy, "The Dark Side of China's 'Aging out Orphan' Program," *Research-China. org* (blog), April 2, 2012, www.research-china.blogspot.com/2012/04/dark-side-of-chinas-aging-out-orphan.html.

44. Hague Conference on Private International Law, 33: Convention of 29 May 1993 on Protection of Children and Co-operation in Respect of Intercountry Adoption. See also China (mainland) annual adoption statistics 2005–09. www.hcch.net/index_en.php?act=publications .details&pid=5158&dtid=32 (accessed September 20, 2015).

45. "3,000-Plus Chinese Children Adopted Overseas," *China Daily*, February 20, 2013, www .chinadaily.com.cn/china/2013-02/20/content_16241325.htm.

46. Sara Dorow, *Transnational Adoption: A Cultural Economy of Race, Gender, and Kinship* (New York: New York University Press, 2006), 100.

47. For a critique of the global orphan crisis, see Kathryn Joyce, *The Child Catchers: Rescue, Trafficking, and the New Gospel of Adoption* (New York: PublicAffairs Store, 2013).

48. Ibid.

49. Dorow, *Transnational Adoption*, 98.

50. Sharon Hays, *The Cultural Contradictions of Motherhood* (New Haven, CT: Yale University Press, 1996), 8.

51. Annette Lareau, *Unequal Childhoods: Class, Race, and Family Life* (Berkeley: University of California Press, 2011).

52. Dorow, *Transnational Adoption*, 201.

53. Tomorrow's Children Foundation website.

54. Tomorrow's Children Foundation newsletter, January 2013.

55. Tomorrow's Children Foundation website.

56. Anna High, "China's Orphan Welfare System: Laws, Policies and Filled Gaps" *University of Pennsylvania East Asia Law Review* 8 (Spring 2013): 127–76, 169.

57. Barbara Yngvesson, "Placing the 'Gift Child' in Transnational Adoption," *Law and Society Review* 36, no. 2 (2002): 227–56, 236.

58. Ann Anagnost, "The Corporeal Politics of Quality (*Suzhi*)," *Public Culture* 16, no. 2 (2004): 189–208, 194.

59. Viviana Zelizer, *Pricing the Priceless Child: The Changing Social Value of Children* (New York: Basic Books, 1985).

60. Joyce, *Child Catchers*.

61. Nili Luo and David Smolin, "Intercountry Adoption and China: Emerging Questions and Developing Chinese Perspectives," *Cumberland Law Review* 35, no. 3 (2005): 597–618.

China's Beauty Proletariat:

The Body Politics of Hegemony in a Walmart Cosmetics Department

Eileen Otis

Introduction

The new millennium was momentous for China's beauty industry. The term *beauty economy* (in Chinese, *meinu jingji*) entered common usage with the country's accession to the World Trade Organization (WTO) in 2001. On the heels of the formal integration into the global economy, government agencies inaugurated the first Miss China pageant, and the nation hosted the Miss World and Miss Tourism beauty competitions in 2003.[1] This, after decades of Maoist socialism that officially rejected the pursuit of feminine adornment. Exploring new frontiers of beauty, the nation launched its first Miss Plastic Surgery Pageant in December 2004. In her best-selling book titled *Beautiful Faces Grow Rice (Meili liandan zhang dami)*, author Lu Junqing articulates what has become commonsense knowledge to many: women's pursuit of beauty is the most certain means of achieving career success.[2]

positions 24:1 DOI 10.1215/10679847-3320089
Copyright 2016 by Duke University Press

The inception of China's beauty industry is part of the recent and dramatic growth of the consumer economy that has been driven by enlarged disposable urban incomes and gives consumers access to a rapidly expanding array of goods and services. The growth of consumption creates new labor markets, new kinds of work, and new gender divisions of labor within workplaces.[3] So dramatic are these changes that some argue consumption has replaced labor as a locus of modern identities; workers no longer claim social recognition as producers but gain status as consumers.[4] Such arguments fail to grasp new and complex interactions between production and consumption that arise with the development of markets for consumer services. With the expansion of the consumer economy, labor has not faded into invisibility but in many cases has transformed into a hypervisible display of gender and class competence.[5] The emergence of a thriving consumer service sector requires armies of new workers who interact with and serve customers in public settings, in many cases, teaching them how and what to consume. At the same time, workers model products on their bodies and become living embodiments of the possibilities of consumption. As a result, consuming proficiently and appropriately is a source of value on labor markets.

As part of this labor process, retailers broadcast myriad messages about management of intimate aspects of the body to their customers, arousing concerns about, for example, odors generated by the body, facial and body hair, fingernail and toenail size and shape, and skin texture, to name just a few. Such messages can be understood as reflecting attempts to configure "body rules": norms for appropriate presentation of bodies of varying types (especially gendered bodies) in specific social contexts. As new retail formats grow in China, workers and consumers negotiate new body rules. By better understanding these negotiations, we can gauge the ways in which the body is used as an index for ethical commitments, a sign of aspirations for class membership, and a vehicle of consumption as part of labor discipline.[6]

In what follows, I examine the proletariat of China's beauty economy through a case study of rural migrant women who have become cosmetics sales representatives (or "reps") in an outlet of a major global retailer in Kunming, Yunnan. I ask, how are body rules generated by the beauty economy used as part of new labor practices in the workplace? The communication of body rules is diffused across a number of sources, with employers being one of many. They are conveyed through customers, products, and product marketing. They are also communicated and mediated through intimate relations with coworkers.

I reveal four components involved in the acquisition of body rules and link these to gendered labor capacities that are naturalized and regulate workers. First, women workers experience cultivation of body aesthetics as pleasurable and part of a personal project of upward mobility. Second, new body aesthetics offers opportunity for creative improvisation, as beauty workers become so many artists. Third, learning new body rules associated with the aesthetic generates physical and sentimental intimacy. Fourth, the sense of community and mutual trust developed through intimacy becomes the basis for an experience of limited autonomy and resistance, which frequently serves the purposes of the employer. In sum, new body rules are learned through intimate relations between workers. As aesthetic discipline and intimacy are simultaneously cultivated, workers are drawn into a new world of consumption and become self-regulating subjects.[7]

In this research, *intimacy* is defined as consensual physical and affective proximity. I find that intimacy is formed through selective reciprocal sharing of personal information on the basis of trust. Intimacy is also formed through explicit and minute commentary about the presentation of the body, specifically, assessment of techniques of presenting urbane femininity. These modes of intimacy lead to affection that in turn maintains the bond of trust.

Acquisition of modern, urban body rules is a basis for an embodied hegemony, a mode of workplace control obtained through learned bodily practices rather than force. Cosmetic workers, who hail from rural villages, voluntarily adopt new body rules out of a desire for mobility and to gain distance from urban perceptions of their rural backwardness and poverty. Learning new body rules is an opportunity to acquire new forms of femininity that offer rural women hope of concealing their rural origins. At the same time, enactment of these rules also represents a form of labor discipline. Moreover, by giving rural women access to new beauty regime practices, they are less apt to question the low-wage and insecure conditions under which they labor. Employers thereby foster consent to low-wage, insecure, low-status labor.

Embodied Hegemony

Hegemony is a form of domination secured through the promulgation of ideas, styles, norms, beliefs, and perceptions that become taken for granted as natural and inevitable.[8] Labor researchers have been interested in forms of workplace organization that achieve hegemony, that is, foster worker consent to work practices, discipline, and remuneration arrangements that generate profits for employers. Most notably, Michael Burawoy, who worked on the floor of a Chicago machine shop, found that self-organized competition between workers in the context of monopoly capitalism maximized worker output.[9] Such competition with fellow workers served as an engaging, and strategic source of play, as well as a distraction from the drudgeries of production. At the same time, workers understood their manipulations of production as "gaming" the system to optimize piece rate wages. Burawoy argues that their games in fact were a mechanism of self-exploitation in the interest of their employer and, ultimately, of capital.[10] In a study of US luxury hotels, Rachel Sherman found that consent to extreme inequality between hospitality workers and their customers took two forms. First, hotel workers considered themselves as morally and culturally superior to customers. Second, customers engaged in gift giving with workers, which reflected sentiments of friendship through reciprocity and moderated employees' feelings of deference and servitude.[11] In research among Hong Kong factory workers, Ching Kwan Lee linked workplace hegemony to an employer's accommodation of women workers' dual roles as both home-makers (who prioritize care for their families) and employees.[12] Supervision and workplace rules were relaxed, and workers developed a sense of camaraderie through their shared identities as mothers and mature women. These studies lend insight into methods of recruiting the hearts and minds of employees so to as to secure their full and willing participation in labor activities, while limiting expressions of defiance. What remains to be understood, however, is the role of the body and bodily aesthetics in cultivating workplace hegemony.[13]

Bodies which enter the workplace already imbued with class and gender attributes may preempt overt modes of labor control, to the extent that employees have already absorbed required practices. Labor requirements like "looking pretty," acting demure, and smiling at the right moment thus seem to emerge from the character of the body and self. At the same time, workplaces may draw less advantaged workers by offering opportunities to learn urbane, middle class styles of self-presentation. The desire to embody middle class respectability can itself become a form of discipline.[14] To fully grasp the relationship between these embodied labor capacities and workplace hegemony, especially in the service workplace, it is critical to shift the focus of analytic efforts from cognitive aptitudes and emotional sensibilities to bodies. Sociologists of service work have conceived of the central task of service work as emotion work in which individual service workers perform labor on their own cognitive-emotional responses so as to project expressions that create a pleasing experience for the customers with whom they interact.[15] According to this approach, service employees use emotional sensibilities learned in their middle-class homes to guide interactions with customers at work. In an alternative approach, Robin Leidner finds other methods of conditioning workers' reactions to customers. One is scripting, in which workers recite preformulated questions and responses, freeing them from the burden of emotional expression. Another is "personal transformation," which refers to altering workers' commitments, practices, and sensibilities so they develop an identification with the firm and the product they are selling.[16] Within this scholarship, the physical/bodily dimension of service labor is neglected.

A more recent contribution in the sociology of service labor moves closer to a full appreciation of embodiment in service labor. Miliann Kang coins the term *body labor* to refer to commercial exchanges "in which service workers attend to the physical comfort and appearance of customers through direct contact with the body (such as touching, massage, and manicuring) and by attending to the feelings involved in those practices."[17] This concept identifies labor enacted by one body onto another through touching, which constructs and maintains hierarchies *through* intimacies between those who treat the body and those who are touched. Kang shows that race and class hierarchies affect how body labor is executed and illustrates the meanings associated with this type of work.

I make a distinction between laboring on a body and laboring with the body. In addition to the labor of working on others' bodies, interactive service work has another central physical dimension; the body is a site for aesthetic reorganization and symbols and signs.[18] The symbolic labor involved in consumer service work certainly recruits the body, as workers' bodies become means of showcasing products like makeup, clothing, accessories, as well as the effects of dietary regimens and even plastic surgery. For example, Pei-Chia Lan investigates the ways labor control is exercised through requirements that workers display products on their bodies. Bodies become models for customer emulation, vehicles of display, and vessels of communication. Employers seek to alter and control this physical capacity, which can compromise a workers' sense of control over the self.[19]

I argue that body rules figure centrally in the control of workers' symbolic displays. Body rules are implicit and explicit norms, standards, and socially enforced expectations for presenting and using bodies. These rules will vary depending on race, class, gender, age cohort, and other categories that divide people based on perceived biological and social differences. Identities are read from bodies—so one can convey an identity through movement, gestures, and ornament. The body is read as a sign of one's commitments to diet, lifestyle, fashion, and consumption. As the body signals the self, its priorities, ethics, morals, and health, its surface becomes a means of displaying such commitments.[20] The body is used to signal conformity to norms and standards, and body rules are adopted to do so.

Workers' bodies bear the rules they have inherited from their gender and class locations. Organizations may seek to amend these rules, imposing new standards and models for behavior, while also introducing social contexts and resources for the revision of rules. Rules are created and altered also through the use of consumer goods that introduce new norms for the disposition of the body, an obvious example being items related to grooming. Pierre Bourdieu argued that the stylized consumption of goods maintains boundaries between social classes by naturalizing refinement and superior taste.[21] This is a particularly useful approach to understanding contests for social recognition in contemporary urban China, where extreme stratification as well as rapid social change breeds tremendous status insecurity. Consumption certainly figures centrally into norms for comporting the body. However, in applying this framework to a case study of work in the retail sector, two adjustments to Bourdieu's theory are necessary.

For Bourdieu, consumption brings status through strategic distancing from a life dictated by struggles to fulfill necessities for food, clothing, shelter, and the like.[22] Bourdieu claims that the working classes and poor develop a "taste for necessity"; they make lifestyle and consumption choices based on utility and pragmatism.[23] This argument may in fact be symptomatic of Bourdieu's emphasis on class reproduction, as opposed to mobility. When one appreciates the social mobility aspirations of the poor and working class their own taste for social status becomes clear.[24] Moreover as growing numbers of the working class labor in retail jobs catering to the middle and upper middle classes, distinction may very well become a necessity. Indeed, I found that rural women working retail develop a taste for status distinction, not only as prerequisite for the performance of retail work but also as a vehicle for social recognition in the urban center. The second revision to Bourdieu's conceptual frame is that struggles for status are contoured as much by gender as by class.

In what follows I show how young workers come to view consumer service labor in a Walmart retail outlet as an opportunity to reinvent their bodies (already imprinted with the effects of a childhood of rural work) as legibly modern and urbanely feminine. These young female cosmetics reps readily appropriate cosmetics as a tool for mobility. On the retail floor, this act of appropriation doubles as an act of consent to the terms of labor. Their reinvention is supported by the intimate labor of colleagues, which figures into both consent to and defiance of rules on the service floor.[25] New body rules associated with gender and class norms figure centrally in the dynamics of workplace hegemony.

Cosmetics in Urban China and in Retail

The modern beauty industry is relatively new to China. It was not until the last twenty-five years or so that this industry began its development, with cosmetics companies mass-producing makeup, face whiteners, and creams. Currently, appearance is no trivial matter in China's urban centers, where quality of self-presentation as well as physical stature can make or break a career. Many of China's state agencies, in their capacity as employers, maintain appearance standards for employment, including minimum height requirements for men and women. One agency reportedly required female breast symmetry.[26] Appearance-based discrimination is permissible and considered a reasonable business strategy; employment discrimination laws are anemic and poorly implemented.[27] These practices place a disproportionate beauty burden on women. In this climate, women turn to cosmetics to enhance their prospects for higher incomes as well as for better marriages.[28]

Foreign cosmetics companies heightened their business activity after China acceded to the World Trade Organization (WTO) in 2001, when import tariffs were slashed. In 2004, the country lifted all restrictions on wholesale and retail distribution by foreign companies in China, as a condition for continued WTO membership. Since then, cosmetics firms have branched out to smaller cities and developed relatively low-cost products for China's mass markets.[29] China's cosmetics market is second only to that of the United States in sales.[30] While most of the three thousand cosmetics firms in mainland China are of domestic origin, 86 percent of the market share is controlled by global firms and suppliers.[31]

Global retailers also enjoy a certain cachet among local consumers in China. For example, while Walmart is widely considered to occupy the low end of the US retail hierarchy offering some of the lowest prices on goods, Walmart's Chinese consumers tend to regard global retailers (which are US and European firms) as offering a higher quality of goods compared to local retailers. Walmart occupies a middling-to-top niche among large general-merchandise retailers in China. Domestic retailers offer the lowest prices and have smaller stores and fewer frills. Wumart is the lowest-price retailer, and its stores tend to be dirty, dreary, and cramped. By contrast, Walmart is cleaner and its prices are higher. It sells some low-cost goods: inexpensive home décor, clothing, and food, but also luxury goods like cognac, California wines, and high-end electronics. The stores thus draw a wide range of consumers—not necessarily the poorest, who can find lower prices at local chains like Wumart. International retailers like Walmart, Carrefour, and Tesco are widely perceived to be less apt to sell fake goods or foods with dangerous additives. In part, this perception derives from the firms' relatively tolerant return policies. Both Chinese and English labels on some goods at Western retailers may also create strategic ambiguity about the origins of products. Walmart's cosmetics department offers a wide range of brands, from moderately priced local labels to expensive French and Japanese items. A middle-class customer shopping at Walmart can conveniently purchase her favorite lipstick or blush along with fresh produce for the evening's meal. Of course, Walmart is not the most luxurious environment in which to purchase cosmetics. Department and specialty stores as well as luxury boutiques cater to the wealthy and women who can afford Western prices for high-end cosmetics. In these stores, customers will find well-trained, attentive staff who are more likely to be urban born. In Walmart (and other general-merchandise retailers), the sales reps tend to not be urban born, nor are they employed directly by the retailer.

Methods

Ethnographic data was collected in 2007 by a researcher who worked as a sales representative for one month in a Walmart retail outlet in the city of Kunming in the provincial capital of Yunnan. The researcher asks to remain anonymous. I will call her Li. Li is a Kunming native and speaks Mandarin and the local dialect fluently. She is female and was twenty-one years old at the time of the data collection and was trained to conduct ethnography. She accompanied me on informal research excursions to different retail outlets in the city, where we both chatted with workers and customers.

Li found a sales position after making multiple inquiries with sales representatives in various Kunming Walmart outlets. They provided her with names and phone numbers of supplier firms. She interviewed with two of these suppliers, a sanitary napkin firm and a cosmetics firm I call Beauty. She was hired to work as a temporary, informal employee for the latter firm. She spent eight hours per day, six days per week, selling cosmetics in Walmart for this foreign firm. She observed interactions between workers, customers, and managers. She also attended weekly meetings convened by the cosmetics firm at an off-site location. The analysis in this article is confined to the cosmetics department.

After each day of work, Li took detailed notes in Chinese, based on her observations of interactions in the workplace. I read these notes and sent follow-up questions to direct her observations and note taking. In addition to Li's observations, I spent considerable time inside multiple Walmart stores in four Chinese cities: Kunming, Shanghai, Beijing, and Changchun, in Jilin Province. I strolled the sales floors and, when the opportunity arose, engaged sales agents in conversation using Mandarin. Workers with few customers were frequently willing to talk to me at some length. I engaged in a total of thirty-four conversations with sales representatives. I asked questions about work history, wages, job experiences, and their relationships with both Walmart and their supplier firms. Occasionally, these conversations were interrupted by customers interested in purchasing the reps' wares, at which point I would often be left chatting with a friend or relative who was visiting the worker. I translated all the fieldnotes into English and coded them by hand, guided by my knowledge of relevant concepts and theories in the literature on work and employment, outsourcing, Walmart, and globalization. I omit any details from the presentation of the data that may reveal the identity of workers or managers. All names used in this paper are pseudonyms, with the exception of the retail firm's name. I have changed the names of the major global cosmetics firms that employ the sales reps to Beauty, Glow, Sparkle, Shine, and Jolie.

Outsourced Labor

Most of the sales staff that densely populate Walmart service floors in China wear the retailer's blue apron and official badges (often with an adopted English name, rather than their Chinese name). But these workers do not receive their wages from Walmart. Vendors who supply products for sale on Walmart shelves hire and dispatch these sales workers (hereafter "reps") to Walmart and other retail service floors. They pay the retailer a nominal sum, usually around $1.20 per day, per worker. Walmart management does not interview these workers; it only enforces the state law requiring that they register for a health card, which involves a health inspection at a clinic or hospital. Each vendor maintains distinctive employment arrangements with their sales staff. Therefore, wages, commissions, benefits, hours, training, and instructions for interacting with customers vary from one employer to another. Hours of work range from short shifts of four hours to twelve-hour days. Some reps are hired temporarily, for a special promotion or to work during a holiday season when sales increase. These reps are usually paid on a daily basis, 30–50 *yuan* a day (US$3.80–4.20), in addition to a 3–5 percent commission that workers receive only after a baseline of products are sold. Exceeding the baseline is next to impossible (a typical number for cosmetics workers was four hundred products per day), and sales depend on customer volume, which in turn depends on location and season. Other reps are hired for one to six months and earn a monthly base wage of 600–1,000 yuan (US$80–120 per month). Some firms that required workers to sign one- or multiyear contracts hold the workers' first month's salary as a deposit, to prevent them from leaving without fulfilling the terms of the contract. A handful of reps receive insurance coverage and subsidies. The insurance usually includes unemployment, medical, housing subsidies, and retirement. One cosmetics rep had been employed with a company for five years, earned 1,700 yuan (US$211) in base pay per month, and received four months of paid maternity leave after giving birth. For long-term workers, suppliers offer three days of holiday for Chinese New Year and one additional day of holiday for each year workers are employed. Sometimes perks are included in the reps' remuneration, with some receiving complimentary supplies of the employer's product. For example, the reps from the French cosmetics company "Jolie" received 1,000 yuan (US$124) of makeup.[32]

This system of vendor-supplied labor emerged in the early reform period when manufacturers did not have a well-developed distribution infra-structure and dispatched workers to manage supplies and sales in various state-owned retail stores.[33] A practical response to the legacy of socialism, the system has the effect today of creating armies of predominantly rural migrant salespeople, mostly women who earn commissions and have little attachment to the retailer. The system survives because there is a surfeit of workers and labor can be paid low wages. It is therefore worthwhile for manufacturers to use this inexpensive method to promote products to con-sumers who have yet to develop strong brand identification in what is still a fairly embryonic market.

At the outlet where Li worked, there were approximately three hundred vendor-dispatched reps, mostly female, whose ages ranged between seventeen and forty-eight. A major exception to the pattern of feminization was found in appliance sales, which was virtually dominated by men.[34] Reps were migrant workers whose original homes were in rural regions of Yunnan, Sichuan, Guangxi, and Guizhou, and occasionally more distant provinces. Kunming had eliminated restrictions on the settlement of migrant workers, and these workers easily rented apartments on the outskirts of the city.[35] These reps worked in proximity to the approximately three hundred workers directly employed by the retailer as managers, cashiers, greeters, and stockpersons, and a few sales staff positioned on the retail floor at the outlet.[36] These workers were typically urban residents; many were from small cities outside the metropolis. Most were between the ages of eighteen and twenty-four. Women were overrepresented among cashiers and greeters, making up approximately 70 percent of the total. Most had completed three years of technical high school.

The vendors were local representatives of suppliers that manufactured products for sale in Walmart. Walmart maintained relationships with more than twenty thousand suppliers in China.[37] Over 95 percent of the products sold in its China stores were sourced from China.[38] Walmart individually negotiated with these suppliers, and many of their local agents (vendors) sent shipments to each store. Some of these vendors also dispatched sales representatives to work on the service floor in an effort to promote their products.

Selling Cosmetics at Walmart, Kunming

Even though salespeople's primary responsibility was to sell the vendor's goods, they were also required to follow the orders of store managers, who could require that they perform nonsales labor like collecting shopping carts or cleaning and stocking store shelves. Despite their formal subordination to retail management, sales reps exhibited little concern about supervision by managers and surveillance cameras suspended above them. In my observations, sales reps were in charge of their time on the sales floor, and they chatted freely with each other, with me, and with relatives who frequently visited. They regularly used their mobile phones on the retail floor. In one Kunming store, I observed a worker casually reading a book. In another store, Li observed tea company reps taking care of one of the employee's children during work hours. Unconcerned about the authority of Walmart managers and agents occasionally sent by vendors to observe them, they did not try to look busy on the retail floor, except when customers were present.

Li was thrust onto the retail cosmetics sales floor with no training. Her vendor simply gave her a uniform and told her when and where to show up. On her first day, she stood behind her small, square counter space, in front of shelves piled high with tiny boxes of creams, eye shadows, and base. She waited for customers, uncertain about what to do should one approach. She looked for cues from her fellow sales reps. Her immediate neighbor, the Jolie rep, was peering in a mirror, sharply focused on her eye as she drew a line around it. Noticing Li, she turned to her, smiled, and asked how she looked. Li responded, "Beautiful." She invited Li over to her counter, pinned her hair back, and began to give her a makeover. Other young reps gathered around, watching and commenting. Li worried, "I was concerned that we were being recorded on the security camera, but I'm not sure if the others realized. It seemed like there was a camera suspended over each rep." After her makeover, Li visited the various reps' small counters, chatting and sampling products. Li wrote, "I finally invited them over to my counter to try my products. I let them try our frosty shadow."

On her second day, Li reported:

> Today after I arrived at work the Blossom rep insisted that I put on makeup. I already had some makeup on, but compared to hers it was fairly light. She pulled me over to her makeup counter and then started making me up. She first spread base powder on my face and them some primer, then frost, and then drew liner around my eyes, eye shadow, mascara, and then blush. The reps all said that I should really take care to put on makeup. I'm much prettier with makeup, and more spirited and lively, they said.

Without any kind of prompting, during their slow shifts each day the reps took the opportunity to practice and develop their cosmetics artistry. In these frequent sessions, they articulated in practice new feminine body rules: women should use makeup to enhance their appearance and look more urbane and alert. By using cosmetics, women signal that they are concerned with and invested in appearance and they care about the impression they make upon others. Using cosmetics, for women, is an act of social respect.

Each day as the reps arrived at work, they took turns proceeding to the women's washroom, pinning their hair back, scrubbing their faces, and returning to their stations. Others remained behind to keep watch over counters and shelves. Pairing or tripling up, they began the process of applying color and creams to change their appearances, using the cosmetics tools at hand to draw more attention to certain facial features and deemphasize others, all the while commenting on qualities of appearance. Makeovers usually began with a base layer of foundation. After studied collective contemplation of hues most suitable for the recipient's skin color, season, time of day, occasion, and clothing—taking into account each of the half dozen or so parameters affecting the overall aesthetic—each selected a blush. Reps investigated all the spectra of eye shadow color, each with ranges of shading and type, in frosted or matte version, used with or without primer.

The efforts were methodical, and the reps brought a range of knowledge acquired from a variety of sources to these projects of self-presentation. In some cases, there were comments remembered from mothers, relatives, and classmates. In other cases, advice drew from beauty magazines, the odd commercial, or a television show. The two reps who received training from their vendors tended to be regarded as the final authorities in aesthetic decision making. The cosmetics counters were daily transformed into a laboratory of experimentation.

Perhaps more interesting than the content of their transformative activity is the fact of their engagement. Their vendors did not direct workers to perform these makeovers, which became a daily ritual. Their direct supervisor, the Walmart floor manager, had minimal awareness of, or concern about, the activity. The reps spent long intervals engaged in the self-organized makeovers. And the activity occupied a liminal sort of space, completely self-organized, not mandated yet not clearly defying firm or store rules. Of course, customers expected to try out the cosmetics on their own faces, and some even succumbed to complete makeovers. Reps learned the skills required to administer cosmetics artfully as part of their sales process. The slow work periods, when customers were sparse or absent, drew reps into nonsales activities but also deepened their interest in and connections to the products they sold.

These activities facilitated learning of new ways of using and presenting the body associated with femininity that reinforced connections between work, the body, and identity. Sales reps learned how to investigate their own and each other's faces endlessly, examining contours, noses, eye shapes, eyebrows, and blemishes. In practice, they contemplated the effects of the various cosmetic hues and textures on features. They analyzed faces with regard to skin tone and type, symmetry, and size of features. They studied which products to use in order to "treat" specific deficiencies of appearance. Perhaps more importantly, the cosmetics themselves (concealers, whiteners, color enhancers, and their systematic directions for use) invoked deficiencies of appearance. The central lesson learned was that appearance could always, indeed *should* always, be enhanced. In short, reps gradually acquired new methods and habits of looking at women that foregrounded evaluation of appearance and features in relationship to an ineffable standard of physical perfection.

Reps were engaged in creative improvisation with their employer's products, using the supplies without approval. But they were also teaching each other the values and skills that would transform their bodies into effective displays of the products they sold. They acquired depth of knowledge about their products, becoming ever more effective at applying them to interested customers. These time-consuming makeovers might be interpreted as resistance to workplace control, but they can also be viewed as consent to deep aesthetic and normative control, as reps learned to use and skillfully display the items they purveyed to customers. This voluntary and practiced incorporation of workplace norms by workers is an instance of embodied hegemony.

Their collective cultivation of a cosmetic aesthetic also served as a kind of social glue: creams, eye shadows, mascaras, foundations, and lipsticks bonded the young women into a more intimate community so that their relationships to each other seemed to transcend their connections to their own firms. The act of applying cosmetics on the face requires spatial and physical intimacy. The applicant of the makeup must position her own face close to the recipient's. Tools like brushes, pencils, puffs, and lipsticks make contact with the skin of the recipient. Sometimes the applicant uses her fingers to spread color on lips or skin. The cosmetics reps gradually learned to moderate their touch so as to gently apply products. As they assessed the aesthetic quality of their use of color and lines, they learned to look directly at the recipient of the makeover, which constituted another kind of intimacy. These forms of closeness drew workers into other kinds of intimacies.

The physical intimacy invited for often intense conversations in which reps shared confidences. During the makeover sessions, workers exchanged stories and personal information about boyfriends, husbands, sexual experiences, vacations, favorite pop singers, and so forth. The Shine rep, married, described details of her sex life with her husband. The Glow rep, who was single, engaged the matchmaking efforts of her fellow workers, who brought eligible bachelors around to the department for the purpose of a casual introduction. The Jolie rep introduced her to a man over ten years her senior, and she rejected him for his age. She became involved with another man who was slightly younger than the first. They dated for a short time, and she shared with coworkers stories from their dates. One day, she showed them an expensive cell phone he gave her. "He is a business man and is rich," she explained. But she lamented that his generosity pressured her to commit to something prematurely and that, in the end, she felt scant affection for him.

Such sharing cultivated intimacy among the reps as their time together lengthened. The intimacy, in turn, lubricated their daily work. Most of the reps earned a small commission from their sales. In theory, they competed against each other for customers. In practice, they felt great mutual loyalty. For example, reps came to each other's rescue when customers challenged their fellow workers. When reps' coffers of complimentary samples and gifts for customers were depleted, and customers made a fuss, a rep nearby would offer some item from her own trove of free gifts to placate the customer.

Each rep was responsible for the care and shelving of her firm's products, and they reported to their vendors the sales and inventory each day (despite Walmart's pioneering, sophisticated logistics technology for tracking inventory). Reps were held personally liable if a bottle of cream or expensive cologne turned up missing; the vendor required the rep to pay for it. Therefore, each rep kept careful watch over her products. This, too, fostered community among the reps. When a rep needed to depart her post, the others remained to watch over her products, aware of the consequences if product went missing. The fellow reps also attended to any customers that inquired about the brand, even selling a fellow rep's products to the customer, with commission going to the absent rep. They exchanged this assistance regularly, so that reliance and trust gradually formed. The mutual dependence reinforced bonds that would eventually override whatever loyalty and attachment they felt for the firms that employed them. After all, they interacted with personnel from their firms only during weekly or biweekly visits to offices, through the occasional call from a supervisor, or from their own daily calls to report the sales. Unlike these fairly superficial, dry, and bureaucratic exchanges, reps' interactions with each other involved mutual trust, as we have seen. Eventually, workers began taking time out of their shift to run errands. Fellow workers readily agreed to cover for each other. Sometimes reps would simply not show up for their shifts. One rep sent her cousin to work for her for the day while she took a school admission exam. If workers' autonomy led them to embrace the beauty products they purveyed, it also led to this fundamental mode of defiance.

An exchange system that developed on the service floor also provided scope for autonomy. Firms distributed free samples of products as well as gifts to customers who purchased a minimum amount of goods. Workers became gatekeepers of these goods, gifts, and samples intended to entice consumers to buy products. Since vendors exercised little oversight of these items, workers dispensed them at their own discretion. The items were treated as a personal stash to use and trade with other employees in exchange for samples and gifts from their companies. Reps exchanged these items with each other, using their own cache of samples and gifts as currency for the cosmetics of other reps. These were sometimes recirculated to families and friends and served as a secondary mode of remuneration to reps whose wages and commissions could be unsteady and low.

The incessant exchange of cosmetic samples and gifts formed an informal economy on the service floor. In this barter economy, reps working for prestigious, popular, and luxury cosmetics firms controlled products of greater worth. Reps quickly learned the differential market value and status of different commodity goods. They learned to place their ownership of such goods within a stratified system of status. In short, they learned to use commodities as a mode of distinction.

Perhaps this sense of distinction gave them a newfound sense of self-possession, for workers found frequent collective catharsis in passing negative judgment on customers who perpetrated incivilities on the service floor. Intimacy by definition must exclude. The closeness shared with coworkers was rarely extended to customers, who were often found to be cold, if not rude. The division only reinforced the sense of camaraderie among workers. One slow afternoon as they gathered around Jolie's counter, the Glow rep described to her colleagues occasions when affluent customers asked her to carry their shopping baskets, like a golf caddy. Despite her dismay, she summoned sufficient calm to decline the requests politely. But the reps did not hide their incredulousness and voiced collective disapproval.

Another typical conflict with customers emerged from the disposition of free gifts and samples. Customers often pressured reps to pass along extra promotion gifts and samples. For example, when Li offered her customer a complimentary jar of cream after making the qualifying 200-*yuan* (approximately $24.00) purchase, the customer's mother, who stood by her side, also asked for one, although she made no purchase. Together, mother and daughter hounded Li until she succumbed. The availability of free items re-creates a barterlike environment in the store as customers try to wrangle items from workers. These kinds of negotiations have resonance with the Maoist socialist period when consumer products were scarce and workers traded goods and favors to acquire necessities.[39] Of course, price negotiations continue to be standard practice at peasant produce markets in cities.

Also irritating to workers were customers who sampled lots of cosmetics without making a purchase. Exasperated by such a customer, the Jolie rep exclaimed, "What a stupid egg!" The customer had engaged in a mind-numbing monologue, to which she was forced to listen. In the end the customer purchased nothing. The others clicked their tongues in disapproval as they listened. They were also critical of customers who openly expressed disapproving surprise at Li's skin tone, which is somewhat dark. Li described to fellow workers an incident she typically encountered: "How can someone with your dark skin sell beauty products?" Indeed, the aesthetic ideal in China for women emphasizes light-colored skin. Sale of skin-whitening treatments is a multimillion dollar business. After hearing about this kind of customer reaction, Li's fellow sales reps became indignant, and they all agreed she should respond to such customers by saying that "dark is beautiful too." Perhaps because these beauty workers had absorbed the body rules of the new economy they felt reasonably empowered to assert their own aesthetics. Indeed, a hegemony grounded in the body certainly allows for creative improvisation without undermining the terms of consent. Reps might alter the standard of beauty without affecting the fact that women are measured by the value of their beauty.

Conclusion

This case study of rank-and-file cosmetics workers reveals what appears to be voluntary invisible sources of workplace control. The reps examined here poured themselves into a transformation of their appearances in the retail workplace, in the process decoding new body rules at play for urban women that were rarely explicitly articulated. They also learned new intimate body practices tied to their work. The reps learned delicacy of touch, to lean in close to others without breathing too heavily in their faces, and to brush, rub, draw, and spread color onto faces decisively enough to create the desired aesthetic effects but softly enough to not hurt the recipient of the procedure. They acquired the capacity and habit of looking at the self in mirrors to assess their appearance. They also learned to perceive other women through these types of assessments. They cultivated a "cosmetic gaze" to diagnose aesthetic inadequacies and treat them with commodities, putting into practice techniques of objectification that prioritize surfaces of the body. In short, they developed a new mode of self-regulation, not only the capacity of evaluating women, including themselves, through a new aesthetic lens, but a habit of doing so. Intimacy with coworkers was both a vehicle of and reward for this mode of self-regulation.

Competencies in the world of cosmetics gave workers the hope of culturally transcending their rural origins and thus being perceived as full-fledged members of urban society. These rural women, traditionally excluded from reigning urban norms of femininity, were less apt to question the low-wage, low-status condition of their beauty labor owing to the perceived benefits of self-improvement realized through their jobs. Their investment in femininity arose from a desire for mobility and inclusion in urban social communities. As they were offered opportunities to learn body rules associated with urbane femininity, body rules which also regulated their labor, they were less apt to question their limited access to economic capital. Workers could overlook their low wages while they gained access to expensive beauty treatments and the skills to use them. Moreover, by learning to replicate dominant urban norms for women's beauty, the sales reps in this study developed a certain aesthetic authority and even a limited empowerment to redefine aesthetic rules, as reflected in the "dark is beautiful" incident. But while cosmetics workers embraced competence in the artistry of makeup application, they were at the same time promoting new norms that placed an inordinate beauty burden on women. The ability to embody new urban norms of femininity and new body rules associated with the development and growth of a market commodity culture in urban China created conditions for a form of embodied hegemony, a mode of workplace consent obtained through transformations of the body. The opportunities offered in retail work to learn how to become urban women and take on new feminine dispositions made rural migrant women largely accommodating to their employers' objectives and also to the larger gender and class hierarchy that excluded them from urban cultural membership in the first place.[40]

By examining a case study of workers engaging in new, ritualized practices that retrain bodies in feminine consciousness of beauty, we can appreciate how new forms of embodiment condition participation in service labor regimes. This, in turn, can illuminate how women and men enter organizations partially predisposed to gendered forms of control, thus inviting a richer understanding of the bodily dimension of personal improvement aimed at obtaining class-inflected ideals of gender. The skills that are at once learned and naturalized as part of women's bodies link women to distinctly gender-delimited markets. As Heidi Gottfried argues, forms of embodiment that qualify women for certain occupations disqualify them from others.[41] However individual and personal these modes of embodiment may be, though, they are learned through intimate physical and social relationships between women in a kind of spontaneous exploration of beauty. This intimacy is also part of workplace hegemony; it enables defiance of workplace rules and regulations, but the space of autonomy formed through this defiance is as often used to incorporate new body rules associated with selling cosmetics as it is to subvert work control itself. This directs us to attend to the embodied, gendered social relations that condition workplace hegemony.

Notes

1. Jie Yang, "Nennu and Shunu: Gender, Body Politics, and the Beauty Economy in China," *Signs* 36, no. 2 (2011): 333–57.

2. Lu Junqing, *Meili liandan zhang dami (Beautiful Faces Grow Rice)* (Shanghai: Dangdai shijie chubanshe, 2004).

3. See Deborah Davis, "Introduction: A Revolution in Consumption," in *The Consumer Revolution in Urban China*, ed. Deborah S. Davis (Berkeley: University of California Press, 2000), 1–24.

4. Pun Ngai, "Subsumption or Consumption?: The Phantom of Consumer Revolution in 'Globalizing' China," *Cultural Anthropology* 18, no. 4 (2003): 469–92; Lisa Rofel, *Other Modernities: Gendered Yearnings in China after Socialism.* (Berkeley: University of California Press, 1999).

5. I use Candace West and Don H. Zimmerman's notion of gender competence to indicate the ways that women make claims to belonging to socially agreed-upon biological categories of sex. See Candace West and Don H. Zimmerman, "Doing Gender," *Gender and Society* 1, no. 2 (1987): 125–51.

6. Eileen Otis, *Markets and Bodies: Women, Service Work and the Making of Inequality in China* (Stanford: Stanford University Press, 2011).

7. Michel Foucault, "The Subject and Power," *Critical Inquiry* 8, no. 4 (1982): 777–95.

8. Antonio Gramsci and Joseph A Buttigieg, *Prison Notebooks* (New York: Columbia University Press, 1992).

9. See Michael Burawoy, *Manufacturing Consent: Changes in the Labor Process under Monopoly Capitalism* (Chicago: University of Chicago Press, 1979).

10. This game unfolds in a larger political context in which the state guarantees workers' rights and limits employers' ability to assign overtime to, penalize, and fire workers. But in an earlier phase of competitive capitalism, the argument goes, workers were coerced by competitive labor markets that gave them little power and few opportunities to earn a living that sustained them. In this economic context, survival dictated the labor process and employers had an upper hand, simply imposing despotic means of control.

11. Rachel Sherman, *Class Acts: Service and Inequality at Luxury Hotels* (Berkeley: University of California, 2007).

12. Ching Kwan Lee, *Gender and the South China Miracle: Two Worlds of Factory Women* (Berkeley: University of California Press, 1997).

13. While studies of aesthetic labor examine the classed corporeality central to service labor,

they do not consider the role of bodies in the dynamics of consent and resistance. Warhurst, Chris, Dennis Nickson, Anne Witz and Anne Marie Culle, "Aesthetic Labour in Interactive Service Work: Some Case Study Evidence from the 'New' Glasgow." *Service Industries Journal*, 20 (2000): 1–18.

14. Otis, *Markets and Bodies.*

15. On the concept of emotion work, see Arlie Hochschild, *The Managed Heart: Commercialization of Human Feeling* (Berkeley: University of California Press, 1983).

16. Robin Leidner, *Fast Food, Fast Talk* (Berkeley: University of California Press, 1993).

17. Miliann Kang, "The Managed Hand: The Commercialization of Bodies and Emotions in Korean Immigrant Owned Nail Salons," *Gender and Society* 17, no. 6 (2003): 820–39, 820.

18. Eileen Otis, *Markets and Bodies: Women, Service Work and the Making of Inequality in China*, (Palo Alto: Stanford University Press, 2011); Christopher Warhurst and Dennis Nickson "A New Labour Aristocracy? Aesthetic Labour and Routine Interactive Service," Work, Employment and Society 21 (2007): 785–98.

19. Pei-Chia Lan, "The Body as a Contested Terrain for Labor Control: Cosmetics Retailers in Department Stores and Direct Selling," in *The Critical Study of Work: Labor, Technology, and Global Production*, ed. Rick Baldoz, Charles Koeber, and Philip Kraft (Philadelphia, PA: Temple University Press, 2001), 83–105.

20. Victoria Pitts-Taylor, *Surgery Junkies: Wellness and Pathology in Cosmetic Culture* (Camden, NJ: Rutgers University Press, 2007).

21. Bourdieu, Pierre, *Distinction: A Social Critique of the Judgment of Taste*, (Cambridge: Cambridge University Press, 2004)

22. Bourdieu, *Distinction.*

23. Pierre Bourdieu, *Distinction*

24. See Hung Cam Thai, *Insufficient Funds: Money and Consumption in Low Wage Transnational Families*, (Palo Alto: Stanford University Press, 2014).

25. Rhacel Parreñas and Eileen Boris, "Introduction," In *Intimate Labors: Cultures, Technologies and the Politics of Care*, ed. Rhacel Parrenas and Eileen Boris (Stanford: Stanford Social Sciences Press, 2010), 1-13.

26. Joseph Kahn, "Chinese People's Republic Is Unfair to Its Short People," *New York Times*, May 21, 2004.

27. Charles J. Ogletree and Rangita de Silva de Alwius, "When Gender Differences Become a Trap: The Impact of China's Labor Law on Women," *Yale Journal of Law and Feminism* 14, no. 69 (2002): 69–96.

28. Yang, "Nennu and Shunu."

29. Barbara E. Hopkins, "Western Cosmetics in the Gendered Development of Consumer Culture in China," *Feminist Economics* 13 (2007): 287–306.

30. P. R. Newswire. 2015. China Cosmetics Market Report, 2014–2017. March 2. Accessed October 2, 2015. www.prnewswire.com/news-releases/china-cosmetics-market-report-2014-2017-300043914.html.

31. Ibid.

32. Drawing on surviving socialist categories, this was termed *laobao*, short for *laodong baoxian* or "work guarantees," echoing the Mao-era work arrangements in which urban workers regularly received quantities of goods in kind from their work units.

33. Amy Hanser, "A Tale of Two Sales Floors: Changing Service-Work Regimes in China," in *Working in China: Ethnographies of Labor and Workplace Transformation*, ed. Ching Kwan Lee (London: Routledge, 2007), 77–98.

34. When Li inquired with a high-speed blender salesman about working for his company, he dismissed her outright, saying "Our company does not hire women to sell its products."

35. With marketization, the Chinese government loosened regulations on movement between rural areas and cities, but it placed restrictions on urban settlement and service provision. Under the residential permit system, rural residents were allowed to stay in cities without dependents only during the time they were actively employed. Dorothy Solinger, *Contesting Citizenship in Urban China: Peasant Migrants, the State, and the Logic of the Market*. (Berkeley: University of California Press, 1999).

36. Walmart also directly employs produce workers and cooks in the fresh-food department.

37. Walmart China Factsheet. 2012. www.wal-martchina.com/english/walmart/index.htm (accessed February 17, 2013).

38. Ibid.

39. Mayfair Yang, *Gifts, Favors, and Banquets: The Art of Social Relationships in China* (Ithaca, NY: Cornell University Press, 1994).

40. Aihwa Ong, *Flexible Citizenship: The Cultural Logics of Transnationality* (Durham, NC: Duke University Press, 1999).

41. Heidi Gottfried, "Temp(t)ing Bodies: Shaping Gender at Work in Japan," *Sociology: Journal of the British Sociological Association* 37, no. 2 (2003): 257–76.

Selling Fantasies of Rescue: Intimate Labor, Filipina Migrant Hostesses, and US GIs in a Shifting Global Order

Hae Yeon Choo

Introduction

Kristin's apartment was filled with the smell of pork adobo and the din of the TV. When I walked in, she was still busy frying the last batch of battered shrimp and warming up rice to feed her fiancé Scott, who came home for lunch in his military uniform. One month earlier, Kristin ran away from Club Heaven, where she worked as a hostess, to live with Scott in a small apartment in a residential area next to the US military camp in Basetown, South Korea, where many US GI-Filipina couples live. "Everything she makes is so good. I've never had Filipino food before, but it is so much better than the canteen food!" Scott exclaimed as he pulled Kristin tightly into his lap and kissed her on her cheek. He then turned back to the TV and hurriedly finished three plates of food before returning to the camp. After Scott left, Kristin murmured, "I don't love him." Startled, I looked out the

positions 24:1 DOI 10.1215/10679847-3320101

window to make sure he was out of earshot. "I had true love before," she said, oblivious to my reaction, and continued, "and this isn't it. But I am still working hard to love him."

Their relationship had begun five months earlier when Scott, a twenty-year-old white GI from rural Kansas, started courting Kristin in the club where she worked. She initially thought of him as one of her customers, laughing off his proclamation of love. Kristin was thirty-four years old, a single mother raising two boys, and she had worked a full-time job for many years in the Philippines. In her eyes, Scott was still a boy. After her ten-year affair with a married man ended badly, Kristin was jaded about romance, but she needed a regular customer at the club, so she was glad to see Scott night after night. After Kristin shared the story of how she had migrated to work as a hostess so that she could support her two children, Scott promised to help and protect her, and he began to woo her with generous tips and gifts.

One night only two months after they met, Scott paid the bar owner $300 to take Kristin out from the club for the night so that he could propose with a cubic zirconia ring. As Scott talked about his plans to form one happy family with her sons, something shifted in Kristin, and she started to think that their relationship could be "something real." She agreed to marry him and ran away from the club soon after. When they moved in together, Scott told her that he wanted to get married after nine months; his term in South Korea would end in three months, and he needed to return to the United States for training. He promised to come to the Philippines after his training to marry Kristin and bring her children to the United States. Although Kristin was uncertain of whether he would keep his promise, she continued to take care of Scott and was "working hard to love him."

Intimate relationships between US GIs and migrant hostesses like Kristin and Scott are the subject of heated debates over the moral boundaries of intimacy and exploitation in South Korea among feminist advocates, US military officers, and Filipina migrant hostesses. While some would accuse Kristin of "using" Scott to earn her commission in the club and to immigrate to the United States, others would blame Scott for "fooling" Kristin into believing that he would marry her when he had no intention of continuing the relationship long-term. In particular, feminist scholarship on military sexual commerce has emphasized asymmetric power relations between US GIs and third world women hostesses as a case of masculine domination and exploitation within racial and imperial hierarchies.[1] Based on twelve months of ethnographic research in a US military camp town in South Korea,[2] this article shows that the shifting dynamics of global power hierarchy, along with the economic ascendance of Asia, have changed the meaning of US military deployment in South Korea and the dynamics of intimate relations between US GIs and Filipina hostesses.

Situating the intimate labor of migrant hostesses in the sociohistorical context of US military camp towns in South Korea, I highlight the shared condition of "indentured mobility,"[3] which brings together US GIs and Filipina migrant women into intimate encounters in South Korea as migrant subjects who are neither simply free agents nor victims of trafficking but constrained subjects in their quest for mobility. Rethinking the power asymmetry between US GIs and migrant hostesses, my ethnography reveals that power differentials are deployed by hostesses as a resource to incite the discourse of benevolence and rescue that attracts US GI customers to the clubs. I examine two dimensions of intimate labor performed by Filipina migrant women in the face of their vulnerable legal and economic conditions in South Korea vis-à-vis US GIs: (1) the labor that they perform as hostesses for the US GI customers in the clubs and (2) the labor they perform on themselves to produce sincere feelings of love and affection. In so doing, I demonstrate how global geopolitics, uneven capitalist development, and transnational migration are entangled with intimacy, power, and emotions to shape intimate labor as migrant women engage in their joint pursuit of mobility and "true love."

US Military Camp Towns and the Club Industry in South Korea

"When I say I am from Basetown, people only think of murders and rape. Because they hear the name on TV when GI crimes happen. They don't know we have a life and good people here."—(Maria, a Korean club owner in Basetown since 1988)

"Basetown," the main site of my fieldwork, is one of the oldest camp towns in South Korea on the outskirts of Seoul, surrounding a US military camp with eleven thousand personnel. Like other camp towns, Basetown is a space of blurred jurisdiction, where the sovereignty of the South Korean state is compromised by that of the US military. Instead of Korean police officers, US military police (MP) patrol the streets of the Basetown, and they possess the power to shut down any club that violates military policy. Korean labor and antiprostitution laws are routinely ignored in the "ville," the club district where 250 to 300 migrant women work. Young soldiers roam Basetown to drink in the foreigner-exclusive clubs in the ville, with names that promise to treat them like a "King," "VIP," or "Pharaoh" and where they can find refuge from their homesickness by falling in and out of love with Filipina migrant hostesses.

US military bases like the one in Basetown are a signifier of US power across the globe, and they are especially concentrated in the Asia-Pacific region.[4] Whereas flows of capital and high-skilled professionals characterize the circuits connecting global cities in Saskia Sassen's framework,[5] the global network of US overseas military bases links cities and towns that are marginalized, underdeveloped, and segregated within the host nation-states. These camp towns are destinations not only for the deployment of US rank-and-file soldiers but also where women migrate internally and transnationally to work in club industries catering to US GIs.[6] I regard US military overseas deployment and the labor migration of club hostesses as an undertheorized circuit of global migrant labor that buttresses the current global order of the US empire.

Camp towns have been present in South Korea for more than sixty years, since the end of World War II, and have been integrated into the national imaginary as a symbol of nationalist shame, of safety and protection under the United States' military umbrella, and of the prosperity and decadence of the West. US GIs entered South Korea at the height of the Cold War as a frontline against the communist bloc in the 1950s, the period during which South Korea experienced severe postwar poverty. While the recent advancement of the South Korean economy is often understood as a product of the growth of the export-oriented manufacturing industry, the service economies surrounding US military camp towns, including South Korean women offering sexual services to US soldiers, have played an important role in the development of postwar South Korea since the 1950s. The South Korean state, especially under the authoritarian regime of the 1960s and

1970s, supported and regulated the camp town sex industry as a source of foreign currency for the national economy,[7] to the extent that state officials visited Korean club hostesses to lecture them about their role as "patriots."[8]

However, since the 1980s, when South Korea began its growth into one of the "four Asian tiger" economies that are ascendant in global financial markets alongside Taiwan, Singapore, and Hong Kong, the place of camp town club industries in South Korea has been significantly diminished. After the US GI salary lost competitive value in comparison to the average income of South Koreans, camp towns were no longer a space of glory and prosperity for South Korean women. Today, these towns are worn and dilapidated, with shops and clubs catering to the limited economic prospects offered by US GIs. As the US military bases no longer offer a highly lucrative source of income for working-class South Korean women, the camp town club industry experienced a labor shortage of Korean women in the mid-1990s, and the clubs are now filled with migrant women predominantly from the Philippines but with a small minority from the former Soviet Union. As club owner Maria lamented, the stigma of the camp towns, long associated with the sex industry and GI crimes, is not decreasing in contemporary South Korea but, rather, is intensifying alongside their shift from US GI-exclusive spaces to segregated spaces where migrant hostesses and US GIs cross paths.

The Indentured Mobility of US GIs and Filipina Hostesses

Encounters between US GIs and Filipina migrant hostesses in camp town clubs illuminate the changing dynamics of global hierarchy propelled by Asia's economic ascendance.[9] Commonly conceptualized as agents of US hegemony and military power, US GIs are often portrayed as problematic figures in feminist discourse as perpetrators of racism and sexism with a sense of entitlement to the sexual services of third world women. Power differentials persist between US GIs and migrant hostesses on multiple levels—as providers and recipients of the intimate labor in the club industry, as stratified citizens in the global hierarchy of nations, and as individuals marked by moral honor through military service or stigma through work in the sex industry.

Yet, these power differentials unfold within a shared condition of both

US GIs and migrant hostesses that propels their encounters in the segregated space of camp towns: that of "indentured mobility." The concept of indentured mobility was used by Rhacel Parreñas to describe a paradoxical state in which participants experience the possibility of upward mobility while they are also bound to servitude and subjugation for the duration of their contract.[10] In order to understand the complexity of intimate encounters between US GIs and migrant hostesses in South Korea, it is critical to recognize that members of these groups are neither freely mobile agents nor victims controlled by their dire circumstances. Instead, each group is composed of actors seeking to realize their desires for mobility under conditions of constrained opportunity in a shifting global terrain.

Filipina Migrant Women in Camp Town Clubs

Relying on South Korean feminist nongovernmental organizations' (NGOs) reports on the camp town club industry in South Korea,[11] scholars such as Seungsook Moon and Jinkyung Lee characterize the migrant flow into the camp town club industry since the mid-1990s as human trafficking.[12] While the intimate labor of migrant hostesses often involves labor rights violations and vulnerability to exploitation, treating all migrant hostesses as victims of trafficking elides the women's pursuit of transnational mobility.[13] For many Filipina migrant women working as club hostesses, migration to South Korea was a "stepping up" experience that provided either their first opportunity to leave the poverty and insecurity of the Philippines or one additional opportunity in a series of overseas contract employment in domestic, factory, and hostess work elsewhere in East Asia. Although some Filipina women were indeed deceived about the sexual nature of the work and self-identified as victims of trafficking, other women entered into hostess work as an opportunity for upward mobility. During their time in South Korea, they supported their extended family's daily subsistence while actively planning for the next step in their transnational journey to uncertain destinations in the United States, Canada, or Europe, where they hoped to achieve greater mobility, permanent residency, and family unification.

For Cecille, a hostess at Club Sky, coming to Basetown in South Korea was a continuation of the short-term labor migration strategy that she used as a single mother to support her son and her parents. During her twenties, she worked in Japan for three years under rotating six-month contracts in hostess bars. She proudly shared that during her contracts, she saved up a significant amount of money and purchased land and a small house in Manila, where she lived with her son, parents, and brother and sister. When her son was little, she stayed in the Philippines to take care of him and worked at various retail jobs, but she later decided to return abroad to work. After being told at thirty-three that she was "too old" to work in Japan, Cecille decided that South Korea was her "second best choice." During her eight months of working in camp town clubs in South Korea, Cecille was disappointed that she could not save as much money as in Japan, but she still considered hostess work better than her retail jobs in the Philippines. Cecille therefore hoped to renew her contract and stay in her current club.

Cecille's desire to keep working in her club did not mean that she was satisfied with the working conditions. The six-month contract with a possibility of renewal offered her indentured labor during that period, and her club owner withheld hostesses' passports to keep workers from running away. The working hours were long, generally starting at 5:00–6:00 p.m. and ending at 12:00–1:00 a.m. on weekdays. On the weekends, hostesses worked much longer days that started at 1:00 p.m. and ended at 3:00 a.m. the next morning. Cecille was given one day off per month, despite a labor contract promising one day off per week. While some hostesses were paid their monthly wage as a lump sum at the end of the contract and had to live off only tips and commissions, Cecille received her wage every month, but delay was still a common occurrence. For the first month of their contracts, she and other hostesses in her club were prohibited to leave the club or their residence on the second floor of the club at any time.

Despite these conditions, Cecille thought her club was better than other clubs where hostesses were never allowed to leave the club or where the club owners or managers pressured hostesses to go out with customers who paid a fee, a practice called a "bar fine." Cecille's greatest concern was that it would take only one phone call from her club owner to the agency that brought her to South Korea to move Cecille to another camp town club with unknown labor practices or send her back to the Philippines. Because she wanted to save money before leaving South Korea and because she was afraid of being sent to a club with worse working conditions, Cecille was in a vulnerable position and unable to discuss violations of her labor contract with her employer.

Despite the challenges of migrant hostessing as contract labor, Cecille felt that these conditions were similar to other types of short-term migrant labor that she, her sisters, and her cousins had experienced as hostesses, domestic workers, and factory workers in other East Asian and Southeast Asian countries. The condition of indentured mobility was an everyday reality that she took for granted and endured. Cecille's family back home also encouraged her to stay abroad despite these labor conditions. She said "This morning, my mom said, 'Stay there as long as you can. Go TNT [undocumented] if you have to.' She was like, 'If they don't extend the contract and if you come home, how are we going to live?' My son says the same thing. He said, 'Don't come home, Mom. I think it is better that you stay.'"

Although Cecille couldn't help feeling hurt when her family urged her to stay away, she understood the reality that her overseas employment was critical to sustain their livelihood. She was tired of the insecurity of short-term contracts, of not knowing when she would return to home, and of being away from her family, especially her son. She often talked about the possibility of settling somewhere permanently like her aunt, who worked in elder care in Italy and who had a stable immigration status there. She wished to save money in South Korea so that she could take the special training course for elder care and apply to go to Italy as well. Cecille also contemplated marriage as an opportunity to settle abroad. "If I marry an American and immigrate to the US," she said, "then all this separation would be over. My son can come live with me there." For migrant hostesses like Cecille, romance and marriage with US GIs represented one potential strategy in a larger pursuit of mobility from insecurity and poverty in the Philippines and from the precarious and indentured conditions of migrant labor in South Korea and elsewhere.[14]

US GIs in Overseas Deployment

The aspiration for upward mobility also propelled many US GIs to move overseas to camp towns in South Korea. Camp towns are a transitory space where US GIs are stationed for a short period of time before relocating to other military bases across the globe. For many young GIs, military service was a secure career option that provided good benefits, the possibility of advancement, and the ability to support a family; for others, it was a short-term job that they utilized to save money and earn support for college or other advanced training. The motivations these men and women had for joining the military were not very different from the desires of migrant hostesses in the camp town clubs.

For John, a twenty-year-old high school graduate from rural Kansas, more than patriotism, a desire to leave his hometown and "do something with my life, maybe go to college" was a strong motivation to join the army. For many GIs like John, South Korea was their first overseas deployment after basic training, and it was often their first experience abroad. No longer powerful agents of the West in postwar, poverty-stricken Asia, US GIs in overseas bases in South Korea often experienced alienation and hostility. As the US dollar's buying power in South Korea declined significantly with the rise of Asian economies, the cosmopolitan and consumerist urban lifestyle of Seoul was out of reach for GIs on a tight salary.

Furthermore, although some US GIs held onto the idea that they were fighting for the freedom of South Koreans, the rhetoric of protecting the country against communist North Korea faltered for many as they experienced the reality of living in South Korea. They faced mixed responses from South Koreans outside the camp towns when they walked around in uniform or even in civilian clothing. Instead of treating them as protectors, South Koreans stared at GIs or walked away for reasons that were difficult to comprehend for GIs who were unaware of the sociohistorical legacy of the US military presence and the anti-US sentiment arising from it.[15] For these reasons, most US GIs avoided downtown Seoul to save on expenses and avoid "hassles," instead spending their time and money in camp towns that are designed to cater to GIs (and sometimes other migrant workers from Asia). Thus, despite their first-world status, US GIs' day-to-day experiences of South Korea—experiences of being contained within the segregated space of camp towns and of hostility from locals—were similar to those of migrant workers from Southeast and South Asia.

In fact, as the number of migrant workers in South Korea increased in the 1990s, some camp town clubs expanded their clientele to include migrant workers from other Asian countries such as Bangladesh, Pakistan, and the Philippines, while others remained exclusive to GIs. Due to frequent fights among Asian migrant workers and US GIs, clubs that serve both groups often segregate their clientele by restricting the entry of Asian migrant workers after the curfew of the military camp. Thus, explaining the system of customer management in her club, Teresa, a Filipina hostess at Club Starlight, told me, "Until 12 a.m., it is GI time, and afterwards it's Asian time." This strategy to maximize profits in the struggling club business while containing conflicts signifies an important shift in the meaning of US military presence in South Korea, where US military power and economic might are no longer treated with reverence. Despite the persistent hierarchies among them, US GIs and Asian migrant workers were both treated and understood as migrant laborers in a space segregated from South Korean citizens.[16]

In this sense, I concur with Jinkyung Lee's argument that US military overseas deployment can be conceptualized as another form of migrant labor. As she states, "If South Korean military prostitution now includes a migrant workforce from overseas, due to the relative wealth of the South Korean national economy, there is a way in which the enlisted ranks of the American military, largely made up of the racialized working class, have become transnational migrant militarized labor, serving the South Korean state and capital."[17] While intimate exchanges in camp town clubs resemble the racialized and gendered relationships between clients from the first world and workers from the third world presented in much of the literature on sex tourism,[18] US GIs did not travel to South Korea for leisure but instead were there as a requirement of their work. They did not choose South Korea as a destination but were deployed there regardless of their preference. Bound by a military contract, US GIs in South Korea experienced a condition of indenture and lacked the ability to control where their next deployment destination would be. This uncertainty created a heightened sense of fear and insecurity during my fieldwork in 2009–10, when GIs watched their comrades deploy to Afghanistan and Iraq, where there was a real possibility of injury and death. For migrant workers like US GIs and Filipina hostesses in South Korea, their aspirations for upward mobility sustain their labor under challenging conditions and motivate them to enter into restrictive contracts. These conditions of indentured mobility—emerging within persisting power differentials between the groups—provide the backdrop for the intimate encounters between US GIs and Filipina migrant hostesses in the camp town clubs.

Intimate Labor to Win the Heart:
Selling Fantasies of Benevolence and Rescue

The most mundane form of intimate labor in the camp town clubs is selling companionship in the form of "juice." When a customer buys a hostess one shot glass of juice—a mixture of juice and alcohol that costs about $10—the hostess is required to sit by the customer's side for fifteen to twenty minutes and receives $2 in commission. What she does during this time varies by club from simple chatting to providing a lap dance. When the time runs out, the woman walks away, and the customer must buy her more juice to keep her company. Club owners often institute a "quota system," requiring hostesses to sell two hundred to four hundred drinks per month. In addition, some clubs also had a "VIP room," where customers could pay for private time with a hostess at about $80 for thirty minutes, and a "bar fine" system in which GIs paid $200–$300 to take hostesses away from the bar for the night. What they do during the bar fine is up to the customer and the hostess and does not necessarily involve sex, though bar fines are used for intimate and sexual exchanges.

US GIs who frequent the clubs as regular customers or "boyfriends" of Filipina hostesses admitted that at first, it was fun to go to different clubs to meet "sweet and hot" young women and to compare "new girls" with their buddies. However, this initial excitement soon wore off. As Steve, a twenty-four-year-old white US citizen from Texas, told me:

> I went down to the ville because my buddies were telling me to come along. As soon as we walked in, the girls there all came after us. They got me a lap dance with one of the girls, and I was really, wow . . . [laughs] So, it was fun at first, but then you realize that they are not after you, they are after your money, because they want you to buy them a drink. And that's no fun. After a while, you get tired of all that.

For US GIs like Steve, experiences of male bonding based on erotic tension and their excitement at meeting the hostesses initially brought them into the camp town clubs, but it did not last long. After they became "tired of all that," GIs might still occasionally visit clubs on the weekends, but this was not enough to establish a thriving business. Only the ability to turn jaded customers like Steve into regulars who buy multiple drinks on each visit and take women out on bar fines could sustain the club business. Thus, rather than rely on high customer turnover, which was impossible in the restricted space of camp towns, clubs cultivated a regular customer base by producing a feeling of sympathy and benevolence on the part of the GIs and by promoting the allure of romantic relationships. In this way, the power differentials between US GIs and Filipina hostesses were actively appropriated by the club owners and hostesses as an integral part of hostesses' intimate labor. The commodity that was bought and sold in the clubs, that attracted US GI customers to intimate relations with Filipina migrant women, was not just sexual gratification but a deep, embodied experience of benevolence. Encounters with Filipina hostesses in the clubs offered GIs a chance to embody the US soldier masculinity that they imagined they would become before deploying overseas as "protectors of the world." While their daily lives in South Korean camp towns were filled with boredom, alienation, and even hostility from the South Koreans they were supposed to protect, their relations with migrant women gave US GIs a concrete opportunity to offer help, protection, and even rescue.

For example, Steve, who thought he was "over the ville" and "wasting money on girls," changed his mind when he met Ramona, a twenty-three-year-old Filipina woman, in Club Mirage: "Even at first, I could tell right away that she did not belong there. She was not aggressive like other girls, but rather shy. She couldn't even look at me directly. I could tell it was hard for her to be there, to throw herself at guys. So I kept going back because I wanted to help her."

Not only did Steve begin to visit Club Mirage on a daily basis, but he also took Ramona out for lunch during his mid-day break and brought food to the club before it opened in the evening. On the weekends, he was a fixture in one corner of the bar where he tried to create as much privacy as possible with Ramona. In doing so, Steve not only differentiated Ramona as someone who "did not belong there" but also differentiated himself from other customers in the clubs who go there to have "fun and play with the girls"; instead, he was there to help as a benevolent hero. After a few months of seeing her almost every day, Steve proposed to Ramona, and they were waiting for her contract to end to get married.

Though not all relationships between US GIs and hostesses were as intense and serious as that of Steve and Ramona, it was not uncommon for migrant hostesses to have one or a few regular customers who would visit them in the clubs on a daily basis, buying them multiple drinks and bringing them food and gifts. Cultivating an intimate relationship with GIs was not an option that an individual hostess seeks but rather an integral part of hostesses' intimate labor dictated by the club industry. It was nearly impossible for club hostesses to meet their quota of drink sales without these relationships with "boyfriends" or "special customers"—a distinction that was often blurry. Hostesses were dependent on GI boyfriends for juice sales in the clubs and to support their daily life in the camp town outside work.

Because receiving "help" from customers was critical to their livelihood, hostesses taught each other techniques to get food and gifts from regulars by appealing to their sympathy.[19] Susan and Anne worked in the same club, and while we were doing manicures in their house one afternoon, Susan talked on the phone with three different men in turn—one Filipino migrant worker and two US GIs. With each, she repeated phrases like "I miss you so much, sweetie" before reminding them of the things she needed. She cajoled, "Please come help me. I have nothing to eat. Can you bring me something to eat?" It was important, according to Susan, to let men know that they were special and that their help and protection were needed. Unlike Susan, Anne described herself as "not talented at all" with these techniques, partly owing to her lack of English fluency but also because of her dislike of asking for things. Anne explained, "I don't want to ask for things, like, 'I have no food in the house, can you please bring me some pork from the commissary, darling?' I don't like that. Why should I always ask and beg?" However, she soon realized that the reason to ask for things was not her own immediate needs, but more lasting feelings of sympathy and benevolence it induced in customers that kept them coming to the club and spending money.

To incite sympathy, many club hostesses selectively presented their life stories. For example, Susan told me that in order to keep regular customers, "you can't say that you are married with kids. Say you are single, or abandoned by your husband back home. And no child, or maybe just one that you need to support." Anne chimed in, "And the age. They can't tell Filipinas' age, so you talk down your age by five, six years. It's not like I want to lie, but if I say I am thirty-five, and my husband is taking care of our children back home waiting for me, who's gonna buy me drinks?" In the clubs, I was able to observe the success of these tactics. Some GIs believed that Susan and Anne were ten years younger than their real age. Anne told GI customers how she missed her son, intentionally omitting her husband and two other children, so some GIs gave her twenty dollars, saying, "Buy a phone card to talk to your son."

The vilification of club owners was another tactic that worked well with customers, as club owners were convenient targets for hostesses. Conflicts and hostility between club owners and hostesses were common, but a sense of solidarity and caring relationships also existed among them. Many South Korean club managers were former hostesses who sympathized with migrant women, like Rachel's club manager Hosoon, who had worked in the camp town clubs in the 1980s, married a GI, and moved to the United States. After divorcing her husband, Hosoon returned to work in the same camp town club, leaving her child behind. Hosoon taught Rachel that if she wanted to turn down a regular costumer's request to meet outside for sex, she should just say "mommy [the club manager] doesn't let us go out," or make up a curfew, two pieces of advice that she followed. Talking about "evil club owners" also made it possible for US GIs to assume the protector role for migrant women. Linda, who had a few GI boyfriends for the four months she worked at the club, recalled her experience:

> GIs are good. Yeah, there are players and all, but some are very kind, and they understand it when you are out on a bar fine and you don't want to have sex. If you say you are just there because *mommy* [the club owner] forced you but you would like to get to know each other first, they get that. They feel sorry for us and take you out to dinner, go club-hopping, and take you to a hotel and let you rest. But Pakistanis and Koreans![20]

They are only into getting into your pants and get really upset when you say no. They are like, "I paid all this money, what are you going to do to make up for it?"

Like Linda, many club hostesses preferred having US GIs as regular customers or boyfriends. GIs had higher average incomes than migrant workers, and because they lived at the nearby military base, they could visit the clubs more often, creating a potential for marriage and migration to the United States. But even women who did not want to marry preferred US GIs because they were more likely to "feel sorry" for the women than Asian migrant workers or Koreans. For GIs, this feeling of sympathy and benevolence was a driving force that motivated them to spend money in the clubs. In this sense, the US GIs' intimate encounters with migrant hostesses were less about sexual gratification and domination than about affirming their masculinity and national superiority. These encounters provided GIs with a way to embody and enact a US masculinity that involves saving and protecting both women and the third world.[21] In particular, these men were attracted to the narrative of rescuing innocent women victims in trouble from the "evil" club owners and managers who exploit them.

After Steve decided that Ramona was a special woman in need of his help, he continued to visit her club almost every day for three months and stayed until the club closed so that she would not have to sit with any other customer. He could not calculate how much money he spent at the club, having bought drinks not only for Ramona but also for other hostesses who were her friends. When he proposed to Ramona, they initially planned to get married after her contract ended, but Ramona did not want to wait. She was afraid of being transferred to another club far away from Steve, and she also felt uncertain about Steve's commitment. As she put it, "It's not that I doubt him. Nothing like that. But he is young, and people say you never know about Americans. They are not like us; once they change their mind, that's just it." Because Ramona could not tell Steve that she was unsure of whether he would change his mind about her, she instead told him that the club owner was forcing her to go out with other men on a bar fine. Steve was enraged by the club owners' purported actions and wanted to fight him, but Ramona begged him to keep his temper. He finally agreed that instead of confronting the club owner, he and Ramona should marry right away. After a few days, Ramona ran away from the club, married Steve, and moved into a rented apartment. Because Steve and Ramona were both in their early to mid-twenties and had not been previously married, the paperwork for the marriage license was not complicated. Soon, Ramona received a spousal visa in South Korea as a dependent of the US military.

When I met with them five months later, Ramona was pregnant, and they were leaving in a few days to return to the United States where Steve would be stationed at a military base in Texas. They looked happy, but Steve was still furious about the "evil" club owner and told me how grateful he was that he got Ramona out of the club before anything happened to her. When Steve left the apartment to return to base for afternoon duty, Ramona told me that she ran into her previous club owner in front of a grocery store. She said:

> He saw me, and he got really angry and started yelling. But there was his wife next to him. She had always been very kind to me when I was there, and she stopped him and asked me whether I am married. When I said yes, she dragged him away. Thank God, I never met him again. I feel sorry for them, because I would be mad too, if I were them, running away like that. But what else could I have done?

Because it was not unusual for hostesses to run away from clubs to live with or marry their GI boyfriends, Ramona did not feel bad about her choice. Her fear that she might be sent away to another club was valid, as was her fear that Steve might change his mind. By portraying herself as a victim who needed immediate rescue, Ramona achieved her goal of marrying Steve and immigrating to the United States. When she told him she needed to work to send money to her family in the Philippines, he responded that he wanted her to stay home during her pregnancy and committed to sending her family $200–$300 every month. After Ramona left the club, her second cousin migrated to South Korea and started working in the same club without the owner knowing their connection. Ramona's departure from the camp town in South Korea effectively ended her current and past cycle of indentured mobility through a series of short-term migrant labor contracts that many Filipina migrant women are subject to in various countries in

East and Southeast Asia. Her intimate labor within the new cycle of indentured mobility continued, however, as she was now bound to Steve's military contract as a wife and might be relocated to other parts of the world in their continuing pursuit of mobility.

Intimate Labor of the Heart:
The Suppression and Cultivation of True Love

This section explores the intimate labor that migrant hostesses engage in within the camp town clubs and beyond to produce and suppress feelings of love in themselves. This labor takes place in tandem with the intimate labor performed under the highly regulated system of juice sales and bar fines, which comes with explicit rules and prices to provide intimacy for US GIs. This was a deeper, less scripted form of intimate labor that women used to reclaim their sense of morality while participating in the commodified exchange of intimacy and pursuing mobility through heterosexual relationships. The internal work of controlling and regulating intimacy was integral to both their formal labor and their mobility strategies, as many suppressed feelings of "true love" until they felt secure about commitments from their US GI boyfriends who could offer material and legal resources. The power differentials between Filipina hostesses and US GIs that were deployed in the clubs to induce sympathy from the GI customers also shaped the intimate labor Filipina hostesses continued to perform after leaving the clubs while facing a vulnerable legal and economic status in South Korea.

The internal labor of producing feelings of love on the part of Filipina migrant hostesses must be read against the backdrop of suspicion about emotions within the commercialized setting of the club industry, where women's intimacy was purchased on a pay-per-time basis. US GIs often held doubts about the authenticity of the intimacy provided in the clubs and felt unsure of whether their partner regarded them as a regular customer or a boyfriend. Hearing stories about their peers who were "played" and women who had "extorted money" amplified their concerns. In order to test whether their intimacy was "real," US GIs frequently asked hostesses to spend time with them "off the clock," by meeting with them during their lunch break, sneaking out at night after the club owner went home, or spending time together during the hostesses' day off. Some hostesses rejected these requests, thinking that the men were "trying to be cheap" and avoid buying juices or spending $200 to take them out on a bar fine. Others who were seriously considering GIs as potential boyfriends and husbands responded positively to these requests, as they too wanted to spend private time together and to save the men money instead of profiting the club owner.

Skepticism about GI-hostess romance and marriage came not only from individual GIs but also from US military officers and South Korean feminist activists who openly expressed their concerns. Some US military officers accused hostesses of being manipulative and "trapping" US GIs to secure the opportunity to immigrate to the United States. Mr. Thompson, a retired US military officer in his fifties who was stationed in Basetown as a civilian employee, thought that Filipina hostesses were duping young GIs:

> Some of them [GIs] are not even drinking age, just right out of high school. For them, the ville is their whole world. After leaving their parents' home, they are on their own for the first time, feeling lonely. They go to a club, and a pretty girl is saying, "Hey! How are doing? Here is lumpya [spring roll] for you," and they get hooked just like that! [laughs] And before they know it, they end up marrying a girl ten years older, and supporting her children!

While people like Mr. Thompson portrayed US GIs as gullible and therefore vulnerable due to their youth and lack of life experience, others blamed US GIs for taking advantage of migrant hostesses' vulnerability arising from their insecure economic positions as third world women and migrant workers. Jiyeon, a staff member at a South Korean feminist NGO for camp town women, had assisted a significant number of migrant women from the Philippines and the former Soviet Union who ran away from the clubs to move in with US GI boyfriends and husbands but then were abandoned as soon as the GIs' deployment ended. Jiyeon was skeptical of the intimate relationships between GIs and hostesses, saying, "The GIs just play around and lie and cheat all too often. Even if they promise marriage and get into marriage, how could their marriages last when they started in the clubs as customers?"

Against widespread skepticism about marketized intimacy in the clubs, many Filipina hostesses as well as US GIs pursued what they called "true love," instead of seeking only limited and bounded forms of intimacy.[22] For Filipina women, it was central to their intimate labor to produce and suppress feelings of true love, depending on the conditions of their relationships because they hoped to use their romantic relationships with US GIs to accomplish two important goals. First, they aimed to lay a material foundation for upward mobility by securing financial support and the ability to migrate to the United States. Second, they sought moral affirmation that their romantic feelings were sincere, not instrumental.

For migrant hostesses, the feeling of "true love" was something that needed to be postponed until they secured from the GIs a promise of commitment that would lead to mobility and financial security, such as a marriage proposal. Many Filipina hostesses distinguished their intimate relationships in the clubs from prior experiences of "true love," with high school sweethearts, extramarital affairs, or intense short flings; whereas those experiences were for love only, now that they had invested money and effort into a path of indentured mobility as migrant labor in South Korea, they pursued a romantic relationship that would fulfill their aspiration of mobility. As such, when some hostesses followed their "hearts" and entered intimate relationships with US GIs or Filipino workers who did not offer material benefits, other women clearly expressed their disapproval.

Kelly, a thirty-one-year-old Filipina woman, told me about her coworker Girlie in Club Peace, who needed to "use her brain." According to Kelly, Girlie often snuck out to spend the night with a US GI who did not give her gifts or money and who offered no formal commitment. Instead, Girlie bought him gifts and took him out for meals because "she was in love." Kelly and other hostesses frowned upon Girlie for spending her precious time and money that way. "We all came here for the same reason, you know," Kelly said. "To make money. If you'd like to fall in love and sleep around, why not just do it back home, not all the way over here?" For hostesses like Kelly, simply following one's heart without considering material conditions was a luxury that they could not afford, as the institution of heterosexual marriage was one of few options to achieve cross-border mobility for migrant women who lacked marketable skills and capital and were restricted to feminized, lower-paid labor markets.

Falling into a reckless romance without the security of marriage posed a particular risk due to the legal and economic vulnerability of Filipina migrant hostesses in South Korea. Because migrant hostesses were in a state of indentured mobility under their labor contracts, when they ran away from the clubs for their GI boyfriends, their visas were voided and their legal status in South Korea converted to undocumented. By marrying US GIs, their legal status could be regularized as a spouse. This dependency of former hostesses' legal status on their GI romantic partners created a power differential that became salient when the boyfriend changed his mind about the relationship. For example, when Amy fell in love and left the club to move in with her US GI boyfriend, Tom, she did not know that his womanizing would continue. Even after Amy was pregnant and gave birth to their son Andy, he kept seeing other women in the clubs, and when Andy was barely two months old, Tom married another Filipina hostess and stopped supporting Andy. Amy sought child support, but because she was not legally married to Tom, she was denied assistance from American Military Family Support Services. To make matters worse, Tom threatened to report Amy to immigration. One day, Tom's friend and fellow US GI called Amy to meet for lunch at the Filipino restaurant in the ville, but she was late because of the baby. Rushing to meet him, she overheard others saying that there was an immigration raid in the restaurant, so she quickly turned back home. She said, "I knew then it was Tom's setup. Now, I am a burden to him, and he wants to get rid of me." Amy was raising Andy by herself, working as a freelancer in another club in Basetown. She was determined not to make the same mistake again and warned her fellow hostesses about the danger of acting on love alone. She advised them to avoid men who offer promises of marriage but do not quickly follow through with legal paperwork.

Even when romance led to legal marriage, the insecurity that Filipina migrant women felt did not disappear because they worried that they might be abandoned when the GI's deployment in South Korea ended. Although there are no statistics to show how frequent such cases of abandonment are, it is telling that the US military in Basetown offers a multilingual hotline for the abandoned wives of US GIs to help them locate their husbands, obtain basic services in the military camp, and secure child support. Ms. Ramos, who was in charge of the American Military Family Support Center that runs the hotline, emphasized the necessity to be careful when choosing a man: "They should find someone sincere. Catholic men are the best, or at least Christians. If they attend the church every week, those guys are okay, but it is rare to find a man like that." She cautioned against young GIs who might impulsively marry but then fall out of love and leave, sometimes without properly filing for divorce or sending child support.

Despite such risks, many Filipina migrant women made the choice to leave the clubs and enter into a romantic relationship with US GIs. The intimate labor they performed in the clubs continued in a different form as domestic labor. In Basetown, former hostesses cooked, cleaned, served food, washed laundry, and cared for their GI boyfriends, often with the promise of marriage. The US GIs who moved in with their runaway girlfriends paid the rent and provided living expenses, and they spent most of their time outside of military duty in rented apartments with their girlfriends, even stopping by lunch to eat a home-cooked meal. In addition to providing intimate labor that made GIs feel loved and cared for, hostesses performed an additional layer of intimate labor: the internal work of producing feelings of love in themselves. While they understood their romantic relationships in terms of potential material benefits, including immigration to the United States, they were also committed to making their relationship one of "true love." They understood this task of achieving sincerity as something they would work on, as a conscious act of labor, as Kristin did in the beginning of the article when she said that she was "working hard to love" her fiancé Scott. Whether she truly loved Scott could not be known by others, and it was not others' judgment that Kristin was trying to satisfy, but her own. As a matter of sincerity, it was her "intent" that mattered, rather than the "content" of the intimate labor she performed for Scott.[23] For many migrant women like Kristin, the labor of cultivating a sincere emotion of love was a way to take care of the self, fulfilling their desire for sincerity and moral legitimacy while engaging in the precarious pursuit of mobility through romantic relationships with US GIs.

Conclusion

In this article, I used the club industry in US military camp towns in South Korea as a lens to examine shifting global hierarchies amid the economic ascendance of Asia in tandem with the decline of US hegemony. No longer a space of economic prosperity in poverty-stricken postwar South Korea as in the 1950s and 1960s, US camp towns are increasingly becoming segregated migrant towns where US GIs and migrant workers from South and Southeast Asia are concentrated, including migrant women from the Philippines who work as hostesses at camp town clubs. Situating the intimate encounter between US GIs and Filipina hostesses in camp town clubs in South Korea in the dynamics of shifting global hierarchies, this article critically revisits the feminist scholarship on military sexual commerce, in which the vulnerability of third world migrant women vis-à-vis US military men was highlighted as a case of exploitation and trafficking. Challenging the dichotomous construction of US GIs as powerful and free agents of US hegemony and of migrant hostesses as victims of trafficking, my ethnography shed light on their shared condition of indentured mobility, in which both groups participated under constraining migrant labor contracts to pursue opportunities for social, economic, and global mobility.

Instead of disputing the power asymmetry between US GIs and migrant hostesses, I have shown that such power differentials were used in unexpected and creative ways by migrant hostesses and club owners as a discursive resource to attract US GI customers into the clubs by appealing to their sense of benevolence and sympathy to rescue third world women in need. In the camp town clubs, US GIs were given the opportunity to enact the role of protector, one that resonated with the US military rhetoric that was betrayed by GIs' experiences overseas. I have also explored how the intimate labor of Filipina migrant women continued after their "rescue" from the clubs, as their legal and economic vulnerability vis-à-vis US GIs intensified after they abandoned their contracts in their joint pursuit of love and mobility. By engaging the US military camp towns in South Korea as a space of migrant encounter from the United States and other parts of Asia, this article challenges the binary between the first and third worlds and illuminates how the interplay of global geopolitics, uneven capitalist development, and transnational migration operates in shaping the practice of intimate labor at a critical juncture in the changing global order.

Notes

I thank the special issue editors, Rhacel Parreñas, Rachel Silvey, Hung Cam Thai, and the anonymous reviewers of *positions*, as well as Nicole Constable, Chaitanya Lakkimsetti, Sharmila Rudrappa, Pei-Chia Lan, Judy Juhui Han, Juno Parreñas, Anna Korteweg, Jennifer Carlson, Ayesha Khurshid, Jessica Cobb, and the Politics, Culture, and Society seminar participants at the University of Wisconsin–Madison. This project received financial support from the Social Science Research Council International Dissertation Research Fellowship, the National Science Foundation Dissertation Improvement Grant in Sociology, and the American Philosophical Society Lewis and Clark Fund.

1. Cynthia Enloe, *Maneuvers* (Berkeley: University of California Press, 2000); Saundra Sturdevant and Brenda Stoltzfus, *Let the Good Times Roll: Prostitution and the U.S. Military in Asia* (New York: The New Press, 1992).
2. The field research for this article took place in the twelve months from February 2009 to January 2010 in Basetown, a US military camp town on the outskirts of Seoul. The migrant hostesses I met were women in their twenties and thirties from the Philippines, and the GIs were mostly young men in their late teens and twenties from the United States; most hostesses and GIs did not remain in South Korea for more than one or two years. In Basetown, I attended the weekly Tagalog Catholic mass, regularly visited clubs to meet with migrant hostesses and club owners, and spent time in the homes of US GI Filipina couples. All the names of people and places are changed in order to protect confidentiality.
3. Rhacel Parreñas, *Illicit Flirtations* (Berkeley, CA: Stanford University Press, 2011), 7.
4. Maria Hohn and Seungsook Moon, eds., *Over There* (Durham, NC: Duke University Press, 2010).
5. Saskia Sassen, *The Global City: New York, London, Tokyo* (Princeton, NJ: Princeton University Press, 2001).
6. The club industry shows striking similarities in organization and work practices across the Philippines, Okinawa, and South Korea. See Sturdevant and Stoltzfus, *Let the Good Times Roll*.
7. Na Young Lee, "The Construction of U.S. Camptown Prostitution in South Korea: Trans/ formation and Resistance" (PhD diss., University of Maryland, 2006). Jin-kyung Lee also notes that the South Korean state played the role of labor broker in the camp town clubs. See Jin-kyung Lee, *Service Economies: Militarism, Sex Work, and Migrant Labor in South Korea* (Minneapolis: University of Minnesota Press, 2010). Grace Cho reports that more than 1 million South Korean women have worked as hostesses in camp town clubs since

the 1950s, although this number is a conservative estimate. See Grace Cho, *Haunting the Korean Diaspora: Shame, Secrecy, and the Forgotten War* (Minneapolis: University of Minnesota Press, 2008).

8. Katharine Moon, *Sex among Allies* (New York: Columbia University Press, 1997); Yonja Kim, *The Big Sister of American Town Yells Out until Her Death* (Seoul: Samin, 2005).

9. On "Asia Rising," see Hijin Park, "The Stranger That Is Welcomed: Female Foreign Students from Asia, the English Language Industry, and the Ambivalence of 'Asia Rising' in British Columbia, Canada," *Gender, Place and Culture* 17, no. 3 (2010): 337–55. Also, for changing racial and national hierarchies in the sex industry, see Kimberly Hoang, "'She's Not a Low-Class Dirty Girl': Sex Work in Ho Chi Minh City," *Journal of Contemporary Ethnography* 40, no. 4 (2011): 367–96; Kimberly Hoang, "Competing Technologies of Embodiment: Pan-Asian Modernity and Third World Dependency in Vietnam's Contemporary Sex Industry," *Gender and Society* 28, no. 4 (2014): 513–36.

10. Parreñas, *Illicit Flirtations*, 121; also see Sealing Cheng, *On the Move for Love* (Philadelphia: University of Pennsylvania Press, 2010).

11. For a detailed analysis of mainstream South Korean feminist organizations' approaches to the camp town club industry and their work with migrant hostesses, see Cheng, *On the Move*, and Hae Yeon Choo, "The Cost of Rights: Migrant Women, Feminist Advocacy, and Gendered Morality in South Korea," *Gender and Society* 27, no. 4 (2013): 445–68.

12. Lee, *Service Economies*. Lee writes, "Korean men now participate in camptown economies, playing a revised role since the earlier era of industrialization, as part of organized crime networks that carry out human trafficking" (130); also see Seungsook Moon, "Camptown Prostitution and the Imperial SOFA: Abuse and Violence against Transnational Camptown Women in South Korea," in Hohn and Moon, *Over There*, 337–65.

13. For how the trafficking discourse presumes migrant women's victimhood and can undermine the rights of migrant women in sexual commerce, see Laura Agustin, *Sex at the Margins* (London: Zed Books, 2007); Cheng, *On the Move*; Parreñas, *Illicit Flirtations*.

14. For an in-depth exploration of the romantic relationship between US GIs and Filipina migrant hostesses in US camp towns in South Korea, see Cheng, *On the Move*; and Sallie Yea, "Labour of Love: Filipina Entertainer's Narratives of Romance and Relationships with GIs in US Military Camp Towns in Korea," *Women's Studies International Forum* 28, no. 6 (2005): 456–72.

15. For rising anti-US sentiment and hostility against US GIs in South Korea, see Moon, *Sex among Allies*.

16. The hierarchical, temporal division between US GIs and Asian migrant workers resonates with the legacy of racial segregation in the United States that played out in camp town clubs in South Korea until the 1970s; see Moon, *Sex among Allies*. During my fieldwork in Basetown, the US GIs were of diverse racial and ethnic groups, including whites, Latinos,

African Americans, Filipinos, and Korean Americans, and there was no longer any explicit segregation in the clubs along racial lines.

17. Lee, *Service Economies*, 179.

18. For example, see Denise Brennan, "Tourism in Transnational Places: Dominican Sex Workers and German Sex Tourists Imagine One Another," *Identities: Global Studies in Culture and Power* 7, no. 4 (2001): 621–63; Kimberly Hoang, "She's Not"; Julia O'Connell Davidson, "The Sex Tourist, the Expatriate, His Ex-Wife and Her 'Other': The Politics of Loss, Difference and Desire," *Sexualities* 4, no. 1 (2001): 5–24; Kamala Kempadoo, "Women of Color and the Global Sex Trade: Transnational Feminist Perspectives," *Meridians* 1, no. 2 (2001): 28–51.

19. On a similar tactic of inducing sympathy and benevolence from Western tourists on the part of Vietnamese sex workers by performing third world poverty and dependency, see Hoang, "Competing Technologies of Embodiment."

20. The camp town clubs are exclusive to foreigners and do not allow Korean customers, but her club owner sometimes brought his Korean friends to entertain.

21. On the savior complex in the United States, see Yen Le Espiritu, "The 'We-Win-Even-When-We-Lose' Syndrome: U.S. Press Coverage of the Twenty-Fifth Anniversary of the 'Fall of Saigon,'" *American Quarterly* 58, no. 2 (2006): 329–52; and Lila Abu-Lughod, "Do Muslim Women Really Need Saving? Anthropological Reflections on Cultural Relativism and Its Others," *American Anthropologist* 104, no. 3 (2002): 783–90.

22. Elizabeth Bernstein offers the concept of "bounded authenticity," which refers to the exchange of emotions and care in sexual commerce that are bounded by the time and place of the encounter. See Elizabeth Bernstein, *Temporarily Yours* (Chicago: University of Chicago Press, 2007).

23. John Jackson Jr., *Real Black: Adventures in Racial Sincerity* (Chicago: University of Chicago Press, 2005).

"From Dance Bars to the Streets":
Moral Dispossession and Eviction in Mumbai

Chaitanya Lakkimsetti

Introduction

In 2005, dance bars emerged as a topic of controversy in the city of Mumbai. That year, the state of Maharashtra banned dancing in particular establishments called "dance bars" on the basis that they were breeding grounds for prostitution. The ban made it illegal for these bars to host live dance performances, and entertainment licenses issued by the state prior to the ban were revoked. The ban put seventy-five thousand dancers (mostly women) out of work and had substantial financial repercussions for bar owners.

The dance bars (described in more detail below) emerged as morally suspect spaces during the late 1990s, when Mumbai's industrial economy was declining while the city developed as a global center of finance and entertainment. Accompanying these developments was the rise of the service sector and a shadow economy generated by "improper" acquisition and spend-

positions 24:1   DOI 10.1215/10679847-3320113

ing of cash in the burgeoning film industry and housing market. Anxieties around the role of illicit cash in Mumbai's economy, along with concerns over "immoral sexualities," were reflected in the trope of men throwing money at women that is often invoked by the opponents of dance bars. The ban on bar dancing was related to moral anxiety around working-class women's sexuality, shifts in the city's spatial and economic organization, and the particular ways cash and capital become antagonists in a global city.

Using discourse analysis of legal documents, newspaper reports, and media archives, I argue that central to the moral hysteria around bar dancing was the perception that bars were places where cash was hypervisible. The explicit flow of cash as tips raised anxieties about shadow economies, and the bars came to be seen as sites where illegal cash was spent. The uneasy and contradictory relationship between unregulated and "unproductive" cash and "productive" capital was highly visible in the debates around the ban. The control of space required to make Mumbai a global city also created conditions of material and moral dispossession for poor and working-class women. Courtroom arguments on the ban had greater implications for the fate of people disposed by the ban and living in the "shadow spaces" of the city's margins. These contestations also reveal that the control and regulation of intimate labor are critical to shaping Mumbai as a global city.[1]

In the following sections, I situate Mumbai in the literature on global cities and discuss the connections between space, sexuality, and class. My focus is on the debates around regulation of dance bars and not so much on the labor practices within the bars. In doing so, I offer an analysis of the ban that moves the focus beyond moral anxiety around sexuality and connects the "moral hysteria" to anxieties around "unproductive" cash and the uneasy relationship between cash and capital in a global city.[2]

Global Cities and the Reconfiguration of Urban Space

As Saskia Sassen shows, global cities have undergone both economic and social restructuring as they transition from industrial to postindustrial economies.[3] These cities have become sharply polarized across class lines, owing to the supply of low-wage jobs required by high-income gentrification in residential and commercial settings. In global and globalizing cities, a new geography of centrality and marginality emerges. Increases in the marginalization of the poor and polarization of city space are associated with increased entry of unskilled and semiskilled workers, particularly women,[4] to the extent that global cities attract more poor people than they can handle and more capital than they can absorb. Thus, these cities often contain shadow economies that are difficult to measure in traditional terms.[5]

Since the 1980s, Mumbai has undergone an economic transformation in which capital shifted from manufacturing to the service and finance sectors and jobs shifted from the formal to the informal labor market.[6] This shift from Fordism to flexible accumulation was accompanied by significant spatial changes. Beginning in the mid-1990s, central Mumbai witnessed a large-scale outmigration of ex–textile workers and slum dwellers to northern Mumbai and the outlying suburbs as the city center became a financial and entertainment center.[7] Manufacturing has been relocated to the hinterlands, where production takes place in small-scale units with a cheap, flexible labor force working on temporary contracts. Financial and producer services, real estate, commerce, and entertainment have emerged as the leading sectors of Mumbai's economy. During the later 1990s, the state implemented proactive policies to make the city a significant center for finance, services, and the TNC (Transnational Corporation) headquarters at the cost of industrial decline in many areas. The poor were pushed from old industrial cores to the outskirts, and ghettoized in peripheral slums.[8]

An additional important change connected to globalization has been the development of Mumbai's underworld. The shadow economy was crucial in shaping the city's transition from Fordist to post-Fordist space, in terms of both disciplining ex-workers' resistance to moving and mediating real estate conflicts between developers.[9] The underworld crime sector includes politicians (with muscle power and money to secure electoral gains) and the construction industry (who use violent tactics to secure land deals and facilitate evictions).[10] The underworld is also linked to Mumbai's Bollywood entertainment industry, which largely runs on illicit funding, so film financing has been associated with "speculation, solicitation, violence and risk, with key players being men."[11]

Mumbai's shadow economy is thus shaped by the unregulated housing market and the entertainment industry. Cash flows from the parallel economy are "everywhere in Bombay's [Mumbai's] 'business' world, in huge rumored payments to government officials or businessmen to get things done, and equally in the daily small-scale traffic in black market film tickets, smuggled foreign goods, numbers racket payments, police protection payments, wage payments to manual labor, and so on."[12]

Although global cities in general may experience similar processes of economic and spatial change, scholars note that as cities such as Mumbai are incorporated into the global economy, they exhibit more diversity and fragmentation than homogeneity, owing to the contradictory relationship between the global economy and local resources and culture.[13] Mumbai's globalization resulted in "decosmopolitization," large-scale dispossession of the poor (in particular, former mill workers and poor city dwellers), and glaring urban inequalities, with local urban development policy since the 1990s increasingly focused on erasing poor and marginalized people from the city center.[14]

Space and Sexual Geographies

Though most of the literature on global cities and urban transformation focuses on class dispossession, feminist scholars have also connected these topics to sexuality and gender. In recent years, feminists have examined postindustrial cities from the vantage point of sexual commerce to understand the relationship between intimate labor and changes in the political economy.[15] For example, Elizabeth Bernstein examines how gentrification in postindustrial cities moved sexual commerce indoors by penalizing visible forms of sexual labor (e.g., street walking). She argues that in postindustrial cities such as San Francisco and Amsterdam, "vice" is not eradicated; rather, the remapping of boundaries has enabled the proliferation of wealthier establishments that profit from sexual commerce.

Bernstein's insights into how postindustrial economies inaugurate new forms of sexual labor may be instructive in accounting for the proliferation of dance bars in Mumbai since the 1990s.[16] The rise of dance bars as a cultural space was tied to changes in the economic landscape. Their number increased rapidly along with the growth of neoliberalism in India:

from twenty-four bars in 1985–86 to twenty-five hundred bars employing around seventy-five thousand bar dancers in 2005. The dance bar phenomenon, which began in southern and central Mumbai, spread to the western and central suburbs, satellite towns, and smaller towns in the state of Maharashtra.[17]

William Mazzarella argues that although the dance bar phenomenon can be viewed as a product of globalization insofar as the bars invoke a postliberalization Indian consumerist erotic, they do not sit comfortably with globalization: "Neither reassuringly world-class nor plausibly traditional, the dance bars rubbed uncomfortably against the blend of cultural essentialism and global aspirations."[18] He argues that dance bars are neither strictly "traditional" nor fashionably "cosmopolitan" because they inaugurate a new form of cultural space by combining popular Bollywood dancing with vernacular folk forms.

Dance bars are neither strictly public nor strictly private. They are indoor spaces, yet their accessibility marks them as public in contrast to three-star hotels and nightclubs that restrict access. The bars are accessible to all classes of male customers seeking pleasure and entertainment. Here, men who may not normally have the cultural and bodily capital necessary for courtship can use their money to gain the attention of beautiful women. Because the bars cater to a male clientele from diverse socioeconomic backgrounds, their association with lumpen and lascivious masculinities mark the bar space as seedy and shadowy.[19]

Dance bars offered a space where young women from marginalized socioeconomic backgrounds—whose only chance for survival are low-paid jobs in the informal sector—could pursue upward mobility and immediate financial independence. A survey by the Forum against the Oppression of Women (FAOW) reported that nearly 46 percent of the sample of five hundred women who worked as bar dancers had no formal education, and only 3 percent were educated at the higher secondary level or above.[20] The vast majority had not been trained in any skill aside from dancing (86.4 percent), and most were supporting dependents (84 percent).[21] Nearly 42 percent came from communities where women were the main breadwinners of the family, through sex work or dancing.[22] Some of the women had worked in other jobs before becoming bar dancers, including domestic work, rag picking, and other informal sector jobs; they made more money in a day as bar dancers than they could make in a month in other low-skill jobs.

Bar dancers are a visible link to the displacement and aspirations created by neoliberal globalization. It is reported that most women working as bar dancers were daughters of former mill workers whose livelihoods disappeared when the mills closed, and who were displaced from the city center to the peripheries where few economic opportunities exist. Women's migration to Mumbai from neighboring districts and states in search of jobs is also linked to neoliberal state policies that resulted in crop failure and the suicide of farmers.[23]

In the bars, young women perform on a central stage, where they dance to popular Bollywood and folk music to entertain an all-male audience. Customers watch the women from a distance, encouraging their favorite dancers through cash tips. Physical contact between customers and dancers is strictly prohibited, and the only time a dancer and customer have contact is when a customer waves cash at a dancer as an invitation for a tip. In addition to bar dancers, women also work as waitresses serving drinks and singers singing with a live orchestra. Although the sale of liquor provides some profit to the bar owners, the cash tips to the dancers generate the greatest revenues. Bar dancers are required to share tips with the bar owners under the arrangements of the particular bar. The FAOW survey also reports that, although the relationship between the bar dancers and owners is not egalitarian, women who work in the bars generally indicated that bars are safe spaces to work, where they do not have to deal directly with police or unruly customers. The number of dancers employed by a particular bar may range from twenty-five to sixty.[24]

Dance bars create new occupational and relational possibilities for bar dancers and their customers. Bar dancers are involved in relational and affective labor, as these bars are supposed to have inaugurated new forms of romance and courtship.[25] Even though interactions between customers and bar dancers are restricted, courtships help women maintain a steady stream of cash and gifts. These exchanges are different from other forms of sexual labor in Mumbai because of the elements of commercial flirtation, courtship, romance, and the illusion of love.[26] Maintaining sexual tension, making the customer feel attractive and desired and withholding sex are all part of the sexual labor performed by the women who work in the bars. Bar dancers are very much aware that once they have sex with their customers, the flow of gifts and money will likely diminish. Thus, the sexual labor in these transactions involves emotions and eroticism, similar to the affective and emotional labor in Filipino hostess bars in Japan described by Rhacel Parreñas.[27] The bars that proliferated in Bombay City beginning in the mid-1990s were mostly hidden because they were perceived as morally suspect. The bars suddenly became visible in the early 2000s because of reports of police corruption and harassment of bar owners and dancers, and of money flowing into bars from scams and illegal trade.

The Ban and Moral Eviction of Bar Dancers

Prior to the ban, dance bars were regulated by the state through an elaborate system of licensing related to food, liquor, and public entertainment, mostly governed through provincial law. This put the bars under the scrutiny of the state for maintaining standards of decency during dances, conforming to regulations on bar hours, and obtaining the appropriate licenses and permits. The state had the power to suspend or cancel these licenses when the bars violated regulations. In addition, the bars were regulated by the Dramatic Performance Act of 1876, the public nuisance provisions of the Bombay Police Act of 1951 (BPA), and section 294 of the Indian penal code of 1860 relating to obscenity.[28] The dances were legal and licensed by the state, but in everyday practice, regulators threatened to use obscenity and trafficking laws to shut the bars down. Thus, even before the ban, dance bars operated in a liminal space where they were regarded as potential breeding grounds for illegality. This threat, at least as much as actual illegal acts,[29] was used by the state as a pretext to close the bars in 2005.[30]

While the system of licenses and permits was in place, reports of tensions between police and bar owners abounded, starting in 1998, when the state government suddenly declared a 300 percent hike in the annual excise fee on bars. In 2004, the bar owners' association filed a petition in the Mumbai High Court seeking protection from police corruption harassment. That same year, bar dancers formed a union to negotiate work conditions in the bars.[31] In the context of this escalating tension, the state banned dancing in bars in 2005: the legislature passed an amendment to the Bombay Police Act prohibiting eating houses, permit rooms, and bars from hosting dance performances. All performance licenses were revoked, and the amendment stipulated a sentence of three months to three years of imprisonment and fines for violators.[32]

The ban on bar dancing is often attributed to a breakdown in negotiations between bar owners and the state over how much money bar owners should kick back to police and other state agents; however, it is worth noting that the amendment had unanimous support in the state legislature. The decision coincided with "moral" pressure to close bars that were purported to promote illegality, crime, and behaviors leading to familial discord. The ban was also supported by women's groups and antitrafficking groups, and a coalition of twenty-four organizations came together under the banner "Dance Bar Virodhi Manch" (Anti–Dance Bar Forum).[33] The bar dancers' union and the bar owners challenged the decision in the Mumbai High Court, supported by feminist and human rights groups in the city. The subsequent legal fight over the ban provides an important window into the ways space and class were regulated in Mumbai, where dancing in specific establishments (not dancing per se) was banned, making questions of space salient. The state justified the ban on the ground that bars were security threats because they were breeding grounds of obscenity, indecency, depravity, and immorality.

To justify the ban, state actors claimed that licenses were granted to bars that operated as entertainment centers but quickly became sleazy and dangerous. They contended that many bars operated without licenses, making dance bars difficult to regulate. Feminist scholars have critiqued the ban for moral hypocrisy and double standards. Building on these critical analyses, I use the legal debates around dance bars in Mumbai to elaborate on questions of class, space, and moral eviction as a form of dispossession in a global city. While sex and prostitution were used as a trope to raise a moral panic around the bars, anxieties over the bars were tied to perceptions of cash.

Opponents of dance bars contended that "dancers were performers with the sole objective of rousing physical lust amongst the customers present. The customers in that state are being provoked and prompted to shower the currency notes."[34] Although no current study examines cash flows in the bars, these opponents used the notion of cash spending to foment moral hysteria around the bars. In Mumbai, excessive flows of cash were associated with illegally acquired earnings and, by extension, with illegal extraction of money by bar dancers through sexual excess and provocation. This is illustrated by the following quote from the opponents' legal petition:

> These girls would dance in a peculiar manner with constant eye contact with certain customers and with such body movements so as to attract the attention of customers and entice them, so that they would be showered with currency notes by the customers. There used to be virtually a competition amongst the dancing girls to attract the attention of the customers so as to be showered with the maximum amount of currency notes. These girls were found to be using various tactics to lure customers and attract their attention. With the kind of cash money that was being generated every night after night at such places, the dance bar activity started being afflicted by various crimes and became pick up joints for prostitution by the bar girls.[35]

As the quote reveals, cash flow in the bars required sexual innuendoes, seduction, and sexually charged exchanges between bar dancers and their customers. Even though male customers consumed alcohol in these establishments in the company of other men, which might induce competition among them, dancers were held responsible for the extraction of cash in the bars. Opponents argued that the cash flow in the form of tips made the bars seedy, discrediting bar dancing as a legitimate form of entertainment. The state went so far as to argue that, rather than legitimate entertainment, dancing was a form of extortion due to the flow of tips.

The state law banned all forms of dance (obscene or otherwise) in the bars, but exempted five-star and three-star hotels and elite clubs where only "obscene" dance can be regulated. A justification for this exemption was the use of cash; state actors argued that the flow of cash tips set dance bars apart as a separate class of establishment. Unlike the dance bars, which could be patronized by any male member of the "public," five-star hotels and clubs served "responsible people who are conscious of social commitments and obligations."[36] This suggested that morally acceptable entertainment was sought in a more discreet manner than in the bars, and hidden forms of spending cash through club memberships were perceived as less vulgar than throwing cash tips. The state further contended that people visiting hotels and high-end establishments were on a different social footing than people visiting dance bars, and that such establishments have to also meet greater degrees of scrutiny from the state to gain that status in the first place.

Another rationale the state deployed to keep the class divide was that dancing is a profession and bar dancing is not a profession. The state government argued that in three-star and five-star hotels the dancers are training in classical Indian and Western dance traditions, and hence dance is a profession of choice for them; whereas for women dancing in the dance bars, it is not a profession of choice but a necessity to earn a livelihood.[37] The government further argued that their economic and social vulnerability pushes them into the dangerous space of the bars: "[The] overwhelming number of dancers are illiterate, poverty stricken women of very tender age who are driven to dance in bars. There is no professional skill involved and hence they can seek employment elsewhere."[38]

The state's contention that bars were dangerous and excessive spaces aligned with popular representations of dance bars.[39] The first film made on the theme of bar dancing, *Chandini Bar*, hyperbolizes the worship of cash in the bars by depicting the most popular bar dancer as adorned by a garland of cash provided by the management.[40] By wearing cash on her person, the dancer performs a fetish that makes cash the most powerful thing in the bar. Displaying the vulgarity and obscenity of cash on a woman's body discursively links her body to morally suspect cash. Cash is thus treated as "powerful in the extreme."[41] Arjun Appadurai argues that cash is a central "signature of the visible" in Mumbai.[42] An excess of cash makes visible its unproductive, illegal, and shadow nature. Showering cash invokes the specter of excess cash that is wasted, unproductive, and capable of making people commit crimes, including prostitution. These representations were also present in the media rumors in 2002 that the perpetrator of a major scam spent an exorbitant amount of cash on bar dancers in a single evening—rumors that reinforced the image of dance bars as dens of criminality.[43]

The fact that other forms of female labor in the bars such as waitressing and singing were not banned indicates the centrality of dancing to the economy of the bars. Banning dancing allowed the state to ban the visual spectacle and the exchange of cash, which the state had begun to lose control over as bar owners and dancers challenged extra-legal forms of control and police corruption.

The state justified the exemption of high-end enterprises from the ban as necessary to promote tourism, consonant with federal and provincial tourist policies. This indicates a tension between the need to retain Mumbai's status as an entertainment destination to attract global finance and tourism and the need to banish forms of entertainment that were not palatable to capital, as the superfluous nature of cash can threaten capital's very existence. Thus, for the state, the bars were connected to all possible social ills, as demonstrated by the following quote from the state's position in the court: "The Institutionalized activity (bar dancing) was having ill effects on society and in particular on safety, public health, crimes traceable to material welfare, disruption of cultural patterns, fostering of prostitution, infiltration of crime, problems of family life of customers and their dependents and self-abasement apart from the degradation of the women themselves."[44] It is also instructive to note that the ban occurred at the time that Mumbai was facing a potential decline because of the collapse of the real estate market, the breakdown of law and order in the city, and increases in ethnic violence.[45] Dance bars—as sites for the production of disorder and crime—were held partly responsible for this decline; as the quote above shows, the bars were considered places where all forms of criminal debasement converged. The ban also coincided with reduced global investment in Mumbai, and the moral panic surrounding bar dancers occurred in a context of anxiety over capital flight. By situating the growth of dance bars and the implementation of the ban in relation to the broader economic and political conditions of Bombay as a global city, we can better understand how multiple moral projects converged to produce hysteria around bar dancing and avoid treating it as merely a case of conservative concern with sexual morality.[46]

Challenging the Eviction:
Bar Dancers Protest Moral and Material Dispossession

Accounts by bar dancers after the ban was imposed defied popular representations of hypersexualized women who used seduction to extract money from male customers. In their public testimonies, bar dancers presented themselves as impoverished wives, daughters, and sisters who were the primary bread-winners for their families.[47] Their earnings were far less than the large sums of cash rumored to be exchanged in the bars, and their stories often reflected dispossession. Most of these women were unable to translate their tips into capital because they lacked access to banks and other institutions that would let them invest their cash in assets. The FAOW survey found that after the bars closed, most of the former dancers were unable to find employment. They survived off their savings and reduced expenses by stopping their children's education, moving from secure housing to cramped abodes, and compromising on household purchases and health care. These reports of impoverishment challenge the narrative of excess in the bars, instead illustrating women's moral and material dispossession in a global city.[48]

Bar dancers challenged this moral and material dispossession and claimed their right to earn a livelihood. They argued that cash in the bars did not translate into sex; tips were remuneration for their hard work of dancing and entertaining customers. They challenged the sexual double standard that made working-class women targets of moral policing while holding elites to a different standard. In doing so, they reclaimed morality as based in hard work rather than as a standard of behavior imposed by elites. The women emphasized their economic dispossession as the primary motivation for their entry into the bars, arguing that if a moral failing existed, it was on the part of the state, which failed to provide economic opportunities for its citizenry. This emphasis on economic dispossession is starkly evident in the testimony of one bar dancer at a public hearing organized soon after the ban:[49]

> Since we are poor, anyone can say anything about us [Humm garib hai too joobhi kyoi booltha hi chall jaatha hi]. . . . I came to this line of work because my parents died and left me with very young siblings. How do I pay for their school fees and how do I take care of them? Because of my family's poverty, I came into this line of work. I am dancing in the bars so that my sisters' and brothers' lives are not ruined; my life is ruined. . . . I don't want that to happen to them. You tell me what I should do. Should I start working on the streets? No one has an answer to that.

Bar dancers saw themselves as victims of a sexual double standard—not of trafficking as claimed by the state—that treated them as morally suspect under the good woman/bad woman binary. These women reversed the morality argument by arguing that for poor women, *izzat* (honor) is achieved through their capacity to feed their families. Bar dancers frequently referred to their income as *izzat kaa kammayi* (hard-earned money), in which *izzat* refers to both hard work and the honor generated by that work. One dancer stated, "Mujee izaath kee jindighi jeena hi, muujhe ohee deedoo. Mujee ohee kaam attaha hi aur kyooi kaam nahi aataa" (I want to live an honorable life, give me back that life. The only way I can make a living is through dance bars, and I don't know any other work).

Bar dancers used their lack of education and other work skills to explain their exclusion from the labor market such that they were eligible only for low-wage jobs under exploitative conditions that would not provide class mobility for them and their families. Lacking educational and cultural capital, these women used their "bodily capital" to pursue a livelihood that would enable their families' survival. While outsiders critiqued the moral value of bar dancing, bar dancers raised voices of protest to argue that honorable women kept their families alive during hard times instead of allowing them to suffer poverty and deprivation.[50]

The voices of bar dancers as mothers, sisters, and daughters disrupted the allegation by supporters of the ban that bar dancing disrupted familial order. These women contended that their right to take care of their families had been violated when they were evicted from the bars. Another bar dancer at the same public hearing testified, "I want to send my kids to a good school. If the kids don't have a good education, I am not sure what future will they have. . . . If you take our livelihood away from us, the government is responsible for the ruin of our future generation." In registering their complaints against the state, former dancers asked, "Will the government [*sarkar*] feed us and our families? Would R. R. Patil [deputy chief minister of the state and the chief architect of the ban] come and feed us or pay the school fee?" These questions not only indicate the immediate consequences of the bar dancers' eviction for their families but also point to the broader dispossession faced by poor communities.

The state's repossession of women's bodies to secure "law and order" in Mumbai was scoffed at by bar dancers and supporters as an example of the ironies in the state's "benevolent paternalism." While the state claimed to protect women from exploitation through the ban, it in fact pushed them into situations that were far more exploitative by sending seventy-five thousand jobless women into the streets. The fact that the state did not consider any alternative forms of employment for dancers before implementing the ban made its claims morally suspect. Bar dancers believed that the state was more concerned with pursuing corrupt policies than with protecting their livelihoods. Though the state claimed that it would rehabilitate dancers after the ban went into effect, this promise was soon revealed as false. The judges highlighted these claims in their remarks:

> It should be pointed out that the statement of the State cannot be relied upon as in the past. The government, despite making promises to rehabilitate the over 1.25 lakh mill workers rendered jobless due to closure of mills, did not do so. It should also be noted that in respect to the devastating earthquake in Latur and the deluge in Mumbai on 27th July, 2005, no effective rehabilitation measures were taken. In addition, with respect to all major projects undertaken by the government, there never has been any effective rehabilitation.[51]

Another way that dancers resisted the state was by demonstrating the moral hypocrisy of evicting women from the dance bars while exempting elite and five-star hotels from the ban. They argued that dancers were penalized for emulating Bollywood actresses, the cultural and social elites of Mumbai, in a clear double standard. In the public hearing above, one dancer argued, "Why should dance be legal in three-star and five-star hotels? Why should there be a different rule of law for the president [elites] and the ordinary people? *If three-star and five-star hotels are to be there, then bar dancers should be there too*, because common man [*jaanatha*] are the ones who elect the president and prime minister. And if *jaanatha* are wronged, then *jaanatha* will raise their voice in protest" (emphasis mine). In critiques like these, dancers claimed that the state was hypocritical for holding different classes to different standards. Many bar dancers argued that they were punished for emulating the popular Bollywood music and dances that were approved by the state's censor board. They claimed that the ban destroyed not only their livelihood but also a major form of entertainment for the working classes and subalterns. By banning dance bars without banning dancing in more expensive establishments, the state helped establish these spaces as subaltern spaces for entertainment that were denied to the subaltern classes. In conflicts like these that centered on issues of space, sexuality, and class in a global city, new class politics and identities emerge, bringing new subaltern spaces and subjects into the spatio-cultural politics of the city.

By highlighting their class marginality, bar dancers and their supporters challenged their eviction from the bars. Dancers confronted multiple layers of dispossession prior to this eviction. As daughters of mill workers, many of these women came from families that were displaced as Mumbai shifted to a post-Fordist economy, and crop failures and suicides among farmers in neighboring districts pushed women to Mumbai in search of work. Some women lived in communities where dancing and sex work were the main source of income, so the ban dispossessed not only individual families but entire communities.

The Mumbai High Court took serious note of these issues and declared the ban unconstitutional in April 2006. In striking down the ban, the judges stated, "There cannot be different standards of morality for the affluent and the rich for availing the means of entertainment in the exempted establishments and any common person who can afford to visit place of entertainment within their reach."[52] While this was a major victory for the bar dancers, whose appeal to their dignity and livelihood was affirmed by the higher court, the state government decided to take the case to the Indian Supreme Court for further consideration. The ban was in effect while the case was pending the Supreme Court, where it remained until July 2013.

Postban Eviction: Visibility without Power

The legal struggle over the ban made bar dancers hypervisible in Mumbai, where they had previously been hidden. This hypervisibility without power made their lives even more precarious, subjecting them to media and police surveillance and forcible eviction from their residences. After the ban was implemented, the media presented stories about the spillover of crime and immorality "from the bars into the streets." The sudden visibility of seventy-five thousand unemployed bar dancers in Mumbai implied a "moral danger" to the city, as described in the following newspaper report:

> Welcome to the sleazy world of Mumbai's bars. Although the Maharashtra government had banned "immoral" activities in its bars since 2005, the girls are back in action. . . . At the Mira Road bar, you can have a beer even as a girl fondles you in your seat. Girls . . . make a living out of giving men a quick erection and demolishing it even quicker. R. R. Patil, the home minister of Maharashtra, had, against much opposition, banned the "dance bars." *But the girls have not gone away.* (emphasis added)[53]

Referring to the bar dancers as "girls" is one method used by the media to undermine their labor claims and hypersexualize their work. The phrase "the girls have not gone away" inscribed the women as migrants who are alien to the city. Describing bar dancers as offering cheap sex legitimized the claim that dancing was disguised prostitution. Many concluded that dancers would be ready to take up sex work as soon as they lost their jobs in the bars. After the ban, police harassment in dance bars reportedly increased, with raids and undercover sting operations conducted with the help of local television channels.

In addition to being evicted from their spaces of work, bar dancers also faced threats of eviction from their homes. These evictions were justified as a way of cleansing residential neighborhoods of "prostitution." The eviction of dancers from the bars gave right-wing groups "moral" justification to evict them from their homes. These groups argued that the dancers' complete eviction from the city was necessary to keep the city safe from "moral ruin and deprivation." Reports of forcible eviction were not uncommon. In July 2007, the *Indian Express* reported the forcible mass eviction of bar dancers from the Thane District of Mumbai, where the Hindu right wing has a foothold. They reported that around one thousand bar dancers left the area after a Hindu right-wing group gave them an ultimatum, and those who resisted were physically assaulted.[54] A public interest litigation was filed in the Mumbai High Court to stop the evictions, but the state government failed to take any action to provide protection to the bar dancers. The state conveniently elided its responsibility by arguing that there were no official complaints of evictions and threats, silently sanctioning the extrajudicial eviction of bar dancers from the city.

It is in this context of the growing opposition to the dance bars that the Indian Supreme Court delivered its judgment on the case in July 2013. The higher court upheld the verdict of the Mumbai High Court and declared the ban unconstitutional, as it promotes class discrimination and class bias. The judges emphatically argued that the state cannot condemn dancing just because it is performed by dancers hailing from socially and economically marginalized groups: "The judicial conscience of this Court would not give credence to a notion that high morals and decent behavior is the exclusive domain of the upper classes; whereas vulgarity and depravity is limited to the lower classes. Any classification made on the basis of such invidious presumptions is liable to be struck down being wholly unconstitutional."[55]

In addition to objecting to class bias, they also took exception to the gender stereotyping and narrow understanding of women's dignity that went into the making of the ban. The patriarchal and patronizing conceptions of honor, morality, and sexual chastity, the court argued, goes against the Indian constitutional values of equality, respect, diversity, and autonomy of women: "Gender stereotyping is also palpable in the solutions crafted by the legislature. The impugned statute does not affect a man's freedom to visit bars and consume alcohol, but restricts a woman from choosing the occupation of dancing in the same bars. The legislation, patronizingly, seeks to 'protect' women by constraining their liberty, autonomy, and self-determination."[56] While installing the bar dancer's right to a livelihood, the judges stated that instead of putting women out of work the state should focus its attention on securing equal rights of women. The judges further directed the state government to focus its energy on proper regulation of the bars instead of subjecting women dancers to the ban.[57]

More importantly to our conversation, the Supreme Court also directed the state to consider the recommendations of the committee that was constituted by the state government in 2004 for better regulation of the bars. One of the major recommendations of the committee was to reroute the cash flow through the management of the bars and ban the practice of "showering money" on the dancers. By recommending the regulation of tips and visible cash flow, the Supreme Court in a way tackled the popular anxiety around "unproductive cash."[58] It needs to be seen how these recommendations might shape the labor practices and the discursive space of the bars as spaces of popular entertainments and even as important markers of Mumbai's nightlife.

Even with these two major legal victories in the higher courts, there is still lingering uncertainty as to when the state government will lift the ban. R. R. Patil, the architect of the ban, is still firm on his stand on the bars, and there are also indications that the state is going to file a review petition in the Supreme Court for further reconsideration. In addition, the state is also finding other ways to continue the ban. This includes restricting the number of new performance licenses, which are mandatory for dance bars; since most bars have stayed shut for many years, their licenses have expired, and they have to apply for new ones. The other option the government is considering is to raise the license fee to a level where most dance bar owners find it impossible to sustain their business from dance performances in the bars.[59] There are also suggestions to revoke the performance licenses from the three-star and five-star hotels so that the government wouldn't be criticized for their class bias. With members of the state legislature, regardless of their party affiliation, staunchly opposing the ban, the dance bars continue to be contentious.

Conclusion

The debates around dance bars help us to understand how practices of intimacy are differentiated and regulated in a global city. Dance bars became contentious, as they are seen as promoting disruptive and unproductive intimacies and perceived as a "threat" not only to the family but also to the security of the city. I used the legal and political struggle around dance bars to show how women's intimate labor becomes the focus of arguments not only about morality but also about the changes and challenges of a globalized economy in a global city.

The dance bars are tied to Mumbai's emergence as a global city. I argue that central to the moral hysteria around bar dancing is the perception that bars are places where cash is hypervisible, with men throwing cash on the dancers. The explicit flow of cash as tips in the bars raises anxieties around the ties between superfluous cash and illegal and shadow economies, making the bars suspect as sites for production of illicit cash. The panic over bar dancing therefore illustrates the uneasy and contradictory relationships between unregulated and "unproductive" cash and "productive" capital. The attribution of the unregulated and unproductive use of cash by dangerous subjects in shadow economies was transposed onto bar dancers, whose sexuality came to be seen as dangerous.

The control of space involved in making Mumbai into a global city created conditions of material and moral dispossession for poor and working-class women. For a brief period, bar owners and bar dancers were able to find livelihoods in the peripheral and shadow spaces that were opened as Mumbai transformed from an industrial to a postindustrial economy. Unfortunately, their livelihoods were soon undercut as they came to be seen as a moral threat to the city. The state played a crucial role in promoting their eviction from the bars.

Dispossession involved complex social reactions that included increasingly conservative articulations of women's sexualities. Global capital interacted with local structures and cultural institutions in complex ways that exacerbated the dispossession of poor and working-class women. Even though bar dancers and bar owners have won two major victories in the higher courts, opposition to dance bars is also growing. This opposition needs to be further examined. In this article, I focused primarily on the state's opposition and its role in imposing the ban; it is not my contention that this opposition is confined only to the state or political parties. In fact, the opposition to the ban also seems to be spreading in middle-class and lower-middle-class neighborhoods as the bars spread from the city center to the suburbs and rural districts. In particular, this opposition is also reported to be coming from those neighborhoods where people are already pushed into the city's margins because of gentrification and skyrocketing real estate prices. The moral panic around sexuality is gaining prominence precisely at the moment when these massive social, spatial, and economic transformations are taking place. The ban should therefore be understood as the convergence of multiple "moral" projects resulting in the eviction of bar dancers from bars and ultimately from the city. Through future empirical work that maps bars in different neighborhoods of Mumbai with plans for the city's development, we can better understand the production of the moral hysteria around the bars.

Furthermore, the ban and the debates surrounding it also help us to ask whether this opposition to the dance bars is also a response against commodification of life in a global city, where real estate and the entertainment industry play a big role in shaping the fate of middle-class and working-class people, and whether, in the push against the widespread commodification of life, dance bars became more "easy," "immediate," and perceivable "threats" and "'targets." Even if this is a misplaced anxiety, the reactions to the dance bars also suggest a rise of conservative voices for which the protection of body and sexuality become the last frontiers to restore "culture," "tradition," and "dignity" in a climate of extreme commodification.

As new forms of intimate labor emerge in a global city, new identities and identifications also emerge. In Mumbai, bar dancers challenged their material and moral dispossession by forming alliances with bar owners and feminist groups. By highlighting their class dispossession and the spatial hierarchies in the city, they were able to garner a positive judicial response. "From the bars to the streets" represents both the precariousness of dispossessed groups and their ability to resist their dispossession.[60] Although the streets have been depicted as places for further moral depravity, they are also symbolic of protest and political subject formation for marginalized groups. Streets are precarious spaces that expose women to danger and violence, but only by taking to streets through protests and public forums could bar dancers resist oppressive moral and spatial hierarchies and refuse to become disposable. This does not mean that bar dancers were able to speak for other groups oppressed by these moral hierarchies; in fact, they distanced themselves from prostitution and any association between their labor and sex. If the discursive struggles around the bars tell us something, it is that alliances on the streets are fraught with contradictions and moral dilemmas. The work of confronting moral and material dispossession should not fall solely on the backs of bar dancers, as they are also the by-product of global economies and neoliberal state policies that require challenges from broader coalitions.

Notes

I would like to thank Rhacel Parreñas, Hung Cam Thai, Rachel Silvery, and the participants of the "Intimate Industries in Asia Workshop" for their comments and valuable feedback on this project. Special thanks to Judy Han for her comments as a discussant of the paper and to Hae Yeon Choo, Sharmila Rudrappa, and Jyoti Puri for offering feedback on the manuscript. My thanks also go to the two anonymous reviewers whose comments have been very critical in revising the manuscript.

1. I use Eileen Boris and Rhacel Parreñas's definition of *intimate labor* as "the work of forging, sustaining, nurturing, maintaining and managing interpersonal ties, as well as the work of tending to the sexual, bodily, health, hygiene, and care needs of individuals." Eileen Boris and Rhacel Parreñas, eds., *Intimate Labors: Cultures, Technologies, and the Politics of Care* (Stanford, CA: Stanford University Press, 2010).

2. To understand the moral dispossession triggered by the ban, I examined media and popular representations of dance bars, as well as legal documents, in particular the High Court and Supreme Court judgments, studies and reports on dance bars, and newspaper databases. My data also include the online archives of a public forum organized by Mumbai-based groups Majlis, Pukar (Gender and Space Unit), and Point of View on August 19, 2005. These testimonials were retrieved from Public Access Digital Media Archive, pad.ma/BT/info.

3. Saskia Sassen, *The Global City: New York, London, Tokyo* (Princeton, NJ: Princeton University Press, 2001). While New York, London, and Tokyo are usually listed as the global centers for finance and business, this geography now includes cities such as São Paulo, Buenos Aires, Mumbai, Bangkok, Taipei, and Mexico City. See also Saskia Sassen, "The Global City: Strategic Site/New Frontier," in *Democracy, Citizenship, and the Global City*, ed. Engin F. Isin (London: Routledge, 2000).

4. Swapna Banerjee-Guha, "Shifting Cities: Urban Restructuring in Mumbai," *Economic and Political Weekly*, January 12, 2002, 121–28.

5. Arjun Appadurai, "Spectral Housing and Urban Cleansing: Notes on Millennial Mumbai," *Public Culture* 12, no. 3 (2002): 627–65, 628.

6. Rashmi Varma, "Provincializing the Global City: From Bombay to Mumbai," *Social Text* 81, no. 4 (2004): 65–89.

7. Judy Whitehead and Nitin More, "Revanchism in Mumbai? Political Economy of Rent Gaps and Urban Restructuring in a Global City," *Economic and Political Weekly*, June 23–29, 2007, 2432.

8. Banerjee-Guha, "Urban Restructuring in Mumbai."

9. According to Whitehead and More in "Revanchism in Mumbai?," Mumbai's high real estate prices were due not only to economic liberalization and the influx of foreign capital but also to the concentration of private land in the hands of only nine developers and trusts. This concentration encourages rent seeking and forcible encroachment, often with underworld

involvement (2431). For further discussion of Mumbai's underworld and its role in facilitating the transition to a post-Fordist economy, see Appadurai, "Spectral Housing"; and Varma, "Provincializing the Global City."

10. Varma, "Provincializing the Global City," 122.

11. Ibid., 80.

12. Appadurai, "Spectral Housing," 633.

13. Critics have argued that Mumbai's rise as a global city has been accompanied by the "decosmopolitanization" through communal politics and provincial identification, with a pinnacle of "ethnicization" of the citizenry in late 1992 and early 1993. As Arjun Appadurai stated, "the decades of this gradual ethnicizing of India's most cosmopolitan city were also the decades when Bombay became a site of crucial changes in trade, finance, and industrial manufacture." Mumbai's emergence as a global city is characterized by the rise of speculative and financial capital, migration, communitarian politics, communal violence, and Hindu right-wing conservative forces.

14. Banerjee-Guha, "Urban Restructuring in Mumbai."

15. Elizabeth Bernstein, *Temporarily Yours: Intimacy, Authenticity, and the Commerce of Sex* (Chicago: University of Chicago Press, 2007); Barbara G. Brents and Kathryn Hausbeck, "Marketing Sex: U.S. Legal Brothels and Late Capitalist Consumption," *Sexualities* 10 (2001): 425–39.

16. Prabha Kotiswaran has argued that neoliberalism is not a useful framework for understanding dance bars because it assumes a coherent national logic. Prabha Kotiswaran, "Labours in Vice or Virtue? Neo-liberalism, Sexual Commerce, and the Case of Indian Bar Dancing," *Journal of Law and Society* 37, no. 1 (2010): 105–22. I agree that there is no coherent national logic, but I contend that it is important to contextualize the emergence of bar dancing within the neoliberal state policies in particular. I use David Harvey's understanding of neoliberalism as a political and economic practice that pegs human well-being to individual entrepreneurial freedoms and skills in an institutional framework characterized by strong private property rights, free market, free trade, and limited state intervention. Thus, even though there may not be a coherent national logic, the neoliberal philosophy has governed Indian state policy since the mid-1990s, when India began to liberalize its economy. David Harvey, *The New Imperialism* (Oxford: Oxford University Press, 2000).

17. Flavia Agnes, "State Control and Sexual Morality: The Case of the Bar Dancers of Mumbai," in *Enculturing Law: New Agendas for Legal Pedagogy*, ed. Matthew John and Sitharamam Kakarala (New Delhi: Tulika Books, 2007), 158–75.

18. William Mazzarella, "'A Different Kind of Flesh': Public Obscenity, Globalization, and the Mumbai Dance Bar Ban," in *Explode Softly: Sexualities in Contemporary Indian Visual Cultures*, ed. Brinda Bose and Shilpa Phadke (Seagull, forthcoming).

19. This is succinctly captured by Sonia Faleiro: "Although their persuasions carried, the clerks and career alcoholics, tradesmen and twenty somethings who walked in were of modest sta-

tus, expectations and income. They knew to go only where they were welcome. In a dance bar, their money could buy the attention of a beautiful woman. And unlike a high-end South Bombay nightclub, it was democratic. There was no entry fee, no sartorial standard, no pressure." Sonia Faleiro, *Beautiful Thing: Inside the Secret World of Bombay's Dance Bars* (New York: Blackcat, 2010), 42.

20. The FAOW conducted a survey of five hundred bar dancers in fifty bars, with the sample designed to identify a diverse group of women and bar types. The first survey, conducted while the state was debating the ban, focused on working conditions in the bar, labor practices, and the women's socioeconomic background. The second survey was conducted after the ban to assess its impact on bar dancers and their families. Forum against the Oppression of Women, "Feminist Contributions from the Margins: Shifting Conceptions of Work and Performance of the Bar Dancers of Mumbai," *Economic and Political Weekly*, October 30, 2010, 51.

21. The survey found that the women were supporting up to ten dependents. Although the number varied between the two FAOW surveys, it is important to note that in both cases the majority of respondents were the primary breadwinners in the family.

22. Many of the women surveyed came from caste communities where women were the main breadwinners and worked as entertainers or sex workers. For these women, bar dancing opened a space where they could earn money without necessarily engaging in sex work. The colonial and social reform movements have stigmatized women from communities where sex work is intertwined with entertainment and ritual functions by reducing their work to stigmatized and criminalized prostitution.

23. Faleiro, *Beautiful Thing*.

24. FAOW, "Feminist Contributions," 52.

25. Suketu Mehta, *Maximum City: Bombay Lost and Found* (New York: Vintage Books, 2004), 369–14.

26. It is not my contention that sex workers only exchange sex and that there is no relational or affective element to the exchange. For bar dancers, affect is the primary mode of offering their labor, because they are expected to titillate clients not through sex but through withholding it.

27. Rhacel Parreñas's work is critical in understanding the moral boundaries between the bar hostesses and the customers and the moral regimes—what constitutes appropriate and inappropriate sexual intimacy—in the hostess clubs. While Parreñas focuses on sexual morality, I build on her work to connect these questions to informal economies and the anxieties around cash economies in a global city. Rhacel Parreñas, *Illicit Flirtations: Labor, Migration, and Sex Trafficking in Tokyo* (Stanford: Stanford University Press, 2010).

28. Kotiswaran, "Labours in Vice."

29. The legislative and legal framework for regulation of prostitution in India is the Immoral Traffic Prevention Act (ITPA, 1986). The Indian statutory approach claims to balance the

views that sex work is immoral, that the sex trade is exploitative, and that sex workers need to be rescued and rehabilitated. The law does not prohibit prostitution per se, but it criminalizes a third party benefiting from prostitution (such as an individual who procures women for brothels), punishes adults over eighteen for living off the income of a prostitute, and punishes any person who solicits or seduces for the purpose of prostitution or engages in prostitution in a public place.

30. Faleiro, *Beautiful Thing*, 39.

31. In August 2004, the Bharatiya Bar Girls' Union (Indian Bar Girls' Union) was formed with five thousand members. Varsha Khale, a Mumbai-based activist, was instrumental in forming the union alongside bar dancers.

32. Section 33A of the Bombay Police Act prohibits holding of dance, of any kind or type, in any eating house, permit room, or beer bar. All performance licenses issued prior to the ban were cancelled with the amendment. It also stipulates a minimum and maximum punishment and fine for violators of the act with a minimum of three months and a fine not less than 50,000 rupees (approximately US$1,000) and a maximum of three years with a fine that may extend to rupees two lakhs (approximately US$4,000). Section 33A is not applicable to three-star and five-star hotels, and their regulation falls under section 33B of the Bombay Police Act. While the dances in these hotels are also under scrutiny for obscenity, at best these licenses will be revoked from the owners of these establishments, and there is no threat of imprisonment. The fact that section 33A prohibits all forms of dancing (obscene or not) makes this act very contestable.

33. FAOW, "Feminist Contributions," 49.

34. *Indian Hotel & Restaurants Association (AHRA) v. State of Maharashtra*, Bombay *Cases Reporter* (2006), 735. (Hereafter cited as AHRA.)

35. AHRA, 763.

36. AHRA, 736.

37. AHRA, 774.

38. AHRA, 749.

39. Jyoti Puri offers a productive way of thinking of bars as spaces of excess and extraction. It is precisely because of the ambiguous nature of the exchange between the dancer and the customer that this exchange is unsettling for the state. The fact that the dance bars became targets, rather than other forms of sexual labor (such as prostitution), illustrates the specific moral anxieties the bars invoked. Jyoti Puri, "States' Sexualities: Theorizing Sexuality, Gender and Governance," in *Handbook of Feminist Theory*, ed. Ania Plomien et al. (New York: Sage, forthcoming), on file with author.

40. *Chandni Bar*, directed by Madhur Bhandarkar, September 28, 2001.

41. Appadurai, "Spectral Housing," 634.

42. Ibid.

43. The Telgi scam of 2002, which involved counterfeit stamps, is often referred to as the

mother of all scams. It was brought to light when perpetrator Abdul Karim Telgi spent exorbitant sums on bar dancers. The investigation into his dealings showed that he spent approximately 2.98 crores (US$450,000) in dance bars. While it is alleged that he spent excessive amounts of money on one particular dancer, there is no way to know whether this is true. The scam shaped the public imagination of bar dancing and bar dancers such that even though most dancers take home only modest earnings, bar dancing became a symbol of excess. The newspapers famously reported that Karim spent 95 lakhs (US$143,000) in one night. See "Telgi's Rs 93-Lakh Gift to Bar Girl," *Times of India*, February 11, 2004, articles .timesofindia.indiatimes.com/2004-02-11/india/28337948_1_bar-girl-bar-owner-dance-bars. In another case, it was reported that a young man named Aman Mishra spent over twenty lakh rupees (US$40,000) on a bar dancer he was infatuated with. Faleiro, *Beautiful Thing*, 51.

44. AHRA, 771.

45. Achin Vanaik, "Rendezvous at Mumbai," *New Left Review* 26 (March–April 2004): 58.

46. It is important to note that the architect of the ban was not the Hindu right wing but the Congress party, which is known for its neoliberal policies.

47. The moral anxiety around working-class women's sexuality is not unique to the case of dance bars. Caitrin Lynch's work in garment factories in Sri Lanka shows how rural Sri Lankan women who entered garment industries had to dissociate themselves from their urban counterparts (*juki* girls), who are perceived as sexually promiscuous. They tailored a "new traditional" identity to be able to work in these garment industries. Here women's entry into public spaces itself is seen as morally suspect or capable of making them sexually corrupt. Bar dancers are operating in a different spatial and moral logic, in a postindustrial city, and their sexual labor is seen as dangerous and corrupting. Caitrin Lynch, *Juki Girls, Good Girls: Gender and Cultural Politics in Sri Lanka's Global Garment Industry* (Ithaca, NY: Cornell University Press, 2007).

48. As Harvey states in *The New Imperialism*, capitalism's other is continually re-created by dispossession. This dispossession can take many forms, including privatization of common lands, state withdrawal from welfare responsibilities, and dismantling of labor unions. Dispossession is also a continuing dialectic that places people "inside" the sphere of capitalism at one moment and undercuts their livelihoods at another. Accumulation through dispossession implies violence, force, and coercion.

49. Three organizations, Majlis, Pukar (Gender and Space Unit), and Point of View, organized a public hearing on the issue of bar dancing on August 19, 2005. These testimonials were retrieved from Public Access Digital Media Archive, pad.ma/BT/info.

50. It is not uncommon in India for urban squatters, landless people, refugees, and others to negotiate with the state from a position of political dependence, citing the government's obligation to look after the poor and needy. These groups make a moral appeal to the state as communities striving to build a decent social life. See Partha Chatterjee, *The Politics of*

the Governed: Reflections on Popular Politic in Most of the World (New York: Columbia University Press, 2004).

51. AHRA, 732.

52. AHRA, 266.

53. "Sex Revives Mumbai Bars," *India Today*, April 4, 2011.

54. "Court Steps in to Check Sena's Eviction of Thane Bar Girls," *Indian Express*, July 5, 2007, www
   .indianexpress.com/news/court-steps-in-to-check-sena-s-eviction-of-thane-bar-girls--------
   /203841/.

55. Civil Appeal No.2705 of 2006, 109.

56. Ibid., 54.

57. The judges directed the state to use the provisions already in place in the 1951 Bombay
   Police Act to regulate the bars; these provisions had already been framed in the interest of
   public safety and to safeguard the dignity of women. Section 33(w) of the Bombay Police
   Act also provides the licensing authority the power to suspend or cancel a license for any
   breach of the license conditions. Sufficient power is already given to these licensing authorities to regulate obscene dancing and exploitation of women. Civil Appeal No. 2705 of 2006.

58. Other recommendations of the committee are around the attire of the bar dancers, in particular, stating that they should not wear revealing clothes that will expose their bodies and
   that restrictions should be placed on dancers wearing tight and provocative clothes. In addition, recommendations were also made to install three-foot railings to separate the dancers
   from the customers. Civil Appeal No. 2705 of 2006, 123–24.

59. "Mumbai Dance Bars May Not Re-open for Months," *Economic Times*, July 17, 2013, arti-
   cles.economictimes.indiatimes.com/2013-07-17/news/40635302_1_dance-bars-maharashtra
   -cm-prithviraj-chavan-review-petition.

60. In recent remarks, the judges are quoted as saying, "We do not want them [dancers] to go
   from the bars and restaurants to the streets," and directing the Maharashtra government to
   examine banning only "obscene and objectionable" forms of dance. "Don't Want Bar Dancers to End Up on Streets: SC," *Indian Express*, September 18, 2011.

Screening Shirtless AZN Men:
The Full Frontal Power of Intimate Internet Industries

Celine Parreñas Shimizu

Introduction

Using the Internet to register one's racial identity and the particularity of one's sexual desires raises provocative questions about how one can forge an empowering identity online, especially for Asian men, whose sexualities are traditionally and widely disparaged in mainstream media.[1] Keni Styles, the first Western heterosexual male star of Asian descent in the global porn industry, counters the depiction of Asian men as asexual, passive, and undesirable through his tumblr blog project in which he recruits other Asian men to join him in achieving porn stardom. When demanding that his candidates not only pose in sexually provocative ways but also show their faces, he demonstrates a high awareness of the relationship between race, sex, and representation. For Styles's project, to show the full frontal power of the face is to participate in a racial project meant to increase the representations

positions 24:1   DOI 10.1215/10679847-3320125
Copyright 2016 by Duke University Press

of diverse Asian and Asian American male sexualities online. At the same time, Asian male sexuality is already present online in the form of gay cruising sites such as grindr, a location-based app with over 4 million subscribers in over 192 countries that helps connect men seeking sexual encounters with other men. In his new video *Look, I'm Azn!*, filmmaker and scholar Nguyen Tan Hoang gathers the ways in which Asian men use such online gay cruising sites to play with the visibility of their racial identity in relation to the sexual practices and partners they desire. But in this context, they refuse to show their faces because the visibility of their racial identity limits their sexual choices and possibilities.

In presenting their bodies and sexualities as both bound to their faces and unbound by them, these intimate Internet industry producers work to provide a better understanding of economies of pleasure across difference and inequality. By "intimate Internet industry" I refer to the online production and consumption of the body. My discussion of the intimate Internet industry focuses more on the construction of intimacy and less on the political economy of the industry. My concern is over how Asian men utilize the Internet to reconstruct images of them as intimate subjects. How do they establish themselves as subjects of pleasure who also are consumers of their racial and sexual images via the Internet? As visual brokers of subaltern intimacy, they engage racialized masculinity as it is produced and redeployed in intimate Internet industries. They do so to subvert established negative representations and defy their sexual racialization. In their use of porn and explicit imagery on the Internet, Asian male sex workers and performers, who are also consumers, combine pleasure and politics to critique the limits placed on their sexual choices and opportunities.

By evaluating the full-frontal casting call initiated by Keni Styles, the first Asian heterosexual porn star, on his LuckyAsianGuy tumblr account, and the art video *Look I'm AZN!* by Nguyen Tan Hoang, who studies the self-representational strategies of Asian men on gay cruising sites, I identify intimate representations as social interventions. I argue that here, representations address inequality at the site of intimacy. Moreover, these performances confront the images of the past with assertions of the present and their presence. These media makers do creative work that uses the Internet to build community, create new aesthetics, and articulate their desires as defiant of the norms. In revealing the limits of existing norms of beauty and desirability in representations that highlight the Asian male face and chest, their new and more inclusive point of view demands new identifications from spectators and other consumers relating to the image of Asian men. These media makers use intimate Internet industries to express their desires to be loved, to be touched, and to have sex; and in doing so, they claim public validation and space for the liberation of their wants, wishes, and lives. Ultimately, I look to Keni Styles's and Nguyen Tan Hoang's projects as more ethical alternatives to the potential of what I call the new Asian American male media empire.

I begin by describing the political economy of the intimate Internet industry as a postmodern regime of accumulation, meaning a decentered and aesthetic-driven economy.[2] In so doing, I establish it as an economy that produces multiple cultural constructions of masculinity, encompassing hegemonic and alternative forms of masculinity. Extending political theorists Michael Hardt and Antonio Negri's conceptualizations of empire and how it can be challenged, I then theorize how intimate representations can make critical social interventions. This context then allows us to delve into how both Keni Styles and Hoang Tan Nguyen harness intimate Internet industries and use the racialized and sexualized bodies of Asian and Asian American men as a site of resistance and redefinition.

Working Intimacy on the Internet in the Context of Asian/American Male Media Empire

The online video *Bananapocalypse*, released in June 2012, announces the launch of the You Offend Me You Offend My Family network (also known as YOMYOMF) on YouTube, a video-sharing site where users can disseminate and consume videos from all over the world. Comprising young, Asian American male producers, *Bananapocalypse* brings together Justin Lin, arguably the premiere Hollywood director of the millennial generation, and two of YouTube's top twenty biggest megastars, Ryan Higa and Kevin Jumba, who each possess millions of followers and over a billion views on their YouTube channels. The five-minute video is a star-studded, action-packed bromance with a racialized agenda. The video depicts strong, sexy

Asian males and humorously refutes key Asian American stereotypes. But it also reveals anxieties about queer masculinity in jokes about cavity searches and the ridiculing of a queer figure (a plump, dark-skinned Indian man in a cropped shirt and Daisy Duke shorts). We also see familiar images of sexy women in servile roles (in this case, delivering a banana that eventually sparks the titular apocalyptic fight scene) and another holding a peeled banana she is about to eat at the close of the video. This video makes clear how Internet industries of entertainment can become terrains of struggle for recognition and representation for minority communities. But in this case, it does so through a show of aggressive male power that ridicules queerness and subordinates women in the narrative. And so, in this new dawn of Internet representation, *Bananapocalypse* perpetuates an aggressive, heterosexual male authorship of Asian American problems of representation, in popular culture and beyond.

At the margins of the Internet, Asian and Asian American men working in pornography and gay cruising sites not only engage the power of Internet pornography to decenter industry representations of Asian male sexuality, but they also use online technologies to directly fulfill desires that those representations do not allow. I further define intimate Internet industries as the engagement of creative labor in the authorship and spectatorship of sexual and gendered representations of race, class, sex, and gender by Asian and Asian American men online. The significance of this engagement can be better understood within the context of Internet porn as an industry, which embodies what David Harvey would describe as a postmodern regime of accumulation as it is decentered, dispersed, based on aesthetics (and not ethics), and reliant on spectacle.[3] The size of the market is very hard to determine, and the numbers vary. The *Smithsonian Magazine* article "The Internet Is Still for Porn . . ." claims, "Some estimates put porn at 30% of all Internet traffic."[4] They juxtapose this against the *Forbes Magazine* interview "How Much of the Internet Is Actually for Porn" with neurologist and coauthor of *A Billion Wicked Thoughts (A Book and a Blog)* Ogi Ogas who describes how a more realistic number requires nuanced explanation: "In 2010, out of the million most popular (most trafficked) websites in the world, 42,337 were sex related. That's about 4% of the sites." Moreover, beginning in July 2009, for a year, "about 13% of Web searches were for erotic content."

Ogas attributes the difficulty of pinning down a number to the enormity of the web and its ever changing "dynamic."[5] Yet, even more recently, the "new porn website Paint Bottle" is quoted in the *Huffington Post* "Tech" page as describing how "porn sites get more visitors each month than Netflix, Amazon and Twitter combined." Indeed, the Paint Bottle infographic claims, "EVERYONE YOU KNOW IS WATCHING PORN," including "70% of men and 30% of women and the numbers are increasing every week."[6]

The market is primarily located in the United States, while its main industry looks out to "the rest of the world" in terms of its future growth.[7] Indeed, the web is decentering its industry production from large adult-video companies such as VIVID to individually produced porn websites by adult stars whose audiences demand more individualized content for pay, as well as sites featuring "amateur" couples who perform certain sex acts at the requests of their live, paying audiences, such as the couple featured on the ABC News show *Nightline*.[8] Porn production on the Internet disperses the center of porn production away from the typical location of California's San Fernando Valley to a proliferation of sites all over the globe. In addition, new laws that place condom restrictions on pornography practices threaten to move the industry out of its current epicenter at Los Angeles, which has seen a decline in the number of production permits for shooting pornography in recent months.[9] The political economy of this industry is changing along with the dynamics of Internet porn production in the United States and beyond. Margret Grebowicz, in her book *Why Internet Porn Matters*, argues that the "Internet fundamentally changes the social meaning of pornography by embedding it squarely in the epistemological shift from knowledge to information [that is] democratically accessible to everyone."[10] She argues that Internet porn is a unique object that "deserves particular attention from feminist and other liberationist projects" for its special ability to wrestle with issues of freedom.[11] Yet she also claims that issues of race have not necessarily transformed in the proliferation of Internet porn, which I dispute. In their self-authored representations online, Asian and Asian American men intimately disclose their anxieties, rather than mask them with a macho posturing that falls into the trap of vilifying femininity, womanhood, and queerness. In the sites I analyze here, Asian American men represent themselves, their identities, and practices in very personal and bodily terms when they attempt to enter the pornography industry or find a sexual partner online. They reveal their own hurt, rather than disparage others.

Intimate Representation as Social Intervention

In the last century, Hollywood extended the imperial reach of the United States, determining a global language of desire and beauty in its own cinematic image—and one that serves its own interests. Michael Hardt and Antonio Negri define imperialism as the "Leviathan that overarched its social domain and imposed hierarchical territorial boundaries, both to police the purity of its own identity and to exclude all that was other."[12] I extend this frame to Hollywood, which partook greatly in what Neferti Tadiar calls the "infantilization" of the third world in a "discourse . . . built up from an exchange of representations that is most evident in the media."[13] Christopher J. Jordan, in his book *Movies and the Reagan Presidency*, argues that Hollywood films spread a view that naturalized systemic poverty to a biological predisposition for laziness while heroizing individuals in an oversimplification of such issues.[14] In *Dream Factories of a Former Colony: American Fantasies, Philippine Cinema*, J. B. Capino illustrates the point: "While the former subjects of U.S. colonialism remain practically invisible in Hollywood pictures, Americans and the states have kept their place as the primary others and elsewheres in Philippine cinema."[15] Capino also points to the "bonds" formed between the "marginal national cinema and dominant global cinema," revealing the dynamic ways Filipinos and third world people recast and transform US fantasies for their own purposes—political and pleasurable.[16] Indeed, the "third cinema" movement from Latin America, Africa, and Asia responded to the imperial reach of Hollywood to craft its own logics, temporal and spatial logistics, and aesthetics as a social and national political movement.[17]

Today, Michael Hardt and Antonio Negri present the death of imperialism and the dawn of empire.[18] They define empire as the "decentered and deterritorializ[ed] apparatus of rule that progressively incorporates the entire global realm . . . [to] manage hybrid identities, flexible hierarchies, [and] plural exchanges."[19] Extending my metaphor, if Hollywood is imperialism, then we now see its twilight, as independent and Internet circuits of production diversify the archive of images circulating the globe. But, while the hierarchy of representation may seem to be decentered, social inequalities have not dissipated but continue to organize access to representation. The digital divide persists, and the new media landscape is still constituted by a constellation of authors with access to power and voice.[20] The presence of Asian Americans at the top of the list of YouTube producers and the launching of YOMYOMF, with its numerous videos since, critique existing US industry representation. However, they do so as agents of empire because of their access to technologies of representation. As such, even as minorities, they do represent a powerful entity of individual authors who influence so many. That is, despite their minority status, they wield the apparatus of representation in the new mainstream in which young people no longer watch network television but free shows online. Thus, they not only critique Hollywood, but their works are also bringing Hollywood to them. They receive success, too, for their content is ultimately emerging from a class-privileged and largely heterosexual male culture. They are markers of globalization in how they move as people, shape markets, produce cool new goods, and earn money that travels across borders. As Hardt and Negri note, in "the lessening of national sovereignty . . . the nation state has less and less power to regulate these flows and impose its authority over the economy."[21] What is more clear now is the presence of what Trinh T. Minh-ha has articulated as the ever presence of "the third world in the first, and vice versa."[22] These particular minority authors of new media represent different regimes that hold power in empire, as captured in the privileging of male subjectivity in their representation of women and the bromance among its primarily male authors.

In light of these persistent inequalities, how do we map the resistance found in new media production by Asian and Asian American men working in pornography and gay cruising sites online? That is, while they are a part of the oppressed minority, they also wield gender privilege. They typically speak for their minority communities even if their subjectivities represent the most privileged constituents. This position at the crossroads, of marginalized minoritization and of wielding industry power, helps to constitute them as part of what Hardt and Negri call the multitude—those with the potential to create counter-empire cultures and provide "alternatives within empire." Hardt and Negri argue that the "realm of production is where social inequalities are clearly revealed and, moreover, where the most effective resistances and alternatives to the power of Empire arise."[23] In comparing the work of YOMYOMF, Keni Styles, and Hoang Tan Nguyen, we can see the conflicting desires and anxieties at work in their Asian American male voices. They express political, social, economic, and sexual struggles through representations of their bodies as platforms for recognition.

Keni Styles's luckyasianguy.tumblr.com

New media forms such as Youtube, Facebook, Blogspot, Tumblr, and the websites of porn stars shift existing hierarchies of representation away from Hollywood and toward a constellation of individual uploads and websites. In the pornography industry, stars offer access to their everyday activities at home, for a fee. Well-known figures like Nina Hartley, Violet Blue, and even the ubiquitous Ron Jeremy work on blogs and maintain a rapport with their avid followers. The first Asian heterosexual porn star in the US pornography industry is Keni Styles, whose debut in 2010 generated great attention and accolades in the form of awards and nominations from Adult Video News (AVN), the Oscars of the pornography industry. As the central character in his new media sites such as luckyasianguy.com, supermanstamina. com, and luckyasianguy.tumblr.com, Styles defies the lack of representation of Asians in the pornography and Hollywood industries. Thai-born, British-bred, mixed-race, slim, and dark-skinned, Keni manages his online presence in a way that gives his fans multiple opportunities to get to know him intimately. He writes on his blog about his experiences on the sets of famous porn films, his impressions as he first meets other actors, and his thoughts in the moments leading to their performances on screen. He features photography of live encounters outside the set.

Almost single-handedly, Keni Styles is utilizing Internet pornography industries to transform the way we see Asian male sexuality. In his blogs, he addresses the distorted way we define sexuality and measure success by the size of the male penis. Instead, he asserts that we need to expand our definitions of sexuality beyond the limited measure of penile size:

The whole size issue is ridiculous. You don't fuck someone with your dick, you fuck someone with your whole body, your attitude, your presence. The moment you say, "Oh, my dick is X inches long," you've let society win the battle of thinking it matters. And it just doesn't. I'm not the biggest there is, and I'm not the smallest, but I've never measured my penis against anything than a girl's vagina. If it fits and she's happy, I'm happy.[24]

A sense of wonder and incredulity permeates his presentation on luckyasian guy.tumblr.com, which includes interviews with the women he has sex with. He expresses disbelief at the hotness of the many women he has sex with in a diversity of daily dalliances, even as he clearly demonstrates awareness of his own attractiveness by exuding a casual confidence in his poses. He showcases their beauty and frames their presence as the most unlikely of events. It is as if he says, "Me with these hot women, and I'm an Asian!" Moreover, he engages with issues of race and sexuality in his interviews with white women and black women regarding their expectations and experiences with him as an Asian man. In these, he offers alternative masculinities that decenter the pornography industry's representations of Asian men, which rarely depict them as possessing desirable and desiring sexualities.

Recently, on his tumblr site, Styles launched an "official casting call to all Asian men interested in creating impact in Adult Entertainment!" He asks provocatively, "Could you be the next lucky Asian guy?" (January 2012). With this wording he identifies his unique position as the first Asian male to achieve straight porn stardom and characterizes his work as intervening in stereotypes attributed to Asian male sexuality. Though he does not specifically name the representations his project aims to challenge, those who respond to his call do. In their auditions or comments on his tumblr account, they consistently note the reputation of lack that places Asian men in a less romantically competitive and sexually desirable role in the West. For example, an entrant or prospect named Kev lauds Keni Styles for representing Asian male sexuality: "While Asian women are considered very sexy by the general public, Asian men are usually looked down upon as being not very masculine or sexy. Caricatures . . . stand out in many women's minds." Clearly, this contextualizes Styles's efforts.

The project aims to populate the pornography industry with other Asian men. Styles invites other Asian men whom he calls "bros" to join him in the adult industry with the clear task of creating better representations that are directly linked to racial diversity in the industry: "I'm looking for Asian male models who are active in expressing their confidence and sexuality. Those willing to 'be the change' and represent a positive image of Asian men." Notable here in his criteria is the search for those Asian men who already defy the reputation of lack and inactivity through their everyday life practices. In effect, Styles wants other Asian men to show that his sexual confidence is not rare, and he wants allies in the industry in order to take on the racialization. And the casting call seeks to find those who defy and challenge, rather than buckle under, the reputation of Asian male sexual weakness. Moreover, they must demonstrate awareness of the moral panics around sexuality and the sex industry so they can deploy the full frontal power of the intimate Internet industries most effectively.

Styles is keen to identify those who are truly unready and unprepared to embrace their sexuality openly, as the adult industry requires. He weeds out those who do not want to show themselves onscreen in the audition process. One entrant writes, "Is there any way I can enter the casting without posting a picture showing my face? My dream job has always been to become a porn star however I am worried about who might see this before my career change, haha." The face has a special significance in representation and in our social relations. The face, according to Emanuel Levinas, is the site that compels responsibility.[25] Keni Styles says he is "fully committed to the success of any guys I select," and the inability and unwillingness of this man to show his face tells him the entrant is not mutually committed to that goal and thus ineligible. Here, we see that the logic of sex panic, which classifies entry into pornography as a site of shame, is not upheld. He clearly states his parameters and his priorities for making the process "transparent": "Everything will be public for all Prospects. If your entry has been posted that is the first part of pre-selection passed." He clarifies that the "first part of the process is to submit [not only your face but also] your shirtless picture accompanied with your email address that I will ensure to keep private and a short paragraph or few describing who you are, your sexuality and your motivation for responding to this casting call." Those who visit the site or are tasked with judging who will be the "next lucky Asian guy" must consider not only the face but also the chest, and the body, in its ability to speak that sexual confidence. The requirement for writing, too, shows us that the subject must also possess the ability to articulate one's philosophy in a thoughtful manner and consciously acknowledge what it means to participate in sexual representation. In a postscript to the invitation to participate in the casting call, Styles adds, "Shots of your dick and only your dick can only tell me one thing, that is all you are . . . smh." The acronym stands for "shaking my head" and indicates Keni Styles's disapproval of this limited way of thinking about one's sexuality.

Those participating in the casting call represent a diversity of young Asian American men with a range of confidence and beauty. What they share is a common demand for more representations that do justice to Asian male sexual diversity beyond what I call the straitjacketed criteria they live under. In the most recent post on February 2013, a twenty-five-year-old named Joe describes himself as "half-Asian" and states that "sometimes we get left out of both sides of the equation. Our Asian side feels like we aren't Asian enough and vise versa [sic]. I want to show that we . . . take traits from both sides and create something unique." In answering the question about who he is, his racial background emerges prominently. Joe has taken his picture with an iPhone. He stands alertly, like a young recruit, facing a mirror in his loose shorts that show a glimpse of the top of his underwear. He has closely shaven hair and a fit, hairless chest. He looks shy, as he smiles with eyes looking down. His peeking big front teeth emphasize his youthful looks. While his chest is fit, his waist widens and looks soft. He clenches his fist by his side in a kind of uncomfortable way while the other holds the iPhone up by his face. As a mixed race or *hapa* man, he identifies in his writing the crossing of borders that his racial composition embodies. Regarded separately, Asian and non-Asian parts remain discrete and insufficient. From there, he makes a link to sexuality, and one that is different. He aligns with the perception of Asians and the need "to change the view that society has [of] us . . . that we are conservative and shy, especially in the bedroom." Ultimately, he wishes for "every race [to be] represented in straight porn for males and females." His overall argument highlights the inability of the stereotype to capture the complexity of his identity, which for him is linked to a love for others, regardless of racial difference.

Jimmy James, who posts on January 2012, presents sexual relations with a diversity of ethnically different women as exciting in itself. That is, he considers himself open to the diversity of sexual excitement in the expression of each woman. In this case, interracial sex scenes, like those featuring Keni Styles, particularly show Asian men "to be empowered sexually." To show and see Asian men sexually engaged with a diversity of partners represents them in a way that should be "encouraged." This text appears below Jimmy James's photograph, as is the format of the luckyasianguy.tumblr.com site. Unlike Joe, however, someone else has taken Jimmy James's photo. The camera is placed below the subject, who then looks down on the viewer. Our vantage point is really at crotch level. We see a big bulky belt over white pants as Jimmy James slouches casually, in a kind of "urban" style. To say so is to racialize him as black or Latino. Jimmy James poses with his hands stuffed in his low-riding pants. Ornate tattoos embellish the bulk of his arms. On his chest, below his shoulder blades, two sharply pointed stars flank letters that read "So Cal," which is emblazoned like graffiti on the flat, muscular space beneath his belly button. Jimmy James's self-presentation equates sexual representation in the porn industry with masculine power that is achieved through the visual evidence of his physical engagement with a variety of women. He writes to Keni Styles twice, actually. And in the brief second letter, Jimmy James states, "We all Enjoy sex and break stereotypes I truly believe Asian men can get lucky." Jimmy James differs from Joe, who prioritizes his unique racial mix. James presents a racialized macho posturing that he identifies as an antidote to the stereotypes that prevent Asian men from getting lucky. In presenting himself as like any other person who "Enjoys" sex, he does so while posturing as urban, or black and Latino, perceiving that he perhaps may get more lucky if he aligns himself with these other forms of racialized manhood.

In the same month, another man posts a picture of himself in action. He bends to watch a woman perform fellatio in a medium-wide profile shot. Taken from below, we see the light fixture and a smoke alarm on the ceiling above them. The text essentializes his identity as a lover of sexual practice. He situates himself as a "struggling college student and like any college student totally in love with sex. I am very experimental and up for anything. . . . I am all about breaking down the stereotypes associated with asians and have proven this point to many a female." Those who simply post that they like to "fuck" are not encouraged nor do they warrant a response from Styles, who encourages "being able to confidently portray other kinds of personalities . . . to succeed as a actor or performer [sic]. Anyone can simply 'fuck lol.' Next." Styles seems to disregard entrants such as this man, who does not present an understanding of performing sexuality on screen, instead of merely loving sexual practice. Key to Styles's criteria is an acknowledgement of the power of sexual representation and not just sexual relations.

The one photograph on his site with an "Approved" mark on its header portrays a young and fit "J," aged 22. Showing off a very ripped torso, he wears black boxers and stands in a bathroom. Behind J on the left, dark clothes hang to frame the black iPhone he holds up with his hand. His other very large and muscular arm hangs casually at his right side. His body stands out against the black coats on the white walls. Behind him on the right, the room deepens with white towels and curtains hanging. The sink foregrounds the shot of J in the mirror. Unlike Joe, the first one I discuss, this photo does not look like a mug shot taken just anywhere. J's text contains four paragraphs that reveal a thoughtful consideration of Keni Styles's invitation. He begins with an argument for his selection because of his ability to deliver an excellent "screen performance." Here, J understands sex is a production, rather than something natural or authentic that can simply be captured. At the same time, he characterizes sexual practice as a demonstration of curiosity that makes his "performance on screen" "passionate." Next, he describes a "diligent" work ethic and an accomplished educational background, as well as his willingness to provide references from ex-lovers. He emphasizes the drive for learning and to "improve myself" before closing with a powerful plea not to allow stereotypes to overwhelm or set the terms for one's self-perception. Instead of feeling "inadequate" and running away from one's "unique racial qualities," to embrace oneself is to "help" others, especially men. This is the spirit of Keni Styles's solution to the problem of the lack of Asian male representation in porn or mainstream popular culture.

Keni Styles responds affirmatively to those who present a more complex understanding of sex, and the role of representation as that which constructs it. But here it is not enough; it must also come with a consciousness about sex, race, and representation as well as a desire to improve sexual relations on the ground. What we learn from Keni Styles's tumblr project is the collective wish to improve both the sexual lives of Asian men and their representation onscreen. We see that representation is a process that requires deliberate decision making; a successful performance requires not only good looks but also a philosophical and analytic approach to both sexuality and representation. For Styles, to be involved in the adult industry requires an awareness of the production of sexuality. The actors must understand sexuality (theirs in relation to others) and representation (the construction of it rather than its simple capturing of authenticity). Keni Styles uses intimate Internet industries in a number of websites to sexually represent the Asian male body as a form of racial resistance. Using a method that differs from the full frontal disclosure of the face, the video art by Hoang Tan Nguyen shows how the face limits the sexualities of Asian and Asian American men online.

Nguyen Tan Hoang's *Look I'm AZN!*

The video artist and film theorist Nguyen Tan Hoang is most known for his short video *Forever Bottom!* (1999), a four-minute classic of queer cinema. It investigates the trope of bottomhood in popular culture for gay Asian men but also celebrates it as a viable way of life and a theorization of power.[26] Rejecting the disparagement and shaming of bottomhood as a passive position in the gay male encounter, Nguyen celebrates the position as active and expressive of desire and as a form of social critique for gay Asian men. His latest video work, *Look I'm AZN!* (2012), a short structured in two parts, amasses the ways in which gay Asian men name themselves and image themselves in gay cruising websites. In four and a half minutes, we see the self-representation of gay Asian men gathered in textual and visual form as he takes their authorships and self-representations off the Internet. Both capture in different ways how gay Asian men define themselves in relation to their social interpellation as racialized and sexualized subjects. In other words, they comment on their racialization in the sexual marketplace through textual and visual creativity. They rewrite the terms that define them in popular culture in order to better express their desires. And when these individual desires are juxtaposed, the homogeneous group classifications explode. Their visual images speak volumes on how they resist the sexuality assigned to them as Asians.

The first part of the video *Look I'm AZN!* collects headers of personal ads in gay cruising sites. Nguyen begins with ads regarding GAMS (gay Asian men), then proceeds to put the names in alphabetical and numeric order. Nguyen begins with *gambit*, a compelling choice of wordplay. *Gambit* indicates risk and calculation, and in the game of chess, it shows the deliberate move of losing pawns to gain advantage when opening the game. To begin with gambit shows us that these Asian gay male subjects are also deliberating and maneuvering, using the terms assigned to them and deploying them as risky, but with an eye to gaining a very real pleasure in identifying their specific desires.

The subjects pair *GAM*, or their self-identification or naming, with other words. We see gambuddy69, GAM_POUNDER, slutbubblegam, gam2play, gam2serviceyou, gam2all, gam4all, gam4bears, gam4black, gam4cauc . . . gam4gam. The litany of text appearing and disappearing on screen, replacing each other conveniently in the same space, convincingly presents the unwieldiness of desire by and for gay Asian men. Through these word pairings, they each characterize their desire through action or preference: "gam4hardbodies, gam4head1, gam4hung, gam4love1," and the list goes on. The first name prefers certain fit bodies; the second, a specific sex act; the third, a particular size of penis, and the last looks for love for one. There are also those who cross boundaries. For example, *GAM 4 Bears* indicates "gay Asian man seeking bears," typically hairy, burly, and big men who prefer similar men. Gay Asian men are typically not bears and typically do not participate prominently in bear culture, though there surely are exceptions. There are enough that they are called pandas and considered rare. In this way, the listing explodes our typical understanding of queer and Asian desires in the marketplace.

Nguyen begins his listing of terms with *GAM*, so as to orient us to the gay Asian male reference. But from there he lists the various ways Asians identify themselves on the Internet. The first grouping is AZN, which is a shortcut for "Asian online," and is at times capitalized and other times not. The sequence of names moves faster onscreen. He begins with "Atypical-AZNbottom, azn11, azn4azn, . . . azn4now, azn4oral, azn4sho, . . . azNerd, aznfratdude, . . . badAzn. . . . ." The term *Azn* is an Internet term, and here it is deployed to represent different queer cultures online. Like the others who identify as GAMs, Azns also link this word with preference, practice, or language play. Those who use the term *Asian* similarly describe themselves as notcuteAsian or smoothbrownasian but also Asian2rideu, Asiananalslut, Asiankat, AsianKen, asiannights, and GoodVibrAsian. A diversity of sexual identities, positions, preferences, and thematics combine here. In *How to Be Gay*, David M. Halperin argues that style, as seen in visible ways of self-fashioning, carry sexual and gender meaning: "Gay male culture is a form of understanding, a way of seeing men, women and the world."[27] In bringing together Azn identity categories with other categories (less likely, such as bears, and closer to common perception, like Adonis), we see an assertion of the specificity of individual desires. It is a declaration of want for others who are considered inappropriate or unexpected. An entire worldview is thus captured in the distilled choice of words. In one, two, or three words, we very clearly see an alignment with a position, a preference, a desire, and a view of the world from their perspective.

This view of the world and one's position in it as an interpellated person whose classification does not capture one's specific desire accomplishes a critique of popular culture. Or at the very least, it establishes a relationship to popular culture in how gay Asian men identify themselves. One calls himself "KarateKid" and another self-classifies in the recognizable image of the clothing brand that is typically white: "Asiabercrombie." These styles that clearly identify a certain look or a certain way of being when associated with Azn, Asian, or GAM, then, make one's identity more readable. Nguyen plays with the articulation of type when he places the following in a sequence: "AznArtFag, AznAthlete and AsianKen, AznRanger, AznSailor, asian_slave, AsianAdonis," or state Asian men's preferences for frat boys, papis, or club daddies. Other terms play with language, such as *Iphoyou*, *oppa*, or *edamamme*. Typically disparaging terms such as *Oriental*, *yellow fever*, and *rice queens* are also rewritten, or reclaimed, in ways that emphasize desire for these terms or identities. In all these, we see the articulation of desire by and for gay Asian men in relation to liberating themselves from the confines of identity categories and the cultures that too frequently limit them. Thus, a new style evolves in the combination of words—one that is more specifically a portrait and that acts as an invitation for sexual engagement. It is a naming that invites a response—to look at the speaker, and to recognize their desire. But what kind of visual image accompanies such a dynamic juxtaposition of namings, categories, and style? How can it emphasize the need to destabilize what *Asian*, *Azn*, or *GAM* means in the sexual market?

The second part of the video assembles shirtless photos posted by gay Asian men on cruising websites. This decision to post chests rather than faces avoids the limitations placed on gay Asian men by their racialization, which is too many times based on the Asian face, as theorized and historicized by David Palumbo-Liu in *Asian/American*.[28] That is, they avoid showing their face so that their racialization as Asians does not limit their sexual choices. They want to be free from the associations typically made for gay Asians and widen the availability of sexual options for themselves in the initial moments of their entry into the Internet marketplace. Here, the face functions differently than in the Styles project, in which the face must be visible. To reveal the face in Styles's project is to be conscious of racial identity in pornography. However, for Nguyen, the face is a limitation. It is a site for others to project and delimit sexuality. To challenge that projection, Nguyen hides the face in order to demand a different relationship to the consciousness that bears it.

In this sequence of images, Nguyen begins with wide shots of men, showing their full shirtless bodies, typically in underwear. The images feature slim, muscular men as well as burly, big men. They display themselves in bed, in the locker room, the bathroom, the backyard, the mirror, on the beach, or outside in the mountains. While we see a diversity of locations, we do not see faces. Nguyen then moves to torsos, similarly shot in a diversity of backgrounds. The images then move to a dancelike phase as arms and hands play more prominently with covering body parts or emphasizing others. The arms and hands move like a dance as we cut from shots of the same size: medium-wide image to medium-wide image. When gay Asian men's arms and hands touch themselves, either to cover body parts or to invite sexualization, the invitation to be touched is clear. We then see a variety of shots connected by each subject holding an iPhone to take pictures of himself. This raises our awareness of the technologies of representation. We then see a series of male torsos as they lie down in bed sheets. The concluding shots feature the men's nipples prominently in the framing of the image. They are dark and set in bodies with differing levels of fitness. Some chests are bursting with muscle, while others remain flat and thin. The images conclude as dandelions rise up in special effects onscreen.

The images described above collect a wide range of self-representations by a large diversity of gay Asian men. When reading them together onscreen, we see that they each attempt to make less prominent the Asian face, which determines and fixes their racial identity. The shirtless bodies make racial identities much vaguer and more difficult to determine. Because the bodies are harder to fix into a classification, they are also freer. Desire is set loose from racialization. In her new book *The Erotic Life of Racism*, Sharon Holland argues that racism enters into our most intimate choices, even the very sites where we seek pleasure. It is a constitutive force that permeates all areas of relationships that we consider our most close. Not only do we feel the other's different body as separate from our own, but we also feel the way touch introduces possibilities for the past, present, and future. Touch has the power to "assume . . . experiential knowledge, while it also calls upon its witnesses and players to testify to it as connection and repudiation, making it part of the person's experience and daring her to dis-own it."[29] In representations of erotics between racial others, she says that "touch is so compelling . . . that the prevailing narrative of race is undone and a multitude of possibilities find fruition."[30] I extend Holland's theorization to the site of intimate Internet sites and the wish for touch that they clearly express, which is oftentimes intertwined with the identity categories that limit them, as well as others. What is so fascinating is that the visceral is at work here. The online sites and art forms I study represent a genre that can lead to action beyond the screen. It is also a medium that can generate self-touch, so that while it looks like a two-dimensional image, it compels and enables a physical experience through the power of the visual, while at first remaining a virtual medium. When the classificatory terms of racism become the material for eroticism, such as when the identity text and the identity image that offers to serve someone else such as GAM4u or GAM4head1, the acknowledgment of such desires does not mean one lives in a state of false consciousness of bottomhood as disparaging or shameful. Instead, it shows that "we are apparently incapable of living without categories of difference, even when those categories are at worse hurtful and at best fictions in and of themselves."[31] These identity texts and identity images are articulations for the desire to be touched and the possibility of becoming both connected to and transformed by another.

In Keni Styles's luckyasianguy.tumblr.com and in Nguyen Tan Hoang's *Look I'm Azn!*, Asian men use both their written text and self-naming in order to make their identities and desires as Azn, GAM, or Asian American men known. They then use images of their shirtless selves to express a relationship to the popular criteria that judges them as desirable or not in terms of their gender and sexual practices as men. In the first case, the Asian/American men seek to address their representations in heterosexual adult industry movies as contrary to or misrepresentative of the active lives they lead off-screen. Styles demands that the contest entrants express awareness of the power of representation to construct the sexualities that viewers consume, and in the process challenge the way their sexuality has been racialized. A notable dynamic in this project is the open way that straight Asian men discuss their heterosexuality. In doing so, they acknowledge the attribution of failure to their racial grouping directly, refusing to ignore it or stay silent about it. It is a brotherly address of a shared racial sexualization that is not common in representations of Asian men, with the exception of the film *Better Luck Tomorrow* and the Harold and Kumar series. Too frequently, Asian men in the movies are alone as characters, with other Asian men nonexistent or underdeveloped.

These two projects also highlight the different dilemmas straight and gay Asian men face. One interaction on Keni Styles's tumblr alludes to this. In response to a viewer who says, "Don't forget your gay fans," Keni Styles acknowledges him and clarifies, "Although I am always aware of my gay fans, this project will focus on heterosexual scenes." In the Keni Styles's heterosexual site, the stigma is in pornification, while in the gay Asian male site, the body is offered for sex online as part of gay social ritual. In this scene, text and visualization work differently. Nguyen's project, situated in the gay and queer Asian sexual marketplace, presents a textual assertion of Asian, Azn, and Oriental gay identities paired with actions, identities, and desires deemed different or disparaging. It reclaims these identities in terms that own those desires. The images that accompany this platform revoke the face's power to determine the racial meaning of these men's sexualities. In doing so, they liberate their sexuality and secure more possibilities for pleasure. In this short film, as they do on the gay cruising sites, gay Asian men deploy textual identity and visual identity in ways that collide and cooperate.

In Closing

The use of the Internet as a means of constructing representation signifies the death of the centralized industry. Yet, decentralization has not necessarily signaled the emergence of a heterotopia, that is, a space that promotes nonhegemonic conditions.[32] To establish the proliferation of a hegemonic masculinity by Asian men, You Offend Me You Offend My Family's *Bananapocalypse* mentioned earlier begins my meditation on intimate Internet industries and Asian male use of this technology in creating Asian male subjectivities. What I fear in this powerful launching, which declares the death of the centralized industry, is the proliferation of a new Asian American male empire of representation that articulates racial problems of representation as male and renders Asian American women as derivative to the narrative, prominent only as banana-feeding dolls, banana-serving hotties, and dancers in the sense of the video ho. Speaking from the margins, Keni Styles and Nguyen Tan Hoang give us hope when approaching the problem ethically. The call straight Styles and queer Nguyen make is succinct. They will not disparage others, whether women or gay men. They each declare through their textual and visual work their demand for inclusion in their sexual networks. They attempt to legitimize their individual desires in the face of their classifications. Nonetheless, they use those namings as part of themselves and declare them a part of their intimate lives: GAM, Azn, Asian. They cannot get away from these racial terms. This is how they are hailed, and so they use them to demand recognition in their own more specific terms. And they do so in order to be seen, to be touched, to be held, to get laid, to come into the light, and to cum.

The shirtless bodies of Azn men critique the limits placed upon their everyday life, especially in relation to their sexual choices. When they pair words like *GAM, Azn, Oriental, Asian,* or other self-identifiers with other names, ways of life, and acts, they attempt to create new spaces, communities, and opportunities. They refute and refuse hierarchies of desire that place them as undesirable and uncompetitive in the marketplace of sex and romance by insistently inviting their potential lovers to look at them anew. The Internet media that they produce while expressing their intimate desires aims to make real a world not yet onscreen. Once we see them, their acts of creation—making images of their version of the world fueled by their own desires—bring us closer to them and make these worlds and desires legible and familiar. These, then, are political representations that transform their lives, as well as the viewers, making them more tangible, touchable, and realizable.

Notes

1. Celine Shimizu, *Straitjacket Sexualities: Unbinding Asian American Manhood in the Movies* (Stanford: Stanford University Press, 2012).

2. David Harvey, *The Condition of Postmodernity* (Cambridge, MA: Blackwell, 1990), 340–41.

3. Ibid.

4. Rose Eveleth, "The Internet Is Still for Porn and Parents Are Trying to Figure out How to Handle That," Smithsonian.com, May 21, 2013, www.smithsonianmag.com/smart-news/the-internet-is-still-for-pornand-parents-are-trying-to-figure-out-how-to-handle-that-75088273/.

5. Julie Ruvolo, "How Much of the Internet Is Actually for Porn," *Forbes,* September 7, 2011, www.forbes.com/sites/julieruvolo/2011/09/07/how-much-of-the-Internet-is-actually-for-porn/.

6. "Porn Sites Get More Visitors Each Month than Netflix, Amazon and Twitter Combined," *Huffington Post,* updated May 4, 2013, www.huffingtonpost.com/2013/05/03/Internet-porn-stats_n_3187682.html#slide=1994670.

7. "American Porn: How the Porn Business Works, What It Makes, and What Its Future May Be," *Frontline,* www.pbs.org/wgbh/pages/frontline/shows/porn/business/howtheme.html (accessed May 24, 2013).

8. Alex Waterfield and Lauren Effron, "Couple Records Sex for Money to Support Toddler" *Nightline,* October 13, 2011, abcnews.go.com/US/couple-records-sex-money-support-toddler/story?id=14724574#.UaAosr8a6gw.

9. Susan Abram, "Porn Film Permits Have Dropped Dramatically in L.A. County," *Daily News,* April 14, 2013, www.dailynews.com/ci_23024668/porn-film-permits-have-dropped-dramatically-l-county.

10. Margret Grebowicz, *Why Internet Porn Matters* (Stanford, CA: Stanford University Press, 2013), 2.

11. Ibid., 12.

12. Michael Hardt and Antonio Negri, *Empire* (Cambridge, MA: Harvard University Press, 2000), xii.

13. Neferti X. Tadiar, *Fantasy-Production* (Manila: Ateneo de Manila University Press, 2004), 54.

14. Christopher J. Jordan, *Movies and the Reagan Presidency: Success and Ethics* (Westport, CT: Praeger, 2003).

15. J. B. Capino, *Dream Factories of a Former Colony: American Fantasies, Philippine Cinema* (Minneapolis: University of Minnesota Press, 2010), xviii.

16. Ibid., xix.

17. Jim Pines and Paul Willemen, *Questions of Third Cinema* (London: British Film Institute, 1990).

18. Hardt and Negri, *Empire*, xiv.

19. Ibid., xii–xiii.

20. See my talk at the Center for Asian American Media at www.youtube.com/watch?v=dw FLyipre2c&feature=youtu.be (accessed October 20, 2013) and the work of Anna Everett, *Digital Diaspora: A Race for Cyberspace* (Albany, NY: SUNY Press, 2006).

21. Hardt and Negri, *Empire*, xi.

22. Trinh T. Minh-ha, "Difference: A Special Third World Woman Issue," *Discourse* 8 (Fall–Winter 1986–87): 10–37.

23. Hardt and Negri, *Empire*, xvi.

24. Jeff Yang, "Mightier than the Sword," *SF Gate*, March 20, 2010, www.sfgate.com/entertainment /article/Mightier-than-the-sword-2481504.php#page-3.

25. Emanuel Levinas, *Ethics and Infinity* (Pittsburgh, PA: Duquesne University Press, 1985), 95.

26. See Nguyen Tan Hoang in Linda Williams, "The Resurrection of Brandon Lee: The Making of a Gay Asian American Port Star," *Porn Studies* (Durham, NC: Duke University Press, 2004), 223–70.

27. David M. Halperin, *How to Be Gay* (Cambridge, MA: Harvard University Press, 2012), 375.

28. David Palumbo-Liu, *Asian/American* (Stanford: Stanford University Press, 2000), 88.

29. Sharon Holland, *The Erotic Life of Racism* (Durham, NC: Duke University Press, 2012), 103.

30. Ibid.

31. Ibid., 100.

32. Michel Foucault, *The Foucault Reader*, ed. Paul Rabinow (New York: Pantheon, 1984).

Deferential Surrogates and Professional Others:
Recruitment and Training of Migrant Care Workers in Taiwan and Japan

Pei-Chia Lan

Introduction

The demand for migrant care workers has expanded globally, owing to the growth of the aging population in postindustrial societies. East Asian countries, facing a similar problem of care deficit, have recruited migrant workers from Southeast Asia in the fields of health and social welfare. Geriatric care, which is traditionally defined and socially located as a gendered form of kin labor, now becomes an institutionally organized form of intimate labor provided by nonfamily, noncitizen employees.

The ethnic boundary and cultural distance between care providers and care recipients pose challenges to the performance of affective labor, which requires physical proximity and the production of affect.[1] Many employers prefer to hire migrant workers for the benefits of status hierarchy and labor subordination, but they are equally concerned about whether these ethnic

positions 24:1   DOI 10.1215/10679847-3320137

others are suitable for the role of fictive kin in a modern household. Southeast Asian women are often associated with essential characteristics, such as a "natural inclination" to care, and therefore considered ideal candidates for the performance of affective labor. And yet, the receiving society also questions their qualification for professional care in a cultural context that is not their own.

Scholars have developed concepts like "global political economy of care,"[2] "transnational care regime,"[3] or "curo-scape,"[4] to describe the emergence of a transnational sphere in which a variety of symbolic, economic, and political exchanges take place between sending and receiving countries, and relatively stable networks are created for the administration and management of care work. However, we still have limited knowledge about how the transnational outsourcing of care operates in different ways across cultural and policy contexts, and how the intermediaries, either commercial brokers or state agencies, participate in the discursive construction and material organization of care work.

This article compares the recruitment and training of migrant care workers in Taiwan and Japan to explore how the intimate labor of geriatric care is culturally defined and institutionally regulated in different ways. Migrant care workers in Taiwan are positioned as "deferential surrogates," while Japan has recruited migrant nurses as "professional others." This comparison allows us to explore the following questions: How does such national variation demonstrate the broader cultural and political contexts characterized by the intersection of migration regime and care regime? Why do commercial brokers or state agencies recruit specific types of migrant workers and view them as proper agents for elderly care? How do these intermediary institutions develop training curriculums to reconcile the paradoxes incurred when outsourcing intimate labor to foreigners? And how do migrant workers themselves respond to these cultural parameters and institutional regulations in the practice of work?

This article is an extension from my previous research on migrant care workers in Taiwan.[5] In that project, I conducted field observation on the recruitment and training of prospective migrant care workers in Indonesia (August 2003) and the Philippines (May 1998). I also interviewed eleven recruitment agency staffers, fifty-eight Filipina workers (1998–99), and thirty-five Indonesian workers in Taiwan (1998–99 and 2002–3). During my visit in Kyoto in the summer of 2012, I interviewed one agency staffer and two Indonesian care workers, and I observed a training seminar for Japanese instructors (with the assistance of a translator). I also collected archival and secondary data in both English and Japanese.

Care and Migration Regimes in Taiwan and Japan

Taiwan started a "guest worker" program in 1992 to recruit low-skilled foreign workers for selected occupations and industries. A substantial proportion of them (42 percent by January 2015) are employed as care workers for the elderly, ill, or disabled and mostly placed in private households rather than medical or care institutions. The total number of migrant care workers by July 2015 exceeded 225,000 and were mostly women from Indonesia (79 percent), the Philippines (12 percent), and Vietnam (9 percent).[6]

By contrast, Japan has been hesitant to open up the employment of migrant domestic helpers or in-home caregivers.[7] Only recently has Japan accepted skilled workers with nursing backgrounds based on the Economic Partnership Agreements (EPAs) with the Philippines (signed in September 2006, effective in October 2008) and with Indonesia (signed in August 2007, effective in May 2008).[8] The EPA is a bilateral economic agreement between partner countries to achieve the liberalization of trade through comprehensive measures such as the deregulation of investment rules and the enhancement of movement of workers and other natural persons.

EPA care workers are divided into two categories: one is "nursing [*kangoshi*] candidate," who is required to obtain a nursing license in the home country and has two or more years of experience working as a nurse. The other is "certified care worker [*kaigo fukushishi*] candidate," who needs to have graduated from a nursing college or vocational school or have obtained a caregiver certificate accredited by the home government. Certified care workers are employed by medical institutions or care facilities to provide support for the elderly or disabled who are unable to independently meet their daily needs. Over eighteen hundred Indonesian and Filipino candidates for registered nurse or certified care workers have entered Japan under the EPA agreements from 2008 to 2014.[9] All of them have a nursing background, and a significant proportion of Indonesian candidates are men.[10] Japan has also signed an EPA with Vietnam (effective in October 2009) with the clause of recruiting care workers, but the first batch of nurse candidates (138 persons) did not arrive until June 2014.[11]

It should be noted that marriage immigrants are another major source of care labor. In Japan, many Filipinas who previously worked as entertainers and later married Japanese men became certified care workers after attending training courses.[12] In Taiwan, taking care of elders and patients is one of the few occupations available to Vietnamese and Mainland Chinese women who immigrated through marriage.[13] This article focuses only on labor migrants recruited through the guest worker program or the EPA program.

The cases of Japan and Taiwan are comparable, given some similarities in their demographic structures. First, both countries have a rapidly aging population coupled with a declining birthrate. The elderly have risen to 23 percent of Japan's population in 2011. This percentage is predicted to reach 32 percent by 2030, and 39 percent in 2050.[14] The elderly population in Taiwan has risen to 11 percent in 2012. With a fertility rate that is currently one of the lowest in the world, the ratio of the Taiwanese elderly population is predicted to reach 20 percent by 2026, and 37 percent in 2051.[15]

Secondly, the populations in East Asia, including Japan and Taiwan, are ethnically homogeneous compared with other parts of the world.[16] Relevantly, these countries have maintained strict immigration policies, including a framework of "ethnicized" citizenship, based primarily on the descent principle (jus sanguinis) and rigid regulations concerning the naturalization of foreigners. Despite these similarities, both countries have adopted divergent ways of recruiting and training migrant care workers that demonstrate broader national diversity in the formation of care and migration regimes.

The concept of "care regime" sheds light on how care work is embedded in particular institutional regimes that organize the public and private in various patterns. Different care regimes can be distinguished by their specific policy logic that divides care between the state, market, family, and the voluntary sector, and by their association with particular cultural scripts about gender and cross-generation relationships.[17]

In Taiwan, taking care of elderly parents is traditionally considered the filial duty of sons and daughters-in-law, and three-generation cohabitation remains a preferred arrangement for the older cohort. According to a 2013 official survey, over 65 percent of the elderly respondents preferred to cohabitate with children, while less than 2 percent considered institutional care as the ideal arrangement. In reality, almost 60 percent of the seniors resided with adult children, while less than 3 percent lived in care institutions.[18] Under the filially pious outlook of extended households, who exactly is taking care of frail parents in Taiwan? Another survey conducted in 2009 showed that, for the elderly who needed assistance with daily needs, their primary caregivers were sons (22 percent), daughters-in-law (15 percent), and spouses or partners (14 percent), followed by foreign care workers (13 percent). The latter percentage rose to 31 percent in Taipei City, even though the majority of elders in this area still lived with their children (62 percent).[19]

The seeming paradox between the normalization of filial duty and the prevalence of care outsourcing is reconciled by the employment of migrant live-in workers. This is what I call a strategy of "subcontracting filial piety."[20] Taiwan's government has coined the term *social welfare foreign workers* to describe migrant caregivers. The state welcomes their arrival to sustain the familistic model of care at low market costs, while excusing its own failure to implement long-term elder care and other social security programs.[21] Migrant domestic care workers, however, are not protected by Taiwan's Labor Standards Law, because they work in the private sphere of family.

The current generation of Taiwanese elders, with preference for and dependence on family care, contrasts markedly with their counterparts in Japan. According to a 2006 survey conducted to compare the family values of East Asian countries (Japan, Taiwan, China, and South Korea), Japanese parents received the least frequent support, either financial or instrumental, from adult children, while the proportion of Taiwanese parents who received financial or instrumental support from adult children very frequently was the highest among the four countries.[22]

The proportion of Japanese elders living with their offspring, especially with married children, has declined dramatically over the past thirty years: In 1980, almost 70 percent of those aged sixty-five years and over resided with children (52.5 percent with married children and 16.5 percent with unmarried children), but the proportion dropped to 54 percent in 1995

(35.5 percent with married children) and 42 percent in 2010 (only 16.2 percent with married children).[23] The restructuring of household patterns has coalesced with the transformation of Japan's welfare state and elder-care policies.

According to Ito Peng, Japan's care regime has undergone several transformations during the postwar period.[24] The welfare state substantially expanded in the 1970s but faced restructuring in the 1980s. The conservative government imposed tight fiscal control to curb the expenses in social security programs, and it rolled back many reforms initiated in the 1970s by reemphasizing the family's care responsibilities. The crisis of declining fertility since the 1990s, acting as a silent protest of younger cohorts of women, has nevertheless pushed the government to adopt policy reforms, including expanding public childcare and opening up employment opportunities for women. The government no longer promotes three-generation cohabitation and recognizes that the responsibility for elders has impeded women's labor force participation. A long-term care insurance (LTCI) program was implemented in 2000 to provide universalized elder care. The care regime has shifted from a "needs-based care provision model" to a "rights-based universal social insurance scheme."[25]

The number of LTCI recipients increased from 1.49 million in 2000 to 3.29 million in 2005, with expenditures nearly doubling between 2000 and 2007.[26] The rapid expansion of social care for the elderly in Japan has created a demand for qualified care workers that cannot be met by current labor pools. Although the government has sought to recruit and train Japanese workers, mostly married women, to work as licensed care workers, job intake has been low, and turnover has been high.[27] The natives do not favor this occupation for the reasons of low wages, long working hours, and inadequate social status.[28] However, the monthly wage of a certified care worker, approximately ¥170,000–210,000, is still about ten times what a nurse could earn in Indonesia or the Philippines.[29]

The second factor that divides the cases of Taiwan and Japan is migration regime, which concerns a multitude of state regulations that promote or discourage the entry and employment of migrants.[30] Taiwan has adopted a guest worker system to fill the labor shortage. All migrant care workers are employed on a contract basis without entitlement to family unification, permanent residency, or naturalization. The maximum duration for their work permits was initially only three years, but it has been gradually extended to twelve years for now.

Taiwan's government has signed bilateral agreements with sending countries, including Indonesia, Vietnam, Thailand, and the Philippines. Mainland (People's Republic of China) Chinese, who share Han cultural heritage with the Taiwanese, are nevertheless excluded from the guest worker program, exactly because Taiwanese society is worried that Chinese migrants would assimilate too quickly and easily.[31] In contrast, the visible differences of Southeast Asians, in terms of culture, language, and physical features, make it easier for the host state to monitor their whereabouts and to define their subordinate status as temporary and disposable labor.

As with Taiwan, Japan in the late 1980s saw a growing number of unauthorized migrant workers, mostly from Southeast Asia. However, instead of legalizing the status of guest workers, in 1989 Japan revised the immigration law to create a visa category of "long-term resident" to accommodate the employment of noncitizens of Japanese descent from Brazil or Peru (*nikkei-jin*). They are preferred for the reason of assumed cultural affinity based on a shared ethnic heritage. In principle, Japan prohibits the entry of unskilled foreign labor, with the exception of admitting foreign workers in the form of "trainees."[32]

Japan's government was very cautious in taking every step during the introduction of EPA workers, including the control of quotas, state-to-state recruitment, and the provision of intensive training programs at great cost. It also made clear that the EPA program aims to recruit skilled foreigners, instead of guest workers, who are expected to continue employment and residency in Japan after passing the national exams to become formally registered nurses or certified care workers.[33] A nurse candidate may take the exam three times within three years, whereas care worker candidates may take it only once over four years, because a precondition for taking this exam even for Japanese examinees includes three years of working experience. Those passing the national exams are eligible for indefinitely renewable visas and can join other foreign residents who have gradually been accepted by the Japanese state and society as "permanently settled residents."[34]

Taiwan: Seeking and Training Deferential Surrogates

Commercial brokers have dominated the recruitment and training of migrant care workers to be placed in Taiwan. Because the contract workforce is constantly replenished with new blood, employers and workers both lack sufficient information about the other party, and they must rely on private agencies as intermediaries.[35] Many Taiwanese brokers have set up overseas branches or acquired agencies in sending countries.[36] This allows them to minimize transaction costs and to maximize control in the recruitment and training process. Or they seek business partners in sending countries to establish stable networks for efficient collaboration and enduring alliances. Through the establishment of a transnational industry, labor brokers are able to oversee and manage the inflows of labor power in order to match the expectations of potential employers.

Mr. Chen, who owned a company with three local offices in Taiwan and overseas branches in Indonesia, Vietnam, and the Philippines, handled the recruitment of eight hundred migrant care workers into Taiwan each year. During our interview, Mr. Chen bragged about the effectiveness of their training program:

> Can you imagine what an Indonesian worker looks like when she first arrives? She wears slippers and carries a plastic bag—not even a handbag! Inside the bag are only underwear and maybe 20,000 Rp in her pocket. Then she says she wants to go to Taiwan! She was like that at registration, but we train her. Now she knows how to dress, she knows sanitation, she speaks Chinese, and she can do things. This is not an easy job. (original in Chinese, my translation)

Mr. Chen boldly discredited Indonesians as being "backward" and "uncivilized." Meanwhile, he emphasized that the ideal workers could be found only in rural areas; "the poorer, the better" is his golden rule of recruitment. Recruiters like him reach prospective workers through the intermediary of local sponsors, also called *niutou* ("the head cow" in Chinese). Sponsors are usually villagers who worked overseas before (with ties to agencies) or who are familiar with local politics (with connections to expedite the processing of documents). The sponsor finds prospective workers in the village, prepares their documents, and brings them over to the agency in the city. In this way, an agency is able to reach the kind of workers they prefer—village women without previous overseas experiences—at low costs. The migrant family also places more trust in a local sponsor than some stranger from the city; they feel more comfortable sending their daughters with a fellow villager to explore the unknown outside world.

Recruitment agencies produce "docile" migrant care workers through a careful screening process. They tend to exclude applicants who "look too smart" and seemingly "have a strong character." They do not prefer those who have worked overseas before or even those of Chinese descent. A familiarity with local society and language is considered not an advantage for job performance but a barrier to labor control. One recruiter explained this, saying, "If they know Chinese, they would ask people, to compare with others. If they have local connections, they run away."

In Taiwan, migrant care workers are expected to provide custodial care and standby service on a live-in basis; their job duties often fuse the categories of domestic helper and caregiver. Both jobs are extensions of women's familial responsibilities defined by the traditional care regime, including the filial duty of a daughter-in-law to look after her aging parents-in-law. Adult children seek outsourcing of elder care for a variety of reasons. The double-earner households need outside help to smooth their time deficit. Some daughters-in-law want to avoid conflicts and tensions across generations. Some want to improve the quality of care for their parents by establishing a network of horizontal cooperation or a stratified division of labor between themselves and migrant caregivers.[37]

The above recruitment strategies help brokers to convince their employer clients, who usually select workers based on limited information in workers' profiles, that migrant candidates referred by them would be reliable and submissive. After being recruited by sponsors, prospective migrants are sent to a live-in training program. In general, a migrant worker stays in the program from two to three months before her departure overseas, but I have heard of people who awaited a job order for as long as six months.[38]

Most training centers in Indonesia are located on the outskirts of Jakarta and Surabaya. The center I visited was composed of four houses—three were dormitories and a larger one was a training center. As there were 450 prospective workers in residence, the living space was very crowded. Fifteen to twenty people shared a room. The staff had just purchased bunk beds and mattresses to meet the Indonesian government's regulations on the basic living conditions of the training centers. This policy has been enforced since only 2003, after nongovernmental organizations reported many cases of abuse, malnutrition, and even mysterious deaths at training centers.[39] Most migrant workers I met in Taiwan were placed in substandard living conditions during the training period: they slept on the floor; they ate only rice and vegetables; hundreds of people took showers together because water was supplied for only one hour a day. One worker humorously described the dreadful environment: "We were like cows, like sheep. You see how they wash cows? We were just like that."

In the center I visited, all the trainees had to wake up at 4:00 a.m. and go to bed at 10:00 p.m. They had classes from Monday to Saturday. Sunday was the only day off, but they could not go out; only visitors were allowed. One worker characterized their days in the center as "staying in prison." At night they were locked in the building, often suffering from hunger because insufficient portions were provided for dinner. One vividly described how they used a rope to lower a basket down to street vendors in order to bring food upstairs.

The training curriculum in this center was as long as 454 hours, starting with 15 hours on moral education, work ethics, sanitation, motivation, and discipline. When I asked Mr. Chen what he considered the most important subject of training, he answered without hesitation: "*li-yi-lian-chi*" (sense of propriety, justice, honesty, and shame). He drew on the Confucian principles of morality to highlight what he perceived the "moral inadequacy" of migrants. These lessons, according to Mr. Chen, fulfill a critical function of taming migrant women's sexual energy and keeping them away from prostitution. More importantly, these moral lessons aimed to discipline villagers into productive and obedient laborers by cultivating an attitude of subservience toward employers. In my observation, the instructor, an Indonesian woman of Chinese descent, preached to the trainees: "Work hard, appreciate the opportunity to make money, don't fight with your employers, and don't fall under bad influences."

A substantive part of training curriculum concerned knowledge and skills for housekeeping (twenty-seven hours), cooking (twenty-four hours), babysitting (twenty-seven hours), and elder care (twenty-seven hours). The curriculum instructed prospective workers not only how to get work done in the house but how to do it in an "efficient" and "proper" way. They also had to learn about table manners and table serving (twenty-seven hours), laundry and ironing (twenty-seven hours), and how to use modern electronic appliances such as vacuum cleaners and microwaves (twenty-seven hours). Such transmission of household skills aimed to correct migrants' "technical backwardness" and reorient them toward the urban lifestyles of modern households.[40] Migrant women's previous experiences of caring for their own family members were disregarded as backward customs without proper sanitation. They were instructed how to take care of babies and elders in a doctor-approved, germ-free way.

A large number of training hours were spent on the instruction of language skills, including English (114 hours) and Mandarin Chinese (138 hours). Chinese language proficiency is the major advantage Indonesian workers have over their Filipina competitors. Taiwanese employers usually hire Filipina migrants for the duty of child care rather than elder care. The lower-educated employers enjoy the extra benefit of English tutoring for their children but worry that their authority may be challenged by English-speaking Filipinas.[41] The transmission of Chinese language skills to Indonesian migrants has its practical function of facilitating communication. Yet, it also carries an underlying purpose of consolidating the status hierarchy by subordinating the servant to the master's language.

The deferential performance of migrant workers is corporeal and somatic; as such, the bodies of migrant women must be transformed during the course of training to mirror the desired images held by employers. Wearing makeup is not allowed, and short hair is the required style at many training centers, although long hair is generally considered an integral element of feminine beauty in Indonesia. Several migrant women I talked to in Taiwan recalled the saddening moment when their long hair was cut off when they registered at the training center. The regulations on hairstyle and makeup aim to repress the feminine look of migrant women and to avoid sexual association in an intimate work setting; the androgynous appearance also matches the image of a servant as being plain and lacking style.

The training programs not only aim to deliver certain skills and capacities to potential migrants but also intend to endow them with proper attitudes and dispositions needed for domestic servitude in a modern household. On the one hand, the curriculum involves speech and bodily discipline for the cultivation of a servile disposition, a mechanism that Daromir Rudnyckyi has described as "technologies of servitude."[42] In the training center in Jakarta on which he conducted observation, the trainees—future workers in Saudi Arabia—were instructed to only speak to their superiors from a kneeling or stooping position. On the other hand, care workers must be transformed to get familiar with the middle-class lifestyle so they can anticipate and meet the demands of employers. The training program aims to cultivate the subjectivity of migrant care workers to "see work from the eyes of employers." A migrant care worker must learn and accept the modern literacy of domesticity as a mediator "between the mind of employers and her own body."[43]

How do migrant workers respond to the situation in which they are forced or compelled to play the role of "deferential surrogate"? Elsewhere I have discussed a variety of ways in which migrant workers negotiate the social boundaries between themselves and Taiwanese employers.[44] Some workers question the status hierarchy and identify themselves as equal human beings or even class peers of their employers. They are mostly downward-mobile college graduates and English-speaking Filipinas. Open confrontation, such as correcting the employer's English mistakes, rarely happens. Most workers choose to "perform deference" in the presence of their employers.[45] Trina, a twenty-nine-year-old Filipina who had previously worked in Singapore prior to Taiwan, explained to me that deferential performance was actually a means for the worker to exert "control" over the employer: "If you are experienced, you know how to control them. You know their personality. Then you know how to talk to them. I know so much about the Chinese personality. They like to have so much control. If you follow, they like you." Some workers cast doubt on their employers' cultural sophistication, such as their taste in fashion or the command of the cosmopolitan lifestyle. They laugh at some "useless" parts of the training curriculum and point out the gap between the imagined lifestyle of potential employers and the actual workplace in which the employers have modest economic or cultural capital. For instance, they learned how to set a formal Western dining table, including the appropriate positions of utensils and napkins, but most Taiwanese households use casual table manners or they are not familiar at all with the Western rules of dining etiquette.

In addition, migrant workers, serving as the fictive kin of Taiwanese elders, may claim the superiority of their home culture in terms of family ties and elder care arrangement. They were critical about the outsourcing of geriatric care in Taiwan: "I will not leave my parents to a stranger." However, the transferring of intimate labor to a "stranger," that is, someone outside the family and cultural terrain, does not necessarily lead to substandard care service or affective labor. The market-based relationship can enable and produce new forms of intimacy and affect, which are not regulated by filial norms and other cultural baggage. When observing the interaction between migrant caregivers and their clients, I was often surprised at the changing behaviors of Taiwanese elders. When the caregivers softly kissed their cheek or tightly hugged them saying "I love you," the elders, who probably never verbally expressed affection to their children in an explicit way, replied in broken English, with a smile: "I love you, too!"[46]

Japan: Recruiting and Training Professional Others

Japan's government did not accept EPA workers with an initial intention to solve the labor shortage in nursing and care work. Rather, the government reluctantly accepted them because the Philippine and Indonesian governments both made strong requests along this line. In order to sell more Toyota, Sony, and other Japanese products to the partner countries, Japan's government agreed to accept nurses and care workers from overseas. The government set up maximum quotas—four hundred nurse candidates and six hundred certified care worker candidates per country—by considering the potential effect on the domestic labor market rather than a measurement of labor shortage.[47]

Different government agencies held distinct opinions regarding the recruitment of EPA workers. The Ministry of Economics, Trade, and Industry (METI) has overseen the overall arrangement and negotiation of the EPA and proposed the mutual recognition of nursing certificates by Japan and partner countries. The proposal was fiercely opposed by the Japanese Nursing Association (JNA) and Japanese Federation of Medical Workers' Unions (JFMWU), who had concerns that this would cause wages and working conditions for local staff to deteriorate.[48] The Ministry of Health, Labor, and Welfare (MHLW) denied that there was a shortage of nursing and care staff, announcing that it accepted EPA workers only in order to achieve "national interests in terms of trade liberalization."[49] Pressured by JNA and other professional associations, MHLW requires that EPA candidates pass Japan's national examinations in nursing or care work, and they need to acquire sufficient skills in the Japanese language and culture.

To ensure the cautious introduction and proper training of EPA candidates, Japan's government has adopted a system of state-to-state recruitment, excluding the involvement of commercial brokers. The Japan International Corporation of Welfare Services (JICWELS), a semigovernmental organization sanctioned by the MHLW, serves as the only matching agency on the Japanese side. It is also responsible for the education and management of EPA candidates and facilitating communication between workers and employers. Upon their arrival in Japan, EPA candidates need to attend a training course run by institutions sanctioned by JICWELS and then work and study at a hospital (for nursing candidates) or a care facility (for care worker candidates) until they pass or fail the national exams to become a registered nurse or certified care worker.

The earlier batches of EPA candidates, who left the Philippines and Indonesia for Japan in 2009 and 2010, underwent a training program for six months upon their arrival in Japan. The Japanese government paid the candidates' travel, accommodations, and daily expenses during their intensive training program, while the employers were responsible for the tuition of training courses. The recruitment and training was very costly—nearly ¥600,000 for each candidate.[50] The EPA workers I talked to recalled the luxury of the lodging during the training period: "It was like a hotel!" Each candidate was offered a twenty-four-hour air-conditioned single room with TV and computer. They studied from nine to five during the week, while being served with three prepared meals and having access to party rooms and a sports center in the dormitory.

In order to economize the government budget, the training locations were adjusted for the later batches of candidates: some part of the training program (two to four months) was conducted in the Philippines or Indonesia prior to their departure by Japanese instructors with the assistance of local instructors. The training program was later prolonged to improve the language capability of EPA candidates. In 2012, an EPA candidate received training for three months in the home country (425 hours) and studied for another six months (855 hours) upon their arrival in Japan.[51] The predeparture training was further extended to six months in 2013.[52]

Unlike the training program offered to caregivers to work in Taiwan with a focus on the "technologies of servitude," the curriculum for EPA candidates is designed based on the belief that linguistic skills and cultural knowledge are essential in the provision of safe and quality care for Japanese seniors. In a 2010 government survey, the Japanese respondents considered the most important qualifications for foreign workers to be "Japanese language skills," "understanding Japanese customs," and "understanding Japanese culture," while "professional skills and knowledge" were considered to be of lower priority.[53] Accordingly, the primary goal of the EPA training is not to cultivate professional skills or a docile disposition but to bridge cultural distance by taming the otherness of migrants. The process constitutes what I call "technologies for assimilation."

A substantial proportion of the curriculum involves the instruction of Japanese language—not just basic vocabulary for conversation but advanced skills in reading and writing (391 hours in predeparture training and 675 hours in Japan). The most challenging goal is the proficiency in Chinese characters (*Kanji*) because Japanese medical specialists tend to use *Kanji*, instead of phonetic writing, in medical documents. A candidate must acquire a JLPT (the Japanese Language Proficiency Test) N1 certificate, which is equivalent to the accreditation exam for the completion of junior high school education in Japan.[54]

The curriculum also highlights the perception of care as a cultural practice and helps EPA candidates to learn about the cultural aspects of "Japanese care work" (forty-six hours in total). Taking a training manual as an example, regarding the assistance with toileting, the candidates learned how to "respect toileting style and custom" and understand how "it relates to human dignity." In order to assist the clients with eating, they learned to appreciate the aromas of special Japanese food, such as *umeboshi* (pickled plum), *yuzu* (Japanese citrus), and *wasabi* (Japanese horseradish). They were also instructed about the correct ways of putting on a kimono (with the right tucked under the left) and the cultural sense of shame in order to offer proper assistance with dressing and undressing.[55]

EPA candidates are also instructed about the difference between Japanese care work and care work in Indonesia and the Philippines. In both the Philippines and Indonesia, daily care for the bedridden or elderly patients in hospitals is normally done by family members or personal helpers rather than nurses.[56] The occupation of a certified care worker is practically nonexistent. EPA candidates, who were trained as nurses back home, generally experience a sense of downward mobility, not only because they are assigned a lower occupational status (care worker rather than nurse) but also owing to the different assignments of work for health care staff in Japan. Personal care duties, such as changing diapers, collecting urine and other waste, and assisting in taking meals and tea to the patients, are conducted by nurses and care workers in Japan as part and parcel of the holistic approach to care.

Utami, a twenty-two-year-old Indonesian registered nurse, joined the first group of EPA nursing candidates to work in Japan. She had long held a dream to work abroad but could not afford the placement fees to go to destinations like the United Kingdom or Australia. The trip to Japan cost her almost nothing, but she was unaware that she came to work as a nursing candidate rather than a nurse. She received little information about the actual working conditions or the difficulty of Japan's national exam during the predeparture seminar in Jakarta. She was shocked and felt demeaned when asked to perform basic care duties in a small Japanese hospital:

> In that time, I did not know. I want to cry. I want to back home. Really, I want to go back Indonesia. For work, I came to Japan. [But] work like this, you know, is really terrible . . . it is really a surprise. I cannot believe it. Our hospital [in Indonesia] is like hotel. And then my hospital in Japan, it's like . . . not so big. And then they ask me to do this, to do this, for example, taking garbage, make me really really . . . I want to cry. (original in English)

Japan's government mandates that the terms and conditions of foreign skilled workers be equal to those of the native labor force. EPA candidates are guaranteed a salary equivalent to that of Japanese care workers without a license (about ¥140,000 per month). There are nevertheless subtle forms of discrimination and uneven division of labor at work. EPA candidates are positioned at the bottom of the status hierarchies along the lines of age, seniority, and citizenship status; they feel it's difficult to refuse requests from middle-aged Japanese coworkers to help with more strenuous or demeaning duties such as cleaning toilets, collecting garbage, and assisting patients to bathe in a tub.

When I asked Utami about the training program, she identified the class on Japanese culture and society (twenty-eight hours in predeparture training and fifty hours in Japan) as "very useful." For instance, the instruction about the cultural sense of "cleanness" in Japan helped her to understand why tub bathing, instead of sponge bathing, is considered such an essential part of quality care for Japanese seniors. She was puzzled at the prevalent use of diapers among seniors in Japan, where the diaper manufacturers now sell more adult diapers than baby diapers. She managed to see the association of adult diapers with autonomy and dignity in Japan's cultural context. The training program aims to cultivate the subjectivity of migrant care workers to see care from the eyes of Japanese clients; it also arranges short-term stays with Japanese households for migrant candidates to immerse them in the local culture and lifestyle.

The two EPA workers I talked to reported no problem at all during the interactions with their patients or wards. Japanese seniors seem to appreciate and enjoy their company, and "they are too polite to complain, anyway." However, both of them found working in a Japanese organization very challenging. This is why the 2012 curriculum included a fair amount of time on the subject "understanding and adjusting in the Japanese workplace" (ninety hours). In Japanese hospitals or care facilities, staff members must follow standardized procedures and write detailed documentation to ensure the conduct of professional care. The working hours tend to be long and rigid, and the status hierarchy at work is evident.

The EPA workers interviewed by me and other researchers aired complaints concerning communication with Japanese staff. The workplace became a "zone of cultural friction,"[57] where cultural differences complicated personal interactions. My informants described the personality of their Japanese coworkers as "shy, not warm," "no answer, no eye contact, no smile" and "not so open-minded toward foreigners." The work ethic in Japan was portrayed as hardworking but overly bureaucratic: "They live for work, work for professional; we [Indonesians] work for life." Japanese staffers as such were criticized for their poor performance of emotional labor. Utami said:

> [Japanese colleagues] work long hours but not generous with emotions . . . .
> but our work is not work with machine. We work with humans. So I think touching and eye contact are really important. They [Japanese wards] like Indonesian and Filipino care workers because we are more emotional and cheerful, not like Japanese workers. They are like robots. . . we make them safe and comfortable even we cannot speak Japanese fluently. Smile is [the] best language. And I see my patients like my family.

Utami characterized her superior job performance with the bodily performance of affective labor—smile, physical contacts, and emotional expression—which can compensate for her short stock in language skills or cultural knowledge. She also utilized the rhetoric of "fictive kin" to emphasize her flexible yet personalized style of care vis-à-vis her Japanese coworkers who only "care by the book." The Japanese owner of an elderly nursing home, interviewed by Mario Lopez, used a similar tone to describe how Southeast Asian women are more inclined to care work:

> The Filipinos I have met are really good at communication. If you want me to give you my opinions of the Japanese now they are like robots. This is why they [the Filipinas] are so good at caring . . . they look after other families' elderly [users] as they would look after their own . . . we don't want to take a policy whereby we demand care workers who are "perfect" Japanese speakers, but speakers who can care. In their cases, they are full of love, so when they speak, words come out naturally.[58]

The Japanese government has spent a great deal of time and money in the efforts to assimilate migrant workers and make them suitable for the cultural practice of Japanese care work. Paradoxically, Japanese employers and migrants themselves also mobilize the discourse of ethnic differences to redefine quality care with the essentialist rhetoric of "migrant women as good carers." The otherness of foreign care workers is constructed as some sort of "affective capital,"[59] a source to create the potential labor of "genuine" affect to vitalize an aging community in the shadow of illness or death, to add personal intimacy to the standardized service and bureaucratic workplace, and to bring energy to an undervalued and demeaned profession. According to a survey of fifty-three Japanese care facilities that accepted EPA care workers, nearly 80 percent of the institutions were satisfied with their performance based on reasons like "the workplace became revitalized," "the elderly became more lively," and "the elderly are pleased to have a cheerful person in their boring daily lives."[60]

However, such essentialist rhetoric has a negative consequence for migrant workers by reducing their affective labor to a natural endowment or an innate proclivity, rather than the outcome of acquired skills or earned knowledge. For instance, Utami felt that her professional skills were never as recognized as her capability to perform emotional labor. She said in a tone of frustration, "The head nurse always says that my *way of care*, not my knowledge or my skill, is good" (emphasis mine). Similarly, Japanese care facility managers in the same survey reported higher satisfaction with migrant workers for their personality ("cheerful") or soft skills ("having respect toward the elderly" and "good at building relationships with the elderly") rather than their professional skills or knowledge.[61]

The likelihood for EPA migrants to gain professional certification and to achieve status mobility in Japan has been extremely low, owing to the high threshold of language proficiency. Takayoshi Shintani, chairman of a medical service company that sponsors EPA nursing candidates, commented, "The exam is to make sure the foreigners will fail."[62] Only nineteen EPA candidates passed the nursing exam in 2011, and forty-seven passed in 2012; the pass rate was very low (4 percent in 2011, 11 percent in 2012) compared to the 90 percent among Japanese examinees.[63] Japan's government had to extend the stay of the EPA candidates to boost the pass rate. In 2013, the pass rate for the nursing exam was 10.6 percent, while 36.3 percent of candidates passed the caregiver test.[64] Another unintended consequence is that among those few who actually passed the exam, many decided to return home. For instance, six out of thirty-five Indonesians who passed certified care work exams in 2012 decided to return home.[65] Despite the institutional possibility to acquire permanent residency in Japan, they still feel isolated and excluded in Japan's social and cultural environments.

Conclusion

With the employment of migrant care workers, a society must engage in discursive reconstruction and institutional reorganization of intimate labor. Cross-national comparison reveals a multiplicity of ways in which the moral meaning and cultural significance of care are constantly negotiated: Should care be seen as a family duty or professional work? Should care be characterized as a culturally embedded practice or a form of market service that can be easily transferred to a foreigner? More importantly, are these categorical divisions in opposition to each other as "hostile worlds,"[66] or are they intertwined with each other and dynamically reconstituted in the practice?

It is often assumed that East Asian societies share substantial cultural affinity because of their intersecting histories and common tradition of Confucianism. Facing the similar problems of population aging and care deficit, Taiwan and Japan have nevertheless adopted divergent approaches to recruiting and training migrant care workers ("deferential surrogates" vs. "professional others"). The comparison between these two cases—Taiwan's guest worker program and Japan's EPA program—is summarized in table 1. This comparative study demonstrates the different ways of defining and regulating the intimate labor of geriatric care embedded in distinct care regimes and migration regimes. It also shows that cultural values and social practices associated with care are subject to transformation under the influence of state intervention and the global market.

The intermediaries, commercial brokers in Taiwan and state agencies in Japan, play a critical role in the operation of the transnational care regime. They not only recruit particular types of migrant labor power in accordance with local care culture but also design and implement training curriculums to cultivate particular forms of body and disposition upon migrant workers in order to reconcile inconsistent or even contradictory images about these racial others. Employers and workers also mobilize ethnic difference in different ways to negotiate the mutual constitution of intimate relations and market processes.

Taiwanese brokers seek village women to meet the servile image of

Table 1. Comparing Taiwan's Guest Worker Program and Japan's EPA Program

	Taiwan	*Japan*
Migrant care worker	*Deferential surrogates*	*Professional others*
Care regime	Familism Care as a filial duty	Institutional professionalism Care as a cultural practice
Migration regime	Preferring temporary labor and visible difference	Preferring skilled foreigners and cultural similarity
Employers	Mostly private households	Medical and care institutions
Recruitment	For-profit brokerage	State-to-state direct hiring
Training	Technologies of servitude	Technologies for assimilation
Ethnic difference	As boundary marker for status hierarchy	As barrier to cultural assimilation or break from cold professionalism
Labor control	Live-in control and citizenship exclusion	Cultural submission and professional exclusion

"traditional women" and to serve as "deferential surrogates" for female employers. The training program not only cultivates workers' dispositions for servitude but also teaches them about the modern literacy of domesticity. The ethnic difference of migrant caregivers is considered a means to rationalize their subordinate status at the employer's home and their social exclusion in the receiving country. Yet, migrant caregivers may also develop new forms of intimacy with their clients when detaching from kinship and cultural connections.

Japan's government recruits only skilled workers from overseas, including both women and men, and limits their workplace to care facilities and hospitals. Japan's distrust of foreign workers goes hand in hand with its emphasis on the cultural significance of care. The training curriculum aims to bridge cultural distance and tame the otherness of migrants, so they can perform not only professional care but also intimate labor as a localized cultural practice. Migrant nurses' mobilization of ethnic differences as affective capital is a double-edged sword, which may increase the economic value of their expressive emotionality but can also downgrade their professional abilities to natural endowment.

My analysis also shows that both systems of recruiting migrant care workers are not sustainable because of some innate contradictions. The "migrant-in-the-family" pattern, prevailing in Taiwan as well as in southern Europe,[67] relies on market outsourcing to sustain the cultural tradition of familism, while it continues to prolong the privatization of welfare and the feminization of care work. Migrant workers are welcomed into the intimate terrain of private homes and even assigned the role of fictive kin, but they are excluded from the Labor Standards Law and placed in a vulnerable status of disposable labor. Although some migrants have stayed in Taiwan for as long as twelve years—in fact, the Ministry of Labor even recently proposed to further extend their maximum duration of stay to fifteen years—these "guest workers" are permanently ascribed a status of "legally temporary."

The "migrant as professional others" pattern in Japan, on the contrary, defines care as social entitlement and holds the state responsible for supervising quality care for senior citizens. The politics of naming—using the terms *candidate* or *human resource* instead of *worker*—allows the government to place EPA workers in a quasi-trainee program or a preparatory stage of talent immigration without challenging the existing migration regime.[68] They are accepted into intimate spaces on the condition of cultural submission. (We will accept you only if you become more like us.) They may even earn a ticket to permanent residency after passing the exams on professional certification. However, the pass rate of the exams has been extremely low because the evaluation of skills is highly embedded in local culture and language. In other words, the EPA program has become a de facto "quest worker" program, and professionalism has turned into a mechanism of exclusion.

Notes

I am grateful to Hong Hui-Ru and Waka Asato for their assistance with data collection in Japan. I also thank the Global COE program at Kyoto University and Emiko Ochiai for sponsoring my visit. Leslie Wong, Ruri Ito, Chiho Ogaya, Reiko Ogawa, Rhacel Parreñas, Hung Cam Thai, Rachel Silvey, and the anonymous reviewers of *positions* have provided fruitful comments during the revision process.

1. Michael Hardt, "Affective Labor," *Boundary 2* 26, no. 2 (1999): 89–99.
2. Nicola Yeates, "A Global Political Economy of Care," *Social Policy and Society* 4, no. 2 (2005): 227–34.

3. Mika Toyota, "Transnational Care Regime in Asia" (paper presented at the conference on "Transnational Mobilities for Care: State, Market, and Family Dynamics in Asia," National University of Singapore, September 10–11, 2009).

4. Mario Lopez, "Reconstituting the Affective Labour of Filipinos as Care Workers in Japan," *Global Networks* 12, no. 2 (2012): 252–68.

5. Pei-Chia Lan, *Global Cinderellas: Migrant Domestics and Newly Rich Employers in Taiwan* (Durham, NC: Duke University Press, 2006).

6. Ministry of Labor, Republic of China (Taiwan), statdb.mol.gov.tw/statis/jspProxy.aspx?sys =100&kind=10&type=1&funid=q13o1&rdm=leabieek (accessed September 17, 2015).

7. Prime Minister Shinzo Abe proposed in May 2014 to grant entry to foreign domestic workers in six strategic zones where bureaucratic regulations for industry will be relaxed in the hope of revitalizing local economies and creating jobs for both women and men. The six zones are greater Tokyo, the Kansai region around Osaka, Okinawa, and the cities of Fukuoka, Niigata, and Yabu. But local communities have responded with skepticism. See "Osaka Zone a Litmus Test of Foreign Worker Policy," *Japan Daily*, July 20, 2014, www .japantimes.co.jp/news/2014/07/20/national/osaka-zone-a-litmus-test-of-foreign-worker -policy/#.VQfs4ot2c1E.

8. Shun Ohno, "Southeast Asian Nurses and Caregiving Workers Transcending the National Boundaries: An Overview of Indonesian and Filipino Workers in Japan and Abroad," *Southeast Asian Studies* 49, no. 4 (2012): 541–69, 544.

9. Japan International Corporation of Welfare Services (JICWELS), *2015 Handbook for EPA Nurses and Certified Care Worker*, www.jicwels.or.jp/files/H27E58F97E585A5E3828 CE38080E38391E383B3E38395E383A.pdf (accessed March 16, 2015).

10. Japan's government has released no statistics on the gender distribution of EPA workers. According to a survey conducted with candidates who attended the predeparture orientation in Indonesia (with 100 percent response rate), 12.8 percent of nurses and 31 percent of certified care workers were males. Women still constituted the majority of EPA candidates from the Philippines. O. Yuko Hirano, Reiko Ogawa, and Shun Ohno, "A Comparative Study of Filipino and Indonesian Candidates for Registered Nurse and Certified Care Worker Coming to Japan under Economic Partnership Agreements: An Analysis of the Results of Questionnaire Surveys on the Socioeconomic Attribution of the Respondents and Their Motivation to Work in Japan," *Southeast Asian Studies* 49, no. 4 (2012): 594–610. It should be noted that nursing started as a male occupation in Indonesia during the Dutch colonization. Rosalia Sciortino, *Care-Takers of Cure: An Anthropological Study of Health Centre Nurses in Rural Central Java* (Yogyakarta: Gadjah Mada University Press, 1995).

11. "First Vietnamese Nurse Candidates to Arrive in June," *Japan Times*, May 30, 2014, www .japantimes.co.jp/news/2014/05/30/national/first-vietnamese-nurse-candidates-to-arrive-in -june/#.VQeLXEt2c1E.

12. According to a survey with 190 Filipina caregivers, 65 percent of them first came to Japan as

contract entertainers. They tend to be older (aged between 35 and 40) and have lower education levels than EPA candidates. Sachi Takahata, Hisako Nagai, Ma Reinaruth D. Carlos, Yumiko Gotoh, and Nobue Suzuki, "2008 Filipino Caregivers in Japan Survey Report" (in Japanese, unpublished report, 2008).

13. Pei-Chia Lan, "Revisiting *Global Cinderellas*: Taiwan's Care and Migration Regimes" (paper presented at the Second World Congress of Taiwan's Studies, SOAS, London, June 18–20, 2015).

14. Ministry of Internal Affairs and Communications, Statistics Bureau, Japan, www.stat.go.jp/english/data/handbook/c02cont.htm (accessed January 31, 2013).

15. Ministry of the Interior, Republic of China (Taiwan), *2008 Population Whitebook 2008*, www.moi.gov.tw/stat/news_content.aspx?sn=7121 (accessed January 31, 2013).

16. Stephen Castles and Davidson Alastair, *Citizenship and Migration: Globalization and the Politics of Belonging* (New York: Routledge, 2000).

17. Mary Daly and Jane Lewis, "The Concept of Social Care and the Analysis of Contemporary Welfare States," *British Journal of Sociology*, no. 51 (2000): 281–98. Ann Orloff, "Gender and the Social Rights of Citizenship: The Comparative Analysis of Gender Relations and Welfare States," *American Sociological Review*, no. 58 (1993): 303–28.

18. Ministry of Health and Welfare, Republic of China (Taiwan), *2013 Report on the Senior Citizen Condition in Taiwan-Fuchien Area* (Taipei: Ministry of Health and Welfare, ROC, 2014).

19. Ministry of the Interior, Republic of China (Taiwan), 2009 *Report on the Senior Citizen Condition in Taiwan-Fuchien Area* (Taipei: Ministry of the Interior, ROC, 2010).

20. Lan, "Revisiting *Global Cinderellas*," ch. 3. Pei-Chia Lan, "Subcontracting Filial Piety: Elder Care in Ethnic Chinese Immigrant Families in California," *Journal of Family Issues* 23, no. 7 (2002): 812–35.

21. The government began to set up a long-term care program in 2002, including an ongoing discussion for a universal scheme of long-term care insurance, but the coverage and progress have been very limited. See Lan, "Revisiting *Global Cinderellas*."

22. Noriko Iwai and Tokio Yasuda, eds., *Family Values in East Asia: A Comparison among Japan, South Korea, China and Taiwan Based on East Asian Social Survey 2006* (Kyoto: Nakanishiya, 2011), 88–89.

23. The MHLW Comprehensive Survey of Living Conditions, www.mhlw.go.jp/english/databas e/db-hss/dl/hs091216f.pdf (accessed February 1, 2013).

24. Ito Peng, "Social Care in Crisis: Gender, Democracy, and Welfare Restructuring in Japan," *Social Politics* 9, no. 3 (2002): 411–43.

25. Ibid., 430.

26. Sonya Michel and Ito Peng, "All in the Family? Migrants, Nationhood, and Care Regimes in Asia and North America," *Journal of European Social Policy* 22, no. 4 (2012): 406–18, 410.

27. Ibid., 410.

28. NHK (Japan National Public Broadcasting Organization) and Sazaki Tokuko, *A Nation without Love: Care Workers Are Running Away* (Tokyo: Hankyu Communication, 2008, in Japanese). Hayashi Naoko and Hayashi Tamio, *The Situation and Problem of Care Work* (Tokyo: Hirahara, 2011, in Japanese).

29. NHK and Tokuko, *A Nation without Love*. My interviews with EPA workers.

30. Helma Lutz, "Introduction: Migrant Domestic Worker in Europe," in *Migration and Domestic Work: A European Perspective on a Global Theme*, ed. H. Lutz (Burlington, VT: Ashgate, 2008), 1–10.

31. The only exception is contract fishermen, who are not permitted to set foot on land. Yen-Fen Tseng, "Expressing Nationalist Politics in Guest Worker Program: Taiwan's Recruitment of Foreign Labor (in Chinese), *Taiwanese Journal of Sociology* 32 (2004): 1–58.

32. The other ambiguous category comprises "entertainers"—mostly young women from the Philippines to work at nightclubs—who are legally classified as "visiting performing artists" and therefore not "workers." Nana Oishi, *Women in Motion: Globalization, State Politics, and Labor Migration in Asia* (Stanford, CA: Stanford University Press, 2005).

33. JICWEL, *2013 Handbook for EPA Nurses and Certified Care Workers*, www.jicwels.or.jp/files/H25E5B9B4E5BAA6E78988E38391E383B3E38395E383ACE3838.pdf (accessed February 10, 2013).

34. Erin Aeran Chung, *Immigration and Citizenship in Japan* (New York: Cambridge University Press, 2010).

35. David Martin, "Labor Contractors: A Conceptual Overview," *Asian Pacific Migration Journal* 5, nos. 2–3 (1996): 201–18.

36. Both the Indonesian and Philippine governments outlaw foreigner-owned agencies, so these host-country agencies purchase only the rights of management while registered under the name of local owners.

37. Lan, "Revisiting *Global Cinderellas*."

38. In such cases the agency often assigns the trainees to local households or the agency owner's family (paid with meager wages) as some sort of internship.

39. My interview with a migrant organization KOPBUMI in Jakarta, August 21, 2003.

40. Shu-Ju Ada Cheng, "Rethinking the Globalization of Domestic Service: Foreign Domestics, State Control, and the Politics of Identity in Taiwan," *Gender and Society* 17, no. 2 (2003): 166–86, 176.

41. Pei-Chia Lan, "'They Have More Money but I Speak Better English!' Transnational Encounters between Filipina Domestics and Taiwanese Employers," *Identities: Global Studies in Culture and Power* 10 (2003): 133–61.

42. Daromir Rudnyckyi, "Technologies of Servitude: Governmentality and Indonesian Transnational Labor Migration," *Anthropological Quarterly* 77, no. 3 (2004): 407–34.

43. Hairong Yan, *New Masters, New Servants: Migration, Development, and Women Workers in China* (Durham, NC: Duke University Press, 2008), 96.

44. Pei-Chia Lan, "Negotiating Social Boundaries and Private Zones: The Micropolitics of Employing Migrant Domestic Workers," *Social Problems* 50, no. 4 (2003): 525–49.

45. Erving Goffmann, "The Nature of Deference and Demeanor," *American Anthropologist* 58, no. 3 (1956): 472–502.

46. Elsewhere I propose the concept "global circuits of care," to replace a linear model of "global care chains" to describe relations of interdependence, mutual exchange, and reciprocal influence, rather than one-way traffic of transfer/extraction, between care recipients and care workers, and between the sending country and the receiving country. Lan, "Revisiting *Global Cinderellas*."

47. Ohno, "Southeast Asian Nurses," 544.

48. Nobue Suzuki, "Carework and Migration: Japanese Perspectives on the Japan-Philippines Economic Partnership Agreement," *Asian and Pacific Migration Journal* 16, no. 3 (2007): 357–81.

49. Wako Asato, "Nurses from Abroad and the Formation of a Dual Labor Market in Japan," *Southeast Asian Studies* 49, no. 4 (2012): 652–69, 654.

50. Ohno, "Southeast Asian Nurses," 546.

51. The details of the curriculum are based on the Philippines predeparture training program conducted by the Japan Foundation (July 2012) and the training program in Japan conducted by JICWEL, *2013 Handbook for EPA Nurses.*

52. JICWEL, *2013 Handbook for EPA Nurses.*

53. The Cabinet Office, "The Survey on the Expectations of International Migrant Workers," released on September 13, 2010, www8.cao.go.jp/survey/h22/h22-roudousya/index.html (accessed February 15, 2013).

54. EPA candidates from Vietnam need only to acquire a JLPT N3 certificate, JLPT website, Japanese-Language Proficiency Test, www.jlpt.jp/e/about/merit.html (accessed February 10, 2013).

55. Wako Asato and "Multicultural Society and Care" Research Team, *Report on "Cross-Cultural Care" in Japan* (Kyoto: Kyoto University, forthcoming), 80.

56. Bachtiar Alam and Sri Ayu Wulansari, "To Stay or Not to Stay: Diverse and Conflicting Interactions between Indonesian Nurses' Socio-Cultural Backgrounds and Their Work Environment," *Southeast Asian Studies* 49, no. 4 (2012): 611–28, 616.

57. Ibid., 612.

58. Lopez, "Reconstituting the Affective Labour," 261–62.

59. Mario Lopez, "From Bride to Care Worker?: On Complexes, Japan and the Philippines," *M/C Journal* 10, no. 3 (2007), journal.media-culture.org.au/0706/04-lopez.php.

60. Reiko Ogawa, "Globalization of Care and the Context of Reception of Southeast Asian Care Workers in Japan," *Southeast Asian Studies* 49, no. 4 (2012): 570–93, 580, 581.

61. Ibid., 584.

62. Hiroko Tabuchi, "Japan Keeps a High Wall for Foreign Labor," *New York Times*, January 2, 2011.

63. Ohno, "Southeast Asian Nurses," 550. Hirofumi Noguchi and Keishi Takahashi, "Hurdles Still High for Foreign Caregivers," *Yomiuri Shimbun* (The Japan News), March 30, 2012.

64. "Filipino, Indonesian Trainee Nurses to Get More Time to Pass Japan Exams," *Japan Times*, February 24, 2015, www.japantimes.co.jp/news/2015/02/24/national/filipino-indonesian-trainee -nurses-to-get-more-time-to-pass-japan-exams/#.VQf1fkt2c1F.

65. *Mainichi Newspaper*, "Foreign Care Workers 'Want to Stay with Family' and Leave Posts to Return Home" (originally in Japanese), May 8, 2012, article.wn.com/view/WNAT1df7 fa099d9046b6972350a40c22e6c8/ (accessed July 24, 2012).

66. Viviana Zelizer, *The Purchase of Intimacy* (Princeton, NJ: Princeton University Press, 2005).

67. Francesca Bettio, Annamaria Simonazzi, and Paola Villa, "Change in Care Regimes and Female Migration: The 'Care Drain' in the Mediterranean," *Journal of European Social Policy* 16, no. 3 (2006): 271–85.

68. I thank Ruri Ito for her insightful comment here.

What to Expect When You're Expecting:

The Affective Economies of Consuming Surrogacy in India

Sharmila Rudrappa

Introduction

"*We* are thirty-two weeks pregnant and everything is going very well. We feel truly blessed and want to thank [doctors' names deleted] . . . and everyone else at [hospital's name deleted]. So here are our two gorgeous babies" (my emphasis). Jocelyn, a forty-year-old straight US woman, writes on her blog. She also posts ultrasound photos of two fetuses. She, however, is not pregnant; the two Delhi surrogate mothers she has contracted with, are. Jocelyn lives in Chicago with her husband of ten years, and after numerous failed in-vitro fertilization (IVF) attempts, she is pursuing surrogacy in Delhi. Claiming the pregnancy as theirs, Jocelyn thanks everyone in India, except those crucial actors in this whole market exchange in babies, the surrogate mothers. Jocelyn's ownership of pregnancy is not an unusual phenomenon. Straight and queer couples/individuals who arrive in India for

positions 24:1   DOI 10.1215/10679847-3320149

cross-border reproductive care make similar pronouncements about their transformed corporeal abilities.

In this article, I build from these sorts of proclamations of "their pregnancy" by consumers of surrogacy to examine two aspects to global affective economies: What are commissioning parents' emotions and expectations—both voiced and felt—regarding surrogacy? And, how do these emotional orientations affect the surrogate mother and her intimate labors so central to making that embryo into a baby?

Much of the literature on caring labor focuses on the workers, often third world women who provide emotional, physical, and intellectual labor to further the comforts of first world individuals. In this article I turn the gaze around. I ask what sorts of demands first world consumers make, that is, the expectations they have that shape the labor experiences of third world women. I examine the specific case of surrogate mothers who provide the intimate labors that go into gestating and birthing babies that make first world parentage possible. The latter's desires for normative nuclear families complete with genetically descended children; their anxieties about India when they have perhaps never traveled outside the United States; their expectations for caring concern; their desires sometimes unspoken, but expected to be fulfilled; their love for "their" babies—often still just fertilized eggs—all shape the work experiences of surrogate mothers who are pumped with hormones, sequestered in surrogacy dormitories away from their own families and children, and, almost always, cut open in caesarian surgeries in order for first world clients to achieve their own nuclear families replete with that priceless baby who nonetheless comes at a market price.

This leads to the second concern: what becomes of the surrogate mother and her intimate labors in making that embryo into a baby, in market-driven, cross-border reproductive care? In this article, I look specifically at the tensions in the market between the disappearance and the reappearance of the surrogate's maternal body. For much of her market-driven pregnancy, the surrogate mother is invisible, but she reappears once the baby is born as maybe the mother who might want to hold, breast-feed, and otherwise nurture the newborn. Building from interviews with seventy surrogate mothers, and thirty-one egg donors in the southern Indian city of Bangalore, and twenty commissioning parents from the United States and Australia, I examine the affective work involved in transnational surrogacy to explain how in Indian cities such as Mumbai, Anand, Hyderabad, Delhi, and Bangalore, surrogate mothers have become empty receptacles, mere body space that is rented; whereas those who commission that labor, that is, first world straight and queer couples/individuals who purchase their labor power, become true creators, progenitors of labor power that begets new life.

Having disappeared from the labor exchange as a producing body because of childbirth, the surrogate mother reenters the scene, this time as a maternal body whose breasts can nourish that baby. It is this reappearance that needed to be resolved by the commissioning parents. If the surrogate mother breast-feeds, then does that make her a mother? What is her social and legal status vis-à-vis the newborn? This need for disappearance and reappearance of the mother workers, driven by client affect, has stark material consequences for the former.

Transnational Surrogacy in India

Transnational surrogacy in India exploded off the blocks when the Indian state commercialized surrogacy in 2002. Though the United States was the leading provider of surrogacy services for couples/individuals around the world, India today has captured that position in the global market.[1] By 2012 it was estimated that surrogacy would generate US\$2.3 billion in gross business profits.[2] While many note that India's popularity is explained by low costs—surrogacy for a singleton baby is between \$35,000 and \$45,000 in comparison to between \$80,000 and \$100,000 in the United States—not all commissioning parents arrive there to take advantage of bargain prices. Instead, they perceive other benefits. In this global assembly line in baby production, sperm can be shipped from the United States or wherever the clients reside. If needed, eggs can be sourced from working-class Indian women, university students in the United States, or women from the Republic of Georgia and even South Africa to match parental racial preferences.

Some interviewees explained that Indian laws are exceedingly commissioning-parent friendly; because eggs are either extracted from the commissioning mother or purchased on the market from a third party, the surrogate mother has no genetic relationship to the baby/babies she bears. As a result, she has little legal recourse if she wants to keep the baby she has gestated for close to nine months. Moreover, the Indian infertility industry is strongly pro-consumer in its orientation; almost all mothers, for example, deliver babies through caesarian sections at weeks thirty-six or thirty-seven of gestation so that consumers are not inconvenienced. They can pick up "their" babies at stipulated times rather than having to arrive and wait until the surrogate mother goes into labor.

In the interest of profit maximization, infertility specialists do not discriminate against the gay men who arrive in India to have babies. This, however, is under legal contestation. Though Indian law has had quite a laissez-faire attitude toward commissioning parents' sexuality up to the present, laws implemented in early 2013 ban gay men, single individuals, and couples married for fewer than two years from entering into surrogacy contracts. There are no clear stipulations for when these laws go into effect, and individuals/couples who currently hold surrogacy contracts, with their surrogate mothers still pregnant, are understandably anxious about the legal status of the fetuses not as yet delivered. Indian infertility assistance providers and brokers of surrogacy services are up in arms regarding these new developments. Dr. Samit Sekhar, embryologist for the Kiran Infertility Centre in Hyderabad, which receives around 120 international individuals/couples every year, says, "A lot of couples who come to us are heterosexual couples but unmarried. In foreign countries, marriage can be an expensive proposition and several couples refrain from it. To deny them the right to have a baby is not correct."[3] Dr. P. Rama Devi, proprietor of Rama's Institute of Fertility, also in Hyderabad, poses rhetorically, "Why should we interfere in their culture. If their country is allowing such a lifestyle, why should we have an objection?"[4] These disturbing homophobic legislative developments aside—which may very well be overturned because of the legal conundrum surrounding the status of fetuses, frozen fertilized eggs, and sperm that legally belong to gay and heterosexual nonmarried clients all over the world—India has up to now been remarkably consumer friendly.

The main reason, however, for India's prominence in cross-border reproductive care is the availability of inexpensive and compliant labor; that is, the large number of working-class women who offer themselves up as surrogate mothers. One infertility specialist, visiting Dallas from Mumbai to recruit clients, said to me, "Any time you decide is right for you, we can work with you. At any given time we have at least two or three women ready to be surrogates. You can choose." The choice for many clients, however, is not one among many different surrogate mothers, but between one or more surrogate mothers. Many opt to contract with two women.

Most commissioning parents explained that they had very high chances of a successful surrogacy pregnancy in India because infertility specialists transfer four embryos each into two surrogate mothers recruited for each client. These embryos are prepared with sex cells that legally belong to the commissioning couple/individual. The doctors selectively reduce fetuses if all embryos begin to grow. That is, they serially inject selected fetuses with potassium chloride to terminate their further development. Thus, each surrogate mother carries one to two fetuses to term, and the commissioning couple can walk away with two to four babies. Most of my interviewees, however, have had one to three surrogated children all born within days or weeks of each other, through two Indian surrogate mothers.

In addition to their availability, Indian working-class women are ideal mother workers.[5] Given the traditional mores of Indian societies, very few working-class women consume alcohol, smoke, or use illicit drugs. They are also acquiescent to upper-middle-class medical personnel's suggestions, submitting themselves to a plethora of hormonal shots and pills, and invasive gestational and birthing technologies that include transvaginal ultrasounds and caesarian sections.

It is small wonder, then, that India has emerged as a "mother destination" for families around the world.[6] New legislation might make the country a desirable site for only heterosexual couples seeking cross-border reproductive services, but up until now, gay men too have arrived in large numbers to have genetically related babies in order to complete their families. The poor availability of assisted reproductive technologies in their own countries because of bans on trade in reproductive materials and services, homophobia, legislation against gay fatherhood, and the exorbitant costs associated with surrogacy propel them toward India.[7] Though the 8 to 10 million Indian couples estimated to be childless could use infertility assistance,[8] such care is outside their economic purview. They remain "reproductive exiles" cast out of the privileged world of reproduction and stigmatized in the pronatalist cultures prevalent in their communities.[9] Instead, upper-middle-class Indians and clients from the United States, the United Kingdom, Australia, Israel, Germany, and Japan come to avail themselves of cutting-edge, cross-border reproductive care.

Transnational Surrogacy as Intimate Labor

The term *reproductive tourism* refers to individuals traveling from their country of residence to another in order to receive infertility assistance that is not available or is expensive in their own country.[10] I use the term *cross-border reproductive care* rather than the more commonly used *reproductive tourism* for two reasons—first, *cross-border reproductive care* recenters the concept of care and the attendant physical, emotional, and intellectual labors involved.[11] Tourism, too, is attended by caring labor provided by men but mostly women in third world destinations.[12] However, the caring labor that underwrites transnational reproductive regimes is fundamentally different from the caring labor involved in tourism, which is centered on the consumption of leisure and recreational services.

Those seeking reproductive services in India are there for procreation and not recreation. Their travels are often a last resort to having children, involving the purchase of eggs, ownership of fetuses, and the exchange and establishment of legal rights to babies. Many heterosexual couples have already undergone painful and expensive infertility interventions in their own countries before turning to India; and many gay couples are unable to adopt because of legal restrictions. Far from the relaxation and rejuvenation suggested in the term *tourism*, they are stressed about egg retrievals, sperm deposits, and making decisions on egg donors or surrogate mothers. They are dealing with unfamiliar legal regimes and cultures of medical practice that are deeply unsettling. As a result, the affective economies that surround the experiences of cross-border reproductive care seekers are profoundly different than what is connoted in the term *reproductive tourists*.[13]

Moreover, clients perform affective work as they transform from being childless to now becoming mothers and fathers. Their identities as parents begin far before the babies arrive in their lives, as they purchase strollers and car seats, remodel homes, hold baby showers, hire nannies, and scope out pediatricians. The market is absolutely central to their ability to actualize parenthood on many fronts; not only are the babies possible through the purchase of cross-border reproductive services but, also, their identities as parents—as with any other "normally" pregnant individuals—are solidified even before the arrival of the newborns through consumption.

The infiltration of the market into intimate spheres of life has been thickly described and analyzed,[14] including the commodification of pregnancy wherein the fetus becomes a real, sentient person through the consumption of reproductive imaging technologies.[15] Building from here, I examine how market consumption makes the fetus a person and the first world clients parents, while simultaneously resulting in the disappearance of third world workers. Jocelyn, whom I quote at the article's opening, illuminates how these processes play out: first, the commissioning parents, whether they are men or women, almost always claim the pregnancy as theirs even when they themselves are not pregnant. It is not the surrogate mother who is pregnant, but *they* are, as her emotional state and bodily efforts are transposed to the commissioning parents who often live halfway across the globe. Second, even at a few weeks of age, the fetus becomes a fully sentient person, complete with a personality. Simultaneously, the surrogate mother loses personhood. She disappears from the scene.

While most laborers disappear from production processes—after all, we do not think of the farmworkers who make our everyday meals possible, or autoworkers when we drive our cars to and from work—such disappearance is central to the production of parenthood in surrogacy. Indeed, through banishing the laborers and the intimate labors they perform, client parents become real parents, the real progenitors of those babies born half way across the world in India. The activity of third world women is converted to passivity, while simultaneously, the inactivity of the first world "parent" is rehabilitated into labor effort. Such a conversion, I argue, is not incidental to transnational surrogacy in which infertile and queer couples/individuals seek cross-border reproductive care; instead, such fabrications are the linchpin on which transnational surrogacy operates. Yet, once the babies are delivered, first world parental anxiety becomes apparent: What if the babies feel closer to the women who bore them? Should client parents allow the surrogate mothers to hold the babies? Breast-feed them? Parental affect, I argue in this article, deeply shapes the processes of labor disciplining and working conditions for surrogate mothers. As often is the case, clients may not even express such anxieties because surrogacy agencies and infertility doctors organize the maternity ward—that final site in the global reproductive assembly line[16]—in such a way as to symbolically and materially transfer parental rights from birthing mothers to client parents.

The rest of the article is as follows: I first describe how clients in the United States and Australia come to experience "their" pregnancy even when they themselves are not. If they are considered pregnant, then what of the surrogate mother? How does she fit into the picture? She does not, at least not until the babies are born. If the surrogate mother's body had more or less disappeared from clients' lives, except perhaps as a "womb for rent," then she now enters the scene as a mother who can breast-feed and sustain the neonatal, often premature infant. I then describe how commissioning parents resolve this reappearance of the surrogate mother. I then conclude with observations on surrogacy as intimate labor.

Expectant Parents and Their Incorporeal Pregnancies

Discouraged by negative stories regarding adoption through public agencies, Jeff and his partner who live in Chicago, both in their mid-forties, had turned to a private adoption agency in the United States that specialized in gay parents. They were assigned to be adoptive parents to twin boys, but the birth mother changed her mind after the babies were born. Jeff was heartbroken but respected the birth mother's reproductive rights; if she did not want to surrender her babies for adoption, then it was her prerogative to do so. However, he did not want to put himself in an emotionally compromised situation once again; so he turned to surrogacy. Surrogacy, Jeff said, granted him greater protection because he had legal rights over the fetus. Priced out of the US market, Jeff and his partner turned to India.

As a gay man, Jeff had never given much thought about what it felt like to be pregnant. Yet upon having received news of their Mumbai surrogate mothers' pregnancies, Jeff claimed, "We're pregnant!" Like Jocelyn quoted at the beginning of this article, Jeff's declaration of his alleged bodily capacity to bear children is not unusual. Another US straight woman, who now has a child through a Delhi surrogate mother, wrote in her blog, "So on Monday we'll be six weeks pregnant. Still a long way where a zillion things could go wrong, but still very exciting when you've never been pregnant before. I am going to have so much fun telling my oncologist (who gave me the fabulous news that I was getting a hysterectomy for my 30th birthday) the news the next time I see him." Yet another straight US client and his wife who had contracted with a Delhi surrogate mother writes in his blog about the anxiety he felt about the surrogate mother's pregnancy and her rising beta human chorionic gonadotropin (hCG) levels, "Even with our beta levels rising as they have, the days in between updates have been torture."

Why do commissioning parents say they are pregnant when they so obviously are not? Not only do they legally own the fetus that grows within the surrogate mother, but they assert ownership over the her bodily processes in growing that fetus; somehow, her beta HCG levels miraculously converted to theirs, and they are, for example, sixteen weeks pregnant or due in five weeks.

I argue that proclamations of "their" pregnancies have to do not just with the anticipation of babies in their lives but also with the palpable fear many commissioning parents felt. Though the fetuses legally belonged to them according to Indian law, this legal recognition changed, depending on the clients' national origins. For example, commercial surrogacy is illegal in much of Australia. Germany, too, does not recognize surrogacy. Moreover, the commissioning parents recognized that the surrogate mother might have a greater moral claim over the baby. After all, the fetus had grown in her body and depended on her nurturance for its development and survival. The commissioning parents worried that the newborn and surrogate mother were closer to each other, both physically and emotionally, than they themselves were to their newly arriving family member. One couple mentioned that they chose India because the surrogate mothers there had few or no rights over the baby they gestated. If the mothers changed their minds, then they would have no legal recourse in claiming the baby, as they might in many other countries. Under these circumstances of morally, though not legally enforceable, competing claims, the commissioning parents' anxieties over the establishment of parental rights over the fetuses through bodily claims were understandable.

Moreover, the fetuses were unfamiliar social "beings" who had to be experienced vicariously. This is the case for all men or individuals pursuing domestic surrogacy; however, transnational surrogacy poses its own challenges, given that the fetus is growing halfway across the globe in a third world woman's body, someone with whom first world clients are unable, or unwilling, to develop empathetic bonds. My conversation with Steve and Stephanie, who are in their mid-thirties and live in Boston, is illustrative. Stephanie has viable eggs but is unable to sustain a pregnancy to term. When Steve suggested that they go to Delhi, Stephanie demurred. She knew that she would not be able to relate to the Indian surrogate mother and would not be able to comprehend what it felt like for that woman to be pregnant with "her" baby. Finally, she relented when faced with the costs of a domestic surrogacy. It seemed that for Stephanie, the surrogate mother was expected to not only give her a baby but also make available for her the experience of pregnancy. That is, the surrogate mother was to elucidate what she was going through, and what it felt like to have that fetus grow within her so that Stephanie could experience pregnancy vicariously.

Stephanie expressed her anxieties about her inabilities to develop empathetic bonds with surrogate mothers; many clients, however, made no such effort. Living in vastly different worlds in Australia or the United States, the only way they were able to concretize the arrival of the babies was through consuming photographs of the mothers' pregnant bodies and ultrasound images of fetuses the Indian infertility specialists updated them with over e-mail. In an attempt to feel connected with the fetuses then, the commissioning parents spoke of the surrogate mothers' pregnancies as their own, and they flooded their blogs with ultrasound images and countdowns to delivery dates.

The commissioning parents labored to make the "baby" less alien, something not achieved through market exchange but birthed through their intentions. But in claiming the infants as theirs, the intended parents mythologized the babies' origins. They claimed the surrogate's pregnancy as their own, declaring themselves pregnant, imaginatively reassigning the surrogate mother's labor to their own bodies. By recasting themselves as "true" parents, they unintentionally and inadvertently but effectively cast out the surrogate mother's efforts in making the baby. She was obliterated.

Instead, in her place the fetus became a person with its own fully developed personality.

Given that they were unable to communicate in one common language, and they occupied vastly different social worlds, the client parents were unable to speak eloquently about the surrogate mothers who worked for them. As a result, they said little about the surrogate mothers, especially in comparison to the expansive descriptions about their experiences traveling to India, and their efforts at parenting once the babies arrived into their lives. Their blogs contained little information on the surrogate mothers. Instead, along with images of ultrasounds, the fetuses had extensive descriptions; they were the size of a "walnut," or they weighed as much as fifty toothpicks. Almost all the clients interviewed, and many who maintained blogs, posted pictures of the fetuses and attributed all sorts of characteristics to them. One couple wrote that one of their twins "looked a bit evil, as if rubbing palms together planning world domination." Another person declares under the picture of the fetus, "I just wanna pinch those little chubby cheeks!!! I think that's his/her little hand in front of his/her mouth. But, I can't help but imagine that he/she is singing a happy tune or whistling the time away. (Now that I look again, maybe it looks like he/she is spitting!)" All that mattered were the growing fetuses and the clients as a nuclear family. The surrogate mothers, never in a relationship with the clients to begin with, disappeared.

Feeding Babies

The surrogate mothers, however, reappeared after the birth of the babies. Their reemergence, though, was fraught; once the babies were born, should surrogate mothers be allowed to handle the babies or, more crucially, be allowed to breast-feed the infants to whom they had just given birth?

Elvia's story is illustrative. A forty-six-year-old dark-skinned Latina from California who had been dealing with infertility for the past decade, she and her white husband traveled to Anand, Gujarat. There, they contracted with an Indian surrogate mother named Bharati to have a baby for them grown from an Indian donor's egg and Elvia's husband's sperm. Elvia explained that upon her caesarian delivery, Bharati had cried uncontrollably. Later she held the baby to her breast and fed him, which Elvia found revolting. The mother's body was dirty, Elvia explained, because she had not cleaned her breasts before feeding the baby. Elvia wanted to contract with Bharati again to have a second child, but this time she said she would take a breast pump so that the mother could express her milk in order to nourish the baby.

While I was quick to make unkind judgments about Elvia, who had found Barathi's body perfectly acceptable for pregnancy but not for nursing, there was more to this story. In subsequent conversations, I came to realize that Elvia's disgust with Barathi was overdetermined by her own social status, and the devaluation of her motherhood because of her race and age. Like most other commissioning mothers who choose egg donors who resemble them in order to perpetuate the social perception that the babies are their genetic descendants,[17] Elvia had requested that a dark-skinned egg donor be selected. The Indian doctor disregarded Elvia's requests and chose an extremely light-skinned donor. The resultant baby was far more light skinned than Elvia had imagined her child could be. In ensuing discussions, Elvia said that because she was an older Latina woman, people refused to recognize her as a mother. Instead, she was repeatedly mistaken as being a nanny to her own son.

Elvia articulates her anxieties about her own systematic, social devaluation through expressing disgust at Bharathi's efforts in mothering the newborn baby. However, she was not alone in her anxieties. Many interviewees said that in order to "protect" the surrogate mother from bonding with the baby, they did not allow her to hold or breast-feed the baby. Instead, they bottle-fed the babies. Thus, their anxieties about establishing their parenthood were recast as an act of benevolence toward the mothers, regardless of what the women themselves wanted.

Some clients preferred to have the surrogate mothers use breast pumps to extract milk and deliver it to them, so that the newly minted first world parents could bottle-feed "their" babies. A straight US married woman, whom I have not interviewed, and now has twin children through a Gujarati surrogate mother named Kailash, writes the following in her blog:

> Everyone knows . . . La Leche has been very successful getting the message out. Breast is better. Well, my breasts don't have any milk in them. . . .

Kailash does have milk in her breasts and *I want it.* . . . Part of the surrogacy contract requires Kailash to provide breast milk for 15 days. After
that, we can have more, but we need to negotiate the details. . . . I asked
for it and Kailash started pumping. She was transferred 2 blocks to the
hospital where the NICU [Neonatal Infant Care Unit] was located for
ease. I asked her to come down to NICU to pump every 2 hours, but
somehow something was lost in the Gujarati-English translation. . . . I
realized *I needed to be managing Kailash.* . . . When we brought the babies
back to [the hotel] things got even worse. Now the milk needed to be
delivered down the street. And the pump needed to be sterilized. Kailash
is back at the . . . hospital where she gave birth. Every 2 hours, we need to
fetch milk from Kailash and bring the pump back to [the hotel] for ster-
ilization. Then the process begins again. . . . I feel like a drug runner, or
a gerbil on a treadmill. I'm almost ready to quit, but working on finding
a runner to pay to do the back and forth. Everything can be outsourced
in India. (emphasis added)

Upon reading this callous and rather disturbing self-representation on her
blog, one cannot help but ask: Why did Kailash have to pump her breasts for
milk instead of simply breast-feed the twins she had just birthed? And how
had her degradation, which included childbirth through caesarian surgery
and the attachment of a machine to extract milk from her breasts, been
converted to the commissioning mother's pain and suffering?

Thus, even when the surrogate mothers reappeared, they were not as full
agents but as bodies that still needed management in order to be harvested.
Their third world bodies were perceived as perfectly adequate for growing
first world babies, but once the babies arrived, it was a different story. The
women fell back to wretchedness; although their wombs were once salu-
brious rental spaces that cultivated first world reproductive materials into
personhood, the women were now too foul to hold the babies they grew.

However, it was not simply a matter of purity or pollution; rather, it was
the active reinsertion of the maternal body as producer of the baby that
troubled clients. If she were indeed the mother, the one who had sustained
and could still sustain that newborn baby, then where did that leave the first
world client? Thus, their anxieties about breast-feeding were not worries

about the contamination of the infant; instead, breast-feeding interrupted their experiences of being authentic parents. These kinds of anxieties about the surrogate mother, though, were resolved through enforcing market relations. The market protected the clients.

The Market as Protection

Pedro Paulo's story of becoming a father through transnational surrogacy is illustrative of the market as protection. Pedro Paulo came from Brazil to the United States as a graduate student and went on to complete his doctoral work in electrical engineering in Canada. Coming from a large family, he always wanted to have children, but being a single gay man in his mid-forties, he felt that his only option was surrogacy. He first worked with a California agency, which charged him over $125,000 for the whole process, which did not include medical insurance and flight charges for the surrogate mother, a woman from Ohio. With $85,000 as down payment, Pedro Paulo started his surrogacy journey in the United States, which did not end well. The Ohio surrogate mother he worked with, a woman in her early thirties, miscarried twice. Given that they had become somewhat emotionally close by then, she persuaded him to attempt an intra-uterine insemination. That is, she would use her own eggs and his sperm to birth a baby. He was unable to extricate himself from how far he and the surrogate mother had traveled on the road to achieving paternity, and he found himself agreeing, although very reluctantly. The third time too, she miscarried.

Pedro Paulo was shattered, and he ended his relationship with the surrogate mother. It was really hard, he expressed; at least when intimate sexual relationships ended there were finger pointing and accusations. But how does one break up with someone who is your surrogate mother, with whom you have a market contract, but also, upon whom you are emotionally dependent, but only because she would give you a baby? He and the Ohio surrogate mother were tied together only because of the possibility of a baby, but how was one to sustain a relationship when the baby did not materialize? Pedro Paulo laughed, "This was the hardest break-up I had. A gay guy like me with a straight woman like her. We were from totally different worlds, but to walk away . . . that hurt." He felt emotionally and financially wrung out. He half-heartedly attempted adoption upon the urging of his mother, but as a single gay man his chances were poor.

It was right around then he became aware of surrogacy in India and decided to work with an infertility specialist in Delhi. When the surrogate mother who had been contracted to work with him miscarried, he said he felt nothing. Because of the repeated disappointments, he had no hopes to begin with, and he felt emotionally dead. The specialist suggested they try again, but this time with two surrogate mothers. He agreed. Finally, in his fifth round of surrogacy, he walked away with a baby boy. It seemed too good to be true, but now Pedro Paulo was finally a single gay father, at age fifty-one.

"You know," he reflected, "surrogacy in India was far easier on me than my experience in the US." Not knowing the Indian surrogate mothers who had contracted with him, not even having met them or spoken with them, he felt protected emotionally. Not only was surrogacy in India cheaper in comparison to the United States but, also, he was afforded far more emotional protection because of the cultural and class differences that put him and the surrogate mother in vastly different social worlds. He felt no obligation to meet her or perform any of the affective work that was expected of him when he worked with the US surrogate mother. He got the baby he wanted, but without having the emotional burdens of caring for the woman who birthed his fatherhood.

Jeff, the Chicago gay father, had a slightly different perspective from Pedro Paulo's. I asked him if he stayed in touch with the surrogate mothers who had made his and his partner's fatherhood possible. He said no. From his perspective as a gay man, the surrogate mothers were "women hired to do a job." He explained that he was afforded complete emotional protection in a way he was not when he had attempted the open adoption; adoption in the United States was emotionally devastating because he had no rights in comparison to the birth mother. Moreover, surrogacy in India allowed him to cut all ties with the Indian surrogate mother in a way he may not have been able to do so with a US woman. In his perception, this was an advantage because it reduced what is described as "post-contractual opportunistic behavior."[18] That is, he worried that the surrogate mothers would make financial and nonfinancial/emotional demands on him and his partner, who might feel obligated or emotionally blackmailed into meeting their demands. He said that while it may sound callous, he stuck to the terms of the contract because he did not want further contact with the surrogate mothers, which could potentially lead to all sorts of expectations on their parts. This did not mean he was not grateful for their efforts, but he did not want surplus emotional ties in his life, which already felt overburdened.

Client parents deferred to the market exchange of wages for babies because by doing so, they established pregnancy as a form of wage labor. To call pregnancy a labor exchange mediated solely by the market, rather than a gift or nonmarket transaction, protected clients in two ways: first, they could walk away from the process and not worry about what surrogate mothers might feel about giving up babies they had just birthed. The clients themselves, especially women who had undergone repeated attempts at pregnancy, were overwhelmed and emotionally exhausted. They simply did not have the wherewithal to deal with yet more social/familial ties and the responsibilities and expectations that went along with such ties. Just as someone who might purchase a car does not express any empathy for the workers who make that car, payment protected clients from engaging in any sort of reciprocal caring with surrogate mothers. They did not have to hear about her anxiety—her sadness about being separated from her own family, for example—or her fears about the impending caesarian surgery, which almost all surrogate mothers undergo in order to give birth to babies. Maintaining surrogacy as a market exchange, then, protected commissioning parents from having to critically engage with the labor process and empathize with surrogate mothers.

Client parents repeatedly expressed in myriad ways that they had been through an emotional roller coaster in their pursuit of motherhood and fatherhood, and they did not have it in them to bring yet another person into their lives and their nuclear families, least of all a working-class woman halfway across the globe who inhabited a vastly different social world. By receiving wages for her labor, the clients asserted, the surrogate mother had agreed to cut all ties to the baby and them for a predetermined payment. Thus, the market afforded clients protection. Contracts safeguarded them from any messy emotions and intimate work they might have to perform in the intimate transactions involved during the surrogate mother's pregnancy.

By deferring to global market exchanges, they kept their relationship at strictly the contractual level, and all social contact was terminated once the babies were delivered. The surrogate mother was exorcized from their lives.

The Market as Exorcist

Intimate labor connotes the purchase of intimacy.[19] Embodying forms of care work, such as domestic service, child care, home care of the elderly, and the provision of haircuts, manicures, pedicures, or sexual services, necessitate the exchange of bodily information and familiarity, often with clients occupying temporal positions of vulnerability vis-à-vis the workers. The client has to rely on the laborer to provide physical and emotional services that fulfill their sexual needs, bodily upkeep, care for kith and kin, health and hygiene maintenance, and help to create and sustain social and emotional ties.[20] However, in this article, I show that this temporal position of client vulnerability is managed through market relations. By sticking to the language of the contract and operating as if the entire intimate labor exchange were modulated by only the medium of money, a barrier is formed between the producer and the consumer, which facilitate the eventual truncation of the relationship to the benefit of the latter.

Transnational surrogacy has superficial similarities to other intimate industries, namely, sex tourism. In both industries there is a global movement of clients and workers, and there is a brisk trade in emotions as bodily needs are assuaged. Yet, surrogacy is fundamentally different because the end product is "customer satisfaction," new life has been created, and babies are exchanged for money between clients and workers. The creation of life does not make surrogacy more sacred, and sex work more profane. Instead, my point here is to think through how different intimate industries are organized based on what is being produced. As a form of intimate labor, transnational surrogacy traffics in reproductive care wherein first world clients' procreational needs are met. That is, they receive genetically descended children who establish their parentage and the continuity of familial lineage. But the process itself is fraught, taxing clients with anxieties over the potential failure of in-vitro fertilizations of surrogate mothers, unsettling interactions with "foreign" doctors and medical personnel, and getting birth certificates, passports, and other such documents that entail coordination between the legal regimes of at least two different nation-states.

Amidst all this emotional instability, the one point of certainty for commissioning parents is that the baby is theirs. They are already parents because they are the source, or at the very least, legal proprietors of the sperm and eggs that go into making embryos that eventually grow to become babies. The surrogate mother is simply a woman who has been hired to grow that baby. She is a canvas, a screen on whom their parental dreams are projected, and their future lives take shape. For all intents and purposes, she has disappeared as a social agent, a person with history, passions, and volition, and as someone who might perhaps nurse budding emotions for the fetus that develops in her. The mediating presence of the mother worker can be disappeared precisely because of the racial/cultural/class differences between her and the clients, and the way the global market is organized to make the most of these differences to the advantage of clients.

The baby's birth, however, brings the surrogate mother's body back into the scene. Commissioning parents are forced to acknowledge that without the surrogate mother's physical and affective labors, the baby would not have an existence. In childbirth she resurfaces as a maternal figure who can provide the newborn with nourishment. But such materialization is forcefully banished once more. The surrogate mothers are believed to have excessive emotions from which the women themselves must be protected, or their bodies are too dirty to breast-feed "first world" babies. This excess manner and bodily material once more needs management. Their wombs already harvested, this time the surrogate mothers' breasts are attached to machines, their bodies reaped of milk to nurture neonatal "first world" life. Through managing the surrogate mother's labor on the shop floor and through sticking to the language of the market, the identity of "parent" is transferred from birth mothers to clients.

The question that arises is this: if pregnancy is wage labor, as avowed by surrogacy agencies, infertility specialists, and intended parents themselves, then is the product of such labor, the baby, necessarily a commodity? Debora Spar notes that we do not like to "think of children as economic objects. They are products, we insist, of love, not money; of an intimate creation that exists far beyond the reach of any market impulse." Yet, she explains that recent innovations in medical technology and business organization have "created a market for babies, a market in which parents choose traits, clinics woo clients, and specialized providers earn millions of dollars a year.[21] In her aptly titled book, *The Baby Business*, Spar maps the trade in infertility services and perhaps even babies in adoption. However, she avers that the defining aspects of the baby trade are the motivations of love and deep commitment parents feel, and thus, "virtually all aspects of the baby trade . . . are technical or social ways for parents to acquire children whom they will subsequently rear and love."[22] The baby business is characterized by the production of "a good that is inherently *good*. It produces children, for people who want them."[23] Partially because of what babies mean, this market does not "necessarily work like the market for pumpkins or mortgages."[24] Prices are not flexible, varying by demand or supply, and, more importantly, "the very idea of property rights—the core of most modern markets—remains either ambiguous or contested,"[25] as it should be with regard to children.

Though the entire process surrounding transnational surrogacy is organized around the exchange of money for eggs, sperm, pregnancy, and finally, a child, Debora Spar asks what is exactly being traded in this market: "Is it babies, or health, or happiness or genes? Is it children or families; bits of protoplasm or the prospect of life?"[26] To call the child a commodity would mean to establish property rights over an individual, and she is reluctant to go in that direction. Instead, she says the money exchanged in the baby business is for the services rendered in making that baby possible, and not the baby itself.

It seems that for Debora Spar, the baby trade, including transnational surrogacy, is directed at procuring custodial rights rather than ownership rights over children. The legal and social demarcation between custody, parental rights, and ownership need to be more clearly understood; but that is beyond the scope of this article. Suffice to say, custodial rights are understood as the right to protect, guard, aid, and raise a child in her best interests. Yet, ownership and custody seem fungible during a surrogate mother's pregnancy and at the child's birth. The language of ownership is routinely inserted in surrogacy transactions. It is precisely because they own the sperm, eggs, or embryos that clients can speak of "my baby." Moreover, the parents themselves engage in "commodity talk" with regard to the babies. They often speak of having given the surrogate mother wages in exchange for a baby or babies, as the case may be.

However, though surrogate mothers receive wages for their pregnancies, the babies they produce are not commodities for all the actors involved, especially for those clients who have made long and heroic attempts to become parents. The language of ownership, tantalizingly close to commodity talk, is a means by which client parents establish that the children do not belong to them but are with them in spirit even before birth. Such language allows them to believe that this baby was always meant to be and always had a place in their hearts prior to even its birth. And once the infant is born, they can walk away with a child that has no social history, and whose origin story begins not with the surrogate mother but with their intentions. They talk about the surrogate pregnancy as pure wage labor and the baby as "theirs" not because they think of these processes as preestablished, already given marketable items; instead, by moving them to the market, they are able to engage in a form of love that feels purer and more authentic to their family-making efforts. The market allows commissioning parents to claim an unalloyed relationship with that fetus. It is precisely because of such commodification of intimacy that love is possible. That is, intimate industries facilitate first world parental love to be established, but only through exorcising the third world mother. This third world mother is not an evil spirit in the sense that she is malevolent and wicked; instead, her continued presence in the life of the child she has birthed disrupts the narrative of the normative nuclear family of two parents and their genetically descended children. There is no place for her in that idyllic intimate sphere, and she must necessarily be exorcised. Sticking to market logic, then, allows her to be banished and births the nuclear family replete with ideals of love, loyalty, and devoted caring.

Notes

1. Lisa Ikemoto, "Eggs as Capital: Human Egg Procurement in the Fertility Industry and the Stem Cell Research Enterprise," *Signs* 34, no. 4 (2009): 763–81; Ruby Lee, "New Trends in Global Outsourcing of Commercial Surrogacy: A Call for Regulation," *Hastings Women's Law Journal* (Summer 2009): 275–300.

2. Amrita Pande, "Transnational Surrogacy in India: Gifts for Global Sisters?," *Reproductive BioMedicine Online* 23, no. 5 (2011): 618–25.

3. Bushra Baseerat, "Surrogacy Business Suffers from Birth Pangs," *Times of India*, January 23, 2013, articles.timesofindia.indiatimes.com/2013-01-23/hyderabad/36504785_1_surrogacy-samit-sekhar-reproductive-tourism.

4. Ibid.

5. Amrita Pande, "Commercial Surrogacy in India: Manufacturing a Perfect-Mother Worker," *Signs* 35, no. 4 (2010): 969–92.

6. Sharmila Rudrappa, "Making India the 'Mother Destination': Outsourcing Labor to Indian Surrogates," in *Gender and Sexuality in the Workplace*, ed. Christine Williams and Kirsten Dellinger, vol. 20, Research in the Sociology of Work (Bingley, UK: Emerald Group, 2010).

7. Turkey, for example, has banned the use of donor eggs, sperm, and surrogacy since 1987. See Zeynep Gurtin, "Banning Reproductive Travel: Turkey's ART Legislation and Third-Party Assisted Reproduction," *Reproductive BioMedicine Online* 23, no. 5 (2011): 555–64. Germany, France, and Italy ban all forms of surrogacy. Commercial surrogacy is illegal in Australia and the United Kingdom. In the United States, a plethora of laws regulate surrogacy; California is extremely commissioning-parent friendly, but New York, for example, does not recognize commercial surrogacy arrangements. Additionally, gay parents may be discriminated against in any of these countries. For example, Israel has historically banned gay men from contracting with surrogate mothers there, though an Israeli Health Ministry committee recently recommended that this ban be lifted. See Roni Linder-Ganz, "Israel to Allow Gay Men to Conceive Children through Surrogates," *Haaretz*, May 20, 2012, www.haaretz.com/news/national/israel-to-allow-gay-men-to-conceive-children-via-surrogates-1.431555.

8. Anjali Widge, "Seeking Conception in India: Experience of Urban Indian Women with In-Vitro Fertilisation," *Patient Education and Counseling* 59, no. 3 (2005): 226–33; S. Sharma, S. Mittal, and P. Aggarwal, "Management of Infertility in Low Resource Countries," *International Journal of Obstetrics and Gynaecology* 116, no. 1 (2009): 77–83.

9. Marcia Inhorn, "Reproductive Exile in Global Dubai: South Asian Stories," *Cultural Politics* 8, no. 2 (2012): 283–308; Roberto Matorras, "Reproductive Exile versus Reproductive Tourism," *Human Reproduction* 20, no. 12 (2005): 3571–73.

10. Matorras, "Reproductive Exile"; Guido Pennings, "Legal Harmonization and Fertility Tourism in Europe," *Human Reproduction* 19, no. 12 (2004): 2689–94.

11. Marcia Inhorn and Zynep Gurtin, "Cross-Border Reproductive Care: A Future Research Agenda," *Reproductive BioMedicine Online* 23 (2011): 665–76; Marcia Inhorn and Pasquale Patrizio, "The Global Landscape of Cross-Border Reproductive Care: Twenty Key Findings for the New Millennium," *Current Opinion in Obstetrics and Gynecology* 24, no. 4 (2012): 158–63.

12. Denise Brennan, *What's Love Got to Do with It: Transnational Desires and Sex Tourism in Dominican Republic* (Durham, NC: Duke University Press, 2004); Kamala Kempadoo and

Jo Doezema, *Global Sex Workers: Rights, Resistance, and Redefinition* (New York: Routledge, 1998).

13. Matorras, "Reproductive Exile."

14. Arlie Hochschild, *Outsourced Self: Intimate Life in Market Times* (New York: Metropolitan Books, 2012); Ellen Boris and Rhacel Parreñas, eds., *Intimate Labors: Cultures, Technologies, and the Politics of Care* (Stanford, CA: Stanford University Press, 2010); Viviana Zelizer, "Risky Exchanges," in *Baby Markets: Money and the New Politics of Creating Families*, ed. Michele Bratcher Goodwin (New York: Cambridge University Press, 2010), 267–77.

15. Rosalind Petchesky, "Fetal Images: The Power of Visual Culture in the Politics of Reproduction," *Feminist Studies* 13, no. 2 (1987): 263–92; Janelle Taylor, Linda Layne, and Danielle Wozniak, *Consuming Motherhood* (New Brunswick, NJ: Rutgers University Press, 2004).

16. Sharmila Rudrappa, "India's Reproductive Assembly Line," *Contexts* 11, no. 2 (2012): 22–27.

17. Charis Thompson, *Making Parents: The Ontological Choreography of Reproductive Technologies* (Cambridge, MA: MIT Press, 2007).

18. Mhairi Galbraith, Hugh V. McLachlan, and J. Kim Swales, "Commercial Agencies and Surrogate Motherhood: A Transaction Cost Approach," *Health Care Analysis* 11, no. 25 (2005): 11–31, 14.

19. Viviana Zelizer, *Purchase of Intimacy* (Princeton, NJ: Princeton University Press, 2005).

20. Boris and Parreñas, *Intimate Labors*, 5.

21. Debora Spar, *The Baby Business: How Science, Money, and Politics Drive the Commerce of Conception* (Boston: Harvard Business School Press, 2006).

22. Ibid., xi.

23. Ibid., 207.

24. Ibid., 196. Emphasis in original.

25. Ibid., 195.

26. Ibid., 207.

Race, Nation, and the Production of Intimacy:

Transnational Ova Donation in India

Daisy Deomampo

Introduction

Jan Marks was thirty-seven years old when she first met her husband, Stephen, in 2005. Two years later, Jan and Stephen were married and in the
midst of expanding their home from two to five bedrooms; already a step-
mother to her husband's sons from a previous marriage, Jan treasured her
family and was eager to fill their home with two more children of her own.
After several miscarriages, however, Jan learned that she had a bicornuate
uterus, commonly referred to as a "heart-shaped" uterus, and it was very
unlikely that she would ever be able to gestate and give birth to a child of her
own. Further, she discovered that because of her age, conception through in-
vitro fertilization (IVF) with her own eggs was not a viable option, and that
they would require the assistance of a third-party egg donor if they ever
chose to pursue parenthood through gestational surrogacy.

positions 24:1   DOI 10.1215/10679847-3320161

Jan was devastated by this news but undeterred in her desire to become a parent. After exploring various options, including international adoption, fostering in Australia, and surrogacy in the United States, Jan and Stephen decided to pursue gestational surrogacy in India. Indian surrogacy appealed to the couple in part because of the relatively low costs and also because they could avoid the long waiting periods and bureaucratic processes associated with international adoption. Moreover, Jan still harbored dreams of having a child that looked like her, so when Jan and her husband booked their first trip to India in December 2008, they made arrangements with a South African egg donor agency to send a white egg donor to India. As Jan explained, "I really wanted a child that looked like me: tall, blond, blue-eyed, that kind of thing. . . . I was really concerned—because I've never had a baby before—that I wouldn't love a baby as much if it didn't look like me."

Yet after several surrogacy attempts ended in miscarriage, Jan had a change of heart regarding the particular phenotypic characteristics she desired in her child. Worried about their shrinking budget, the couple decided to continue pursuing parenthood through gestational surrogacy, but with an Indian egg donor whose fees would be significantly lower than those of the South African donor.[1] When I asked her about this change, Jan replied, "When I'd flown in this South African donor and it didn't work, part of the grief was, 'Oh my god, I'm never going to have a blond-haired, blue-eyed child now!'" But she went on to elaborate that she felt "quite proud" of her decision to use an Indian egg donor. While Jan described herself as "quite fair," she explained that despite her Polish-Scottish heritage, most of her family has darker, olive-toned skin: "A dark child is actually going to fit in well with the family! And honestly, she [the egg donor] is the spitting image of my sister when she was younger. . . . So I carry that donor's photo around with me in my wallet, because I'm just—I'm going to get emotional—but I'm just so grateful." Interestingly, as Jan navigated the disappointment of not being able to have a child that resembled her physically, she took comfort in the fact that her Indian egg donor resembled her sister, and that the child would fit in with her darker-skinned extended family.

This article explores the ways in which commissioning parents pursuing surrogacy in India negotiate the process of third-party egg donation. Indian medical doctors draw attention to the marketlike aspects of gestational surrogacy and egg donation, comparing the process of creating a life (with specified phenotypic or skin color characteristics) to simple consumer choices. As one doctor states, "The womb is like an oven. It merely bakes the cake. Whether you insert a chocolate or strawberry cake is for you to decide."[2] I examine how intended parents and doctors navigate such choices through the practice of transnational egg donation. In particular, I analyze the ways in which commissioning parents construct relations with the anonymous egg donor—the genetic parent of the child—as well as with the child conceived through egg donation, IVF, and gestational surrogacy. I also explore the means through which doctors organize practices of transnational and local egg donation. While egg donors undoubtedly play a central role in this process as the providers of genetic material, in what follows, I focus primarily on the perspectives of doctors and commissioning parents, as I am interested in how these actors, the organizers and consumers of assisted reproduction, deploy notions of race, nationality, and skin color in the context of egg donation. By examining doctors' and parents' narratives, I illustrate the heterogeneity of approaches to egg donation in the context of neoliberal global forces that place the onus on egg purchasers to "choose" the genetic material of future children.

Moreover, I analyze transnational egg donation as an "intimate industry," extending Michael Hardt and Antonio Negri's concept of "immaterial labor" to include the intimate labor that sustains assisted reproduction.[3] I use the term *intimate industry* to refer to intertwined actions that foster intimate relations and organize intimate matters of care and reproduction. In particular, I focus on the ways in which such industries construct intimacy and intimate social relations among various reproductive actors, including commissioning parents, surrogate mothers, and genetic donors, who may remain anonymous or meet only briefly through interactions mediated by doctors and surrogacy brokers. These industries, which foster and commodify intimate relations of reproduction and family making, provide a key lens through which to explore the gendered and racialized inequalities that emerge through transnational linkages and technological advances. By emphasizing the social relations among those involved in transnational reproduction, I consider "intimacy" and intimate relations to involve elements such as "shared secrets, interpersonal rituals, [and] bodily information."[4] Here, I focus on the shared genes and reproductive tissues that individuals exchange and commodify; it is through these genes and tissues that actors construct intimate relations of family and kinship, particularly across boundaries of class and nation.

Similar to the editors and fellow authors of this issue, I draw attention to how intimate relations traverse unequal terrain by attending to the complex ways in which actors comprehend emotional ties and relationships. As Western parents pursue surrogacy and egg donation in India, they make reproductive decisions within a framework of transnational inequalities, including along racial, ethnic, and class lines. I found that for many parents, this process is most intense and intimate within the context of egg donation, and their narratives reveal the diversity of ways in which parents address issues of race, genetics, and kinship. In contrast to dominant assumptions that intended parents primarily seek donors who match their own racial/ethnic backgrounds, I found that of the nineteen mostly white couples/individuals I interviewed who used donor eggs in their surrogacy process, fourteen commissioning couples/individuals sought Indian egg donors with darker skin tones. I suggest that while such actions appear to subvert dominant racial hierarchies that privilege white skin, revealing potential spaces of resistance to racialized preconceptions about kinship, they in fact rely on essentialized notions of race and beauty and reflect new articulations of biological race.[5]

A Note on Nomenclature

Everyone involved in transnational reproductive services refers to the women who undergo hormone stimulation and egg harvesting for payment as "donors." Yet, to call these women donors would be inaccurate; their explicit task in this global reproductive economy is to sell their ova for a specified sum of money. Indeed, all the egg providers I spoke with, both Indian and some South African, said they pursued egg donation because of financial need.

Following Michal Nahman,[6] I refer to these women as "egg providers" or "egg sellers," to call attention to the participation of purchasers and providers of ova in a wider global economy. Doing so confronts the discomfort that egg donation evokes, particularly for those disturbed by the commercial aspects of assisted reproduction. Identifying those who receive eggs as "purchasers" and women who provide them as "sellers" also highlights the positionality of participants. The prospective parents who commission surrogacy arrangements and donor egg IVF typically come from wealthier countries than those from which egg providers and surrogates originate. These distinctions underlie the complex ways that global ova donation and surrogacy reflect broader patterns of stratified reproduction.

Defining Race and Skin Color: Identity and Notions of Essentialism

Jan's story of her path to transnational surrogacy and egg donation raises several questions. How do commissioning parents navigate the process of selecting an egg donor, specifically for the purposes of conception via IVF and gestational surrogacy? What factors might prompt a Western couple pursuing surrogacy in India to select a white egg donor from another country? Alternatively, why might a couple select a darker-skinned Indian egg donor? How do Indian doctors convey the various options available to clients, in terms of race, skin color, or ethnicity? These questions point to broader issues about the intersections among race, kinship, and assisted reproduction: What do these stories tell us about how intended parents understand the relationship between race, nationality, genetics, and kinship? What do these narratives reveal about the broader stratification of reproduction?

In addressing these questions, it is important to first clarify how Western commissioning parents and Indian doctors understand notions of race, skin color, nationality, and ethnicity. In the context of transnational reproduction, I encountered a range of systems of racial and skin color classification among non-Indian commissioning parents and Indian doctors and surrogates. These actors, hailing from different nations, often expressed different understandings of race, skin color, nationality, and ethnicity, which at times intersected and overlapped in the process of transnational reproduction. Here, I explain the ways in which these actors defined and, at times, conflated notions of race, skin color, nationality, and ethnicity.

Foreign commissioning parents traveling to India, for instance, tend to rely on racial categories that reflect Western notions of race based on phenotype. Parents of children conceived with Indian donor eggs and the intended father's sperm often described their children as "biracial" or "mixed-race," meaning they were part Indian and part white, with the understanding that Indians were racially classified as "Asian" as per US census categories. Several parents expressed essentialist views of race in their descriptions of their encounters with Indians during their surrogacy journeys. One Australian woman, for instance, related her belief that Indians "are just an amazing race. They are so kind. They dress so well and look after themselves so well, even when they have nothing." Commissioning parents often conflated this notion of race with ideas of nationality and culture, in ways I will discuss further in this article. Some intended parents, for example, believing that eggs from an Indian woman would make their child "part Indian" through conferral of certain skin color and other physical characteristics, simultaneously felt a responsibility to teach their children about their "Indian heritage." These parents spoke of educating their children about Indian foods, culture, and religious rituals. Further complicating this picture is the belief of still other parents that it was not genetics but gestation that bestowed on children some degree of "Indian" heritage and identity.[7]

In India, on the other hand, the category of race is a complex issue. During British colonial rule in India, there were various attempts to classify the Indian population according to a racial typology, reflecting the predominant racial theories popular in nineteenth-century Europe. Following India's independence from British rule, the 1951 census of India abolished racial classifications, and today the national census does not recognize any racial groups in India. Social conflicts in India are better described in terms of "communalism," in which hierarchies of community, caste, and religion organize social relations. Thus, Western notions of race make little sense in the context of Indian "communal" conflicts. However, with the increase in global consumers of assisted reproductive technologies (ARTs) traveling to India, Indian doctors increasingly adopt the language of race in their interactions with foreign clients. This adds yet another layer of complexity to understandings of race in India as Indians, who rely on categories of caste and religion in their own social contexts, utilize Western categories of race in the global spheres of transnational reproduction.

While Western notions of race remain unusual in India, preferential treatment based on skin color, or colorism, is widespread. In the context of egg donation, then, skin color, not race, is perhaps the most salient organizing feature. By "skin color," I refer to subjective understandings of skin color or tone, which span different terminologies, depending on the context. Many South Asian languages, for example, have terms to refer to different shades of skin tone. In Hindi, *gora/gori* refers to fair or light-skinned individuals, *saanwala* refers to wheatish brown skin, and *kala/kali* means black, or dark skin. In Punjabi, a person's fair complexion is compared to the color of milk (*dudh waken*) or to the color of the moon; a dark person's complexion, on the other hand, is likened to that of a crow or the back of an iron skillet.[8] In one Mumbai IVF clinic, skin color is described on an egg donor profile form along a spectrum of shades, including dark, dark wheatish, wheatish (light brown), light wheatish, fair, and very fair. While individuals of fair and dark skin tone can be found at all levels of caste and class in India, in general, individuals with fair skin enjoy greater wealth and social status.

These categories—of race, nationality, skin color, and ethnicity—and the varied ways in which actors understand, conflate, and define them, hold critical implications for notions of identity and essentialism in the context of reproductive technology. In recent decades, anthropologists have examined the ways in which "identity" is an unstable object of inquiry. Rather than something immutable, identity is not a fixed essence, and scholars have explored how individuals craft their identity through social performances. However, with the increasing availability of and reliance on reproductive and genetic technologies, essentialist identities have grown ever more powerful. New genetic knowledge, with the cloak of prestige lent by "objective science," has propelled the notion that one's identity is an innate, natural, and immutable quality. Gamete donation, for instance, has precipitated a return to ideas of genetic and racial essentialism, in which sperm and egg donor profiles are scrutinized for certain traits, with the promise of inheritable phenotypic and skin color characteristics, among other features. This resurgence has startling implications for those concerned with the feminist and bioethical issues at stake. Cynthia R. Daniels and Erin Heidt-Forsythe, for example, show how sperm and egg donation practices in the United States reflect positive eugenic beliefs in new and more subtle forms.[9]

Reinforcing the belief that idealized (and often nonbiological) human traits are transmitted genetically, gamete donation propagates views of the eugenics movement.

Within donor agencies, there is a marked preference for matching physical characteristics, and the language of "resemblance" and "matching" serves as a neutralized proxy for race.[10] As Charis Thompson notes, in the case of eggs, sperm, and embryos, "the cells themselves are raced in ways that affect not just their availability and who can benefit from them, but the market value and the perceived kinship to recipients of the cells, even when detached from the donor."[11] Ben Campbell, too, explores these problems in the context of gamete donation in three European countries, in which governments require donated gametes to match the physical characteristics of the recipients.[12] Campbell argues that, by analyzing ethnic matching of gametes, biology and culture are separated and then reassembled with the intention of creating offspring who resemble their parents. The meaning of race hovers over biology, inherited physical appearance, and culture, harkening back to the eugenic era though reconfigured as consumer choice. This is what Karen-Sue Taussig, Rayna Rapp, and Deborah Heath have called "flexible eugenics."[13]

This resurgence of genetic essentialism in the context of gamete donation has important consequences for notions of identity and belonging, because to claim a certain social identity always implies particular rights and obligations. For instance, articulating what counts as a mother-child relationship in the world of surrogacy and egg donation determines what mothers and children owe each other. As Paul Brodwin argues, we must ask difficult questions: "How does new genetic knowledge change the ways people claim connection to each other and to larger collectivities? How, in turn, does this process change the resulting webs of obligation and responsibility: personal, legal, moral, and financial?"[14] As gamete donation has led to the increasing biologization of race, these questions are of particular import in the context of ova donation across racial and national lines.

Egg Donation Practices in India

My fieldwork, based in several clinics in Mumbai, included a diverse sample of thirty-nine commissioning parents (or twenty-six couples/individuals) pursuing surrogacy, including twelve gay couples/individuals and fourteen heterosexual married couples from around the world, primarily Europe, North America, and Australia. Of these twenty-six couples who pursued surrogacy, nineteen couples/individuals (twelve gay, seven straight) relied on the assistance of donor egg IVF in their surrogacy arrangements. For these clients, the process of egg donation represented an intensely personal transaction in which skin color and nationality, among other factors, were considered in their decisions about who would provide the genetic material for their child.[15] The process of family making thus became a remarkably high-tech enterprise—including egg donation, IVF, and gestational surrogacy—and the process and experience of donor selection proved to be one of the most stressful and agonizing aspects of their conception and kinship narratives.

Surrogacy guidelines in India dictate that the surrogate may not provide any genetic material in the conception of the child; if the commissioning mother's eggs are not viable, the commissioning parents must purchase eggs from a third-party egg donor. These guidelines emerge from the view that without a genetic connection to the child, the surrogate will be less likely to bond with the child and therefore have little difficulty handing the child over to the commissioning parents. But the guidelines also support many nations' citizenship laws, such as those in the United States, for example, which assert that legal parenthood is conferred through genes, not gestation, thus removing any possibility that the gestational surrogate may claim the child as her own. Here, the intimate industries of surrogacy and egg donation clearly define what constitutes intimacy and intimate relations. In order to support medical guidelines and citizenship laws, the industry emphasizes the significance of genes and genetic relationships, thus excluding and silencing the surrogate mother herself, who performs the most important intimate labor in the project of family making through assisted reproduction.

Thus, for couples who pursue gestational surrogacy with donor eggs in India, donor selection typically includes choosing between a "local" Indian provider or egg provider agencies outside India, which may offer for a higher price a white egg provider. Some foreign egg providers travel to India; others undergo extraction in their home countries for fertilization, freezing, and shipping to India. Typically, if they can afford the higher costs, a commissioning couple will opt to fly an egg provider to India in order to achieve pregnancy through fresh embryo transfer (instead of with frozen embryos), as the rates of success with fresh embryo transfer are higher. In rare cases, a couple may bring a friend or family member to India as an egg donor.

Nationality and skin color, too, deeply influenced payment, though in complicated ways. In the global spaces in which transnational surrogacy occurs, one finds intersecting ideas of race, beauty, and value, emerging in distinct ways at varying local/global scales, revealing local and transnational inequalities. For instance, white providers received higher pay than Indian providers; in my study, in 2010 Indian providers typically received between US$180 and US$360, while white providers from South Africa received US$2,200.[16] Yet in a global economy, ova providers of similar racial/ethnic background, too, are differently positioned to one another in terms of their relationship to the state, power, the global economy, and ova recipients.[17] Indeed, commissioning parents desiring white donors often opted for donors from countries in Eastern Europe or from South Africa, where donor payments were significantly lower.

In this study, however, a minority of parents opted to purchase eggs from a white egg provider. Of the nineteen couples/individuals who used egg donation, only four (approximately 21 percent) chose to use eggs from a white woman. Three of these couples were white heterosexual married couples, and their donors originated in South Africa, Eastern Europe, and Canada; one gay male couple also opted for a white donor from South Africa. One individual (a single, white gay male) opted for an Asian egg donor from China, the country in which he was then living and working. The remaining fourteen couples/individuals who used egg donation opted for Indian egg providers. Of these, the majority (ten couples/individuals) were white, gay males, with the exception of one white/Asian couple and one white/Latino couple. Four heterosexual married couples also opted for

Indian donors; these, too, were primarily white, with the exception of one African American woman (with a white husband).

As commissioning parents navigate the process of egg donation across racial, ethnic, and national lines, it is important to contextualize these negotiations within the transnational hierarchies in which they occur. Here, I turn to Howard Winant's explicit call to link globalization with imperialism: "Globalization is a re-racialization of the world. What have come to be called 'North-South' issues are also deeply racial issues. The disparities in status and 'life chances' between the world's rich and poor regions, between the (largely white and wealthy) global North and the (largely dark-skinned and poor) global South have always possessed a racial character. They are the legacy of a half millennium of imperialism."[18] As Winant argues, globalization is a "racialized social structure,"[19] and it is within this structure that commissioning parents confront the transnational inequalities that privilege their capacities to become parents while relying on the reproductive labor of women in the global South.

As transnational egg donation involves the movement of donors, gametes, and embryos across borders, I found that commissioning parents dealt with stratification in diverse ways. In what follows, I detail the ways in which doctors hierarchically organize donor profiles along lines of class and skin color, shedding light on how parents understand and negotiate this process. I show that while Indian doctors rely on kinship models that privilege whiteness, Western commissioning parents often rejected such models and opted for Indian egg donors for varying reasons.

Stratifying Donors and Divas

I first came to realize that the system of transnational reproductive services values donor eggs by skin color in an interview with Dr. Guha in October 2010. Dr. Guha was the managing director of a well-known agency that facilitated surrogacy arrangements between surrogates and intended parents, the majority of whom are foreign clients who travel to Mumbai from all over the world. We spoke about his work in the surrogacy industry; however, as we concluded the interview, Dr. Guha suddenly lowered his voice and said, "Now, I have a personal question I would like to ask you." He continued, "It's just a thought, so don't feel offended or anything—but we get a lot of queries for Oriental donors.[20] Would you like to be a donor?" Somewhat taken aback and unsure I had heard him correctly, I asked for clarification and he continued, "Yes, Oriental donors. The compensation we give is very different from others; we can give a compensation of more than US\$2,000. See, if you want a Caucasian donor or an Oriental donor, it's more worth it [to clients] if you are already here—so you don't have to fly them [donors] to India and pay travel costs." Though he couched his inquiry in terms of my potential financial windfall as a prospective Asian egg donor, I quickly gathered that Dr. Guha was at least partly motivated by the prospect of offering his foreign clients the best deal he can.

As Dr. Guha told me of the many inquiries he received from couples in Hong Kong and Taiwan, as well as from Chinese or Japanese couples who live in the United States, Canada, and Australia, he turned to his computer to show me his confidential database of donor profiles. As I scanned his computer screen and debated how to respond to his query, something on the screen caught my eye: two distinct categories, "Diva donors" and "regular donors," marked each profile. When I asked about this distinction, Dr. Guha responded, "Normally, the donors you would get from India are from the same background as the surrogates. They are not very educated, not very gorgeous or beautiful. . . . [Diva donors] are highly educated. She's from a 'Harvard' background. She's highly professional. Their compensation is different."

Here, Dr. Guha subtly indicates the ways in which the medical establishment determines what kinds of women are appropriate for different kinds of ART labor. While the bodies of lower-status women are deemed appropriate for surrogacy, they can also provide the genetic material used in IVF (albeit at a lower price). Eggs of higher-status women, however, were more highly valued on the market and thus received higher compensation than "regular" women. But these women were not considered "good" candidates for surrogacy. One doctor explained the difference between working with women of different class and educational backgrounds in the following way: "The good thing is that they [higher-educated women] can read a prescription. The bad thing is they think they're smarter than you. The others will take your word as god's. With simple things, they will not shake without asking if it's ok. But the ones who think they're super smart, they'll just do whatever they want on their own." For doctors, lower-class, uneducated women represent docile, submissive bodies, ideal for gestational surrogacy. On the other hand, upper-class women, perceived as strong willed and insubordinate, are more suited for the shorter-term commitment of egg donation and rarely were recruited as surrogates.

Moreover, photographs accompanied Dr. Guha's egg donor profiles, and I could see that the regular donors who were "not very educated, gorgeous, or beautiful" were almost uniformly dressed in traditional Indian wear, that is, a *salwar kameez* or sari, with simple, unsmiling mug shots. Doctors described them as having "dark" or "dark wheatish" skin color, and they typically had low levels of education, with "professions" listed as domestic work or "housewife." The diva donors' photos, on the other hand, resembled professional photographs one might take in a photographer's studio: the women wore makeup and Western clothing (a shirt or blouse with denim jeans, for instance), and soft lighting framed their smiling faces. Moreover, all the diva donors were fair skinned with lighter colored eyes and taller-than-average height, and they shared a range of profile characteristics, including personality traits, profession, and education.

Dr. Guha's donor database commoditized markers of class, skin color, and social status. He recruited low-income, darker-skinned Indian women as the providers of "regular" eggs, while women of higher social status provided the genetic material with highly desired characteristics. At the same time, Dr. Guha's database illustrates the organizing principles of egg donation: notions of beauty and desirability overlap with education, class, and modernity, while his database rates the less attractive, that is, "not very gorgeous or beautiful" women as, like surrogates, low status and not ideal sources of genetic material for Western couples. Race, to be sure, is an organizing criterion for egg donation, and medical practitioners perpetually reify race as a valid classificatory system when assessing patients.[21] Indeed, I witnessed this firsthand as Dr. Guha informed me that my own Asian/"Oriental" features could fetch high payments and a spot in the diva donor database.

These divisions also reflected regional inequalities and prejudices between North and South India. In a burgeoning surrogacy clinic in Delhi, I found that, like Dr. Guha in Mumbai, Dr. Verma categorized her profiles of egg providers hierarchically. When asked to describe her clinic's database of egg providers, which, like Dr. Guha's, included only Indian women, Dr. Verma began by describing the categorization of women's profiles:

> I have two categories: the A-list are highly professional, models, absolutely stunning women. I have a doctor who's an egg donor. A lecturer at a university here. They get up to US$2,000. Usual egg donor compensation is around US$630. See, here (*turning her computer screen toward me*) this is one of my A-list egg donors. She's a model. She was here in the clinic the other day and everybody in the hospital was going gaga. I have a few who are like that. You can't see but she has green eyes. That's very unusual for India. She's a university graduate. Here's another one; she's also a university graduate. Then I have some "Asian-looking" profiles; see, she's Asian looking, so if we have an Asian-looking intended parent, they can have her.

Dr. Verma continues to show me profiles of engineering students, university graduates, and other women with professional backgrounds and emphasizes, "Being in the north of India, you'll see that people here are different from Bombay or the south because people here have fairer complexion, sharper features. They are more smartly dressed. It's just a culture thing in Delhi. So there is a better choice of egg donors here." Eventually, she shows me a few profiles in the less desirable category, the "D-category," in which the women are "uneducated young girls."

Interestingly, caste rarely surfaced in interviews with doctors or intended parents, except in my conversation with Dr. Verma. When asked whether other factors might play a role in egg donation and surrogacy, Dr. Verma disclosed, "Yes, but not for the surrogate. I had one couple who were Muslim and from a Muslim country somewhere in the Middle East. They wanted only a Muslim surrogate and a Muslim egg donor. That was the only case I've encountered." With respect to surrogacy, on the other hand, Dr. Verma indicates that caste became an issue only in relation to the health of the baby:

> The only thing people might be concerned about [with respect to caste] is that in India, some higher-caste Hindus are vegetarian. They are concerned with the nutrition of the baby. So we absolutely load [the surrogate]

with nutrition. There's this girl who's in charge of nutrition at the home [where surrogates stay during their pregnancies] and she has a goody bag that's filled with biscuits, vitamins, and other snacks. So it doesn't matter if they're vegetarians. Most of our babies are three kilos (about six and a half pounds). In the North, people are taller, broad-shouldered, so they are able to carry the pregnancy just fine.

Dr. Verma's comments illuminate how social hierarchies work in India. Framed in terms of "choice," Dr. Verma places North India, and specifically the cosmopolitan city of Delhi, at the top of the list from which egg purchasers may select "A-list" eggs, owing to its culture and reputation in India as well as the prevalence of people with lighter-skinned, "sharper features" less common in the South. She also underscores the role of caste in surrogacy, again highlighting regional difference as she moves from descriptions of nourishing higher-caste Hindus to claims of better physical fitness for childbearing.[22] Such practices elucidate the ways that physicians work to reinforce skin color and other physical characteristics (attributed to regional difference) as biologically inheritable; doctors, who have culturally sanctioned authority that extends to reproduction,[23] are in a unique position to perpetually reify skin color and other forms of difference as valid systems of classification. Here, we see the salience of skin color as a classificatory system in egg donation, revealing hope for or a belief in some kind of biological persistence of skin tone.[24]

In India, skin color matters, and donor eggs were valued in an economy of color reflective of a history of colonialism and racism. A light complexion confers symbolic capital in marriage negotiations among South Asians,[25] and financial capital in negotiations between South Asians and prospective parents. Most doctors had separate files or databases for fair- and dark-skinned donors, and as the following narratives illustrate, in these files skin color nearly always overlapped with education, class, and beauty.[26]

In my fieldwork, I found that other doctors crafted their presentation of their egg seller profiles in much the same way as Dr. Verma and Dr. Guha, according to their perceptions of what clients would find desirable. Yet, at the same time, I found that many intended parents did *not* explicitly desire the fair-skinned, highly educated egg donor. Moreover, as I will discuss, parents described Indian donors as desirable precisely because of their "otherness" or exotic beauty, in which racialized perceptions of beauty both opened up a space for resistance to whiteness but also a reinforcement of racial/racist stereotypes.

"Appropriate" Matches and the Reproduction of Whiteness

Ethnographic research on egg and sperm donation indicates that prospective parents commonly seek phenotypic, personal, and cultural "matching"— seeking donors who share a similar racial/ethnic background, personal qualities, and phenotype—between egg donors and intended mother or sperm donor and infertile male partner, and agencies or doctors commonly encourage the practice.[27] Such matching appeared to keep assisted reproduction as "natural" as possible, while also allowing families to be discreet and maintain secrecy regarding donor use, giving parents full control over domestic decisions about disclosure to their children about their "origin stories."

Infamous ART cases around the world reinforce this presumption of ethnoracial matching and reveal the desirability of racial purity. The media and public reaction in response to these cases are telling. In a 2002 case in which a white couple had mixed-race twins after an Asian man's sperm was mistakenly used to fertilize the intended mother's eggs, the woman was later quoted as saying, "All we wanted was a family. Instead we were landed with a nightmare that will last forever."[28] Seline Szkupinski Quiroga has noted how media accounts referred to the case of an African American woman inseminated with the "wrong" sperm (from a white man) as a "dream . . . turned into a nightmare," "unthinkable," "a fertility screw-up," and a "fiasco."[29] Drawing on such examples and her own fieldwork on gamete donation, infertility, and race in the United States, Quiroga asserts what while the stated goal of the US infertility industry is to "create families," what remains unspoken is "the desire to create a certain type of family, one that closely matches, and thus reproduces, the heteropatriarchal model of a white nuclear family."[30] Quiroga ultimately argues, "ARTs's privileging of genetic relatedness is currently deployed in ways that support a white heteropatriarchal model of family in which race and whiteness are reified as inheritable."[31]

Throughout my own research, I confronted many examples of ways that IVF, egg donation, and surrogacy in India bolstered white, heteropatriarchal kinship patterns and reflected fears about race mixing. For instance, Dr. Singh, a Mumbai-based IVF specialist, discussed her surprise at how often her clients, particularly her clients in same-sex relationships, opted for Indian donors with darker skin:

> I kept pushing the lighter skins [on same sex-couples], because I feel it's hard for a child to go through life with two dads, and then you put the child through color difference in a society. It's something that's going to bother them later. So if they do agree, I can tilt them towards, you know, "These are the options and that's what you can use, but think about it really hard before you choose a darker color skin." . . . Children do not understand racism, but they do understand color and they do understand difference, like, "Why are you so different from your parents? Why do you have two dads?"

Dr. Singh found it difficult to accept that a couple would want to conceive a child who would be a racial mismatch to its own family. Indeed, as the doctor and facilitator of surrogacy arrangements, she often used her position of authority to attempt to influence prospective parents' decisions in egg donor selection.

Moreover, Dr. Singh found it troubling that same-sex couples in particular expressed preference for donors with darker skin, even as same-sex couples clearly have no option of concealing the use of assisted reproduction. I found, just as Dr. Singh described, that same-sex couples rarely made matching racial/skin color characteristics a high priority. While Dr. Singh described this preference for nonwhite donors or donors with darker skin tones as signaling an increased "sensitivity" and openness on the part of her gay clients, she thought that the stigma of being a child of same-sex parents was all the more reason for same-sex parents to avoid dark-skinned donors.

Marlene Sawyer, an African American woman in her late forties and mother of a two-year-old son born through surrogacy in India, also reported that her doctor had an opinion about her taste in skin color in an egg provider. Marlene's husband is white, and they needed the assistance of donor eggs. According to Marlene, "I sent her emails and said, 'Here is a picture of me and my husband. As you can tell, I am a dark, black woman. Please give us the darkest donor you have.' What do we get? The whitest donor she has!" I asked Marlene what she thought about why her doctor had taken matters into her own hands, and Marlene said, "I have no idea. I think she probably was looking at it for my husband, because my husband is a white male. So I thought maybe she was thinking, culturally or something, since the men are so dominant, 'Oh, we'll give her someone that looks like her husband.' I mean, I showed you the picture of Sean [Marlene's son], right? (*shows picture*). He's white as white can be." Marlene's experience as an African American woman contrasted sharply with the majority of intended parents who traveled to India, who were white. While Dr. Singh expressed concern over the multiple boundary crossings committed by same-sex parents who seek darker-skinned egg donors—parents who challenge heteronormative models of kinship and resist expectations to reproduce whiteness at the same time—Marlene's doctor ignored her request for a donor who matched her own skin color, a move that Marlene believes has impacted her own experience as a black mother. Marlene divulged, "Even though I love Sean, I don't want to feel like an outsider. Even though he never makes me feel that way, he loves me and he's my baby, I want him to get a little darker!" When asked about challenges or concerns that have come up for her since the birth of her son, Marlene replies:

> People don't understand; they think I'm the nanny, or they say, you must be babysitting today. When little kids say it I don't care, but when adults say it, I say *I'm* his mother. And they're kind of caught off guard. I'm like, I don't have to explain Sean's existence to anyone. When Sean is of age and he wants to tell his story, he can tell his story. I feel like, as a black woman, why are you questioning me? That kind of stuff, I'm trying to figure out how to deal with it, where I'll feel comfortable.

Liz's story, like Marlene's, elucidates the problems and anxieties that stem from lack of transparency and trust in the doctors who arrange surrogacy packages from half a world away. A US mother of twins born through surrogacy in India, Liz was fifty-four years old at the time of their birth. Liz had previously been married twice; she had five children with her first husband, whom she divorced after eleven years because of his escalating struggle with alcoholism. With five small children to support, Liz decided to enroll in college, and completed one year before she met her current husband. The couple went on to have eight children together before they decided to adopt an infant from Guatemala. With fourteen children (including the children from Liz's previous marriage), Liz took on the work of educating her children at home, while her husband supported the family through his job in systems management.

Even though they had an already full family, the couple hoped to adopt still another child from overseas. Yet their plans fell apart when evidence of corruption halted their adoption process in Vietnam. Somewhat disillusioned with adoption, it was around this time that Liz learned about surrogacy in India. Though she had heard that most doctors would accept only childless clients with histories of infertility and within a certain age range, Liz had also heard that some doctors did not adhere to this rule. After sending several inquiries and receiving multiple rejections from doctors, they found Dr. Sen in Delhi.

Because Liz was menopausal, the couple would need donor eggs in their surrogacy process. When asked about her experience with egg donation, Liz explained:

> We were eager to have the donor be Indian as we had this idea of a sort of transworld cosmic connection through that, since we had really wanted to adopt [internationally]. We did tell them we hoped she [the egg donor] was reasonably attractive and healthy and intelligent, but we did not do any selecting, since they didn't offer it, and we knew that they would be able to select based on medical criteria. We suspect that he did not actually use an Indian donor because they stressed how they needed a picture of me to choose a suitable person, and the babies are very very fair. . . . [Dr. Sen] made mention of how he uses his best judgment on egg donors, and I got the distinct impression that he would do just what he thought best. . . . He wanted LOTS of sperm samples from John, even after the day that they did the egg retrieval and fertilization for our twins. . . . It honestly never crossed either of our minds that any doctor could be so lacking in ethics to do such a thing as "borrow" other people's genetic material without disclosing that it would be given out to other strangers.

I don't know how to even deal with this. We were told just about nothing of the egg donor. John asked and was shown an indistinct photo of an Indian woman.

Liz believed that Dr. Sen committed various offenses—ignoring her request for an Indian egg donor, using John's sperm to fertilize another woman's eggs even after the initial IVF for her twins—and I frequently heard such stories of misdeed circulated among parents pursuing global surrogacy. In the absence of any formal legislation or regulatory mechanism regarding the use or provision of ARTs in India, parents such as Liz—who lived beyond India's borders and thus had little recourse to take any legal action—often resign themselves to speculation about the source of their children's genetic material. Liz's experience also reflects issues that arose in many of my interviews with intended parents; foremost among these was the issue of trust between client and doctor, and fears about what could happen when the commercial exchange takes place across multiple geographic/cultural boundaries. Many parents, indeed, spoke of the need to "blindly trust" their doctor in order to move ahead with surrogacy in India.

Marlene's and Liz's stories reflect the power that doctors hold in defining what is "desirable" in a donor and creating "acceptable" families. Similar to Elizabeth Roberts's finding that Ecuadorian clinicians frequently aimed to make whiter children through sperm and egg donation,[32] my study, too, reveals how doctors view themselves as key players in a whitening project and deliberately select donors based on their lightness, regardless of what the intended parent may request.

Yet, what motivates an intended parent to request a donor of a different racial, ethnic, or national background; or, more specifically, what motivates white intended parents to select Indian egg donors? Liz's narrative reveals a common thread among intended parents who explicitly desired an Indian egg donor. Liz and her husband specifically hoped for a child who might reflect and fulfill her desire for some kind of a "transworld cosmic connection," a connection rooted in her desire for a family filled with internationally adopted children. As I will discuss in the following section, couples more frequently opted to forgo ethnic or skin color matching in favor of donors from nonmatching backgrounds (phenotypic, ethnicity, race, culture, etc.). Indeed, of the nineteen couples/individuals who used donor eggs, only four parents purchased eggs from donors of matching (white) background. Of those who opted for eggs from Indian women, four couples/individuals took into account the woman's skin color, indicating a preference for fair- or dark-skinned donors, depending on the commissioning couple's own skin color. The majority (ten out of fourteen couples), however, selected Indian egg donors with skin tones darker than their own. This desire reflected in part a "primordial ethnic authenticity,"[33] in which expressions of desire for children who "looked Indian" were often interchangeable with expressions of desire for a child who "looked exotic." As I describe below, such wishes reflect the complex dynamics of reproductive tourism, in which intended parents' desires for exotic-looking children tangle with essentialist ideas of cultural heritage and Indian identity.

The Biologization of Race, Skin Color, and Nation

While rates of compensation, doctors' practices, and beliefs about matching revealed the stratification of egg providers according to skin color, in practice, intended parents select egg donors based on a range of "qualifications." The process of egg donation in India differs vastly from the process in countries where most intended parents originate. For instance, based on their knowledge or experience with agencies in the United States, Europe, or Australia, many intended parents expected to receive basic information about ancestry, medical history, and personality characteristics. Practitioners in India made much less information available.

In this context, what "qualifications" did commissioning parents look for? Patricia, a forty-four-year-old US mother, would have liked to use eggs from a white egg provider but couldn't afford the higher costs. When she and her husband decided to choose an Indian egg provider, she explained how she sought more information about the women's background:

> I did actually try to develop a little questionnaire to ask our egg donors some questions, to try and find out a little more about her potential. It didn't work very well. . . . I tried to ask questions in a way to try to uncover her potential rather than her actual, things she had achieved.

But it did make me aware that the circumstances that she lived in didn't really give her any possibility of exploring her potential. It was a little bit of a fruitless exercise and it made me a little bit sad, just knowing how limited her options had been. Basically we picked someone who we thought was pretty. And that's not what you ideally would want to base your decision on.

After asking her doctor to share the questionnaire with potential egg providers, Patricia recognized the social and economic constraints that limited Indian women's access to education. Thus, she accepted that she had to use much simpler criteria for selection, such as beauty.

When asked to expand on her process of selecting the egg donor, Patricia underscored that skin color also factored into her decision:

> We picked one of the fairer egg donors that we found. There was something about her face that reminded me of people on my side of the family. It's funny, because even my father, not knowing that, said that he [my son] looks like his brother. And that's exactly the side of the family that her face shape had reminded me of. There were a lot of factors in the looks that we considered, and definitely someone who would "blend" into our family was one of them. We were totally shocked though that he ended up having blue eyes and reddish hair! Of all the things I expected when picking an Indian egg donor, that would have been at the bottom of the list. It's just completely a genetic surprise.

Here, Patricia (like Jan, whose story opens this article) engages in a kind of "resemblance talk."[34] Patricia and Jan, among other parents in this study, recognize the cultural significance of resemblance, and they searched for familiar qualities in their egg provider regardless of her ethnic background.

Similarly, Mark and Lionel, an Australian-Italian couple in their early thirties and parents of a son born to a surrogate mother in Delhi, ultimately settled on an Indian donor they felt was "beautiful" and evoked a kind of Indian "authenticity":

> **Lionel:** We received a number of profiles, which basically consisted of age, initials . . .

Mark: Some of them would have a picture and a few words, others would have all these . . .

L: . . . blank fields. We just sat there and went through and had very distinctive feelings about, "Oh, no way," and "Oh, she's so pretty," or "Oh, she likes confetti, that's quirky." But we both felt that we were attracted to a story.

M: Yeah, we said, "Can we have more information about *her?*"

L: Some of these profiles are, you know, the shots that you take when you're "Miss India," ten superhot gorgeous, over-make-upped—

M: Yeah and the background, everything is like "mistyland" or something.

L: We were like, no, we wanted something *authentic.*

M: All of JM's photos, they were just very natural. Very simple shots, and that's what we like, I guess. That's how we chose, basically. At the end of the day, it was just a sense of warmth . . .

Lionel went on to explain their desire for an Indian donor: "We actually always thought that, because India is allowing us to do this, it was natural to have the child be . . . of India. In a way our child belongs to India. The other thing is, Lionel and I don't care what race the child is. Actually I was surprised to learn that a lot of couples were still seeing egg donors from outside of India."

Patricia's, Mark's, and Lionel's comments reflect those of many parents I interviewed, who mentioned a variety of reasons for selecting an Indian egg donor. While Patricia cited cost as a major factor, Mark's and Lionel's comments reflected essentialized beliefs about race. As they sought a kind of Indian "authenticity" that was "natural" and "simple," they simultaneously expressed an understanding of race as a persistent biological category, with their belief that their child is "of India."

Several parents shared this conviction that genes from an Indian woman conferred an "authentic" Indian identity to the child born through egg donation and surrogacy, though occasionally, couples disagreed. The story of Matthew and Anthony—fathers to three girls born through surrogacy in India—illustrates the complexities of transnational reproduction and the questions that many couples face with respect to kinship and ethnic identity. Two surrogate mothers carried the three children—twins and a singleton—

who were conceived with the eggs of one Indian egg provider and sperm samples from each father. As a result, each partner was genetically related to at least one child, and the children were "connected" through a single genetic donor. Thirty-six-year-old Matthew described the complicated nature of this twenty-first-century family: "Imagine the first day of school. We've got—these are triplets, in a sense, but there are different birthdays, and different fathers, but the same mother, and different last names." Interestingly, Matthew attributes motherhood status not to the surrogates who carried and birthed their children but to the egg provider who contributed the genes in the conception of the three girls.

As Matthew and Anthony pondered what they would tell their daughters about their family's unique history, Matthew enthusiastically shared his views on his daughters' ethnic identity: "I love that our children are Indian. And that makes me a little bit Indian, too. So I want to make sure that they have a connection to their heritage. I expect we're going to go back someday. You know, I don't know when, but now India is a part of our children's heritage." However, thirty-eight-year-old Anthony heartily disagreed. Born and raised in China before moving to the United States at eighteen, Anthony claimed, "Well, the Indian part is nice, but I'm Chinese, so they're going to be more Chinese." Indeed, Matthew and Anthony chose their egg provider because, hailing from northern India, "she looked Chinese," and Anthony felt ambivalent about their children's identity as Indian. As Anthony argued that the girls would be "more Chinese than Indian," Matthew conceded his point yet noted the complexity of their family's story, reiterating, "But India is a part of our children's heritage. It's a part of our history now. And it always will be."

Martin's story further illustrates the role that skin color plays in transnational reproduction. Martin, a forty-two-year-old gay male expecting twins with his longtime partner, discussed his approach to selecting an egg provider and described the process as "the most emotional and traumatic part of the entire process." This was due, in part, to the lack of information available: "You have a picture, you have height and weight, and you know whether they're Hindu or Muslim. That's about it." Martin went on to explain:

The hardest thing is you sit there and you look at these women, and you try to picture her as the mother of your child. It's so beyond even looking at her facial features and looking at her smile; it's like, do they look like a happy person? We narrowed it down to five or six that we felt fit our vision of what would be attractive. We looked for women who were relatively fair skinned. Although we know the child's going to be part Indian, we didn't want it to come up with a really dark complexion. And it says that on the profile: fair, medium, or dark. So that was part of it for us. We also definitely intentionally chose someone who was Hindu. We intentionally did not want a Muslim. I'm Catholic and I studied religion in college and I just didn't really want that connection to Islam. And I love the Hindu faith, the deities, everything about the way they worship. I thought that, for me, I would be a lot more interested in telling my child, "This is the background that I came from, and this is the background that your mother came from," and introduce them to both and let the child select which of those they'd be interested in. I didn't know that much about Islam and I didn't really want to go down that path. We want religion to be a big part of our children's lives and so for me, I would rather present to them those two options. And obviously if they want to go a different route, they can, but in my mind I like the idea of Hinduism.

Like many parents I interviewed, Martin ascribed motherhood status to the genetic donor, not the surrogate mother, which contributed to the stress and tension that surrounded the process of selecting an egg provider. Indeed, when asked what he knew about the woman who was carrying his future children, Martin replied, "Very little. And you don't typically pick the surrogate. The doctor picks her for you. I know that she has a child and that she's married, but I don't know anything more than that." While Martin described a deeper emotional investment in selecting the egg provider, the future "mother" of his children, he also revealed an emotional detachment from the surrogate, indicating the complex ways in which parents construct intimacy and intimate relations with the various reproductive actors who contribute to the conception and birth of a child. Martin, like other participants in this study, constructed a deeper intimacy with the "mother" of his twin boys, based on a genetic, not gestational, relationship.

But precisely what is transmitted through this "intimate" genetic relationship? For Martin, notions of beauty clearly overlapped with fair skin. Yet he believed that religious identity, too, was embedded in genetic ties. Thus, he sought to circumscribe the realm of religious possibility for his children by choosing a Hindu egg provider. As I have previously argued, "understandings about a child's biogenetic origins emerge in tension with a child's right to identity."[35] While many parents I spoke with expressed a strong desire to "maintain the Indian element" in their children's identities, for Martin, biogenetic origins also intersected meaningfully with religious identity.

Other parents, particularly white parents, articulated racialized notions of beauty in their discussions of Indian egg donation and "mixed-race" children. Marla, a thirty-two-year-old Norwegian mother of a baby girl born via surrogacy in Mumbai, explained:

> Since we had to have a donor, I told Roland that I didn't mind having an Indian donor. But then he said that it would be a lot easier for us to explain to governments and a lot of neighbors—everything—if she's white. I said, "I don't mind and I know that it's good to mix races." I told him that, "It's actually not a bad thing. It's a good thing." Indian mixes or the Indian and the white mixes that we have seen, the children are so beautiful. They are absolutely beautiful. They are lovely. So, I told him that. To me, it doesn't matter, but he wanted to try it [donation with a white donor] one time.

Though Marla claims she would have considered an Indian egg donor because of the "loveliness" and "beauty" of children of mixed descent, she ultimately decided to go with a white egg donor from Eastern Europe, mostly owing to her husband's wishes to maintain resemblance and secrecy regarding surrogacy.

Conclusion

Scholars have recently paid close attention to the commodification of intimacy and intimate labor.[36] Sociologist Arlie Hochschild has found that "on issue after issue, people sought to protect the personal from the purchased, the village from the market, the self from a strange new emotional capitalism."[37] In the context of transnational egg donation, I have shown how parents negotiate the process of egg donation across racial, ethnic, class, and national boundaries. Across these overlapping and fluid lines, I suggest that parents employ a range of strategies to create intimacy and closeness—with the egg donor and the child conceived through egg donation—even as they acknowledge the commodifying aspects of this particular form of family making. In confronting the anxieties associated with the intimate industry of egg donation, and evading the marketlike aspects of their family's origin stories, parents engaged in discursive strategies that inject intimacy, emotion, and affect into a relationship that is otherwise anonymous. These strategies, too, seek to reconcile tensions inherent in the transnational structures of inequality in which egg donation takes place.

As I have discussed in this article, transnational egg donation encompasses multiple racial and national projects. In some cases, parents may explicitly seek to reproduce whiteness or resemblance. In other cases, however, parents sought to subvert dominant kinship models that privilege whiteness, by deliberately selecting Indian egg donors that reflected notions of mixed-race beauty or a kind of Indian authenticity. Such actions, nonetheless, maintain racial/racist structures that rely on essentialized notions of culture and racialized beauty. Moreover, transnational egg donation underscores the salience of donor skin color (often conflated with race or nationality) in donor selection, even though genetic determination of skin color, among other traits, is unpredictable at best. Ultimately, as doctors and parents organize and negotiate the process of transnational egg donation, the social constructs of race, skin color, and nationality become ever more biologized within transnational relations of power.

Notes

I would like to thank Rhacel Salazar Parreñas, Rachel Silvey, and Hung Cam Thai for organizing the Intimate Industries workshop and for their feedback on this article. This article greatly benefited from the comments of fellow participants in the workshop, particularly Purnima Mankekar, as well as the anonymous reviewers. Finally, I am grateful to everyone who agreed to be interviewed and, for funding, to the National Science Foundation, Wenner-Gren Foundation, and Ford Foundation.

1. In general, parents who wished to purchase eggs from a white woman paid approximately US$10,000–11,000, while eggs from an Indian woman cost around US$700.

2. Bella Jaisinghani, "Maid-to-Order Surrogate Mums," *Times of India*, April 11, 2010, timesofindia.indiatimes.com/articleshow/5783263.cms.

3. Michael Hardt and Antonio Negri, *Empire* (Cambridge, MA: Harvard University Press, 2001).

4. Viviana A. Zelizer, *The Purchase of Intimacy* (Princeton, NJ: Princeton University Press, 2005), 14.

5. Charis Thompson, "Skin Tone and the Persistence of Biological Race in Egg Donation for Assisted Reproduction," in *Shades of Difference: Why Skin Color Matters*, ed. Evelyn Nakano Glenn (Stanford: Stanford University Press, 2009).

6. Michal Nahman, "Nodes of Desire: Romanian Egg Sellers, 'Dignity' and Feminist Alliances in Transnational Ova Exchanges," *European Journal of Women's Studies* 15, no. 2 (2008): 65–82.

7. See Daisy Deomampo, "Gendered Geographies of Reproductive Tourism," *Gender and Society* 27, no. 4 (2013): 514–37.

8. Jyotsna Vaid, "Fair Enough? Color and the Commodification of Self in Indian Matrimonials," in *Shades of Difference: Why Skin Color Matters*, ed. Evelyn Nakano Glenn (Stanford: Stanford University Press, 2009), 148–65.

9. Cynthia R. Daniels and Erin Heidt-Forsythe, "Gendered Eugenics and the Problematic of Free Market Reproductive Technologies: Sperm and Egg Donation in the United States," *Signs* 37, no. 3 (2012): 719–47.

10. See, for example, Andre Gingrich, "Concepts of Race Vanishing, Movements of Racism Rising? Global Issues and Austrian Ethnography," *Ethnos* 69, no. 2 (2004): 156–76; and Peter Hervik, "The Danish Cultural World of Unbridgeable Differences," *Ethnos* 69, no. 2 (2004): 247–67.

11. Charis Thompson, "Race Science," *Theory, Culture, and Society* 23, nos. 2–3 (2006): 547–49, 548.

12. Ben Campbell, "Racialization, Genes and the Reinventions of Nation in Europe," in *Race, Ethnicity and Nation: Perspectives from Kinship and Genetics*, ed. Peter Wade (New York: Berghahn Books, 2007), 95–124.

13. Karen-Sue Taussig, Rayna Rapp, and Deborah Heath, "Flexible Eugenics: Technologies of the Self in the Age of Genetics," in *Anthropologies of Modernity: Foucault, Governmentality, and Life Politics*, ed. Jonathan Xavier Inda (Malden, MA: Blackwell, 2008): 194–212.

14. Paul Brodwin, "Genetics, Identity, and the Anthropology of Essentialism," *Anthropological Quarterly* 75, no. 2 (2002): 323–30, 326.

15. It is worth noting that sperm donation is rare in the context of surrogacy. In my study, there were no cases in which sperm donation was necessary; typically, the husband/male partner provided the sperm that would fertilize the donor egg through IVF. In the case of gay male couples, the couple would negotiate which partner would provide the genetic material; I encountered several cases in which both partners opted to become genetic parents through IVF with one egg donor and two surrogates.

16. In contrast, Rene Almeling found that due to the difficulty of maintaining a diverse pool of donors in the United States, often agencies will increase the payment for donors of color, particularly Asian American and African American donors. She illustrates how in the US market race is viewed as biological, and egg cells from women of color are perceived as scarce, contributing to their increased value. Paradoxically, this results in a situation in which donors of color are more highly valued than white women, an unexpected consequence given that the reverse is often true in other contexts, such as in transnational egg donation. See Rene Almeling, *Sex Cells: The Medical Market for Eggs and Sperm* (Berkeley: University of California Press, 2011).

17. Nahman, "Nodes of Desire."

18. Howard Winant, *The New Politics of Race: Globalism, Difference, Justice* (Minneapolis: University of Minnesota Press, 2004), 131.

19. Ibid.

20. Dr. Guha's use of the term *Oriental* may reflect the influence of British English in Indian speech, where the term may not be considered particularly offensive, and it is generally used to refer to people from East and Southeast Asia. He was the only doctor to use the term, and other doctors I interviewed used racial categories such as *Asian* to refer to people of Asian descent. It is perhaps worth noting that Dr. Guha was one of the few doctors I interviewed who had not received any medical training outside India. All other doctors were educated abroad, reflecting perhaps a cosmopolitan understanding of the various racial categories used in different contexts.

21. Richard Garcia, "The Misuse of Race in Medical Diagnosis," *Chronicle of Higher Education*, 49, no. 35 (2003): B15.

22. In my research, I found that most foreign clients expressed no preference regarding caste in egg donation or surrogacy, and that a high proportion of women who opted to become surrogate mothers came from lower caste backgrounds. Yet caste remains an implicit organizing criterion within assisted reproduction in India. Indeed, Indian consumers of ARTs frequently take into account caste background in their decisions regard-

ing gamete donation and surrogacy. See Saritha Rai, "More and More Indians Want Egg Donors, but Only If They're from the Right Caste," *MinnPost*, September 22, 2010, www.minnpost.com/global-post/2010/09/more-and-more-indians-want-egg-donors-only -if-theyre-right-caste; Amarnath Tewary, "At a Sperm Bank in Bihar, Caste Divisions Start before Birth," *New York Times*, July 12, 2012, india.blogs.nytimes.com/2012/07/12/at -a-sperm-bank-in-bihar-caste-divisions-start-before-birth/.

23. Brigitte Jordan and Robbie Davis-Floyd, *Birth in Four Cultures: A Crosscultural Investigation of Childbirth in Yucatan, Holland, Sweden, and the United States* (Prospect Heights, IL: Waveland Press, 1992).

24. Thompson, "Skin Tone."

25. Vaid, "Fair Enough?"

26. Almeling, *Sex Cells.*

27. Gay Becker, *The Elusive Embryo: How Women and Men Approach New Reproductive Technologies* (Berkeley: University of California Press, 2000); Charis Thompson, *Making Parents: The Ontological Choreography of Reproductive Technologies* (Cambridge, MA: MIT Press, 2005).

28. NewsCore, "London Sperm Bank under Investigation after Couple Has Baby from Different Race," *FoxNews.com*, April 29, 2012, www.foxnews.com/world/2012/04/29/london -sperm-bank-under-investigation-after-couple-has-baby-from-different-race/.

29. Seline Szkupinski Quiroga, "Blood Is Thicker than Water: Policing Donor Insemination and the Reproduction of Whiteness," *Hypatia* 22, no. 2 (2007): 141–60, 160.

30. Ibid., 144.

31. Ibid.

32. Elizabeth F. S. Roberts, *God's Laboratory: Assisted Reproduction in the Andes* (Berkeley: University of California Press, 2012).

33. Thompson, "Skin Tone," 143.

34. Gay Becker, Anneliese Butler, and Robert D. Nachtigall, "Resemblance Talk: A Challenge for Parents Whose Children Were Conceived with Donor Gametes in the US," *Social Science and Medicine* 61, no. 6 (2005): 1300–1309.

35. Deomampo, "Gendered Geographies," 530.

36. Nicole Constable, "The Commodification of Intimacy: Marriage, Sex, and Reproductive Labor," *Annual Review of Anthropology* 38 (October 2009): 49–64; Eileen Boris and Rhacel Salazar Parreñas, *Intimate Labors: Cultures, Technologies, and the Politics of Care* (Stanford: Stanford University Press, 2010); Arlie Russell Hochschild, *Outsourced Self: Intimate Life in Market Times* (New York: Metropolitan Books, 2012); Arlie Russell Hochschild, *The Commercialization of Intimate Life: Notes from Home and Work* (Berkeley: University of California Press, 2003).

37. Hochschild, *Outsourced Self*, 13.

Contributors

Danièle Bélanger is professor of geography at the Université Laval in Québec City. Her recent research focuses on migrants in precarious situations, including low-skilled migrant workers, undocumented migrants, and marriage migrants in Asia and North America. She recently published the article "Labour Migration and Trafficking among Vietnamese Migrants in Asia" in *The American ANNALS of Political and Social Science* (2014) and is the coeditor of *Reconfiguring Families in Contemporary Vietnam* (2009).

Hae Yeon Choo is an assistant professor of sociology at the University of Toronto. Her research centers on gender, migration, and citizenship. Her work has been published in *Gender and Society* and *Sociological Theory*. Her book, *Decentering Citizenship: Gender, Labor, and Migrant Rights in South Korea*, will be published in 2016.

Nicole Constable is J. Y. Pillay Global-Asia Professor of Social Sciences (Anthropology) at Yale-NUS College, Singapore, and professor of anthropology at the Dietrich School of Arts and Sciences at the University of Pittsburgh. Her most recent book is *Born out of Place: Migrant Mothers and the Politics of International Labor* (2014).

Daisy Deomampo is assistant professor of anthropology at Fordham University. Her research focuses on the globalization of assisted reproductive technologies and its implications for gender relations, family formation, and social stratification. Her book *Transnational Reproduction: Race, Kinship, and Commercial Surrogacy in India* is forthcoming from New York University Press.

Akhil Gupta is professor of anthropology and director of the Center for India and South Asia (CISA) at UCLA. He has taught at the University of Washington, Seattle (1987–89), Stanford University (1989–2006), and the University of California, Los Angeles (2006–present). His most recent books are *The Anthropology of the State* (2006, with Aradhana Sharma), *The State in India after Liberalization* (2010, with K. Sivaramakrishnan), and *Red Tape: Bureaucracy, Structural Violence, and Poverty in India* (2012).

Chaitanya Lakkimsetti is an assistant professor in sociology and women's and gender studies at Texas A&M University. Her research centers on sexuality, law, and globalization. She is currently completing a book manuscript on sexual politics, law, and citizenship in India.

Pei-Chia Lan is professor of sociology at National Taiwan University. She was a postdoctoral fellow at University of California, Berkeley, a Fulbright scholar at New York University, and a Radcliffe-Yenching fellow at Harvard University. She has authored *Global Cinderellas: Migrant Domestics and Newly Rich Employers in Taiwan* (2006). She is working on a manuscript on parenting, globalization, and class inequality.

Purnima Mankekar is professor of gender studies, Asian American studies, and film, television, and digital media at the University of California, Los Angeles (UCLA). She has taught at Stanford University (1993–2006) and UCLA (2007–present). Her research explores media, gendered subject formation, and transnationality in postcolonial contexts. She has published *Unsettling India: Affect, Temporality, Transnationality* (2015) and *Screening Culture, Viewing Politics: An Ethnography of Television, Womanhood, and Nation in Postcolonial India* (1999) and has edited two books, *Caste and Outcast* (2002, coedited with Gordon Chang and Akhil Gupta) and *Media, Erotics, and Transnational Asia* (2013, coedited with Louisa Schein).

Eileen Otis is an associate professor of sociology at the University of Oregon. She is the author of the award-winning book *Markets and Bodies: Women, Service Work and the Making of Inequality in China* (2011). Her research has been published in the *American Sociological Review*, *Politics and Society*, and *American Behavioral Scientist*, among other journals. She is currently working on a book about Walmart retail workers in China.

Juno Salazar Parreñas is an assistant professor of women, gender, and sexuality studies at The Ohio State University. Her article in *American Ethnologist*, "Producing Affect: Transnational Volunteerism at a Malaysian Orangutan Rehabilitation Center," won the 2013 American Anthropological Association's G.A.D. Award for Exemplary Cross-Field Scholarship. She is currently working on a book manuscript, "Decolonizing Extinction: An Ethnography of Orangutan Rehabilitation."

Rhacel Salazar Parreñas is professor of sociology and gender studies at the University of Southern California. Her current research examines the intersections of human trafficking and labor migration. The author of four books and numerous articles on women's labor migration, her latest book, *Illicit Flirtations: Labor, Migration and Sex Trafficking in Tokyo*, examines the effects of anti–human trafficking campaigns on Filipina migrant hostesses.

Sharmila Rudrappa is associate professor in Sociology and the Center for Asian American Studies at the University of Texas at Austin. Her research explores emerging markets in bodies in South India.

Celine Parreñas Shimizu is a filmmaker, film scholar, and visiting professor of cinema and sociology (sexuality) at San Francisco State University. A former full professor at the University of California at Santa Barbara, she coedited *The Feminist Porn Book* (2013) and authored *Straitjacket Sexualities* (2012) and *The Hypersexuality of Race* (2007). Her award-winning films include *The Fact of Asian Women* (2004) and *Birthright: Mothering across Difference* (2009). For more information, go to www.celineshimizu.com. She completed this article as a visiting faculty fellow at the United States Studies Centre at the University of Sydney.

Rachel Silvey is associate professor in the Department of Geography and Planning, University of Toronto. Her research focuses on gender politics, labor migration, and economic development through the lens of migrant workers from Indonesia. Funded by the Fulbright New Century Scholars Program, the US National Science Foundation, and the Social Science and Humanities Research Council of Canada (SSHRC), she has published numerous journal articles and book chapters.

Hung Cam Thai received his PhD in sociology at the University of California, Berkeley, in 2003. He is the author of *For Better or for Worse: Vietnamese International Marriages in the New Global Economy* (2008) and *Insufficient Funds: The Culture of Money in Low Wage Transnational Families* (2014). Thai is associate professor of sociology and Asian American studies at Pomona College and the Claremont University Consortium, where he is also director of the Pacific Basin Institute.

Leslie K. Wang is an assistant professor in the Department of Sociology at the University of Massachusetts, Boston. Her research investigates issues related to gender, family, and childhood that are linking China with the global North. Her book *Outsourced Children: Orphanage Care and Adoption in Globalizing China* is forthcoming from Stanford University Press.

Printed and bound by CPI Group (UK) Ltd, Croydon, CR0 4YY

13/04/2025

14656483-0001